BENEDETTO CROCE AND THE BIRTH OF THE ITALIAN REPUBLIC, 1943–1952

FABIO FERNANDO RIZI

Benedetto Croce and the Birth of the Italian Republic, 1943–1952

UNIVERSITY OF TORONTO PRESS
Toronto Buffalo London

Toronto Buffalo London
utorontopress.com

ISBN 978-1-4875-0446-5

Toronto Italian Studies

Library and Archives Canada Cataloguing in Publication

Rizi, Fabio Fernando, 1935–, author
Benedetto Croce and the birth of the Italian Republic,
1942–1952 / Fabio Fernando Rizi.

(Toronto Italian studies)
Includes bibliographical references and index.
ISBN 978-1-4875-0446-5 (hardcover)

1. Croce, Benedetto, 1866–1952. 2. Croce, Benedetto, 1866–1952 – Political and social views. 3. Italy – Politics and government – 1943–1947. 4. Italy – Politics and government – 1945–1976. I. Title. II. Series: Toronto Italian studies

B3614.C74R593 2019 945.092092 C2018-904968-5

University of Toronto Press acknowledges the financial assistance to its publishing program of the Canada Council for the Arts and the Ontario Arts Council, an agency of the Government of Ontario.

Canada Council for the Arts Conseil des Arts du Canada

Funded by the Government of Canada Financé par le gouvernement du Canada

To my sisters,
Marisa De Chellis and Mirella Diano,
and their families.

Contents

Acknowledgments

The writing of this book created many debts of gratitude that I now have the pleasure to acknowledge. Over several years, a number of booksellers dealt with my orders with speed, efficiency, and good humour; those entitled to special thanks are Mario Ciccoritti of Toronto's Librital; Casalini Libri (Fiesole); and Licosa Sansoni (Florence). Rocco Capozzi, long a pillar of the Department of Italian Studies at the University of Toronto, now a professor emeritus, followed my work with keen interest, read the manuscript at a critical moment, and gave valuable advice for revision and improvement. My former thesis supervisor, Bill Irvine, now professor emeritus at York University, just as in the good old days, read my manuscript with cheerful enthusiasm and then was full of astute observations and encouragement. Michael Lettieri, acting head of undergraduate studies at University of Toronto Mississauga, offered some pertinent comments and several pieces of advice. The official readers for the University of Toronto Press also deserve a note of thanks for reading my manuscript with great attention, for submitting their reports promptly, and for their critical observations, which led in due course to a more focused narrative. Ron Schoeffel of the University of Toronto Press accepted with enthusiasm my proposal for a new book on Croce and remained ever supportive. Unfortunately, he passed away, suddenly and prematurely, before the book's completion. I am only one of many authors and colleagues who mourn his loss. Fortunately for us, Ron's successors at the Press, especially acquisitions editor Stephen Shapiro, continued his legacy and carried on their task with enthusiasm and intelligence, providing support and advice at each stage of the process, from the first submission of the manuscript to its final acceptance for publication. The final draft of the manuscript delivered to University of Toronto Press was copyedited by Anne Laughlin. Formerly managing editor at the Press, and now in active retirement as a freelance editor, she gave the manuscript the benefit of her long familiarity with academic publications, making astute observations and suggesting subtle changes that enhanced the clarity and fluency of the text. Three fellow graduates of the Liceo Classico Ovidio, in Sulmona, Italy, deserve to be singled out. Bruno Caccavella, a cousin by marriage, retrieved old periodicals and out-of-print books and sent them to Canada free of charge. Unfortunately, he died, still young, in late 2016; I will miss his support and his enthusiasm. Giuseppe Evangelista, former principal of our old high school, has shown a generous interest in my work over the years. Luciano Angelone, a lawyer by profession and a liberal by political inclination, was instrumental in obtaining from the Luigi Einaudi Foundation in Rome a photocopy of the unpublished diary of Alfredo Parente, a close friend of Croce's and one of the leaders of Naples' insurrection against the Germans in September 1943. Marta Herling, secretary general of the Istituto Italiano per gli Sutdi Storici in Naples, promptly and graciously responded to my appeals for assorted information and bibliographic material. The librarians of the Stouffville Public Library were pleasant and efficient when dealing with my interlibrary loan requests. Laura Nesci, a graduate of the University of Toronto, transformed my manuscript, typed on a venerable Olivetti Lettera 22, into a computer file. My wife, Joan, during the years of researching and writing this book, has shown understanding and patience while also providing, when it was most needed, critical support. I thank other members of my family, too, for their love, support, and generosity, without which this book would never have seen the light of day: my daughter, Margaret, her husband, Paul, and their daughter, Samantha; and my son, Richard, his wife, Joanna, and their children, Chiara and Arianna. Last but not least, my editor, Curtis Fahey, was a most attentive reader; his comments, questions, and changes have improved the book considerably.

Introduction

This book analyses in detail the political activities of Benedetto Croce, one of the most important Italian intellectuals of the twentieth century, in the years 1943–52, from the fall of Mussolini to the consolidation of the republic under the leadership of Alcide De Gasperi. It aims to correct longstanding misconceptions, and to offer a better understanding of Croce's contribution to Italian political life and to the rebirth of Italian democracy during that turbulent time.

The research relies on extensive published writings by Croce and numerous primary sources and personal documents that have become available in book format over the years, resources that were formerly available only in various archives scattered in many locations. In chapter 1 and the conclusion, I have added information on Croce's life to give today's reader an overview of his main activities and achievements before 1943 and after 1948. The narrative takes a chronological approach in order to avoid generalities and to explore in depth Croce's participation in events, even if running the risk in the process of some repetition. Sometimes, when issues overlap in time, several chapters are devoted to a single year. A number of chapters thus deal with the so-called Kingdom of the South, at a time when Croce acquired a leadership role in dealings with the king, the Allies, and various political parties. This period encompasses the most tragic years of modern Italian history: the peninsula was politically cut in two, invaded by foreign armies, and ravaged by civil war; the monarchy came to an end and the republic was proclaimed; an old order collapsed and new political leaders emerged. For most of that time, Allied troops were present in Italy, and no Italian government, even in liberated territory, enjoyed complete freedom. To appreciate Croce's position fully, one must place his political activities in this context, and stress the constraints it imposed on his choices.

In many ways, this book is an elaboration on the last two chapters of my previous work, *Benedetto Croce and Italian Fascism.* Naturally, the research done for that book proved useful, directly and indirectly, for this one as well. The material I consulted in the national archives of Rome, and the books I read in Toronto, established a deep familiarity with Croce's personality and political and philosophical ideas. I also acquired an awareness of the issues associated with his participation in public affairs. Perhaps most importantly, I became acquainted with Croce's modus operandi: all his life, even during the Fascist regime, he spoke his mind openly and without reticence – *giocare a carte scoperte,* in his own words.[1] There are no secrets in Croce's life to be discovered in the archives of Rome or Naples. What he wrote in his diaries and letters coincided with what he said and did in public – a fact supported by statements in the diaries and correspondence of his contemporaries, in official documents, and in the reports of police informers.

The new research done for this book confirms that earlier discovery, which makes Croce's diaries all the more valuable. There can be no doubt that Croce's writings, public or private, are the best sources of information on his political activities, as well as the most important guide to understanding his goals and to following his changing positions under the constraints imposed by the social and political conditions of the time. For this reason, the story told here draws extensively on Croce's diaries (both those long in print and those recently published), his political speeches, occasional papers, and philosophical essays, and his published correspondence, which already spans more than twenty volumes. My research also draws on a series of personal and official documents collected by Croce himself and published in book format in 1988, edited by Maurizio Griffo and introduced by Gennaro Sasso.[2]

In working with this vast amount of material, I rely, first and foremost, on Croce's diaries. These include the *Taccuini di Lavoro,* work notebooks or diaries covering the period from 1901 to 1949. These were printed in six volumes in 1987 in a private and limited edition, which was subsequently graciously donated by his daughter Alda to the University of Toronto at the time I was writing my earlier book. For 1943–5, however, pride of place goes to the *Taccuini di Guerra* (War Diaries), published in 2004, which offers the full text of Croce's diaries for those years. In this regard, it has to be noted that historians of an older generation, including Giorgio Candeloro and Charles Delzell, were at a disadvantage in assessing Croce's political activities, since they had to rely on a shorter version of his diary, the *Quando l'Italia Era Tagliata in Due,* published by

Croce himself in 1946 and translated into English in 1950 as *Croce, the King and the Allies.* That version was severely edited by Croce to avoid the "touchiness and susceptibilities of others." In a letter to Ivanoe Bonomi, the former prime minister, he wrote that "in some places I had to suppress or attenuate certain particulars and judgments which would have caused pain and discomfort to our common friends." Bonomi himself would have been the first to feel the sting of Croce's observations.[3]

Despite the wealth of writings by Croce at my disposal, I made a special effort to hear the voices of others who were involved in the same events, whether they acted in collaboration with Croce or in opposition to him. The list of sources that contain primary documents on this score is long and covers a variety of subjects. Among the official documents are the minutes of the Committee of National Liberation in Rome; the official proceedings of the Bari Congress and the minutes of the Giunta created by that Congress; and an unpublished report on the Bari proceedings, found among Croce's papers and marked "secret." The latter was provided to the author by Marta Herling, Croce's granddaughter and secretary general of the Italian Institute for Historical Studies in Naples (IISS).[4]

My research has greatly benefited from a series of volumes containing documents and writings pertaining to the Liberal Party and its national leaders. These include the clandestine publications of the party before the fall of Mussolini; the diary and speeches of Luigi Einaudi, the future president of the republic; the speeches of Vittorio Emanuele Orlando, the prime minister who guided Italy to victory in the First World War; a selection of the personal papers of Niccolò Carandini, then ambassador to London; the unpublished diary of Alfredo Parente, a close friend of Croce, provided to the author by the Einaudi Foundation in Rome; and, finally, a long and detailed account of the Liberal Party's policies from 1943 to 1945, written by Leone Cattani, its secretary general in those years.[5]

To achieve a better understanding of Croce's relationship with other political figures, I turned to a number of volumes, each including his correspondence with a particular individual; among these politicians were Alessandro Casati, Vincenzo Arangio Ruiz, Guido Calogero, Carlo Antoni, Adolfo Omodeo, Luigi Russo, Leone Cattani, and Mario Pannunzio, the editor of the Liberal Party newspaper *Risorgimento Liberale.*[6] On another subject, the position of the Vatican on the referendum, the constitution, and the beginning of the Cold War, I have found useful three books recently published by Father Giovanni Sale, SJ, that contain documents from the archives of *Civiltà Cattolica,* an Italian Jesuit periodical that is reputed to be the mouthpiece of the Vatican, especially on political and theological questions. (Its editor meets regularly with the pope and always before the publication of a new issue.)[7]

To ascertain the views of the monarchy, biographies of the king, Vittorio Emanuele, and his son, Umberto, were valuable, as were the diaries of two aides-de-camp and two ministers of the royal household.[8] For clarification of events relating to the Kingdom of the South, I found extremely useful the diaries of Oreste Lizzadri, a Socialist leader, and Filippo Caracciolo, a former ambassador, a leader of the Party of Action, and a secretary to the Giunta. These diaries are barely mentioned in general histories of the period.[9]

For events that took place in Rome before the fall of Mussolini or after the liberation in 1944, I have consulted with great advantage several other diaries, specifically those of Ivanoe Bonomi, chairman of the Committee of National Liberation and future premier; Pietro Nenni, leader of the Socialist Party; Giulio Andreotti, a young man then but already the right-hand man of De Gasperi, leader of the Christian Democrats; and Umberto Zanotti Bianco, a member of a clandestine organization in touch with members of the court and anyone else who counted in the circles of power.[10]

I also examined the writings and recollections of some contemporaries of Croce who were directly involved in the same events or who had been eyewitnesses to them. These include Enzo Storoni, on the ousting of Mussolini; Leopoldo Piccardi, on Badoglio's so-called Government of Forty-Five Days; Palmiro Togliatti, on his return from Russia and his participation in the Badoglio cabinet in Salerno; Max Salvadori, on his experiences in Southern Italy as a British officer with the Special Operations Executive (SOE); Leo Valiani, on his trip north to join the Resistance; Raimondo Craveri, on his underground organization in aid of the Northern Resistance; Luigi Barzini and Paolo Monelli, on the referendum; Giuseppe Dossetti, on the constitutional debates; Giulio Andreotti, on the break-up of the Tripartite coalition in 1947 and the expulsion of the Communists from power; and Guido Carli, a former governor of the Bank of Italy, on Italy's economic reconstruction after the war.[11]

On the Allies' conduct of the war, and their policy towards Italy, I read not only general histories but also works of a more personal nature. Unfortunately, the memoirs of Robert Murphy, American ambassador and political adviser to Supreme Allied Commander Dwight Eisenhower, were without much interest. Much more useful were the *War Diaries* of Harold Macmillan, the future British prime minister, who during the war was Winston Churchill's special emissary to Italy and minister resident in the Mediterranean theatre. Immensely valuable, too, was the *Secret Wartime Correspondence* of Churchill and US President Franklin Roosevelt, a source that sheds light on the Allies' interference in Italian affairs, the rivalry among the Great Powers, and the shifting fortunes of the British Empire and the United States.[12] Also useful for my purposes were some works of fiction, written by newspaper correspondents and other contemporary authors, which provide graphic depictions of wartime living conditions;[13] in particular, two books, one by Herbert Matthews of the *New York Times* and the other by Richard Malone, a Canadian Army officer, offer astute observations on Croce's personality and his political standing in Italian and Allied circles.[14] I consulted as well several volumes of government documents, both Italian and English, some with profit, others with disappointment. Definitely in the latter category were the series *British Documents on Foreign Affairs* and *Foreign Relations of the United States,* the first for the years 1943–5 and the second for 1943–7. Here, I carefully perused the material dealing with Italy and the Vatican; but while this material is important, even essential, for other purposes, it sheds no light on Croce's political activities. In both collections, Croce is rarely mentioned, and when he is, he is usually relegated to a junior position behind Carlo Sforza, the former and future Italian minister of foreign affairs.[15]

By relying on these official records, a reader not fully versed in Italian political history and cultural traditions runs the risk of forming a distorted view of the events unfolding in Italy during the war and immediate post-war period, and also of Croce's special position among Italian political leaders. Used to well-organized political institutions in their own countries, and trained to operate in clearly defined lines of command, most Allied officers failed to grasp that Croce's influence was informal and personal, emanating much more from his moral and intellectual reputation than from his party's position.

Marginally more fruitful, but only for a few episodes, are the three volumes of the *Verbali del Consiglio dei Ministri,* minutes of cabinet meetings, from 1943 to the end of 1944, edited and introduced by Aldo G. Ricci. These minutes record the date of the meeting, the agenda, the final decision, and sometimes the decree enacted, but not the discussion. Often, however, the minutes provide insights into the role of individuals and relationships between them, as well as issues before the government. In one respect, Croce's war diaries are a necessary supplement to the *Verbali*: the meetings of the inner cabinet of Badoglio's last government do not appear in the *Verbali* but are mentioned in Croce's diaries. The same applies to his personal intervention in the meetings of the Bonomi cabinet after June 1944.

In terms of secondary literature, a great deal of scholarship covering the period under discussion has appeared in Italy and elsewhere during the period in which I was researching and writing this book. Also, several new essays have been published on various aspects of Croce's life and ideas.

When dealing with historical events and political leaders, or providing background information, I took great care to rely on the most recent publications and the most authoritative scholars. Piero Craveri's superb biography of De Gasperi has been particularly valuable;[16] the same is true of Paolo Pombeni's biography of Dossetti and Luca Polese Remaggi's biography of Ferruccio Parri.[17] Surprisingly revealing were two books by the late Victor Zaslavsky, *Togliatti e Stalin* (with Elena Aga-Rossi) and *Lo Stalinismo e la Sinistra Italiana,* based as they are on secret Russian documents that became available after the collapse of the Soviet Union. Especially rich in information and insight have been several essays written for academic periodicals and scholarly conferences, notably those appearing in the journal *Ventunesimo Secolo* and those published in book format by Rubbettino Editore, under the title *I Liberali Italiani dall'Antifascismo alla Repubblica,* in two large volumes.[18]

Among general histories, two books by Simona Colarizi, a student of Renzo De Felice and one of the best historians of her generation, are noteworthy: *La Seconda Guerra Mondiale e la Repubblica* and *Storia dei Partiti nell'Italia Repubblicana.* To my pleasant surprise, three old books – Charles Delzell's *Mussolini's Enemies,* Giorgio Candeloro's *Storia dell'Italia Moderna* (vol. 10), and Federico Chabod's *L'Italia Contemporanea* – are still admirable for their wealth of information, their soundness of judgment, and, unlike other works, their care in treating events in the North and South of Italy with equal attention. Reading or re-reading the books of those great historians, now long gone, made me realize the validity of Croce's claim, which he formulated as part of his theory that history is always contemporary history, that in the narration of historical events the most important element is not the documentary record itself but the intelligence, the wisdom, and the personality of the historian who gives meaning to it.[19]

In the world of Croce scholarship, the extensive writings of Gennaro Sasso and Giuseppe Galasso, often published in large tomes and long essays, have benefited me greatly. Whether the subject is Croce's philosophy, historical works, or cultural activity, the knowledge of these scholars remains unmatched and their arguments difficult to challenge.[20] However, strange as it may seem, despite the vast literature devoted to Croce's intellectual pursuits and to his philosophical system, a gap in his biography still remains: there is not yet a published work devoted entirely to Croce's political activities from 1943 to 1952 that explains his actions in detail and does justice to his contribution to the revival of democracy following the end of fascism and the war. No historian has seen fit to place Croce at the centre of a new narrative focused on this period and to assess fully his role in Italian political life, drawing both on documents long in print and ones newly available. Given Croce's importance at the time, this omission is surprising and regrettable, and needs to be addressed if we are to have a complete view of the events unfolding in those years.

Besides the publication of Croce's full wartime diary in 2004, and of several volumes of his correspondence more recently, there are other weighty reasons that justify revisiting this period, making Croce the centre of attention, and offering a new perspective. After the fall of Mussolini, Croce had unequalled authority among Italian anti-Fascist leaders, and few enjoyed more popular support. Once the Italian government left Rome for Southern Italy in September 1943, seeking the Allies' protection, Croce became the leader of the liberal-democratic opposition, and he played a key role in dealing with the king, Prime Minister Badoglio, the Allies, and other Italian political parties. People from all quarters expected him to play a prominent role in the new government. Every time a position of national importance had to be filled, Croce's name was put forward. Had he been more confident of his political abilities, or more driven by personal ambition, he could have replaced Badoglio as prime minister, certainly in Southern Italy during the Kingdom of the South and perhaps later in the country as a whole, and in 1946 he had a fighting chance of becoming president of the republic.

As president of the Liberal Party, Croce also occupied a strategic position in the political landscape of the time. In the party's executive in Naples, or in Rome after its liberation, his voice and influence were paramount; hardly any decision was taken without seeking his advice or consent. Moreover, the Liberal Party had been a founding member and was an essential component of the Committee of National Liberation. In that organization, until the general election of 1946, each of the six parties enjoyed a position of parity, and each decision required unanimous consent. The national government in Rome was based on an agreement reached by the committee's six parties, and it acted according to the same principles. The views of the Liberal Party therefore had consequences for the cabinet. Croce's position, as president of the party, carried weight in the highest councils.

Nevertheless, for various reasons, the lacunae regarding Croce have remained, and so have the misconceptions. In general, historians have not been fair to the Liberals and to Croce in particular. Quite often their role has been downplayed, or dealt with in a cursory way, if not completely ignored, as Giovanni Orsina and Fabio Grassi Orsini have forcefully argued. The achievements, real or imaginary, of the Communist Party and the Party of Action have been stressed to the detriment of the Liberals, the Christian Democrats, and the Socialists, and the history of the Northern Resistance has received greater attention than the events that took place in Southern Italy. In both cases there are evident partisan preferences and slanted accounts.[21]

Consider, for instance, that even Claudio Pavone in his massive *Una Guerra Civile* does not say much about Croce and the other political figures of Southern Italy, focused as he is on the Northern Resistance and its protagonists, big or small. The most glaring example, however, is the treatment of the 1944 "Turn of Salerno," referring to the Communist Party's decision to accept the continuance of the king on the throne and to support a new coalition government led by Badoglio, a decision that represented a complete abandonment of its previous policy. In acclaimed works by Roberto Battaglia, Antonio Gambino, Antonio Lepre, and Paolo Spriano, the role of the Communist Party leader, Palmiro Togliatti, in that event is emphasized and the contribution of Croce minimized. For these authors, Togliatti's return to Italy from the Soviet Union and his unexpected initiative in 1944 broke a political impasse and made possible the formation of a new coalition government supported by the anti-Fascist parties.[22] Typical of the existing, and long-lasting, bias is the judgment offered by Ernesto Ragionieri, a Marxist historian, in his influential *History of Italy*, published with great fanfare by Einaudi in 1975: "Despite the slow steps forward made through the actions of Croce, and the propitious atmosphere that these had created, a political initiative [by Togliatti] was necessary [in 1944] that would lend a new direction to the discussions underway, changing radically the logic in which they had been entangled since the beginning."[23]

In the face of such bias, the defence mounted by Croce's admirers has been rather generic and often not based on solid arguments. For example, in 2014 Giancristiano Desiderio published a lively and very appreciative biography of Croce that went through three reprints in less than a year. But Desiderio focused mainly on Croce's intellectual pursuits and cultural achievements. In a book of almost five hundred pages, he devoted only a few pages to the political activities of Croce in Southern Italy during the war, and without offering a detailed analysis of the events in which he was directly involved.[24]

Things, however, are slowly changing. In recent years, not without some difficulties, a group of liberal-minded historians has given a more positive assessment of the Liberal Party's contribution to the Resistance and to the social and economic reconstruction of Italy after the war.[25] One of these historians, in a long essay, has claimed that Croce was not only a great philosopher but also a distinguished statesman and skilful party leader.[26]

This book shares that view, and provides the evidence to support its claims, narrating the events from 1943 to 1952 in which Croce was among the chief protagonists of Italian political life.[27] In the process it dispels a few misconceptions and at the same time clarifies several issues. It shows that Croce, among other things, was the real deus ex machina of the Turn of Salerno. He played a leading role in the Congress of Bari and was instrumental in preventing that body from collapsing in discord. He guided the democratic parties in the South away from empty rhetoric towards a more realistic stance. He assured the unity of the anti-Fascist leaders, demonstrating unsuspected diplomatic skills along the way, and compelled the king to retire to private life. He was the driving force behind the formation of the third Badoglio cabinet, and shaped its program. He blocked a drift to the right by the Liberal Party in the post-war years, and put an end, through his alliance with De Gasperi, to the Jacobin aspirations, or temptations, of the radical parties, thereby assuring that Italy remained anchored in Western traditions, the Atlantic alliance, and the European Union. The analysis presented here provides a fuller and more accurate interpretation of Croce's political philosophy, showing that his liberalism was characterized by a dynamic conception of life, was open to reform, and had a progressive inclination, even if it favoured personal initiative, individual responsibility, and respect for tradition, understood as the work of previous generations.

In summary, this book fills a gap in the biography of Benedetto Croce; it covers aspects of his public life that have often been overlooked and analyses in detail the events in which he was involved, thus going beyond the usual generalities. Furthermore, the research on which the book is based draws on some of Croce's writings that are regarded to be of minor importance by those who are more concerned with his philosophy but that in fact are essential to understanding his political actions – and even his political theory. In short, this new study of mine does for Croce's political activity from 1943 to 1952 what my earlier book did for his anti-Fascist efforts under Mussolini's dictatorship from 1922 to 1943. It recounts what he did, said, and wrote during these years, and it puts the reader in a position to appreciate Croce's significant contribution to the return and vitality of democratic life after the fall of Mussolini and in the aftermath of the war. My hope is that others, after reading my account, will agree with me that Croce deserves to be ranked among the founding fathers of the Italian republic, and belongs to the pantheon of the nation.

Finally, a few editorial notes. All of Croce's quotations are my own translations, and I have tried to maintain the rhythm of his classical prose. In a few cases, to make the text clear to a modern reader, I have made minor adjustments, adding punctuation or even a noun here and there. Sometimes, a long sentence has been broken up into shorter ones. I have taken these liberties with some reluctance, but in the realization that, in an electronic age accustomed to short messages, long and complex sentences, with the harmony achieved through subordinate and relative clauses, are no longer fashionable. I usually prefer to quote Croce directly rather than paraphrase him, because, more often than not, the meaning of his words is clear. Also, I wanted the reader to hear his voice, so as to better understand his feelings and his ideas.

The book capitalizes the names of discrete political groups and parties (such as Liberal, Communist, Socialist, Fascist) and uses the lower case for the names of the ideologies they represent (liberalism, communism, socialism, fascism). Also, with regard to the Committee of National Liberation, the Italian form of this name was Comitato di Liberazione Nazionale, and all sources, Italian and English, contemporary and later, use the Italian abbreviation "CLN" rather than the English "CNL." That is also the abbreviation used here, even though the full name is given in its English form. The same logic applies to the Committee of National Liberation for Upper Italy (CLNAI).

BENEDETTO CROCE AND THE BIRTH OF THE ITALIAN REPUBLIC, 1943–1952

1
Croce and Italy in 1943

In 1943 Italy entered one of the more tragic periods of its history, reaping the bitter fruits of fascism and of Mussolini's imperial adventures. As a nation it was no longer able to wage war or to achieve peace; it had become a rudderless boat in a stormy sea and with no port in sight. That year the Italian army and the German Afrika Korps were defeated in North Africa, and the Allies landed in Sicily while their bombs rained down on Italian cities. In July, in quick succession, the king, Vittorio Emanuele, ousted Mussolini and the Fascist regime collapsed. After twenty years in power, Mussolini became a captive and Marshal Pietro Badoglio formed a new government. In September, an armistice between Italy and the Allies was signed. Then the king and Badoglio left Rome for Southern Italy, and the Germans invaded the country and returned Mussolini to nominal power in the North. At the same time, a Resistance movement arose in Central and Northern Italy, while the Allied armies continued their slow advance from the South.

The king's ouster of Mussolini, prompted less by internal unrest than by military defeats, occurred on 25 July 1943. Thus, after twenty years of complicity, the long dictatorship came to an end, not by a popular insurrection, but by royal intervention supported by disgruntled generals and disillusioned party leaders. Once the duce was in captivity, the Fascist regime melted like snow under the sun, in Hitler's words. Throughout the country the population applauded the king's action. Yet, welcome and necessary as the king's initiative was, it had come several months too late, when the military situation had deteriorated, the position of Italy had been severely weakened, and the presence of German troops, already strong, had increased throughout the peninsula. Always uncertain in his deliberations, the king had waited too long and wasted precious time.

By now, Italy was no longer able to continue the war, but the strengthened presence of the German forces made it difficult to reach peace with the Allies. The king then made another blunder. Against advice from different quarters, Vittorio Emanuele refused to allow the formation of a government of national unity that would embrace all the reborn democratic parties and include anti-Fascist leaders. Instead, Badoglio, a man of considerable military reputation, but with a controversial past, as former Chief of Staff under Mussolini until 1940, became head of the new government; he then formed a cabinet consisting of uninspiring civil servants and mediocre generals, all of them without political experience or moral authority, none possessing strong leadership abilities.[1]

When the invasion of the country appeared imminent, a group of liberal leaders re-emerged from the catacombs, where they had been relegated by the Fascist regime, and began to reorganize their forces. They held meetings among themselves in Rome and in other cities of Italy, and some of them met with the king in the spring of 1943 and urged him, to no avail, to fire Mussolini, form a new democratic government, put an end to the war, and seek peace with the Allies.

Among these old political leaders, Benedetto Croce enjoyed a special status, both for his intellectual renown and for his long opposition to the Fascist regime. Croce was born in 1866 into an upper-class Neopolitan family that had remained faithful to the old order and immune to the ideals and passions of the Risorgimento, the cultural and political movement that called for the unification and independence of Italy under liberal institutions and the House of Savoy. At one time his ancestors had been shepherds and then over the years became owners of sheep farms in the region of Abruzzi, constantly increasing their wealth and their herds. After they moved from the countryside to the capital of the kingdom, they acquired extensive landholdings in the provinces of Campania and Apulia. Their upward mobility continued through the generations; Croce's grandfather married into the provincial aristocracy and ended his career as a judge of the Supreme Court.

At home and at school, Croce received a traditional Catholic education. A voracious reader from an early age, he lost his faith while attending high school, when one of his teachers, a devout priest, encouraged him to read books of philosophy. In time, he developed a more humanistic and secular conception of life, but the basic tenets of Christian morality remained central to his personal and intellectual outlook, informing his private and public life.

In 1883 Croce and his family suffered a tragedy: his parents and a sister died during an earthquake on the island of Ischia, near Capri, where they were on holiday. Another brother, away at the time, was spared, but Croce himself remained buried under the ruins for a full night, suffering a broken leg and bruises all over his body. Rescued by soldiers, he quickly recovered, but the experience left a deep emotional scar that never healed, making him subject to depression, even to the point of contemplating suicide. In the process, he acquired a tragic view of life, despite the image of Olympian calm that he presented in public, as revealed by his diaries.

After this episode, Croce spent two unhappy years in Rome under the tutelage of his paternal uncle, Silvio Spaventa, a leading liberal politician of the time and, by philosophical persuasion, a Hegelian. In the house of his uncle, which was a gathering place of major politicians and intellectuals, Croce for the first time came into contact with national issues and listened to free-wheeling philosophical discussions. There he met Antonio Labriola, a university teacher and Marxist philosopher, who became his intellectual mentor. Meanwhile, he also attended university, but, unimpressed with academic life, he dropped out after a year, without regret. He never enrolled again in university, becoming instead a self-taught scholar.

In 1886 Croce returned to Naples and entrusted the management of the family's holdings to his brother, devoting himself with great discipline to wide-ranging intellectual pursuits, including research first on local traditions and later in the areas of history, literature, and philosophy. For a short period, under Labriola's influence, he fell under the spell of socialism and Marxism, as was fashionable among youth at the turn of the century. In the 1890s he wrote several essays on Marxism that greatly impressed Georges Sorel in France, Eduard Bernstein in Germany, and Filippo Turati in Milan.

From 1900 to 1910, Croce published at regular intervals the fundamental works setting out his philosophical system, works that gained him a national and international reputation as a leading philosopher of the Hegelian school. He was particularly noted for his theory of aesthetics, in which he viewed art and poetry as forms of lyrical intuition, and his idea that history is always contemporary history. In 1901, with the collaboration of Giovanni Gentile, Croce launched a bimonthly periodical, *La Critica*, which quickly was recognized as one of the most important journals of the time, especially for its essays on history, literature, and philosophy. The same year he also began a close and fruitful association with the Laterza publishing house that would endure for the next fifty years, an association that helped to shape the cultural landscape of the country.

In 1910 Croce entered national politics when he was named a senator for life by royal decree, as was then the rule. Though not a great orator, and not interested in politics as a career, he took his duties as senator seriously; he spoke only a few times in the Senate, but he participated in all the important votes. At the outbreak of the First World War, he campaigned for Italian neutrality, incurring for that stand the everlasting wrath of the nationalists and other interventionists of a democratic bent. During the war he was a member of various committees engaged in supporting the war effort and providing assistance to veterans. At the same time, in the press and in his own periodical, he defended freedom of expression and condemned the exaggerated claims of nationalist propaganda that poured forth from both warring camps.

After the war, in 1921, he became minister of education in the last cabinet of Giovanni Giolitti, and in that post he strove to recreate the cultural cooperation that existed before the war among European nations and academic institutions; above all, he prepared the ground for an ambitious reform of education which would be carried out with great energy by Giovanni Gentile two years later under Mussolini. Following the March on Rome in 1922, Croce initially took a benevolent stand towards the coalition government of Mussolini, hoping that fascism would restore the weakened authority of the state without departing from the liberal traditions of the Risorgimento and without changing the institutions of a free society. But, in the summer of 1924, when the Socialist leader, Giacomo Matteotti, was murdered by a gang of Fascist thugs who had close ties to the Fascist Party and easy access to government offices, Croce changed course. That summer, he gave a newspaper interview critical of government actions and sponsored a motion in the Senate calling on the government to restore the rule of law, protect freedom of expression, and put an end to all violence. In the fall he broke off his friendship with Gentile, who had become an enthusiastic supporter of Mussolini.

His anti-government activity intensified in 1925 after Mussolini embarked on a systematic destruction of the liberal state, and the construction of a dictatorial regime in its place, by means of altering the constitution of Italy, suppressing the basic rights of citizens, and outlawing opposition parties. From that point on, Croce maintained a "constant and resolute opposition" that found expression in the realms both of culture and of politics. In quick succession, he joined the Liberal Party in 1925 and became an active member on its behalf; wrote a "Manifesto of Anti-Fascist Intellectuals"; established a close friendship with Giovanni Amendola, the leader of the opposition; expressed public solidarity with anti-Fascist figures harassed or persecuted by the regime; published articles in the press critical of the government and leaders of the Fascist Party; and wrote essays for *La Critica* in defence of liberalism and the ideals of the Risorgimento. Later on, in the Senate, he voted against all the laws abrogating freedom of expression and association, and, in 1929, he spoke and voted against the ratification of the Lateran Pacts between the Italian state and the Vatican. In 1931 he resigned from the Academia dei Lincei and other learned bodies when members were required to swear allegiance to the Fascist regime; in 1938 he publicly criticized the Racial Laws aimed at Jews; and, throughout the late 1930s, he made known his opposition to military adventures and the alliance with Nazi Germany.[2]

During Mussolini's dictatorship, Croce never entertained the idea of going into exile, nor did he join any underground organization, aware that he did not possess the personal qualities that such an activity required, "used as I am to speaking my mind freely." Yet, through his frequent trips throughout Italy and Europe, his regular correspondence, and the hospitality of his house in Naples and his summer residence in Piedmont, he remained in close touch with the old political leaders, with the anti-Fascist exiles, and with the young people involved in the underground resistance, often supporting them in their political and economic difficulties.

For his opposition to the regime, Croce incurred the hostility both of the authorities and of Fascist militants. One night in 1926, after a failed assassination attempt against Mussolini in Bologna, his house was invaded and ransacked by a group of Fascist thugs. Afterwards, the house was put under police surveillance, his movements abroad and in Italy were often monitored by police agents, and his mail was frequently opened, sometimes even confiscated. The regime also recruited spies among his entourage and among Laterza employees to keep him under close watch. In response, Croce took some elementary precautions, but mostly he continued to live a normal life, following his usual routines.

In so doing, he exploited with great skill the margin of freedom that he enjoyed on account of his national and international reputation and his immunity against prosecution as a member of the Senate. The results of his efforts were impressive, as shown by the sheer number of books, essays, and other writings he was able to produce during these difficult times. He became internationally known as a fearless defender of the liberal ideals of the Risorgimento heritage and a powerful symbol of opposition to Mussolini's dictatorship. His writings influenced generations of Italians; a few of his books became bestsellers, despite the official boycott of his writings in the Fascist era. Some of his historical and political essays provided inspiration for political activity and offered nourishment to those who were active in the underground resistance or suffering in jail or living in exile. *La Critica* even increased its circulation and was avidly read by friends and foes alike; especially popular was a column in which Croce regularly denounced the peccadilloes of those intellectuals who had once been liberal democrats but suddenly became admirers of Mussolini and supporters of fascism.

As a result of his moral and intellectual influence and personal contacts, Croce was able to generate a peculiar ethical-political movement, the "Italian Family," as he called it, or a "centre of business," as defined by a police informer. This movement was loosely organized and without written rules but united by moral ties. Members of this movement lived mainly in major urban centres throughout Italy and comprised influential intellectuals, university teachers, and former politicians. In the past they had been of various political persuasions, but now they were united by their love of freedom and opposition to the authoritarian regime. After the fall of Mussolini, some of them joined the Liberal Party or the Socialist Party, but the majority went on to form the Party of Action. Quite a few played leading roles in the Resistance and after the end of the war held influential positions in the republic, displaying in both cases a special Crocean flavour, admired by some, resented by others.[3]

In 1943 Croce was seventy-seven years old, still enjoying good health and a vigorous mind. Amid the worries and difficulties created by the war, and by the frequent bombardments suffered by the city of Naples, Croce's literary output remained quite remarkable, in both quantity and quality. His periodical, *La Critica,* was still published regularly every two months, and he continued to offer advice to the Laterza publishing house. A passion for hard work had always been a characteristic of Croce's personality, providing a therapeutic defence against the danger of depression. But, after the fall of Mussolini, more and more of Croce's time was devoted by necessity to political affairs and public obligations.

When the armistice was signed between the Italian government and the Allies in September 1943, and the king and Badoglio, to avoid German capture, fled to safety in Southern Italy, Croce's villa in Sorrento – where he had then moved – became almost a seat of government in exile. Assuming the role of leader of the opposition, he became the centre of all the democratic forces opposing the king and his current government. He was the most famous intellectual in Italy, and one of the most respected political leaders in the South. Nobody was better known, or enjoyed equal prestige at home or abroad, and especially among the Allies. A political power to be reckoned with, he found himself at the centre of political negotiations affecting the future of the king, the monarchy, the formation of a new government, and the relations with Allied authorities.[4]

Max Salvadori, as a member of the British Special Operations Executive and an expert on Italian affairs in contact with high-ranking Allied officials, witnessed the influence that Croce enjoyed. He wrote: "We have to remember that ... Croce was then the Italian figure best known and esteemed in democratic nations; his position was taken into consideration not only by intellectuals but also by politicians; his statements arrived on the desks of the few who were sitting at the top of the Allied command administration ... During the crucial and difficult months of the fall of 1943 and the winter of 1944, the central point of the Italian political situation was Croce, and not Badoglio; for, in the eyes of the Allies, Croce was universally known and esteemed while Badoglio was equally known but little esteemed."[5] By coincidence, British minister resident Harold Macmillan had a low opinion of the new cabinet: "The Italian government then consisted of a fugitive King and Prime Minister, two Germanophile generals, and a rather crooked courtier, huddled together in a fortress in Brindisi."[6] Salvadori concurred, repeating probably what he heard among his British colleagues. "The Allies have no confidence in the Italian government ... How different would it be if there were a complete break with the past, and people like Croce and Bonomi were to form a new cabinet, joined by those who have spent long years in prison."[7] Salvadori's assessment is echoed in the memoirs of Richard Malone, a captain in the Canadian Army Corps. In civilian life, Malone would become a fine military historian, and during the war, as a liaison officer assigned to General Bernard Montgomery's headquarters, he participated in the planning of the landing operations in Sicily and Calabria. In his official capacities, Malone was in a position to know the plans and opinions circulating among Allied officials. In those quarters, he wrote, "the famous and much respected Italian philosopher and historian" was mentioned as a possible candidate "of a temporary civilian government till the whole country was liberated."[8]

During those months, Croce was urged repeatedly to assume the top leadership post in the government not only by his liberal friends but also by Ugo La Malfa of the Party of Action. Even the king at one point made an offer, which was firmly refused. Yet, while lacking personal ambition, Croce was ready and willing to play his part in the creation of a more democratic government. He pursued his goals with determination, but also with moderation. He showed common sense and political realism, and even unsuspected qualities of diplomacy, always acting with patience and dignity whether dealing with Italian politicians or with Allied officers. His main objectives were to regain prestige and respect for Italy among the Allies, and to increase or restore the authority of the Italian government. To achieve those aims, as Gennaro Sasso has indicated, he proposed and pursued three main points: abdication of the king, who shared some of the responsibility for fascism, to mark a new political beginning; creation of a government of national unity, supported by all the anti-Fascist parties; and an increased war effort beside the Allied forces to speed up the liberation of Italy from the Germans. Croce did not always have his way; he suffered some disappointments, and the hard reality of the times often compelled him to accept honourable compromises, or to change his views. But, in time, his main goals would be realized.[9]

Despite the isolation of Sorrento, Croce became one of the best-informed men in Italy. From Sorrento, or from Capri during the few weeks he lived there, Croce kept in touch with political events by listening to the radio, exchanging letters with his friends, and sending and receiving emissaries to and from Naples, Rome, Brindisi, Bari, and other cities. For a while his son-in-law, Raimondo Craveri, acted as his special envoy. He was visited often by Badoglio's ministers, Italian army officers, and civil servants, all seeking advice, bringing news, or venting their frustrations. Almost every day, he received political leaders of the anti-Fascist parties from Naples, Rome, or Bari. Like many others in those days, Italians or foreigners, when ambassador Filippo Caracciolo met Croce for the first time he was greatly impressed. "I have experienced one of the most important moments of my life. I have been admitted to the presence of true greatness. With absolute modesty and integrity this man personifies the highest ideals, those moral and civil ideals that could unite the best Italians of today. For all of us he is a source of strength and inspiration ... His person, his intellect, his ideas are a precious element of nobility and offer authority for our struggle."[10]

Croce was consulted often by Allied officers and members of the intelligence agencies. Among these were many former acquaintances, sons of old friends, or more often readers of his books and students of philosophy in American or British universities. Croce had meetings with American, British, French, and Soviet ministers attached to the Allied headquarters of General Dwight Eisenhower, among them Harold Macmillan, publisher of some of his books, and the "inscrutable" Andrey Vyshinsky, the cold mastermind of Stalin's purges and now an equally sour diplomat. Able to speak English, French, and Spanish, Croce gave frequent interviews to American and British journalists, often friends from the pre-war years, like Cecil Sprigge. But more often these were young war correspondents, not familiar with Italian history and culture, all seeking a better understanding of the country's present predicament. And all were cordially received by Croce, who answered their questions with remarkable patience, in some cases with amusement but rarely with rudeness.

The foreign correspondents no doubt learned a great deal about Italian affairs, past and present, from their meetings with Croce. But the meetings must have been useful for Croce too. He had the opportunity to ask questions and to learn first-hand about the war aims of the Allies, not to mention the mood of international public opinion or the results of the international conferences where post-war settlements were discussed. Croce used his sessions with journalists to explain his position and to make known his political aspirations, but above all to defend the general interests of Italy and the needs of its people.[11]

In all of this, Croce was not acting alone. He was president of the Liberal Party, which was a member of the Committee of National Liberation (CLN). He had sympathizers in all political parties and among the educated public. The presidents of the CLN branches in Naples and Bari, the organization's basis of power in Southern Italy, were close friends. He could count on the solidarity of newspaper editors in Bari and Naples and in other cities. He was at the core of a group of strong figures who shared the same hopes and goals, notably opposition to the king and to the Badoglio government. Including Carlo Sforza, Enrico De Nicola, Alberto Tarchiani, Vincenzo Arangio Ruiz, Adolfo Omodeo, and Alberto Cianca, this group had tentacles stretching throughout Southern Italy and was in constant communication with Rome and other centres of political activity. Its members could pursue policies of their own, and enter into negotiations even with the king or Badoglio, but they always consulted with Croce. No decision was reached without his knowledge or taken without his approval, after some discussion. In the end, contrary to conventional wisdom and accepted accounts, it was less the intervention of Palmiro Togliatti than the cooperation of Croce and De Nicola that produced a compromise with the king which made possible the third Badoglio cabinet and the first democratic government after fascism – a development that has passed into history as the "Turn of Salerno."[12]

Croce also found support within his family; his daughters acted as his secretaries; his son-in-law became a roving ambassador and special messenger, travelling to Rome and Bari or meeting Allied officers in various places. Croce's villa in Sorrento functioned as a sort of hotel, hosting friends from Rome, Naples, Bari, and elsewhere. On a few occasions, out of respect for his age, cabinet meetings took place there. In Croce's diary, his wife is rarely mentioned, but Adelina Croce must have struck quite a figure. She was the one who maintained order, made sure that everything was clean and washed, and above all put regular meals on the table. To assure the requirements of an enlarged household, she had to deal daily with local suppliers or vendors from the countryside, or perhaps with their own tenants not far from Sorrento. This was not an easy task in those troubled times, and required organizing skills, force of persuasion, and a great deal of personal stamina. Herbert Matthews of the *New York Times* captured well the atmosphere of the Croce household. For many newspapermen, he said, "it was a great consolation" to have "fascinating talks" with Croce "in rooms lined with books" and then to enjoy "pleasant luncheons" that were "provided and presided over by his charming wife." These encounters also had intellectual rewards. "A conversation with Croce was always stimulating, even when one disagreed with him." Matthews reported that "it is in such gatherings that one finds the permanence of all that is good in Italy." He ended his reminiscences on this subject with an astute observation on Croce's changing mood. When he first met him, "there was an aura of rejuvenation about the gentle old man," but later, as the war continued and Italy's suffering increased, "he lost that happy feeling."[13]

The actions of the king and Badoglio after the fall of Mussolini added to his anguish. The government that held office in Italy from 25 July to 8 September 1943 is known in Italian history books as the Government of Forty-Five Days. Mussolini had been ousted from power and jailed; Badoglio had replaced the dictator and formed a new cabinet, but the authoritarian structure of government remained in place. The war against the Allies continued; the alliance with Germany was not yet repudiated. Italy was in a state of siege and ruled by martial law; public order was entrusted to the army; political demonstrations were dispersed by force; military tribunals were kept in operation and applied the rules with full rigour. Political parties were still outlawed, and censorship of the press continued. Freedom of expression was limited; it was impossible to criticize the king or the government openly and directly. For the most part, it was almost a new incarnation of fascism, only without Mussolini. Unlike the former regime, however, the new one wanted to end the war, somehow.

By historical necessity, Italy had returned to the status of an absolute monarchy, and by personal inclination the king had no intention of restoring the rules of a democratic society; he also had no desire, perhaps did not possess the moral energy, to undertake radical changes or bold initiatives, either in internal affairs or in foreign policy. He had refused Badoglio's advice to include moderate anti-Fascist leaders in the government and had assembled a cabinet of civil servants used to following orders. Left to his own devices, he would have included in the new administration moderate Fascists, like Dino Grandi, without realizing the inappropriateness of doing so. As a result, the new government had no moral standing, and no precise plan of action. It was concerned only with law and order; it wanted to assure the authority of the state and to protect the safety of the king and, with him, the permanence of the monarchy.

But events moved forward, sometimes contrary to the king's expectations. Strangely enough for a military man, Badoglio showed, on many occasions, a mental elasticity far superior to that of the king and his closest advisers. The old marshal realized that changes were necessary, even inevitable. Despite numerous obstacles, political parties were being reorganized, if in a semi-clandestine way. Their leaders had formed, first, the National Committee of the Opposition, and later were united in the Committee of National Liberation under the chairmanship of a former prime minister, Ivanoe Bonomi. The Fascist Party was outlawed; the mass organizations of the regime were disbanded; the Special Tribunal for the Defence of the State was suppressed. The trade unions were put under the direction of Socialist and Christian Democrat leaders, even of members of the Communist Party. Bruno Buozzi, the old trade unionist, friend of Socialist politician Filippo Turati, resumed his former positions as head of the Industrial Workers Federation and chairman of the General Council of Labour and played an influential role in labour relations. Political prisoners were slowly released, and political debate began to resume.

But the fundamental problem faced by the king, Badoglio, and the Italian people was how to end the war. Unfortunately, before and after the fall of Mussolini, no decision was made on how to deal with the Germans or how to get in touch with the Allies. No preparation had been undertaken to change sides. No avenues for possible peace negotiations were explored in advance. Everybody knew that the war was lost and that the time had come to seek peace. But the king and the generals were incapable of taking a bold decision for fear of incurring the wrath of the Germans. So the king and Badoglio tried to gain time – in a situation where time was of the essence. Precious days were spent in hypocritical meetings with the Germans and in sterile negotiations with the Allies for better terms that were no longer in the cards. The consequences of delay and uncertainty would be catastrophic for Italy, and fatal for the monarchy.[14]

During this period, Croce was living in Sorrento. He had left Naples in the winter of 1942, following the advice of friends who were concerned for his safety. Industrial cities and maritime centres, like Naples, were then being subjected to heavy bombing to disrupt the movement of troops and the production and transportation of goods. Croce agreed to make the move despite his reluctance at his age to leave familiar surroundings. The decision, however, proved wise because his Naples neighbourhood was later badly damaged. When the family finally returned home in 1944, months after the liberation of Naples and Rome, Croce found, to his surprise, in one of the closets a still-live bomb, which, before calling an army specialist, he then carried to a balcony, "gently," as he wrote in his diary.

On the night of 25 July 1943, close to midnight, when Mussolini's fall from power was reported over the radio, there was joy, commotion, and confusion in Croce's household as in all of Italy. He was roused from bed; friends who had just left for the day came back, and those in the vicinity came over to discuss the news. The end of the dictatorship was received with jubilation by the Italian people, from North to South. Croce's reaction was no different. As he wrote in his diary: "My feeling is one of liberation from an illness that weighed at the centre of the soul: damage, pain, and danger remain, but that illness will never return."[15]

Like most Italians in those days and afterwards, Croce spent time grasping at news, making conjectures, and seeking information, all in the hope of receiving solid facts instead of rumours. As had happened in 1925, when the Fascist regime began, so now, at its end, there was the spectacle of turncoats, people disclaiming their pasts or proclaiming their innocence, and even boasting of a record of courageous opposition to the dictatorship not seen before by others. "Not unforeseen but always repugnant is the show we are witnessing of sudden political changes," Croce wrote. Still, Croce, like others who later remembered the same events, also noted something different – and certainly more appealing: "an effusion, a joy for the return of the name and appearance of freedom ... which seems sane and sincere: a sign, one may hope, that the oppression and the corruption of fascism had not succeeded in destroying that idea in the hearts of Italians."[16]

Under Badoglio there was still censorship of the press, though controls were loosened. Editors who had compromised with fascism were replaced by others more in tune with the new reality. Sometimes old editors, ousted by Mussolini, were given back their former positions. As during the Fascist regime, some editors were more daring than others and were not afraid to bend the official directives. Gaetano Afeltra of *Corriere della Sera* and Alberto Bergamini of *Giornale d'Italia* were among them.

For the first time in his life, Croce became a contributor to the *Corriere della Sera*, then and later the leading Italian newspaper. He was among those liberal writers who, in the pages of that paper, as Afeltra wrote, "during the 45 days condemned the Fascist regime, denounced its violence and arbitrary acts, and also pointed out its ridiculous side." In particular, Croce called attention to the official textbooks that, during the Fascist regime, the public schools were compelled to adopt as part of the curriculum and that were instrumental in inculcating the cult of "Il Duce." According to Afeltra, his intervention had an effect. "The government abolished those textbooks, whose principal aim was to shape the minds of young people and to foster the idolatry of Mussolini." Later, when Mussolini returned to power in Northern Italy, he demanded a list of all those who had written articles critical of his regime in the *Corriere della Sera*. Croce's name was prominent on that list, a fact that, for him as for others, "could mean arrest, deportation and even death."[17]

Croce's most significant newspaper article at this time appeared in August in the *Giornale d'Italia*. The article resembled a political program. He defined his priorities, expressed his fears, and at the same time clarified the nature of his liberalism. Croce was convinced that the fight against the dictatorship and the oppression suffered by all democratic parties had created a new and stronger sense of unity among political movements and the Italian people. Yet he also saw signs of future danger, notably the radical aspirations evident in some demonstrations and written into the platforms of some of the political parties. These radical proposals were put forth not only by the traditional left-wing parties but also by those democratic leaders who had a Jacobin conception of politics and were ready to use government intervention, and to employ force, in order to achieve their goals. Croce was afraid that, driven by enthusiasm and impatience, Italy could share the tragic fate of Spain at the end of Primo de Rivera's dictatorship. "Spain, once it regained freedom, wanted then to undertake and to solve, all together and at the same time, problems of a different nature, from the struggle against the church to agrarian reform; as a result, her people became divided, and her land was soaked by rivers of fraternal blood."

To avoid the repetition of the same events in Italy, and to prevent a possible return to dictatorship, it was essential to have a clear set of priorities. Not surprising, for Croce, "the restoration and protection of freedom was fundamental" and took precedence over anything else. Before any social problem could be addressed in a democratic way, "freedom has to enter the minds and fill the hearts of people." To forestall new oppression, "freedom has to become the common platform of all parties, and it has to be accepted and respected by all in the political arena." As he had done under the Fascist regime, Croce stressed again the distinction between liberalism and *liberismo,* or the free-market economy, and especially that between the theory of freedom and the problems associated with economic and social issues. This position reflected, not "indifference towards those issues," but a clear understanding that such issues could be resolved only when the distinction between freedom and matters of public policy "is observed and maintained."

In the weeks after the fall of Mussolini, some leaders of the radical parties invoked the use of force to achieve social revolution. In his *Giornale d'Italia* article, Croce reminded his readers that all parties have the right to fight for their cause, but none has the right "to call for force and make recourse to violence," let alone invoke a temporary dictatorship, even in the name of the proletariat. The article ends with an eloquent defence of the ideals of freedom and political unity as the best protection of Italy's newly regained liberty. "Let all of us, belonging to different parties, old and new, unite our forces to give strength to our common aspiration and foundation: freedom." There is also a call for moderation and realism and the avoidance of partisan fanaticism. "Let us remain vigilant against the deviations that can be produced by our particular aspirations which for too much impatience could destroy freedom and with it even the possibility of their own fulfilment."[18]

In November 1943 Croce republished this article in a booklet together with other short political essays dealing with the nature of liberalism and issues of the moment. In the introduction to that booklet he made another recommendation, dictated by the changed circumstances following the German invasion of Italy. Political debates were necessary and fruitful in the new life of Italy, but now, Croce added, "I want to stress that there should be a temporary truce, and we should turn, in full agreement, all the force of our minds and our wills to the main aim of liberating our land from the German invader."[19] As he had done during fascism, Croce continued his relentless polemics in defence of liberalism against all his political and philosophical adversaries. In the political arena, however, a government of national unity among democratic forces, and unity in the fight against Germans, remained his top priority.

Another of Croce's articles in the *Giornale d'Italia* dealt with the matter of the Academy of Italy, created by Mussolini between 1926 and 1929. As often happened in those days, whenever there was an important position to be filled, the name of Croce was mentioned. However, when it was proposed that he become the new president of the academy, Croce not only refused the nomination but suggested instead the outright abolition of that body – which for him was beyond redemption – and the restoration of the old and more illustrious Accademia dei Lincei that Mussolini had suppressed. As Croce explained: "The Academy of Italy has been created notoriously as a means of inducement and enslavement for the men of letters and science, and unfortunately has largely fulfilled its corrupting task."[20]

In that article there is also one of the first mentions of a question that would trouble Italian political life for the next few years. How should those members of the Academy of Italy who had fatally compromised themselves by wholly adhering to the Fascist regime be distinguished from those who deserved to be included in the new Lincei by virtue of their scientific achievements and upright character? Here Croce announced the criteria that should guide the purge of Fascist militants, the so-called cleansing or *epurazione.* "There are in this Academy some worthy men, besides members without any merit and who did not maintain their moral dignity." Such individuals could again be elected members of the new Lincean Academy, following, however, some special screening procedures which should avoid "vengeance and cruelty" but instead promote the principles of "discernment and justice, united at the same time with some compassion and leniency." These were noble principles, no doubt, but difficult to apply amid the passions of civil war.[21]

From July to September 1943, Croce, with the help of friends, undertook to reorganize the Liberal Party in various parts of Italy, and especially in Naples and other cities in the South. To clarify the party's political program, Croce wrote several essays. He also encouraged the Neapolitan section of the party to publish a series of pamphlets dealing "with the most urgent economic, financial, constitutional and cultural problems." The publishing activity of the party during that time, and the essays written later by Croce himself, or by Luigi Einaudi and by Guido Carli, both future governors of the Bank of Italy, show that the Liberal Party possessed clear political and economic ideas, moderate but suited to the needs of the time. What the Liberal Party always lacked was not ideas but a solid organization equal to that of the new mass parties, as modern politics required. Instead, it remained, then and later, a party of elites, which included people of ability and stature but also, especially in the South, old notables and their clientele.[22]

Some consideration of Croce's liberalism is in order here. Croce was an atypical liberal, and, as a result, his political beliefs have given rise to much controversy. He certainly subscribed to liberalism's central tenets – the freedom of the individual, the sovereignty of conscience, and the separation of church and state – but fundamentally Croce had a religious conception of freedom, which he regarded in almost divine terms. He viewed history as the story of liberty. Freedom, for him, defines the nature of man and acts as the agent of his creative powers, thus underlining a dialectic tension between the volition of the individual and the volition of the universal, or, in Crocean terms, between vitality and ethics. "Est deus in homine," he could have repeated with the Platonic philosopher of the Renaissance. By philosophical training and personal inclination, Croce was closer to German idealism than to British empiricism, and he had no use for the utilitarian tradition. That explains why he delegated to others the task of writing about economic, financial, and constitutional issues. In his own writings on liberalism there are philosophical arguments in favour of freedom as a political concept, but few reflections on the elaborate architecture of institutions associated, in the Western world, with a free society and democratic government. Furthermore, while freedom has an assigned transcendental nature and is defined as the essence of man, institutions are regarded as practical means, or instruments devised by historical experience, and as such can be altered as needs change and expediency requires. In the final analysis, freedom is superior to the institutions in which it finds its embodiment from time to time. Also, for Croce, the traditional liberal institutions and the rules that go with them were certainly important and performed ethical-political functions. But by themselves they were not sufficient to avoid the collapse or to guarantee the survival of a free society, as recent Italian and European history had shown. Only the energy of freedom, animating the minds and hearts of the people and informing and shaping the will of the polity, can assure the vitality and protect the safety of a free society – and the institutions that underpin its structure.

The absence in Croce's writings of commentary on institutional architecture has created some unfortunate misunderstandings, suggesting to some that Croce was indifferent to the subject and regarded it as having little importance. In fact, this is far from the truth, especially for men of Croce's generation and his background, who had seen the progress achieved by Italy under liberal institutions and then witnessed the calamity of fascism and the dictatorship of Mussolini. In Croce's thought, the importance of constitutional guaranties, liberal institutions, and the separation of power between them, is implicit and fully present, even if not plainly stated. All of his life he was admirer of the British political system and the loyalty it had inspired among the people who lived under it. This admiration, however, tended to be expressed in his historical writings rather than in his philosophical essays, which are more concerned with the essence of ideas. In his historical works, the role of liberal institutions in promoting and enriching the lives of men, the welfare of society, and the wealth of nations is argued with force, and sometimes with great eloquence. One must also remember that Croce had a dialectical conception of life and reality. For that reason, his liberalism could include features and endorse proposals that liberals with a conservative bent or more traditional outlook could not accept, or found questionable.

From Croce's political essays, written after the fall of Mussolini, it becomes evident that for him the Liberal Party ought to be a moderate party, but certainly not a conservative one; it had to belong to the centre, not to the right of the political spectrum. To achieve that ideal position, Croce looked for an example to Cavour, the main architect of Italian political unification. For Croce, rather than "a liberal conservative," Cavour was a "radical liberal." Accordingly, he could write: "Our aim is to bring the Liberal Party back to the pure source of Cavour's tradition, avoiding any contamination, either of a conservative or revolutionary nature, but keeping it open to all the new needs and measures, to be achieved, however, always by means of freedom." Those who wanted progressive reforms were assured that "the future Liberal Party … acting in conformity to its nature and its mission, will not reject a priori any economic reform, but it will demand that each such reform be discussed in a context of freedom, and adopted only when time and conditions are ripe; this way, reforms will not be a cause of regression but will lead to what is their supreme goal: better social conditions and increased human freedom and activity." To those who gave supremacy to law and order, Croce replied that "liberalism does not renounce force, which is the foundation and the warranty of the State; but it uses that force to protect liberal institutions (freedom of expression and of the press, freedom of association, equality before the law for all, political parties and free elections, and all the others) and not curtail the freedom of other members of society, as happens in abhorrent and disgraceful regimes of an absolute and totalitarian bent."[23] Here, one detects a criticism of those Italian political figures (perhaps including Croce himself) who had opposed the use of force and thus had failed to protect liberal institutions from the assault of fascism.

In these essays a pedagogical purpose is evident. After twenty years of dictatorship, Croce wanted to offer to the younger generation a new set of ideals. He also wanted to refresh the memory of the older generation and allay the concerns of those who saw only danger in free discussion and political activity. "The liberal idea wants freedom for all, and for this reason wants the birth of different parties; without these, political life could not be, because it would lack vitality." The old and new generations were reminded of an ancient truth. "The true liberal wants to fight his adversaries; he does not want to suppress them, because, if he were to do this, he would violate his own inner essence." In a time when the king and Badoglio acted in secret and never contemplated the recall of Parliament or the holding of new elections, Croce pointed out that in the history of Italy there had been a different period when other methods were employed. "Cavour used to say that he never felt so strong and so secure as when parliament was in session and he was under the scrutiny of and subject to the attack of the opposition."[24]

In these essays Croce's relations with other parties also begin to be clarified. One notes a new attitude towards Catholics, especially liberal Catholics. Croce was never a traditional anti-clerical in the Jacobin tradition. Throughout his public and private life, he was always respectful of religion. Some of his best friends were practising Catholics, as was his wife; his daughters received a Catholic education and were left free either to embrace or to reject religion in their later lives. During the Fascist regime, and especially after the Lateran Pacts, he had criticized the pope, Pius XI, for forging a quasi-alliance with Mussolini's dictatorship and describing liberal ideas as "old fetishes." But, in the early 1940s, Croce appears to have thought that a new posture was necessary in order to face common enemies and a difficult future. No doubt his meetings and conversations with the old leaders of the Popular Party, like De Gasperi and Don Luigi Sturzo, which took place in Italy and abroad, had helped both sides to overcome reciprocal misconceptions. Croce now told his more radical friends of the Party of Action that the old anticlericalism was no longer possible, that relations with liberal Catholics had to be cultivated. "We should not forget," Croce wrote, "a little detail, which is that the great majority of the Italian people are Catholic, and their feelings should not be offended, and it is necessary that even the more radical rationalists keep this fact in mind and act accordingly."[25]

While relations with liberal Catholics improved, those with the Party of Action became more difficult. In dealing with at least some of his young friends in that party, Croce, it seems fair to say, showed impatience and undue severity; he was not always fair-minded or able to recognize the positive features of their proposals and the value of their arguments. As a result, disagreements gave rise to acrimonious debates that did harm to all concerned. Some differences were clear-cut and self-evident, but often it is hard to say who was right and who was wrong, or why it was impossible to find common ground in certain areas and compromise in others. In any event, there certainly was bitterness on both sides.

A few of Croce's essays of this period were aimed specifically against the Party of Action's policies. In November 1943 he republished the essays in booklet format, with this statement in the introduction: "These essays stress again and again one point: that freedom, in a civilized country, has to be the foundation of all economic programs, and for this reason it cannot be identified, in a preliminary and absolute way, with any of them in particular." Then Croce made clear the object of his criticism: "My polemics were directed in particular against young friends, with whom I have agreed and cooperated, and agree and cooperate even now, in almost all points of practical action." Notwithstanding their friendship, Croce had fundamental disagreements with some Actionists which had to be frankly expressed since they involved the ideas of freedom and justice, and whether one or the other took primacy.

Until 1942, Croce and members of the future Party of Action had been able to collaborate against fascism, and afterwards they had joined forces in a loose organization called the Anti-Fascist Collaboration. In fact, their relations had been rather close; even before the fall of Mussolini there had been frequent meetings and exchanges of views.[26]

This began to change in July 1942 when the Party of Action was founded in a clandestine meeting in Rome. The new party brought together members of different affiliations, especially veterans of Carlo Rosselli's Giustizia e Libertà and followers of the democratic tradition associated with Giovanni Amendola. In the new organization, the movement called liberal-socialism, the brainchild mainly of Guido Calogero, had a strong theoretical influence. Croce found Calogero's attempt to reconcile freedom and justice, liberalism and socialism, unpalatable, seeing in it the long shadow of Giovanni Gentile and his conception of the ethical state as well as a possible point of vulnerability and weakness for the liberal state in its relations with the Communist movement, against whose aims liberals and democrats had to remain ever vigilant. Moreover, in January 1943, without prior consultation with Croce, the new party published its political program, which called for a radical reform of society, including the nationalization of major industries and key financial institutions, the abolition of the monarchy, and the immediate proclamation of a republic. From then on, disagreement between Croce and the Actionists increased and cooperation became difficult. A typical comment by Croce is this August 1943 diary entry: "Much upset about the attitude of members of the Party of Action, who mix contradictory ideas, propose an impracticable program, and make accusations and issue excommunications which are foolish and factious."[27]

The capital sin of the Party of Action, according to Croce, was the dualistic nature of its program. It tried to "join in a strange union a burning liberal faith and an authoritarian practical method." It wanted to realize, at the same time, "the proclamation and realization of freedom and a total social reform," the latter of which would require the use of force to put into practice. The stated aim of the Party of Action was to realize a synthesis between liberalism and socialism, freedom and justice, but many members of the party gave priority to socialism and justice, proposing a planned economy, nationalization of key industries, and the expropriation of large estates in order to solve, once and for all, the long-standing structural problems of Italian society. Such a program, and the thinking underlying it, was unacceptable to Croce. In his philosophical system, freedom took primacy over justice, not because he was against social justice, but for a more fundamental reason: "Freedom is the essence of man, and he possesses it in his quality as a man." There is no need, then, to unite freedom and justice, because freedom coincides with morality and as such is the creating agent of justice. "Freedom ... has in itself the virtue, and with it also the duty, to face and resolve all moral problems that arise." From this premise, it follows that the duty of man is to promote freedom, and in doing so he also realizes justice.[28] One can also maintain that Calogero, starting from a different point and using different arguments, reached the same conclusion. For him, "freedom walks together with justice," as Sasso has written.

On economic matters, Croce had a position different from that of traditional liberals and supporters of the free market and laissez-faire economics like Einaudi. He certainly disliked rules and regulations that are dictated from above and was in favour of individual responsibility and private initiative and risk taking. But on problems of an economic nature, he had an open mind, devoid of ideological rigidity. For him, the state could play a direct role in the economy, and be a positive force, depending on the circumstances; industries could be nationalized, if that policy would increase the production of wealth or assure a better distribution of goods. "For its own purpose, to achieve civil progress, freedom can adopt different means; it can use the free-market economy or even state intervention." But Croce issued a warning to those who were too eager to achieve justice, even at the expense of freedom. "Economic problems have to be solved with their own appropriate means, but the means and the solutions have always to promote freedom, and as a result they have to increase the freedom of man." "The end of freedom is to enhance and elevate life."[29]

The Party of Action was composed of competing groups, each led by a strong personality. Not surprisingly, therefore, it had a tormented and brief, if heroic, life. From the beginning, it was divided into two main factions, one attached to the ideas of liberal democracy, the other sharing the views of the maximalist wing of the Socialist Party. In the end, the internal feuds destroyed the party, thereby dashing the hopes it had aroused and leaving behind deep regrets over unfulfilled dreams.

In view of its internal conflicts, Croce, in conversations with Omodeo at the end of 1943, expressed his hope for a separation in the Party of Action between those who favoured a liberal and open society, and gave the primacy to freedom, and those who wanted to realize social equality above all and to this end gave preference to justice. "Because the whole matter is a question of method, and those who want the method of discussion, of elections, of assemblies and votes, with a majority and a minority, and do not wish a dictatorship in any form or shape, however mild it would appear or how temporarily disguised, belong to a liberal movement; those who prefer the opposite method and want to undertake an economic revolution and to place on top of it the so-called true freedom do not know what freedom is and tend instead towards a dictatorship, be it Fascist or Communist."[30]

In the following years the debate continued with new intensity, though personal friendships remained intact. In April 1944, during a national meeting of the Liberal Party, Croce criticized, again, the policies of the Party of Action, but at the same time he made a revealing statement. "I like to renew my feelings of friendship towards members of that party, remembering the ties that I had with them during the Fascist oppression, and also mindful of the frequent collaboration for common purposes that are continuing even in the present situation."[31] Still, friendships could not be a substitute for common programs and joint initiatives. Disagreements between Croce's Liberals and the Actionists weakened both parties, diminishing the appeal of liberal ideals to the new generation and strengthening the Christian Democrats and Communists, not only in the political arena but also, and in a more pervasive way, in civil society. The result was that the heritage of the Risorgimento, and the public ethos that had animated its ideals and institutions, was seriously undermined and never regained its former eminence.

During the Government of Forty-Five Days, the most pressing problem for Italy, and the most difficult, was to find a way to end the war, either by agreement with the Germans or by peace negotiations with the Allies. For a while, the king and Badoglio chose dilatory tactics, unable to make a clear choice, fearful of German reactions, unaware of Allied plans. When they finally decided to enter into negotiations with the Allies, the task was entrusted to General Giuseppe Castellano, a man without diplomatic skill and unable to speak English; few people were involved, and only a small group was informed about the undertaking and the outcome, in order to avoid German suspicion and reaction. Croce was among the few who were kept informed, in a general way, every time a significant step was taken. On 8 August 1943 he made this comment in his diary: "Omodeo has come back from Rome with very bad news." Omodeo had probably talked with Alessandro Casati, Umberto Zanotti Bianco, or Carlo Antoni, all of whom had relations with members of the government and elements of the court. Their reports reflected the ambivalence, uncertainty, and disagreements of the ruling elite. But that same day Croce also made this diary entry: "I went to see Giuliana Benzoni, who has just arrived from Rome, and from her I had more precise news about the negotiations undertaken by Badoglio in order to get out of the present absurd situation." Benzoni, a member of the aristocracy with a villa in Sorrento, a woman of charm, daring, and intelligence, had close relations with the crown princess, Maria José, wife of the heir to the throne, Umberto. On this occasion Benzoni was probably relaying a message from the princess herself, known to be in touch with liberal anti-Fascists and also well disposed towards Croce.[32]

On 12 August, finally overcoming its doubts, the government sent its emissary, General Castellano, to Portugal to negotiate an armistice with the Allies. As a sign of continuing disarray on the Italian side, however, the negotiations proceeded in a rather leisurely way, with trains rather than airplanes being used for secret trips. In fact, on 24 August, there is this worried note in Croce's diary: "About the armistice negotiations, which I am assured are under way, there is no effect yet." But better news came soon. On 27 August, the same day that Castellano returned to Rome, Croce wrote: "I received a letter from Giuliana Benzoni, announcing that an agreement with the Anglo-Americans has been reached, of which we shall soon see the effect." The effect would come a little later. For the moment, the welcome development produced only acute excitement, as usually happened when Croce was confronted by news of some import, personal or national: "The news so excited my mind that I could do nothing for the rest of the day." However, the joy was mixed with feelings of a different nature, as is shown by this comment: "Happiness? No, but a feeling of relief that we are ending an intrigue and starting on a new road, rough but straight." No doubt Croce was thinking of future difficulties associated with a sudden shift in alliance, in the middle of a war, done without preparation, in a position of weakness and in the face of a determined and ruthless opponent.[33]

The armistice between Italy and the Allies was finally signed by General Castellano at Cassibile in Sicily on 3 September 1943. The next day, the king and Badoglio, despite some last-minute hesitation, accepted the terms of the so-called Short Armistice, which consisted of only twelve articles. This time Croce was informed by his old and trusted friend, Raffaele Mattioli, who, as president of the Banca Commerciale Italiana, was in touch with the powers that be, inside and outside the government. That day, 4 September, Croce received a cryptic message, necessitated by government censorship of the mail and by the need for secrecy about the outcome of the negotiations. "A friend has relayed a phone call from Rome, made to the local branch of Banca Commerciale: 'The patient has recovered. Inform Senator Croce of this.' This we interpret as the announcement of the conclusion of the awaited agreement." But on 7 September, a day before the public announcement of the armistice, Croce made a note in his diary that was full of foreboding, reflecting discussions with friends. "As usual there is fearful news on the future awaiting Naples and Italy." Finally, after further misunderstandings on both sides, signs of vacillation among the Italians, and some arm twisting by Eisenhower, the armistice between Italy and the Allies was announced to the Italian people by Badoglio on the evening of 8 September 1943 at 7:45 p.m. Unlike many Italians Croce did not hear the broadcast but was told the news by his wife. "At six thirty [sic], I was coming home from a small walk, when Adelina told me she had heard over the radio that the armistice has been reached with the Anglo-Americans." That night, rejoicing Italians filled the public squares. Only a few paused to reflect "on the fearful future awaiting Italy."[34]

2
Waging War

The events of 8 September 1943 left Italy irreparably damaged. Even the disaster of Caporetto during the Great War, when the Austrians overran the Italian army, pales in comparison. On that occasion, only part of the Italian army collapsed, and soon afterwards the army and the country rallied around the king and the government, all forces bent on stopping the invading enemy. In contrast, on 8 September 1943, the entire structure of the state crumbled and the army ceased to exist, collapsing in disorder. There were acts of heroism, but on the whole the political and military leaders left their positions, concerned primarily with their personal safety. A mood of defeatism seemed to grip the entire nation. As Claudio Pavone has observed, for most civilians and soldiers, the armistice meant peace and a return home, not the continuation of the fight or the beginning of a new struggle alongside a different ally. It took time and German brutality before the will to fight back returned. Meanwhile, the Italian people were left to fend for themselves in the midst of chaos.[1] In doing so, they proved to be quite resilient and resourceful, even creative.

September 1943 clearly marks the end of a historical period, if not, as some have argued, the death of the fatherland or the birth of a new nation. As in all the great historical upheavals, something old died and something new was born. However, the tradition of the Risorgimento – the union of the fatherland and liberty, Crown and Parliament, along with the devotion to public institutions – had been weakened by twenty years of dictatorship, and on 8 September 1943 it was torn asunder completely. From then on, the Risorgimento ceased to be a driving force in Italian politics. The main political parties that came to dominate the life of the future republic, "the Blacks" and "the Reds," the Christian

Democrats and the Communists, were independent of that tradition, and sometimes even resentful of it. Three months later, reflecting on the events of that time, Croce entered in his diary this sad meditation: "Last night, between two and five, I remained awake for a few hours, my mind set on the thought that everything that Italians had built politically, economically, and morally over a century has been irremediably destroyed. All that survives are the ideals in our hearts, with which we have to face a difficult future without looking back any more, refraining from regret."[2]

One of the ideas that perished, or was greatly damaged, was the love of fatherland. Already in June 1943, in a note for an underground publication, Croce had lamented the disappearance, especially among the younger generation, of the word "fatherland" and "the love of fatherland." For this he blamed with good reason the Fascist regime, "because the love of fatherland was not only perverted but also supplanted by nationalism."[3] In the age of dictators, the humanitarian patriotism of the Risorgimento, friendly to other peoples and generous to oppressed nations, was transformed into imperialism and imbued with a spirit of conquest and oppression. For the patriots of the Risorgimento, the nation was a historical creation, while under fascism it acquired racial, ethnic, and ideological connotations and became identified with the leader and the party in power. Devotion to the state and its institutions was replaced by the adulation of Mussolini, who was treated as almost the living symbol of a new divinity.

To understand better Croce's feelings, one has to remember that in his *Storia d'Italia dal 1871 al 1915*, published in 1928 to critical acclaim and commercial success, he had given a positive assessment of that historical period and praised "those three generous and industrious generations" for achievements realized "under the aegis of liberal institutions." In that work and in other historical essays written before and after, he had shown – without ignoring the negative side of the ledger – that Italy in these years had made great progress in every field, overcoming the burdens of a long period of neglect and decadence. Also, he had stressed the beneficial influence and new vitality brought to public life and mores by the spirit of freedom; under liberal institutions, freedom of expression and freedom of association had spurred new ideas while also reviving old ones that had languished under the old regime. Finally, in this book Croce had celebrated Italy's return to the European cultural and political arena as an equal partner "among sister nations" and with a voice and personality of its own, made possible by the unification and independence of the country and by the end of the foreign oppression that the Italian people had suffered since the time of the Renaissance. It is thus evident, from his historical and autobiographical writings, that Croce saw the Risorgimento – and the ideal of freedom that inspired and sustained it – as in reality the rebirth of the Italian nation and its people. For that reason, the heritage of the Risorgimento was to be cherished, especially in the midst of a war and in the face of a possible return to the divisions and oppression of the past.

On the evening of 8 September 1943, the armistice with the Allies was broadcast to the nation by Badolgio. The next morning, to avoid certain capture by the Germans and deportation to concentration camps, or even possible death, the king, the royal family, Badoglio, and the General Staff fled Rome, and by land reached first Pescara and Ortona on the Adriatic coast and later, by sea, Brindisi in Southern Italy. With that hurried flight, "la fuga di Pescara," as it is known in Italian history, the continuity of the state was assured and the government preserved, and with that the terms of the armistice could take effect and become binding. Any other government on Italian soil would now be regarded as illegitimate. All of this has to be regarded as a positive achievement, painful but necessary. But the price paid was high indeed.

The flight of the king and Badolgio from the capital, done in haste and confusion, without leaving behind precise instructions, created a power vaccum at the top of the administration, generating the collapse of the state's central authority and the dissolution of the armed forces. Within days, hours in some cases, the Germans, already present on the peninsula with increased strength and in control of strategic points, invaded with fresh troops and took control of Central and Northern Italy. Paratroopers rescued Mussolini from captivity and brought him to Germany; he was then returned to power as head of a puppet government by Hitler, enjoying neither authority nor influence, his old energy now gone.

With a few notable exceptions, the military authorities did not offer much resistance to the German invasion and occupation of Italy. Most army units were disarmed without a fight, and in many cases commanders fled before the new enemy arrived. The political and military elites, created and nourished by fascism, utterly failed to carry out their obligations. Despite a few individual acts of dignity and courage, their conduct was on the whole deplorable. Badoglio's proclamation was clear on the main points: an armistice had come into effect and the hostility between Italy and the Allies had come to an end. But the Italian army had to respond and fight back "against assaults from any other side." When the assaults came, in many cases there was no reaction. Generals accustomed to taking orders from above were unable to take bold initiatives. Even after the war, when generals wrote or reflected on those events, they blamed others; hardly anyone was ready to admit or assume responsibility for what, after all, had happened under their command.

The facts speak for themselves. The navy, and part of the air force, remained operational, obeyed orders, and reached their assigned locations, under Allied control. But the army's collapse was almost total. Out of more than eighty divisions, only three remained intact, twenty-nine offered some resistance for a while, and fifty-one surrendered without a fight. The Germans captured a vast quantity of materiel. The human loss was staggering; 40,000 soldiers were killed or wounded, 20,000 remained missing, and more than half a million, perhaps 700,000, soldiers were taken prisoner and brought to Germany, where they remained in concentration camps until the end of the war, ignoring Mussolini's appeal, and German pressure, to join his camp. The conclusion of Domenico Bartoli, journalist-turned-historian, is fair: "Italy was involved in a struggle for world domination that was much beyond her means. To get out of that tragic adventure, which was necessary and urgent, she was fatally bound to suffer damage, human loss, and humiliation. There was no easy way out, not without pain. But to exit that predicament there needed to be found more dignified ways."[4]

When it became evident that the power of the state had disappeared, new authorities began to emerge in the cities and the countryside. At the local level, groups of citizens organized civic committees to deal with the most pressing needs. Sorrento, where Croce was then living, experienced the same chaos, anxieties, and difficulties as other parts of Italy. The entries in Croce's diaries after 8 September express his personal feelings and display his lack of solid news; they also show the quick progress of the German occupation. On 10 September, Croce wrote: "In the afternoon, hopes and anxieties over the military events and the episodes of Italian resistance to the Germans. But in the evening, we learned of the German occupation of Rome and of the flight of the king and Badoglio, who have retired to a safe place. We are now worried for all our friends, who are in Rome, all of them engaged against fascism."[5] The next day, there was more bad news from Naples. "Friends who came from Naples brought the news that the city has been occupied by the Germans, and that there have been conflicts with the population, and dead and wounded."[6] The diary entry for 13 September underlines Croce's anxiety in the face of so much uncertainty: "We are in complete isolation. For a week, there has not been any mail delivery; for two days, newspapers from Naples have not arrived – probably because they are no longer being published; for two days, any communication by land and by sea with Naples has been interrupted; today, because of British bombardment of Torre dell' Annunziata [a city nearby], resulting in the loss of electricity, everyone has been without light and water. Tonight the radio stopped broadcasting, and for this reason we know nothing of nothing, and only hear the rumours of canons and the explosions of bombs."[7]

On 14 September, Croce participated in the formation of a citizens' committee. As his diary says, "there has been agreement for the formation here in Sorrento of a committee to deal with the dangers of the uncertain situation ... fearing [as we do] a sudden attack from these [Germans] and the last surviving Fascists emboldened by the recent events [liberation of Mussolini and the German occupation]; but above all worried by the grave discomfort of the population, which for a few days has been without bread."[8] As an example of the confusion of the times, a small episode is revealing. The Salerno committee sent the former mayor to the Allies to apprise them of the precarious conditions of the population and to ask for immediate supplies of food. The Allied officers, fearing an ambush, arrested the mayor, accusing him of being a former Fascist. When the news reached the family, his two daughters rushed to Croce's villa, begging for his assistance, and he had to intervene on behalf of the unfortunate former mayor, giving reassurance on his intentions and true purpose.[9]

Despite the relative isolation of Sorrento, and the protection of his friends, Croce still ran the risk of being kidnapped by Germans and then held hostage for political ransom, as happened to others in those days. Also, there was the threat posed by local Fascists; from these, Croce received anonymous and threatening letters. To avoid unpleasant surprises, a friend organized regular patrols of the villa in which Croce was staying, and even provided hand grenades to the defenders of the philosopher. The mood of Fascists found clear expression in a message on the national radio service, now controlled by the Germans: "Benedetto Croce and the others, who, like him, have abused the patience of the regime, will be rigorously punished." For his safety, Croce was urged by his friends in Sorrento and Naples to move to the island of Capri, where he could be better protected by Allied and Italian boat patrols. He agreed, but with some reluctance. On 15 September 1943 he was taken to Capri by British sailors and Italian soldiers, accompanied by his three daughters; his wife and the fourth daughter joined him the day after, escorted by Malcolm Munthe, the head of the SOE mission. This was probably one of the first successful rescue operations of the Allied forces in Italy or in Europe. Croce and his family remained in Capri until the middle of October, when they returned again to Sorrento, which was then free from German occupation and safely in Allied hands.[10]

Croce's account of the whole affair, from the preparation to the conclusion, is factual and without much detail. But there is another, more colourful description of the incident. Adrian Gallegos, the British officer in command of the rescue boat, reported that Croce "gave me a strong impression of great serenity." He also added a romantic touch. When the boat with its precious cargo reached its destination, "a clear-cut moon rose over the horizon and over Capri, as clear and as serene as the mind of the great philosopher." However, to his surprise and amusement, the silence was suddenly broken by the dashing appearance of the Hollywood movie star Douglas Fairbanks, who, strangely attired, sword in his hand, soon was shouting orders of disembarkation from the bow of a boat. Gallegos never saw Croce again after that night in Capri. But he was pleased when he saw his name mentioned in Croce's diary. In his own memoirs, "the rescue of the great philosopher of world repute" marked a high point in special missions during the war.[11]

The Allied authorities gave great importance to Croce's rescue and safety. Many realized, as Gallegos wrote, that "the most esteemed champion of freedom in Italy" "would have been of immense value in German hands," if only for propaganda purposes. Inside and outside the Special Forces, Croce's rescue almost came to equal the liberation of Mussolini from Gran Sasso, carried out a few days before by German paratroopers. As a sign of his international standing, the day after his arrival in Capri, Croce received a courtesy visit from Admiral J.B. Moore of the British Royal Navy. The admiral was probably on an exploratory mission to ascertain Croce's political plans, or even to discuss his future role, either as the leader of the democratic forces in Southern Italy or as a welcome addition to the cabinet of Badoglio, with whom the Allies at that time were not too pleased. At the end of the meeting, however, the admiral's adjutant asked for more mundane information: a list of former Fascists who could still be dangerous in Sorrento. The reply of the old philosopher was prompt: "I begged to be excused because, at my advanced age, I did not feel like doing something that I had never done in my whole life." The admiral and his adjutant understood and did not press the matter.[12]

It was in Capri that Croce began to emerge as the leader of the opposition to the king and his government. While there, he undertook important political initiatives and remained in touch with his friends in Naples and in Rome. He had visits from Allied officers, who had read his books, and he granted interviews to British and American journalists. The *New York Times* published one of Croce's essays on fascism. His daughter translated Herbert Matthews's *The Fruits of Fascism.* Croce established or re-established cordial, and useful, relations with Malcolm Munthe and another British SOE officer, Max Salvadori. One day, an amused Croce and his family had to pose for several pictures for *Life* magazine. Thanks to Henry Luce's publication, millions of American readers came to know, probably for the first time, a famous Italian philosopher who had opposed the Mussolini regime and was now in disagreement with the king and his government.

In Capri, Croce met anti-Fascist leaders just released from jail, including Tito Zaniboni, a former Socialist member of Parliament, and two exiles recently arrived from London, members in France of the anti-Fascist movement Giustizia e Libertà and now leaders of the Party of Action. "Today besides Fausto Nicolini," Croce wrote in his diary, "came [Alberto] Tarchiani and [Alberto] Cianca, just returned from America, whom I had not seen for the last ten years; with them I talked for three full hours, giving and receiving news about Italian events; we found ourselves in agreement about men whom I have known and they have encountered in France and in America." The people being referred to here probably included Gaetano Salvemini, Carlo Sforza, and Luigi Sturzo. In Capri, the three old friends agreed on a common policy for the future. Especially with Tarchiani, Croce was in full agreement about the political initiatives to be undertaken and about the relations to be maintained or to be established with the Allies, the king, and Badoglio.[13]

While in Capri, Croce's most important meeting was with General William Donovan, a confidant of President Franklin Roosevelt and director of the Office of Strategic Services (OSS), forerunner of the Central Intelligence Agency (CIA). The meeting took place on 23 September 1943; also present were James Whitaker, head of the Psychological Warfare Branch (PWB), and Peter Tompkins, an OSS officer in charge of relations with the Italian Resistance. Before the war, Whitaker and Tompkins had been newspapermen in Italy, the former for the *Chicago Daily News* and the latter for the *New York Herald Tribune.* Both were familiar with the Italian cultural landscape and able to appreciate Croce's intellectual and political importance.

During the discussion, prodded by Croce, Donovan promised flour deliveries to the people of Naples, soon after the Allied occupation of the city, and he urged Croce to exhort the Resistance forces in Naples to protect the port facilities from German destruction. After the preliminaries came the important part of the discussion, which was the main reason for the meeting. Croce's diary entry reads: "To the question of General Donovan about feelings and disposition in Italy, I have answered that the formation of legions of fighters under the Italian flag, cooperating with the Anglo-American armies for the liberation of Italy from the Germans, is something that all the best Italians desire and that would give them confidence; and since he asked if there was somebody who could command such formations, I have given the name of General Giuseppe Pavone, who belongs to an old liberal and patriotic family of Southern Italy, and at the present is a member of the Party of Action."[14] The general had been recommended to Croce's entourage by Ugo La Malfa, one of the leaders of the Party of Action and a member of the CLN in Rome.

Donovan was evidently impressed by Croce's proposal. The day after the meeting, he wrote to General Mark W. Clark, commander of the US Fifth Army, recommending the "organization of Italian Operational Groups for the Employment with Allied Forces." In the letter, Croce is described as "since 1924, the most courageous, aggressive and effective opponent of fascism." Donovan also wrote that, "by published articles and open statements," Croce "has denounced totalitarianism and attacked Fascist rules in Italy."[15]

Croce and his friends in Capri acted with equal speed when they learned that Donovan had agreed with Croce's proposal and had recommended its acceptance to General Clark. Craveri got in touch with General Pavone and brought him to Capri; together they had another meeting in Paestum, this one with Donovan, Tompkins, and Munthe and Salvadori of the SOE. At the same time, to facilitate communication between the two camps, a liaison committee was established, composed of Craveri, Pavone, Tarchiani, and Ambassador Filippo Caracciolo for the Italians and Whitaker and Tomkins for the Americans. More importantly, on 24 September, Croce, Pavone, Tarchiani, and Craveri constituted themselves into an Executive Committee of the National Liberation Front (NLF), with Croce as president. A letter was immediately sent to General Eisenhower in England, apprising the supreme commander of the meeting between Croce and Donovan and the agreement reached, as well as the creation of the NLF.

For Croce, the NLF in Capri had to be the nucleus of something wider. As he wrote to Eisenhower, "as soon as contacts will be established, the

Executive Committee of the National Liberation Front will be enlarged in such a way as to include the representatives of all the forces of Liberation now existing and organized, and of those which may arise in various parts of Italy."[16] Word of the NLF's founding quickly spread, as evident in Salvadori's later reflections: "The formation of the Committee of National Liberation, of which Croce was the president, a few days after the landing, was in that time the most important political event in Southern Italy, more important than the arrival of the king and his prime minister in Brindisi."[17]

Interestingly, all these meetings and communications at the highest levels were taking place merely three weeks after the military armistice, before Badoglio met Eisenhower in Malta on 29 September to sign the Long Armistice, and before Italy declared war against Germany on 13 October 1943.

On 1 October 1943 Croce sent Craveri and Tarchiani to Brindisi, then the temporary seat of the Italian government, to inform Badoglio of their initiative and to ask for his support. He also wrote to Badoglio, making it clear that he hoped to reach a mutual understanding given their common interest in "the dignity and future of Italy" and the need "to participate militarily in the war to expel the Germans from our land."[18] Despite transportation difficulties, Craveri and Tarchiani reached Brindisi in a short time and a cordial meeting took place. Badoglio approved the idea of Italian "operational groups" fighting alongside the Allied forces; he had words of praise for Croce and promised help. Though his support was full of political qualifications and technical reservations, Croce was convinced that an agreement had been reached. As he wrote in his diary, there was no doubt in his mind, after the return of Craveri and Tarchiani, that "with Badoglio they found full agreement, in the sense that we will operate independently of the king's government, and Badoglio will not create any obstacles against us."[19]

Craveri and Tarchiani's account of their mission in Brindisi is an interesting document. It sheds light on recent historical events and on social conditions in Southern Italy. It reveals some traits of Badoglio's personality: his ability to be flexible, to sound friendly, and to temporize at the same time. Above all, it reveals the weakness and lack of autonomy of the Italian government and the dominant role of the Allies. Badoglio himself stressed his precarious position and the government's lack of power. "He recognized that in Brindisi there was not a government but only a few generals." In his memoirs Harold Macmillan was even more precise; in Brindisi there was just an old king and an old marshal.[20]

During the conversation Badoglio mentioned the distressing social conditions of Southern Italy, where corruption was rampant and the political parties were clamouring for posts in the civil service and in the mass organizations, trade unions in particular. Badoglio talked of the different positions he had held under the Fascist regime, and he also offered some useful details on the conspiracy to oust Mussolini from power, on the flight from Rome, and on negotiations with the Allies. Badoglio "was pleased to have already obtained the status of co-belligerent and hoped to gain soon the status of Ally." Unfortunately, Italy never attained that status and remained a defeated nation, under the terms of unconditional surrender: the harsh terms of the Peace Treaty of 1947 reflected that reality. Nor would Badoglio be able to realize another goal. Once back in Rome, he intended to enlarge his cabinet, bringing in representatives of the new political parties. As it turned out, however, after the liberation of Rome, the CLN leaders would compel him to resign and retire to private life. At one point, to avoid arrest, he also had to seek refuge in the British embassy. Turning to the present situation, Badoglio talked about the relative strength of the various parties that were members of the CLN. Among these, according to him, only the Christian Democrats and the Communists had a mass organization. As he put it, using military language, "these two have a general staff and troops, all the others have only generals; they have not been able to organize troops, including us Liberals."[21]

As was to be expected from a general, Badoglio made astute military observations: enthusiasm was not enough in modern warfare – modern armies required well-armed troops, well-trained soldiers, and good means of transportation; Germans were capable, seasoned soldiers and there was a need to be prudent in organizing fighting groups against them, to avoid failures and disappointments, or *brutte figure.* Badoglio reminded his guests that he too was trying to reorganize the army, in the midst of great difficulties and lack of materiel. For that reason, he was ready to accept help from any organization willing to fight against the Germans. He himself was in favour of "small and agile units of guerrilla fighters," to be employed in the mountains of Abruzzi, beyond enemy lines. This idea was similar to the Allies' thinking but different from what Croce hoped for.

In a roundabout way, Badoglio stressed some unpalatable truths about the present political reality that Italian politicians tended to ignore or forget. He told Craveri and Tarchiani that, by the terms of the armistice, his administration – serving at the behest of the king – was the only legal government in Italy; he also stressed that now there was an Allied Control Commission (ACC) "with the mission to put into practice the agreements reached in Malta between Eisenhower and Badoglio," and that "all the military questions in Italy and the reorganization of the Italian armed forces had to be approved by that Commission, together with Badoglio and his general staff."[22]

There were some heated exchanges. Tarchiani pointed out that General Donovan was also an influential American politician and a friend of President Roosevelt, and as such was able to pull powerful strings to achieve his goals. Badoglio's reply was disarming but appropriate. "Marshal Badoglio observed with much frankness that often Anglo-American generals undertake divergent initiatives that generate differences and conflicts among various departments."[23]

Tarchiani put forward political arguments which were shared by Croce. "We have come to Brindisi to inform the marshal of our initiative. We do not want in any way to give the impression to the Allies of a dualism or to show a willingness to act against the knowledge and the authority of the legal government." In fact, the fighting groups advocated by Croce "would not be in conflict with the formations of the regular army that Badoglio intended to organize." Tarchiani also stated that it was important not to leave the initiative to organize bands only to the Communists, "because in the future such bands could have a grave political influence."[24] Badoglio replied that he did not fear a victory of the radical parties because the Allies had enough power to maintain order. Here Badoglio proved to be prophetic.

In the end, Badoglio, for the third time in the conversation, "declared explicitly that he would support our initiative." Badoglio also read and approved of Croce's draft manifesto inviting Italian citizens and former soldiers to join the fighting groups. But he advised that the manifesto should not be made public until "the initiative was approved definitely by the Allies." That is, in plain words, until the old fox had discussed the proposal with the ACC and given his considered advice.[25]

Two weeks after the meeting in Capri between Croce and Donovan, OSS headquarters, in a letter dated 5 October, notified Croce and Pavone that General Clark had formally approved their initiative for "the organization of Italian Operational Groups." The letter also stated, in general but clear terms, the conditions under which the groups were to be organized. "The Groups shall be composed of Italian military personnel under Italian leadership; they shall be non-political; they shall make no effort to oppose the king or General Badoglio; and their operations shall be under the direction and control of the commanding general, Fifth Army." The OSS assured Pavone that "it stands ready to assist in any way." Even more importantly, Pavone was invited to come to Naples as soon as possible and to move into the OSS's headquarters for the time being, "in order to begin this work which we all believe will assist the Allies and serve, in some way, to unite the Italian people."[26] Soon afterwards, on 8 October, Croce and Pavone received a second letter of approval, which made it clear that the matter had been further discussed in depth among the Allied officers, including members of the British SOE. In this document the instructions were more precise and more detailed and included almost a timetable of action. "Since time is of the essence in connections with the undertaking, OSS has undertaken to procure food, arms and equipment, office and housing facilities, and a training area. OSS will provide such funds and such instructors ... as may be necessary in making effective the program approved by the commanding general."[27]

General Pavone answered these two letters. "It is necessary to state – for a clear understanding of the Italian Operational Groups – that these groups – as agreed upon – will be under my direct orders although all operations shall be made in perfect accord with the Commanding General of the Fifth Army and, of course, under his discipline."[28] A careful reading of this correspondence suggests that from the beginning there were misunderstandings, or at least conditions under which misunderstandings could arise. The Americans made it clear that the Italian groups were to be under the complete control and direction of General Clark. Pavone instead stressed that the groups were under his "direct orders" and that operations had to be undertaken in "perfect accord" with Clark and "under his discipline," which is not precisely the same thing. With regard to the composition of the Italian groups, the American always talked of military personnel, made up of officers and soldiers, and organized by small units for special actions. Croce at least, and probably also Pavone, referred more generically to Italian volunteers, or to "volunteer formations of free Italians," fighting beside Allied soldiers. Above all, the Americans' detailed plan of implementation required an energetic general with clear ideas and organizing skills who would be able to produce results in short time and in a difficult environment: a leader, in short, capable of infusing respect and enthusiasm among his men. It remained to be seen whether General Pavone had these qualities.

Once the approval of the Allies had been obtained and the support of Badoglio assured, Croce and his associates went into action. General

Pavone, Alberto Tarchiani, and Raimondo Craveri travelled to various towns to undertake the task of recruiting, housing, and training the volunteers. On 10 October, the National Liberation Front issued a press release, written by Tarchiani and approved by Croce, announcing the creation of the Gruppi Combattenti Italia by a decree of General Clark and in agreement also with the proper British authorities. The communiqué went on to explain that these groups "are made up of Italian soldiers and officers, under Italian command, with the Italian tricolour flag; and on their uniforms there will be written Italia." "These groups will fight beside the Anglo-American formations for the liberation of our country from the Germans and the Fascists, accomplices in the ruin and dishonour of Italy." The communiqué also gave the name of the commanding officer, Giuseppe Pavone, "tenacious in his anti-Fascist faith and with proven military competence." It indicated the place of the groups' headquarters, the Mueller Hotel in Naples. It stated that "the Gruppi Combattenti will report to the National Front of Liberation, which undertook the initiative and obtained official support for it, and whose executive consisted of Croce and Pavone, soon to be joined by Carlo Sforza." The press release ended with a stirring appeal. Italians were invited to emulate Garibaldi and repeat the deeds of the Risorgimento, to be the avant-garde of a people's army, to fight not only for the liberation of Italy but also for the freedom of Europe, "so that Italy, through the valour and the sacrifices of her sons, could regain a fraternal parity among the nations, which are engaged in the great struggle to secure and defend a world of freedom, justice, and peace."[29]

Like the press release, Croce's public manifesto inviting Italians to join the Gruppi Combattenti was distributed to newspapers and Allied-controlled radio stations and was posted in public buildings in Naples and other cities of Southern Italy. It is really a short historical essay, more than two pages long, directed to officers rather than to ordinary soldiers. But it has effective and stirring parts, and makes certain points clear. The Germans were singled out as the enemy; they were burning buildings, destroying industries, killing and deporting people. The Steel Pact, negotiated by Mussolini with Hitler, was contrary to Italy's traditions and interests; the alliance with Germany was against Italy's past and present, "and surely against our future" because a German victory in this war would result in the enslavement of Italy and Europe. Croce presented a sad truth: long before their invasion, the Germans, with the consent of Mussolini, had taken control of Italian industrial and military affairs. Now, as other people were doing in other regions of Italy and other parts of Europe, the time had come to fight the Germans, to regain the honour of Italy, and to prepare a better future. Croce also stressed a legal point, much debated then and later. The war against the Germans was a legal war, because in Italy there was only one legally recognized government, "the one that has concluded the armistice with the Allies." The manifesto, like the press release, ended with an invitation for Italian men to join "the Gruppi Italiani Combattenti, with the Italian tricolour, who are co-operating with the Anglo-American Forces to expel from Italian lands our common enemy."[30]

Through the press release and Croce's manifesto, the work of the NLF's Executive Committee was much facilitated. The first results were encouraging; two thousand volunteers were recruited in Salerno, and a few more hundred in Bari and other cities. Ambassador Caracciolo, just arrived in Naples from Switzerland, was impressed by the auspicious beginnings, as he writes in his memoirs. "The initiative was in full development, and promised good results; young people, coming from different places, were joining in great numbers; the training of soldiers and officers was proceeding well and apace; among the volunteers there was a great deal of enthusiasm and fighting spirit." The Gruppi Combattenti attracted some outstanding people, Aldo Garosci and Giaime Pintor among them, both, it seems, enjoying the support of the British SOE. Leo Valiani, on his way to Rome and Northern Italy, where he played a leading role in the Resistance as a leader of the Party of Action, got in touch with members of Croce's committee, and approved of and encouraged the initiative. In his memoirs, written in 1945, Valiani also provided one of the best descriptions of Croce's plan. "The idea was to organize a volunteer armed unit of Italian anti-fascism, and to participate through this in the war of liberation."[31]

While Craveri, Pavone, and Tarchiani were busy trying to organize the Gruppi Combattenti – and faced some difficulties in doing so, both with the Allies and with Badoglio – Croce had the task of defending the work of the NLF against critics from the right and from the left. At the beginning of October, he met with Tito Zaniboni, a distinguished First World War officer and former Socialist member of Parliament. He had spent years in prison for a failed attempt against Mussolini's life in 1925. Now, out of jail, he wanted to play a meaningful role in the struggle against the Germans, but in complete independence of the king and Badoglio. For that purpose, he had proposed to American officers the creation of an Italian Legion, composed only of Republican elements, fighting under his direct command and employed beside the American army as an equal ally. Croce explained that such a request was unrealistic and also impractical, in his own words, *campata in aria* (pie in the sky), since every proposal had to be approved by the Allied authorities and also by Badoglio. He tried to persuade the old Socialist that, in the present circumstances, the volunteer legions had to follow the example of Garibaldi and be composed of Italians of different political persuasions, belonging to the monarchical or republican camp, but united by the common ideal of fighting the Germans. Croce also urged Zaniboni to join forces with Pavone – advice that Zaniboni was unable or unwilling to follow. Meanwhile, Zaniboni crossed paths with Pavone, quarrelled with Craveri, and caused disagreements with others, all without achieving, in the end, any results.[32] Nor was his experience unique. Many who had been imprisoned by the Fascist regime, or spent considerable time opposing it, came to believe that they were entitled to high-level positions. These naive expectations were crushed first by the harsh reality of the military struggle and then, in the post-war era, by the new rules of the political game, dominated by mass parties. A sense of injustice and bitter resentment often ensued, clouding their judgment.

A few days later, Croce met with an old friend, Joyce Lussu, the sister of Max Salvadori of the SOE and the wife of Emilio Lussu, one of the most radical leaders of the Party of Action in Rome. Like her husband, she was a fine writer; before the war, Croce, who thought highly of the couple's literary talents, had helped Joyce to publish a book of poetry. She had spent years in exile like her brother but now was a sort of roving ambassador for that party, often employed on dangerous missions successfully carried out with panache and daring. As was to be expected from a member of the Party of Action and a staunch republican, she made a radical request, and a rather simplistic one. As Croce wrote in his diary: "In the name of her husband and their friends, she asked that our actions in the war against the Germans be undertaken not only behind the backs of the king and Badoglio but against them." Croce tried to demonstrate that her request was unreasonable, because the Anglo-Americans had signed an armistice with Badoglio and recognized the king's government as the only legal government of Italy. He also stated that "we have to organize groups of volunteers, who will give an oath of allegiance neither to the king nor to Badoglio, who will not make monarchical or anti-monarchical demonstrations, but want only to fight the Germans and wish to achieve honour."[33] Despite her admiration of Croce, Joyce Lussu remained unconvinced. Her views would be expressed later on in Northern Italy by various factions of the Resistance, some of whom were uncomfortable accepting hard realities and the compromises they imposed.

In *Una Guerra Civile,* Claudio Pavone (no relation of the general) has expertly analysed the different ideals that animated individuals and movements in the struggle against fascism.[34] Contrasting views about the past, the present, and the future generated heated debates. But the solution found in the South and in the North would be along Croce's lines, or Togliatti's, one may add. The political parties recognized that all forces had to be united in a common front and the priority had to remain the war against the Germans and the liberation of Italy; the institutional question – the choice between republic and monarchy – could be resolved later by elections, once peace had returned and the war ended.

In order to assure the success of his initiative, Croce also sought the support of an old friend, Vincenzo Arangio Ruiz, a man of liberal persuasion, a fine jurist, then a member and later chairman of Naples' CLN. After a long conversation, Ruiz wrote to Croce on 14 October, the day after Italy declared war on Germany, raising knotty legal points and weighty political questions that could not then and cannot now be easily answered, let alone simply dismissed. "I believe that, especially now that the war has been declared against Germany, the national army is the only body that has the right and the duty to wage it. To leave to individuals the choice to serve in the Italian army or in other formations would be an evident sign of disunion, before ourselves and before the Allies." He made a distinction between political issues and military matters. Political parties had the right to have different ideas about the institutional problem and its solution in the future. "But now Italy is still a monarchy, ruled under the Albertine Statute, and the king is the commander-in-chief of the armed forces, and these forces are the only legal ones." Ruiz also raised the issue of the volunteers' pay. If the payments came from the Italian government, "the army so paid and supported would be an Italian army." If, on the other hand, the volunteers were paid by the Allies, "they would resemble mercenaries rather than free citizens, eager to fight against a foreign enemy." At the centre of Ruiz's concerns was the future of a free country and the integrity of a nation and the authority of the state. No less than Croce, Ruiz was not moved by a desire to protect the monarchy; he was focused only on the unity of the nation, hoping that Italy would "remain intact after the tremendous crisis we are going through."[35]

Ruiz also raised a matter not usually mentioned in discussions of the Resistance. "Don't you find it rather singular that, just relieved from the tyranny of a man who built his dominion on the use of armed squads, we start soon after to organize new armed bands, that will be at the service of a party or a group of parties? Could it not be that tomorrow the new chief would impose his conditions on the government, abandoning completely once more the method of freedom?"[36] Ruiz's main worry was that the Communist Party would organize armed groups for its own purpose, employing them to seize power in the future. His fear was shared by others.

Echoing Ruiz, the Naples CLN passed a resolution "against the formation of volunteer groups, fearing that this would raise the institutional question, and the choice between the monarchy and the republic." Croce, however, was not impressed by Arangio Ruiz's legal arguments, and regarded the Naples resolution as a mistake, "a decision that is not useful and helps to destroy the enthusiasm of the volunteers, which we have accepted whether we are monarchical or republican, following the spirit of Garibaldi."[37]

In essence, Ruiz's position was a legalistic one which ignored the political necessities of the moment. The king was no longer an agent of unity; his collusion with Mussolini and his present policies created resentment and disunity. In Southern Italy there were officers and soldiers eager to fight but who refused to join the regular army, unwilling to serve under the king or to swear an oath of allegiance to the monarchy. As we learn from Croce's diary, officers from Central and Northern Italy who shared these feelings continually arrived at his home, seeking his advice. Croce's initiative offered a way to harness the enthusiasm of those young men, thus contributing to national unity and to an expanded war effort.

Little attention has been paid by historians to Croce's political efforts during this period. Few have recognized the value of his contributions, yet many have questioned, just as some contemporaries did, his intentions. Croce's aim was not to bring the anti-Fascist forces under moderate and monarchical leadership, as Roberto Battaglia claims in his book on the Italian Resistance.[38] Croce soon realized that participation in the war beside the Allies was indispensable if Italy was to regain its lost prestige. He tried to make a contribution towards that end in the only way possible. He wanted a military formation without partisan affiliation but officially recognized by the Italian government and supported by the Allied authorities.

Something of a similar nature would find final shape a few months later: the Brigata Maiella in Abruzzi. Once fully organized, this brigade depended on the Italian government for its administration and pay; it was attached to the British Eighth Army, worked closely with the Polish Corps, and retained autonomy of command. It was not required to swear allegiance to the king, but carried the Italian flag and its soldiers and officers had the tricolour on their epaulettes. Even the Germans regarded the Brigata as a military unit and its members as regular soldiers, protected by the Geneva Convention. At its maximum strength it numbered fifteen hundred men. It fought well from Abruzzi to Northern Italy; it gained the respect of the British, the affection of the Poles, and the admiration of the Italian people. More importantly, in Abruzzi it had the support of the population and in other regions did much to make the Resistance popular among the common people. In Abruzzi, members of the Brigata were always referred to as "patriots" rather than "partisans." After the war, whenever "the Patriots of the Maiella" participated in military parades, they were greeted in the cities and towns of Abruzzi with general enthusiasm. There were several reasons for its success. The Brigata Maiella had committed soldiers and motivated officers, all of whom had volunteered and were united by a common idea of patriotism. Moreover, the two leading commanders showed skill and dedication in military and political leadership throughout the campaign, qualities often lacking in those times among traditional and regular army officers.[39]

Unfortunately, Croce was not able to repeat the success of the Brigata Maiella with his Gruppi Combattenti. On 16 October there is a note of distress in his diary: "I am very sad to have learned about the opposition undertaken against our volunteer groups, not only by Badoglio, but also by monarchical elements." On the 31st, there is another observation in the same vein: "Unfortunately, things are going badly for the groups. General Pavone has answered my questions with evasions, and the Americans accuse him of having done nothing concrete until now."[40] The groups were officially dissolved on 1 November 1943, an outcome that Caracciolo blamed on the scheming of Badoglio and the bad faith of the Allies. Both of them had always disliked the groups' spirit of independence, particularly their refusal to accept fully the authority of the king or to embrace Allied policy without question. Croce, it seems, never completely understood the reasons for the groups' dissolution. Perhaps, as he said, the fault rested with "the little ability and slow pace of General Pavone, as many say"; or perhaps with the desire of the Americans to abandon "what they had promised before," or with the "intrigues and pressures from the king and Badoglio."[41] The last entry in Croce's diary on the Gruppi Combattenti, on 13 November, expresses continuing puzzlement about the failure of an initiative that had started out so promising. "I had obtained, without begging and while preserving Italian dignity, an agreement with the Americans that would allow the creation of volunteer corps under the Italian flag. But I have not yet understood if afterwards the Allies wanted the failure of that initiative, one that they had to accept since it came from General Donovan but with which they were not happy from the beginning, or if the king or those around him expressed opposition to the Allied command, or if the Italian general chosen by us was neither active nor capable enough. The fact remains that the corps has been disbanded."[42]

It is now clear that Croce's initiative failed for several reasons. First of all, the initiative was sabotaged by the king and was met with hostility from his generals. The traditional generals, prisoners of the old rules, resisted change and did not grasp the importance of Croce's military and political enterprise. Moreover, Badoglio did not provide the cooperation he had promised; instead, he worked for its failure, telling the Allied authorities that he was against any recruiting of volunteers outside of the regular army. At the same time, he promised the Allies that the government and the regular army could give them better assistance. At the beginning of October, he even issued a decree prohibiting the formation of volunteer groups. His chief of staff, General Vittorio Ambrosio, then invited the volunteers to join the royal army. It is interesting to note that the Badoglio government recognized the Brigata Maiella only after Giovanni Messe, a younger and more modern general, replaced Ambrosio as chief of staff. Moreover, elements of the court and their agents spread lies and rumours about the groups, accusing Croce of promoting the formation of a republican army. General Pavone in fact was quite blunt in his accusation against Badoglio and the king's entourage. "I have to tell you that the entire government of Badoglio, certain well-known generals, and also political elements of the court and local politicians have worked against us."[43]

Moreover, the opposition of the monarchical groups was not balanced by the support of the anti-Fascist forces. The left-wing parties looked with suspicion on Croce's initiative, resented his position of leadership, and did not like the prominent role of members of the Party of Action in the Gruppi Combattenti. On the other hand, Tarchiani himself did not enjoy the full support of his own party; some members of that party did not share his moderation and were suspicious of his close ties with the Allies and with Croce. Pavone also blamed the Americans for their obstructionism. According to him, the Americans did not remain faithful to the agreement. Sometimes recruits were used for purposes other than those originally agreed upon, and even without the general's knowledge. The supply of food, clothing, and transportation equipment was never sufficient. After the publication of the first press release and Croce's manifesto, the Allies did not permit the publication of newsletters or the posting of notices, which would have provided important information to those who wished to volunteer.[44]

Finally, there was dissension among the members of the liaison committee. The committee at first worked well. Its members travelled to various cities, trying to give shape to the organization. But soon there were disagreements about the nature and function of the groups. Carracciolo quickly lost confidence "in the ability of our general"; relations between Pavone and Craveri deteriorated rapidly. Craveri wanted no more than two thousand volunteers. Pavone dreamed of a regular army corps, with platoons, companies, and divisions. But, according to Craveri, Pavone himself showed no energy or sense of urgency, took no decisions, and gave no orders; though a great talker and a pleasant raconteur of old stories, he did not display organizational skills. Pavone was an old-fashioned general, not attuned to the requirements of a modern army or with the needs of a resistance force. He looked back to the First World War and continued to speak of mules as a means of transportation in a time of jeeps and armoured vehicles.[45] While never questioning Pavone's motives or his character, Croce seems to have agreed with this assessment. Historian Claudio Pavone, among the few who has studied in depth the Gruppi Combattenti, has come to a fair conclusion: "General Pavone was an anti-Fascist army officer, an honest and brave man; however, he was not equal, from a technical and political view, to the task of guiding such a difficult undertaking."[46]

The effort to organize the Gruppi Combattenti was not completely in vain. On 31 October, when Croce learned that the groups would be disbanded, he made this revealing note in his diary: "I have spoken with Tompkins, and I believe that those nuclei of the volunteers will be disbanded; but we had an exchange of ideas and discussed how, in that event, to undertake a similar initiative."[47] In another document, Croce adds this important comment: "The person who has remained more disappointed and has shown more irritation than anyone else is Raimondo, who hopes to carry out a different initiative, but one equally useful to the struggle against the Germans and to the liberation of the Italian land."[48] In fact, with the consent and the support of Croce, Craveri immediately "began to organize a new but smaller group of volunteers, the Operazione Resistenza Italiana, or ORI." As Craveri writes, this would be "a secret organization, made up of Italian volunteers, that operated in Northern Italy, with the aim of providing military information to the Allies and at the same time helping the Committee of National Liberation and the partisan groups in the North in any way possible."[49]

The ORI was mainly the result of Raimondo Craveri's efforts. But he received much help from Peter Tompkins of the OSS. They recruited a group of Italian volunteers, highly motivated and able to speak English, all sworn to secrecy, who received instruction in Italy or in Algiers by American officers and were then trained to conduct sabotage and maintain radio communication behind enemy lines. This time there were written agreements, and clear lines of responsibility were established between the ORI and the OSS. Motivation, organization, and training assured the success of the ORI, but there were also other reasons for the good results. The ORI could rely on the support of a number of young OSS officers, usually of Italo-American origin, who understood the political value of the Italian Resistance and were willing to trust its leaders, Ferruccio Parri of the Party of Action in particular. Most of them were supporters of the Democratic Party and Roosevelt's New Deal. Craveri enjoyed friendly relations with some British officers of the SOE, such as Salvadori, who offered assurances, if not of cooperation, at least of non-interference. Craveri kept not only Croce but also key members of the Italian government, who were in agreement with his aims and could provide help when needed, fully informed of his efforts.

From 1944 to 1945, the ORI undertook more than twenty missions behind enemy lines. It was instrumental in providing military information to the Allies and the Resistance alike, as well as arms and ammunition to the latter. In the opinion of an American historian, the "ORI became the communication hub of the entire Northern underground." It also paid a heavy price. Many of its members were killed in action, or captured and tortured to extract a confession and valuable information. Unfortunately, their contribution to the Resistance had to wait a long time before it was fully recognized.[50] The Brigata Maiella has recently attracted more attention, but the ORI, like the Gruppi Combattenti, is barely mentioned in most histories of the Italian Resistance.

3
The Matter of the King

Besides the creation of the Gruppi Combattenti, the other issue, at the end of 1943, that concerned Croce deeply involved the abdication of the king and the formation of a new government. In the fall and winter of 1943, everybody agreed, Italians and Allies alike, that the Badoglio government was weak and unrepresentative and that it needed to be strengthened by the inclusion of representatives of the democratic parties.

The achievement of that goal proved to be difficult for several reasons. Often the interests of the parties and the leaders participating in the negotiations were divergent. The king and Badoglio disagreed on the nature and the scope of the change required and pursued different solutions, entering into negotiations independent of each other and sometimes with conflicting goals. Liberals and other moderates, at least the better-known ones, demanded the king's abdication as a condition of their participation in a new cabinet. The radical parties of the left insisted on the abolition of the monarchy and the proclamation of a republic. Inside the CLN, pragmatic solutions were accepted in the interests of internal unity. But sometimes the committee itself was in a belligerent mood. In the middle of October, the Rome CLN, supported by the Naples committee, in a wordy resolution, probably the result of a difficult compromise, demanded "national unity" in order to wage "a war of national liberation"; and, since this was not possible "under the leadership of the present king and the Badoglio government," it proposed "the constitution of an emergency government that would be the expression of the political forces which fought constantly against fascism and have opposed the Fascist war since 1939." Even the Communist members voted for the motion, forgetting the Stalin-Ribbentrop Pact.

The Allies, for their part, certainly wanted a more representative government with the participation of political parties and supported by anti-Fascist elements, but they were opposed to any change in the status of the monarchy, at least before the end of the war, and were not favourable to replacing Badoglio as prime minister. For that reason, the king and Badoglio, weak in other respects, were in a stronger position than the democratic parties. In a divided country, and in the middle of a civil war, the king and the monarchy represented the continuity of the state and the source of legality, and they also controlled whatever remained of the armed forces. Furthermore, the king and Badoglio, as signatories of the armistice, enjoyed the protection, if not the full confidence, of the Allied powers and, more importantly, could count on the support of Churchill and the British cabinet. The British prime minister did not trust anti-Fascist leaders and was adamantly opposed to the abolition of the monarchy and the replacement of Badoglio. At the end of 1943 and the beginning of 1944, then, the obstacles to forming a more democratic government were substantial and came from different sources. Many efforts would be needed to overcome those obstacles. In the end a compromise was found, different from anything ever anticipated.[1]

Croce's attitude towards the monarchy was more emotional than rational and not without contradictions, but one theme remained constant: the need for the king's abdication. He repeated the same terms to all concerned, Italians and the Allies alike. He demanded the abdication of the king as a condition of his participation in a new government. To this end, he put forward a practical and reasonable solution, and pursued it with determination and tenacity, employing various means at his disposal. Croce made a distinction between the institutional question and the personal fate of the king; the first could be postponed until the end of the war, the other had to be solved in the present, the sooner the better.

For Croce, the monarchy had been beneficial to Italy; it had guided the process of national unification and assured the progress of the country, and it could still play a useful role in the future as a symbol of tradition and unity, and also as a counter-attraction to the Vatican. He was also fearful that, among the chaos of the war, the proclamation of a republic could be the first step to an authoritarian government, even a new dictatorship. But Croce had a strong dislike of the present king; in his opinion, Vittorio Emanuele had betrayed the Albertine Statute – the constitution of the Italian state created in 1861 – by identifying the monarchy with fascism; he had approved of or tolerated all of Mussolini's crimes, and finally, together with Mussolini, had brought Italy to ruin. As a sign of a clear break with a shameful past and as an indication of a new beginning, the king and his son must abdicate and be replaced by a regency council, in favour of his grandson. For Croce, the abdication of the king was necessary, first of all, because of "the deplorable conduct of the king during fascism," but also because of the illiberal and dangerous policy he was following in the present. The king and his close advisers were then in favour of an authoritarian policy, fascism without Mussolini, as it was then called. The king felt comfortable with moderate former Fascists and with generals of questionable repute. On 10 October 1943 Croce wrote this revealing note in his diary: "From information that I have received and documents that I have read, I have come to the conclusion that the king and the sycophants around him believe and hope that it is possible to save the monarchy with the support of the majority of the former Fascists; for this reason, the king is protecting them as best he can, so that they do not suffer any harassment, and are able to keep offices and stipends. The king asks for only a profession of monarchical allegiance, and with that he accepts and employs all, even the Communists."[2]

There was also another, equally important, consideration. For Croce, an increased war effort beside the Allies was essential to gain their confidence and to change the terms of the armistice so that Italy might acquire the full status of an ally rather than remain in the ambivalent condition of a co-belligerent. He soon came to realize that the presence of the king was a hindrance to that aim. As already recounted, he met frequently with army officers who had come to Southern Italy from the North willing to fight but unwilling to serve under the king, and he was also told that many young men had no desire to join the army as long as the king remained in power as head of state. The king was associated with the crimes and mistakes of the past; he was no longer a unifying force as he had been during the last war – now he had become a source of division.

To these reasons, a few months later Croce added another. In the course of events, he had come to suspect that the Allies were not keen on turning Italy into a full-fledged member of their alliance, because they wanted "to have a free hand in the future peace conference." That perhaps explained why the Anglo-Americans wanted to keep in power a monarch "with the character and the weakness of the present king," who was unable and unwilling to rally the nation to increased participation in a common war.[3] Croce was not alone in his suspicions, according to various sources, including Macmillan's *War Diaries.* "We hold no brief for the King and Badoglio," Macmillan wrote, "but at the present time they can be useful to us and do what we tell them."[4] Croce's experience of dealing with the Allies and observing their policies at close range probably accounts for this reflection on the nature of the present war, which in some respects contradicts his other assertions on the same subject: "For my part, I have come to the conclusion that this is not a war for freedom, but, like all the other wars, is for independence, for dominion, for economic and political advantages, and that the war for freedom will have to be fought later, and with means different and more suitable than arms."[5]

Croce often discussed the king's refusal to abdicate in his diary. Every time the judgment is critical and severe; the king's obstinacy "created great damage to the future of Italy" and "showed an absence of moral sensibility." In fact, the stubborn refusal to abdicate was the last disaster inflicted on Italy by the king. It showed an undue attachment to personal interest, and a failure to understand the new reality. His attitude weakened the authority of the government, and in the end it would prove fatal to the monarchy itself. It created a great deal of difficulty for the democratic anti-Fascist forces and especially for the old Liberal leaders. Above all, it transformed an internal problem and a personal decision into an international issue, one that damaged Italy's position by allowing the Allies to play one party against the other. It also compelled political leaders to devote time and energy to the institutional problem instead of concentrating all their thoughts on the war effort and the pressing needs of the country. Croce himself had to discuss the institutional question with British and American journalists when his international prestige could and should have been fully used for changing the terms of the armistice or for creating better feelings towards the new Italy that was emerging painfully from the ruins of war.

In his contest with the king, Croce soon found an ally in Carlo Sforza. The former minister of foreign affairs in Giovanni Giolitti's last government in 1921 had just returned to Italy after twenty years of exile, spent in genteel poverty, first in Europe and then in America. He had departed from the United States, hoping to play a leading role in Italian affairs. That aspiration was more than justified. He had "a keen intelligence"; he was among the few then who had prior government experience; he enjoyed the backing of influential members of the American administration; and, perhaps most importantly, at the beginning he had the support of Churchill, who had received him in London with great courtesy, discussing Italian issues for hours. As a result, when Eisenhower met Badoglio at Malta to sign the Long Armistice, he had spoken in his favour and asked Badoglio to include Sforza in his government. Afterwards, however, Sforza's position began to unravel. In Washington, he had promised Adolf Berle, undersecretary of state, "to rally the Italians around the king and Badoglio," and he made the same vow in London to Churchill. But, once in Italy, from what he saw and what he was told, he became critical of the king and his government, and he joined Croce in demanding the king's abdication, refusing to participate in the Badoglio cabinet despite several invitations. Churchill was furious, regarding Sforza's about-face as a blatant betrayal. From then on, he and Foreign Secretary Anthony Eden vetoed Sforza's appointment to government positions. Moreover, in his feud with the British leaders, Sforza did not receive the kind of support from American officials that he expected. Unknown to him, the Americans had been informed that Sforza was persona non grata to the Vatican. Eisenhower's departure from the Mediterranean theatre and American deference to Britain on Italian affairs did the rest. In a short while, for those trying to bring about a new government, Sforza went from being a powerful force to a liability.

Sforza himself did not play his cards well, quickly squandering his political assets. He did not have an organized party behind him; his only strengths were the perceived support of the Allies and his own reputation; the first soon evaporated and the second was irremediably harmed by Sforza's own conduct. After his return to Italy, Sforza did not show the temper and the toughness of leadership, revealing instead personal "limits and defects" and "changing views a little too quickly." On many occasions he was carried away by circumstances, making, as Croce put it, "imprudent utterances" that were "not expected from a future head of government." In meetings with foreign military officers, or Italian ones for that matter, he indulged in gossipy conversation during which his ego appeared too much in evidence. As Macmillan wrote after their first meeting: "The Count appeared to go for a moment or two into a trance and then, in spite of a sore throat and a heavy cold, he poured out a continual stream of words in his peculiar English." Macmillan reported that "he said some witty, some interesting and many revealing things" – "the same as Croce, but with a lot of embellishments and much court scandal."[6] Even more worrisome, in dealings with the Allies, or with some of their leaders, Sforza was not careful with his promises, and these were usually accompanied by several qualifications that, made in wartime to harried men, could be easily forgotten or misunderstood, especially when it was convenient to do so. To Churchill, Sforza had promised to support the king, but then he had immediately added: "if the king was doing the utmost to fight fascism and the Germans." Churchill regarded the king as a useful and reliable ally, and the Allies much preferred pliable figures to those who questioned their aims or could hinder their plans.

Sforza also stretched himself too thin. He had a compulsion to be omnipresent; he never refused an invitation to speak at a political rally, however small, or to appear at a ceremony of insignificant value. He intervened in local politics and took positions in personal rivalries, alienating possible allies or former supporters. Croce and others noted this weakness and tried to warn him against the harmful results of his innocent vanities, or "romantic nature" as Sforza preferred to call it. One day Croce drew his attention to the scene in Shakespeare's *Henry IV* where the king tells his son how he behaved to achieve support before his accession to the throne: "Thus I keep my person fresh and new; / my presence, like a robe pontifical, / never seen but wondered at: and so my state, / seldom but sumptuous, showed like a feast, / and won by rareness such solemnity."[7]

Sforza's acceptance of Croce's position on the monarchy, therefore, further complicated negotiations with the Allies. In a conversation in the summer of 1944 with Umberto Zanotti Bianco, a common friend, Croce recapitulated his changing attitude towards Sforza. In Bianco's words, "Croce told me that when Sforza had been in America, he had regarded him as a future prime minister. When he met him again after his return to Italy, he noted that the count had not aged well, and some of his youthful shortcomings had worsened; with age he had become more impulsive, full of himself, inconstant, and not careful in his judgments. When he spoke he boasted of the support of the Allies, and alluded that they wanted him as prime minister, but then in public he used a language not appropriate to a prime minister. At the end his manners and his way of talking lost him sympathy and support in Italy and abroad."[8]

Even Badoglio and the king realized the need for a more representative government. But they disagreed on the means to achieving that end. As a result, their personal relations deteriorated, and on some issues their positions were in open conflict.

Typical of the negotiations then taking place at various levels and in different cities was a meeting on 13 October 1943 between Croce and Leopoldo Piccardi. Piccardi was one of the few civilian and Liberal ministers in the Badoglio government. And on this occasion he definitely was engaged in an exploratory mission on behalf of Badoglio, who wanted to show the king that his policy was supported by important figures in the country. The questions posed by Piccardi to Croce were clear, as recounted in Croce's diary: "Piccardi asked my opinion whether, with the imminent liberation of Rome, it was opportune to form a new political cabinet instead of the present one made up almost completely of military personnel; whether it was necessary to keep Badoglio as prime minister or to replace him; and what position was to be taken on the institutional question." Croce's answers were also clear, if slightly different from some previous ones, reflecting changed circumstances or changed opinions: "I have answered 1) that it is necessary to form a political ministry; 2) I believe that, the war against the Germans being the most urgent problem, it is not convenient at this time to relieve Badoglio from his position, since, because of his military ability and his pledge undertaken in the present crisis against fascism and against the Germans, he is the person more suitable than anybody else; 3) That we must now put aside the institutional question, which will be solved in the course of events, but Badoglio should advise the king, on his return to Rome, to abdicate in favour of his son." Piccardi assured Croce that Badolgio was in agreement with him on all these points.[9]

As a result of Piccardi's report and his own findings, Badoglio, on 24 October, wrote a formal letter to the king asking him to abdicate and to create a regency council. The old king was not amused. He undertook consultations of his own, sending faithful emissaries to various cities.[10] On the 28th, Croce had a meeting with Pietro Acquarone, then the minister of the royal household and the king's chief political adviser. In a circuitous way, Acquarone sought Croce's support for the cause of Vittorio Emanuele, or at least he hoped to enlist Croce's help in persuading Sforza to serve under the king in a new government. Acquarone was not highly respected by democratic leaders, a standing later confirmed by historians of the period. In dealing with Croce, he was not straightforward and at times less than candid, even misleading. As Croce wrote, it was "an hour of a painful dialogue." Acquarone tried to persuade Croce to accept as an "experiment" the continuance of King Vittorio Emanuele on the throne in order "to achieve the cohesion of the Italian forces in the war against the Germans." Croce replied that the king had lost all moral standing among the common people and political leaders. "Because of his adherence to fascism," he had become a hindrance to national unity and an obstacle to a government of all democratic parties. Acquarone pointed out that "the Allies demanded that the king remain on the throne and nothing could be done in the face of their determination." He also added that "the Allies wanted the institutional question and the choice between monarchy and republic to be postponed till the end of the war." As he had done before, discussing the same subject with others, Croce made a distinction between the king's abdication and the institutional question. "I told him that the question today concerns a person, and the monarchy could remain undiscussed, if a regency council were created." In the end, Acquarone did not change Croce's mind or his "disposition of spirit" towards the king. No promise of future collaboration was made. The mission was a complete failure. But Acquarone had been reminded that the question of abdication rested only with the king, and it was a personal choice, depending on his sense of responsibility and morality.[11]

The day after the meeting with Acquarone, Croce met those who really held the keys of the kingdom. Evidently even the Allies were trying to find a way to bolster the Italian government's authority by obtaining the support of the democratic parties or at least of the most representative political figures in Southern Italy. On the institutional question, Croce had a meeting with Harold Macmillan and Robert Murphy, the political ministers of the United Kingdom and the United States at Eisenhower's Allied headquarters in Algiers. As Croce reports in his diary: "They asked me to explain the political situation in relation to the monarchy question: and I have done so."[12] With a sense of amusement, and a hint of criticism, Macmillan wrote that Croce "spoke for almost an hour and a half without catching his breath."[13] One is left with the impression that neither Macmillan nor Murphy grasped Croce's political and cultural importance at the time. The meeting or Croce's name is not mentioned in Murphy's memoirs. Macmillan was in a better position to know; his family's firm, after all, had been the publisher of Croce's books in English. Yet, though a man of learning and an avid reader, he seemed out of his depth in dealing with the Italian philosopher. He admired the vitality of the old man, and also was impressed by the clarity of his ideas on the present political situation. But, as a member both of the British establishment and of the Conservative Party, he made disparaging remarks about Croce's wealth, his "old fashioned liberalism," and "the obscurity of his books." On another occasion, he expressed his annoyance at the frequent requests for publication of new editions of Croce's works, without grasping the importance of spreading Croce's ideas – for the present and future alike. Unlike William Donovan, Macmillan probably did not bother, or did not have time, to acquire up-to-date information on Croce. Used to organized, well-structured parties and political freedom in their own countries, Macmillan and Murphy did not realize the special position held in Italy by public intellectuals. It never crossed their minds that Croce's views carried more weight than the opinions of Sforza or anyone else, at least in Southern Italy before the liberation of Rome.

The final round of negotiations to find a way out of the impasse took place in Naples. Croce and Sforza had meetings with Badoglio and tried to impress upon him that the king must abdicate "because there was no other solution." Apparently, Badoglio agreed with their assessment. He even assured them that he was willing to be head of a regency council in the event of the king's abdication. For the present, however, he made a strong plea for them to join his cabinet. But a careful reading of Croce's account of those meetings leaves no doubt that, as he had done before with Craveri and Tarchiani, Badoglio was also indirectly telling Croce and Sforza some unpleasant truths and reminding them of some hard facts: the king was absolutely opposed to abdication, enjoyed the support of the Allies, and could always find a more pliable general, one of those with an authoritarian bent, eager to carry out his orders and less favourable to liberal ideas and personalities than Badoglio was.[14]

As a result of all these negotiations, and pressure from the Allies at the same time, Badoglio formed a new ministry, his second, on 16 November 1943. He had failed to persuade Croce and Sforza to join this new cabinet. But he was able to replace several generals and civil servants with moderate and conservative liberals, some of them on cordial terms with Croce. Some of the new ministers were men of ability and political standing, as would be shown by their future careers. The few existing newspapers announced the event with great fanfare. In a subtle way, rumours were also spread that Croce supported the new government. Many friends of Croce sought his advice, asking whether they should support or oppose the new cabinet. "I gave answers to their questions and strongly advised them to maintain their opposition and continue a policy of the most rigorous intransigence."[15]

The formation of Badoglio's second cabinet showed both the strength and weakness of the Liberal Party. In Southern Italy the party had well-known public figures. But it lacked an organization and the propaganda machinery suitable to a modern party. It was centred around strong personalities, but, as noted in chapter 2, the majority of these were notables, often famous professionals or landowners, surrounded by their clientele. Many of them tended to act as individuals, sometimes out of personal ambition, often out of sheer isolation and lack of communication.

A common policy was hard to achieve and difficult to maintain, and usually was the result of personal meetings with Croce, causing delays and missed opportunities. The lack of a modicum of party discipline allowed the king, or Badoglio for that matter, to follow a policy of divide and rule. When Croce proposed the organization of Gruppi Combattenti, and was trying to organize them, Liberals in Naples opposed that initiative, fearing the breaking up of the Italian army into factions. In another instance later on, when Croce had persuaded the Allied authorities to name a professional journalist with true liberal qualifications as editor of Naples' newspaper – the only one then allowed to operate – Liberals in that city instead suggested one of their own, because he was from Naples, had had the job before, and in any case had a family to support. While the Liberals were playing an open game, in another political party something different was happening: a modern party organization was taking shape and a new way of doing politics was emerging. The Christian Democrats in Southern Italy were then discussing and approving in semi-public meetings the document prepared and written in Rome by their undisputed leader, Alcide De Gasperi: *Ideas for the Reconstruction of a Christian Democracy*. That document was brought from Rome to Southern Italy and then copied and distributed to small and large cities by special emissaries. The ensuing discussions prepared the ground for a mass party, with a shared program and a cohesive leadership, possessing the means to influence public opinion and to achieve and exercise power.[16]

The creation of Badoglio's second cabinet, and the meetings and negotiations preceding it, persuaded Croce that the king would change his mind only under pressure from the Allies, and perhaps from national public opinion. Accordingly, he now worked on those new fronts. First, he enlisted the help of Anglo-American journalists working in Italy. He had several meetings and interviews with Herbert Matthews of the *New York Times* and with his old friend, Cecil Sprigge, then working for the Reuters Agency and later with the *Manchester Guardian*. During an interview with Matthews, Croce "told him clearly all that I think about the monarchy question and the person of the king." On another occasion, "we had a discussion about the king, and his obstinacy in clinging to power, which is creating great damage to Italy." Finally, Croce told a group of American journalists that "it is impossible to keep the king and his son in power, but it is possible not to abolish the monarchy, creating a regency council in favour of the little prince of Naples." The conclusion of that meeting was gratifying to Croce. "After several questions and answers, they accepted my arguments and promised to support my position in their newspapers and with the American authorities."[17]

On 18 November 1943 Croce, with the help of Peter Tompkins, sent a long letter to Walter Lippmann, then and later one of the most influential American columnists, a former editor of the *New Republic* and a public philosopher writing for the *New York Herald Tribune* and other papers. The letter is full of keen political and philosophical observations. It represents a recapitulation of Croce's reasons for desiring the king's abdication. It is also an appeal to an old friend and a kindred soul, one able to shape public opinion and influence official policy. In many ways, the letter was a brief for the prosecution, in which Croce offered Lippmann arguments for asking the American administration to change policy and to pursue a course in Italy more attuned to democratic ideals. Lippmann was not the only one to receive or read that document. Sometime later, Carlo Sforza sent a copy of it to Ivor Thomas, an influential Labour member of the British Parliament favourably disposed towards Italian democratic parties.

In the letter, Croce pointed out the contradictions of Allied policy in Italy and the present and future dangers of that policy. The Allies wanted to eradicate fascism from Italian society, but at the same time they were supporting the man who as "the head of state had been the principal figure responsible for fascism," a king who had violated the constitution on many occasions and who from 1922 "had been completely at the service of the Fascist dictatorship." It was true, Croce conceded, that the king had ousted Mussolini from power and signed an armistice with the Allies, but since then he had been defending only his dynastic interests and "his policy has been to maintain and protect as much as possible the men and institutions of the old regime." Furthermore, after declaring war on Germany, the king began reorganizing the armed forces as a private army "so that it will be able to support his permanence on the throne," and for this reason he accepted into the new army even old Fascist generals guilty of war crimes. With a direct reference to the formation and failure of the Gruppi Combattenti, Croce also informed Lippmann that the king was discouraging, even sabotaging, "with direct or indirect means," the recruitment of volunteer fighters. And for this reason, many young people who had come to Southern Italy to volunteer now felt discouraged and disappointed. At the same time, on account of the king's past crimes and his present authoritarian policy, democratic politicians were refusing to join a new ministry because of their unwillingness to swear allegiance to the monarch. As a consequence, the absence of a cabinet formed by old and trusted politicians together with young leaders of the anti-Fascist parties weakened the authority of the state and created a paralysis in Italian public life. This state of affairs was not conducive to public order, did not facilitate the solution of social problems, and would only create troubles even for the Allies.

Croce also dealt with the main argument used by those who preferred the status quo. "We are told that now no change is possible, because the British and the Americans want to maintain the monarchy for the time being and leave the Italian people after the war free to choose the institution they prefer." Croce assured Lippmann that he and his friends agreed. While the war lasted, there was no need to choose between a monarchy and a republic. At the moment there was not an institutional question but a personal one, the abdication of a king no longer fit to remain in power by reason of his past behaviour and present conduct. The abdication of the old king and his son, and the creation of a regency council in favour of his grandson, according to Croce, could be useful in the future to the monarchy itself but, above all, "in Italy would produce a spiritual unity and the feeling of a complete separation from the past."

The last part of Croce's letter offered a criticism of the general policy followed by the Allies in North Africa, in Italy, and even in Europe. Their stated aim was to restore freedom, but in practice they did not support the forces of liberation; instead, they favoured conservative elements and the creation of semi-fascist regimes, moved by a desire to protect their interests and also by fear of communism. For Croce, that policy was dangerous for Italy and for all of Europe, and contrary to the liberal and democratic ideals of the Allied nations. It was vital that public opinion in Great Britain and the United States of America force a change in direction.[18]

The fear of an authoritarian resurgence was emphasized again by Croce in a speech delivered to an assembly at the University of Naples organized by Adolfo Omodeo, then president of the institution. Omodeo was afraid that, without public support, the democratic opposition to the king would fail just as the Aventino against Mussolini in 1924 had failed, and so he wanted to bring the institutional question to the attention of a larger audience.[19] In his speech Croce accused Vittorio Emanuele of protecting men and interests of the former regime. "The army that is being reorganized has become a refuge for Fascists," and the king is making clear that "he counts on them to put in place a semi-fascism under liberal forms, which is the danger of today and tomorrow of our unfortunate country." Once again Croce defended the monarchy as an institution, and at that point was loudly jeered by the people and students, encouraged by members of the Communist Party who were present. But he received a warmer reception when he forcefully demanded the king's abdication for his betrayal of the Albertine Statute, support of fascism, and failure to fulfil his constitutional duties. Croce reminded the king that abdication was a personal act and in making his decision he should be mindful of Italy's future above all else. Because the choice was personal, it did not compromise the institution and could not be vetoed by the Allies. As Croce said, "abdication is a voluntary act, dictated to the king by the voice of his conscience, and, in the present circumstances, by the necessity to make a full break with the past's dangerous heritage, and also by the opportunity to remove an obstacle ... to achieving concord among the Italian people and the full cooperation in the struggle to liberate the country from the invading Germans, who, after they have brought destruction, are now trying to create a cruel civil war."[20]

This appeal to the king's conscience was repeated by Croce in a letter to the editor of Naples' newspaper. The letter was a reply to a recent statement by Badoglio, in which he had declared that the king had not abdicated and could not abdicate because the Allies would not allow him to do so. It was a compelling argument but it cut no ice with Croce. "The abdication had to arise, as was long expected, spontaneously in the conscience of the king, as a result of his moral sensibility, and he had to put it into effect without asking somebody else's judgment and approval." Croce made another point that shows the bitter animosity that the old liberal elite harboured against the king. For most of them, Vittorio Emanuele bore a greater responsibility than Mussolini for the misfortunes of Italy. "It was not their fault that the king joined body and soul with fascism, and assumed a responsibility bigger than that of Mussolini, who was a poor devil, ignorant, short of intelligence, and made drunk by easy demagogical success, while the king had received a proper education and had ruled a liberal and civilized Italy."[21]

By December 1943, the political situation in Southern Italy was still at a stalemate. Croce and Sforza demanded the abdication of Vittorio Emanuele; Badoglio agreed with that proposal and had even suggested to the king that he step down; but the king refused to budge. A new cabinet had been formed in the middle of November after long and contorted negotiations, but the government remained without much popular support. Negotiations among Italian leaders, under pressure from the Allies, continued in order to find a solution acceptable to all. Yet, so far, all these efforts were leading nowhere.

Soon, however, the elements of a compromise began to emerge and took the shape of a rather peculiar constitutional proposal, devised, this time, only by Italians. At the very end of the year, on 30 December 1943, in Naples, Croce and Sforza had a special meeting with Enrico De Nicola, the last speaker of the Italian Parliament before Mussolini's dictatorship. De Nicola had been a follower of Giolitti and a member of his cabinet. He was also a famous lawyer and a fine jurist; more significantly, he was at that time the most important and popular Liberal leader in Southern Italy. He enjoyed universal respect, and his advice was valued by the king; his personal integrity was proverbial. Under Mussolini, he had remained aloof from official functions, devoting all his energy to the legal profession. During those years Croce and De Nicola met only a few times, conversing cordially but never discussing political affairs. Still, this time Croce and De Nicola found themselves in agreement on the most important issues. Without success, Croce even urged him to to assume the leadership of the Liberal forces, as the heir of Giolitti, allowing Croce to take a step back. As a result of these meetings and discussions, a warm personal friendship developed. Even more importantly, a political partnership was born.

At their meeting on 30 December, as Croce writes in his diary, "De Nicola has told us that he is in full agreement with us on the point that the king and his son, the prince of Piedmont, have, in one way or another, to abdicate. But he has doubts about the regency." De Nicola was afraid that a regent could use his position to pursue an undemocratic course and even become a new dictator. Instead of a regency, De Nicola "proposed a lieutenancy, which would last two or three years, until the Italian people could be consulted and give its response on the institutional form to be adopted." Under this proposal, the king would not formally abdicate but rather just retire to private life and name a lieutenant general of the realm to take over the royal duties; this would not represent an abdication by another name, but the effect would be the same. The suggestion had precedents in the House of Savoy and was used during the First World War, when the king left Rome and moved to the front, where he remained for the duration of hostilities. As was natural, Croce expressed a few doubts. First of all, a lieutenancy seemed to him to carry more dangers for the monarchy itself than a more traditional regency. Once the continuity of the institution was broken, it would be difficult to put it back on the same pedestal, especially if the vote on the institutional question after the war was delegated to the Constituent Assembly. To that objection, De Nicola, claiming "a better intuition ... of the king's character," replied with great assurance: "The king will oppose abdication, but you will see that he will accept the lieutenancy."[22]

Encouraged by such self-confidence, and trusting in his negotiating ability, Croce and Sforza agreed to let De Nicola submit this new proposal to the king; they also agreed to maintain a strict secrecy on their new course of action, which was consonant with De Nicola's own modus operandi. Also in the interests of discretion, Croce wisely refused to suggest a name for the position of lieutenant, a matter deemed of no importance at that stage. Though during the discussions the name of Prince Umberto had been mentioned, Croce and Sforza had soon discarded that possibility "as not only unacceptable to us, but also to the king himself, as a diminution of his son."[23]

Croce's opposition to the old king never changed, but his demand for abdication had gone through several stages and was not without some contradictions. First there was the request for an abdication of Vittorio Emanuele in favour of his son, Umberto. Then Croce demanded an abdication of both the king and Umberto, and the creation of a regency council, under Badoglio's chairmanship, acting on behalf of Umberto's young son. The lieutenancy proposal would be the last attempt to remove the king from centre stage, and De Nicola and Croce would spend the next three months trying to persuade the stubborn king of its inevitability. The clash paved the way for the destruction of the monarchy, but it also divided the liberal forces at a time when unity was of the utmost importance. Croce's opposition to the Badoglio government and his call for the king's abdication were resented by monarchical elements, and were also criticized in moderate quarters as divisive and even unnecessary. But his position was justified. There are the elements of Greek tragedy in the unfolding of these events. Croce, Sforza, and Vittorio Emanuele seemed fated to follow their chosen paths. The king could not accept his share of responsibility for the present misfortunes of Italy or for twenty years of complicity with Mussolini. He never realized that he had become a hindrance to the interests of the country and the destiny of his own house. Sforza and Croce's overall policy could be better carried out from inside the government and with the full support of the state, using the levers of power, and Croce himself recognized the necessity for unity and deplored unnecessary disagreements. But he could not stomach the idea of serving under the king; all his past and current beliefs rebelled against such an accommodation. Had he done so, he may have better advanced his cause, but his personal reputation would have suffered and his political effectiveness would have been diminished. Sforza faced the same predicament. Had he ignored his reservations, and been ready and willing to collaborate with the king upon his return to Italy from the United States, he certainly could have been minister of foreign affairs, perhaps even prime minister in due time. But, as Caracciolo tried to explain to a group of baffled British diplomats: "If Sforza would make an agreement with the monarch, he would lose authority, prestige and influence in the country; moreover, he would be immediately disavowed by the Party of Action, by the CLN and by all the other parties."[24] In other words, he would have been reduced to political impotence.

At the end of an eventful year, Croce's diary, as during the Fascist period, is full of lamentations for the present, doubts on the right course to be chosen, and sometimes even despairing contemplations of the future. Yet he concluded a review of the year on a positive note: "Despite the unhappy ending of my honest attempts, I find a few positive results." After the fall of Mussolini, Croce had reorganized the Liberal Party and given it a more modern program, trying to avoid the pitfalls of radicalism and conservatism. He had made a contribution to the renewal of Neapolitan journalism, and had persuaded the Allied authorities to appoint a liberal-minded professional as editor of the only paper published in that city. He had tried to organize Gruppi Combattenti operating beside the Allies but under the Italian flag. He had refused to join the Badoglio government or to support the position of the king, but instead "had engineered a public trial of the king," demanded his abdication, and at the same time had suggested a dignified way out of his dilemma with the institution of a regency council. Above all, Croce had revived a political opposition which had been absent from the Italian scene for more than twenty years. Refusing radical solutions, stressing moderation, appealing to realism, he had become a de facto leader of the opposition. While defending his ideas with tenacity, using the power of persuasion and the art of diplomacy, he had been able to maintain the unity of the anti-Fascist forces; and, finally, by appeals to national and international public opinion, he had compelled the king and the government to make some changes, and had persuaded the Allies that a more representative government had to come into existence in the new year.[25] These, one might say, were not small achievements in wartime conditions.

4
The Congress of Bari

In 1944 the so-called Kingdom of the South faced much political strife. The Badoglio government was weak and unrepresentative, and, despite the recent shuffle, it did not enjoy much authority. Croce and the democratic parties refused to support the new cabinet and continued to demand the abdication of the king as a condition of their participation. The institutional question still dominated public debate, overshadowing other problems. In the middle of the war, among social upheavals unprecedented in scale, it came to monopolize political energy. None of the political parties had a strong organization, nor did they enjoy a great deal of popular support. They were also often divided into factions, split by personal rivalries or hindered by local animosities. While their leaders frequently gave rousing speeches, few were able to offer concrete and realistic solutions. CLN branches existed in various cities, but their influence was not widespread and they often lacked the ability or even the means to coordinate initiatives. Filippo Caracciolo, a man known for astute observation, offered a realistic assessment: "The Committees of National Liberation are all improvised entities, devoid of political experience, often made up of heterogeneous elements, well-meaning in many cases but rather weak."[1] At best, they could organize public demonstrations, when authorized by military authorities, but were not in position to effect political change, let alone to set new directions.

Against the weakness of the political parties stood the authority of Croce. His international reputation was one of the few real assets of the anti-Fascist forces. He enjoyed a dominant presence in the political landscape and his leadership was widely recognized. The Socialist Oreste Lizzadri, recently arrived from Rome, noticed to his surprise and amusement that Croce's name was mentioned in every conversation, his ideas debated in every gathering. "Croce has said; Croce wants; Croce here; Croce there. Even on the streets and the walls there are many posters with bold letters: Long live Croce."[2] Croce's standing was also high in the Allied councils, as is shown in Richard Malone's memoirs. Malone wrote:

> Many complications arose when the Fascist Grand Council deposed Mussolini and Italy sued for peace. In legal jargon Italy then joined the Allied cause as a "co-belligerent," whatever that meant ... In reality ... while the Germans had established military control over the major part of Italy, there was confusion over civilian authority in Calabria and the South ... In these circumstances, it was determined that AFHQ [Allied Forces Headquarters] in Algiers would simply appoint a temporary government till the whole of the country was liberated. To avoid untold political squabbling, it was first decided to establish a presidential type of administration with the presidency offered to Benedetto Croce, the famous and much respected Italian philosopher and historian. Because of his age, the old man turned down the job. I had the good fortune to meet this fine gentleman before I left Italy, and was much impressed with his wise views on this troubled world.[3]

When Croce fell and broke his left arm in February 1944, Caracciolo noted that "the consequences of his removal from political activity, even for a short period, would be serious ... His existence alone gives to our struggle and to our hopes a tone and a meaning that would be unthinkable without his presence."[4]

Similar feelings were expressed in Florence by Piero Calamandrei, a leader of the Party of Action and one of the future fathers of the Italian constitution. Early in 1944, Calamandrei, by listening to a poor-quality radio broadcast, had come to believe that Croce had died. He remained "deeply shocked" for the entire day and kept meditating on the meaning of such a loss for the country. "I have been saddened by the news, for his family naturally ... but especially for Italy, which needs him more than anyone else in these difficult times. His death raised an immediate and anguishing question: Who now is left to Italy? Whenever one searched for a person who could show that Italy was still alive, that Italy could still cooperate with the rest of mankind and teach something to the world, one soon thought of him, of this old man." Calamandrei then added: "One immediately thought of him when looking for a man who could speak with authority to the winners at a peace conference, or ... could be president of the republic ... in the future."[5]

Meanwhile, the Allied armies continued their slow advance but were meeting stiff German resistance, stronger than anyone had anticipated. In January their landing on the beaches of Anzio almost turned into a disaster and had little effect on the military outlook. No breakthrough happened, and the Germans remained well fortified behind the Gustav Line, their next line of defence. The disappointment in Allied circles was well expressed by Harold Macmillan, who lamented that "a high opportunity was lost" and "hopes were shattered." That same month, the Allied forces reached the ancient abbey of Montecassino, where they remained stuck for four months, suffering heavy casualties. As a result, the liberation of Rome took months rather than weeks, upsetting military and political plans. Today, several military cemeteries dotting the area with long rows of white crosses remain a harrowing witness to poor military planning and generalship.[6]

Badoglio obtained some success both in foreign-policy and in domestic affairs. Against the will of the Anglo-Americans, and practically behind their backs and without their knowledge, the Italian government and the Soviet Union negotiated a diplomatic agreement in January 1944. Italy sent an ambassador to Moscow, and the USSR dispatched a "direct representative" to Salerno. In response, the United Kingdom and the United States named "high commissioners," but, reflecting Allied displeasure with this turn of events, Italy was not allowed to send ambassadors to London and Washington. While nothing of real substance changed, Badoglio had succeeded in breaking Italy's diplomatic isolation, and Stalin found a clever way to influence Italian affairs and to gain a foothold in the Allied Control Commission, from which the Soviet Union had been excluded.[7] The Allies also returned to the king's government the administration of the liberated provinces, which until then had been kept under direct Allied control. Badoglio moved the seat of government from Brindisi to Salerno, but several ministries remained scattered in various cities, creating administrative confusion and communication delays. In general, Badoglio, operating in precarious conditions and contending with different and meddlesome masters, had not been able to improve the efficiency of his government, nor had he been able to enlarge Italy's contribution to the war effort, as he had promised.

Badoglio's task was complicated by the often unreasonable, sometimes contradictory, demands of the Allied armies. His government's room to manoeuvre was constricted by the terms of the Long Armistice signed in Malta on 29 September 1943 by Badoglio and Eisenhower. Even when Italy declared war on Germany on 13 October and became a co-belligerent, its legal status remained much the same; it was still a defeated nation that had surrendered unconditionally, the Allies retaining full military, economic, and political control. By the terms of the Long Armistice, Italy came under the control first of the Allied Military Government (AMG) and later of the Allied Control Commission, which lasted until the end of 1945. The ACC had complete authority over financial institutions, communication facilities, and administrative structures. In Italy, the Allies followed an occupation policy of indirect rule. The Italian government was required to give all financial, economic, and political assistance to the ACC and its more than fifteen hundred experts, who often meddled in affairs they knew nothing about, guided by "wooden heads and desiccated hearts," according to Macmillan. Even more important, Badoglio's government could not take any action without the prior approval of the ACC. In 1944 Italy was no longer an independent nation; politically it was in a very weak position, it was internationally isolated, and many former enemies were clamouring for revenge. Above all, everything depended on the generosity of Allied powers, which alone had the ability to deliver the necessities of life to the population.

At the same time, the situation was made more difficult by the fact that Italy was part of the British sphere of influence. Because Britain wanted to restore its imperial position in the Mediterranean, it was determined to prevent the re-emergence of a powerful Italy. To that end, the British government, as it had done in French North Africa, pursued a short-sighted, sometimes even vindictive, policy in Italy, one that supported traditional institutions, favoured conservative politicians, shunned democratic parties, and hindered leaders who questioned its objectives and actions. The incongruence of that policy was criticized by American journalists stationed in Italy, both in their correspondence and in briefings to American officials. "Italy afforded the first great test of the United Nation's policies for the reconstruction of the world," Herbert Matthews wrote, "and the democratic nations made a signal failure of it." C.R.S. Harris concurred: "Allied policy consistently discouraged liberals and democrats," and as a result, "what we did was to bolster the forces of conservation."[8] But, despite American grumbling, Winston Churchill and Anthony Eden continued to support the king and to trust Badoglio. They also were adamantly opposed to any institutional changes, even the replacement of Badoglio, while the war lasted. To make matters even worse, Churchill had no confidence in anti-Fascist leaders, disliked left-wing parties, and continued to harbour an intense animosity towards Carlo Sforza.

Alongside these political problems were social and economic ones. In late 1944 food and goods of every kind were scarce, and even basic necessities were in short supply. There was widespread unemployment in the cities; the old industries of Taranto and Naples were completely idle for lack of raw materials. On the other hand, there was an acute lack of manpower in agriculture, and many fields remained fallow, since many young men had been drafted into the army or were now prisoners in foreign lands. From the beginning, the Allies had assumed that Italy was self-sufficient in foodstuffs and that local resources could feed the population and the Allied armies alike. When they recognized their mistake, military requirements imposed other priorities; there were not enough ships to bring adequate food and merchandise into Italy, and there were not enough trucks to transport the goods for distribution in the countryside and into the cities. The consequence was that the average Italian consumed only 600 calories daily, one-third of what was needed to survive and one-half the average intake when Italy was occupied by the Germans. Allied policy created novel problems in other ways as well. The Allies issued an enormous quantity of occupation money, not really justified in a poor environment and in a small country but which the Italian government, nevertheless, was required to honour. Also, the exchange rate favoured the pound sterling and the dollar. The huge amount of money in circulation, and in the hands of soldiers, increased the price of food and goods, creating inflation, corruption, and an underground economy. A kilogram of bread or pasta had an official price of ten lire but could be bought only on the black market for ten or twenty times more. Making the matter even more difficult for the Italian middle class, wages, stipends, and pensions remained the same as before the war. Historian Giorgio Candeloro summarized the situation perfectly: "The result was a worsening of the economic and social conditions, and an increased diffusion of black-market activity, hence poverty, robberies, corruption and prostitution in the cities and a return to barter in the countryside."[9]

Operation Overlord had a deleterious effect on Southern Italy. The more capable officers and soldiers were sent to England to prepare for D-Day. The soldiers who remained were not so well trained, came from diverse national and ethnic backgrounds, and proved difficult to discipline. French colonial troops especially were guilty of grave crimes against the local population; they inflicted violence on men and women, young and old, and went unpunished by their superiors. Young American soldiers, not used to driving on narrow streets or winding roads, but eager to show their prowess, killed or seriously injured more than twenty-five thousand people and did much damage to property.[10] All of this left a lasting resentment among the people that influenced politics even after the war.

The misery of these times has remained a vivid memory for all those who lived through it, whether common people or members of the elite. One such person was Communist Party leader Palmiro Togliatti, who addressed the subject in a speech given in the 1960s, twenty years after the war. He had returned to Italy in the spring of 1944 from the Soviet Union, via the Middle East and North Africa. He must have seen a great deal of destruction and suffering in those lands. Still, what he saw in Southern Italy made a lasting mark on him. There was destruction everywhere. In the countryside, lands remained uncultivated; in the cities there were no longer any functioning factories. The steel works of Bagnoli had been destroyed and the workers were unemployed. The port of Naples was not operational and was full of sunken ships and destroyed and idle boats. Transportation was either non-existent or unreliable: many bridges had collapsed; trains did not run on time and their service was sporadic. Commerce between the cities and the countryside had stopped or was difficult to carry out. The roads were full of people, animals, and strange but ingenious means of transportation. Prices were high everywhere; food was scarce in the cities; clothes were not available in the countryside. Many buildings were damaged and no repairs were under way. Allied troops often acted in a rough and summary manner with the Italian people. There was corruption at all levels, and prostitution was widespread. The black market had replaced normal commerce and involved thousands of Italians and a similar number of Allied soldiers and officers of every nationality. Government did not have the means to carry out its functions.[11]

The experiences of Pietro Nenni, the leader of the Socialist Party, were even more harrowing. He saw devastation everywhere on his way from Naples to Rome.

> Naples and the region of Salerno are congested with American troops, and everywhere there are the inconveniences brought by overcrowding. Prostitution and begging are common. It is disheartening to see on some buildings in the cities and in the countryside the capital letters D.V. [venereal disease]. On the Appian Way on the road to Naples and on the Casilina towards Rome there are only ruins, ruins, and more ruins: not only material but also moral. According to police reports, in the province of Frosinone there have been 396 rapes, involving people of all ages, women, men,

children ... terrible! We passed Cassino, which offers an hallucinatory view: its ruins seem to belong to a prehistoric world.[12]

The material destruction inflicted by the German army was later graphically described by Farley Mowat, then a young officer with the Canadian army. "Not a bridge along the few snake-gutted highways, byways and even mountain tracks remained undestroyed. There was hardly a culvert or an overhanging cliff that had not been demolished to form an obstacle. And everywhere – along the road verges, at blown bridges, in the exit from roads and tracks, even in the few level fields where vehicles could be dispersed and men could camp – there were mines, mines, and more mines."[13]

The British writer Alan Moorehead, for his part, painted a detailed picture of the grim conditions then prevailing in Naples. "For anyone who loved Italy, it was a bitter experience to come to Naples. The traditional talents of the people, their charm and generosity, seemed to have vanished in the savage and abject struggle for existence." The imperative of survival overshadowed personal dignity. "The animal struggle for existence governed everything. Food. Food for the children. Food for yourself. Food at the cost of any debasement and depravity." In the absence of normal commerce, or employment, "to live you had to deal in the black-market ... it seemed that all pride and dignity had gone out of men's minds." Yet Naples had to endure another calamity: the collapse of private and public sanitation created a medical emergency. "In Naples typhus broke out," and because the means to deal with the disease were far from adequate, if available at all, an epidemic ensued.[14]

Nature itself seemed bent on increasing the country's troubles and the people's miseries. On his return to Italy, Togliatti found that "Vesuvius was in eruption and on the roads there was a high stratum of ashes, on which we had to walk, making treading quite difficult." On landing in Naples' airport, Harold Macmillan was greeted by an apocalyptic view. "The Bay of Naples and the surrounding area was almost obscured by an immense pall. The high wind then carries the ashes as far away as Sorrento, and across the Apennine mountains as far as Bari and the Adriatic coast."[15] In Sorrento, Croce, too, experienced "the bad day," observing "the rain of ashes from the Vesuvius eruption and the darkening of the sky." The ash penetrated inside houses; it had to be removed from roofs and cleaned from each room, but remained stuck on furniture, windows, and mirrors.[16]

The eruption of Vesuvius occasioned philosophical reflection, as during a visit of Richard Malone to Croce's villa. "While waiting for my plane ...

in Naples … I made a point of visiting Benedetto Croce, the great philosopher," Malone wrote. "The old man told me much about Naples … We talked of the frailties and foibles of mankind, of human ambition and the futility of war. From where we sat, we could see out over the Bay of Naples and, in the distance, Vesuvius, which had suddenly, after many years, started to erupt once more. As Croce remarked, Vesuvius through many centuries had witnessed countless invasions and wars. When the Hitlers and the Mussolinis were simply names in some ancient history book, Vesuvius would still be there, marking future centuries with periodic rumbles and fiery protests."[17]

Not surprisingly, Croce's mood at this time was sad. In his diary there can be found laments for a dangerous present and forebodings of an uncertain future, together with nostalgia for old times. Several reasons, public and private, explain Croce's feelings. After breaking his left arm in February 1944, he made a quick recovery but was handicapped in his movements for several weeks; he then began to worry that his physical weakness would affect not only his political activity but also his mental ability. The deliberate burning of Naples' National Archives by a young German officer, and the Allies' wanton destruction of the Montecassino Abbey, like that of other monuments, gave him "a sleepless and very sad night"; he wrote that the monuments destroyed and the historical documents lost "are not mere material objects but means of spiritual life."[18] At the same time, his dealings with the Allied authorities had produced few concrete results and made him realize that British foreign policy towards Italy was dominated by hostility: a hostility deep-rooted and hard to change, despite the personal niceties and the occasional promises made by Allied officials. "Their policy is to keep Italy under their feet, preventing her from rising and fighting again, and achieving a renewal … This is the anguish that is at the depth of my soul, as it should be of every Italian mindful of our fatherland's future."[19]

But there was a deeper anguish yet: the realization that the European civilization of the nineteenth century, of which liberal Italy was a part, was coming to an end. "In the depth of our heart we still hope that one day may return a world resembling the one that existed before the War of 1914: a world of peace and work, of national and international cooperation. In this is the source of our anguish, because that hope is fast disappearing and becoming increasingly dim. Instead, we have to expect not the return of that world, its continuance and improvement, but, for at least another fifty years, a series of changes and upheavals brought by wars and revolutions that may even lead to the end of Europe, *finis*

Europae." Amid personal pain and public ruin, as was typical of Croce, his determination was severe. If the events pointed in a clear direction, men had to accept the new reality, face the challenge, and act accordingly, shedding nostalgic illusion and bitter regret. "We have then to part from those hopes with resolution, accepting a life without stability, and without the possibility of organizing, as in the past, an orderly regime of personal and social activity; taking life day by day, a practice so repugnant to those of us who used to follow well-planned programs and to realize our works with calmness." In Croce's philosophy, the acceptance of the hard facts of life never led to moral relativism, to hedonism, or to the renunciation of one's duties, public or private. "On this ground shaking under each step, we have to do the best we can, and to live a worthy life as men, thinking and working and loving. We have to be ready to relinquish our fond hopes, but without losing faith or courage in ourselves ... and without ever plunging into indifference."[20]

Finally, Croce was slowly coming to the realization that his rhythm of life was broken forever, and that his involvement in political affairs was not an exceptional event, and was not likely to be followed by a full return to intellectual pursuits as before. "It is necessary that I accept, with resignation and at the same time with resolution, that my scientific life, in large part, has come now to a conclusion ... I will continue to read and to study, in order not to lose the ties with great books and thoughts, and to keep in touch with developments in my favourite fields ... But for the rest I will continue to give my contribution to public life without protest ... and will accept with patience its vexations and even its waste of time." As always in Croce's life, once a decision was reached, the conclusion was the same, a stoic decision to do one's duty. "With courage, then, as best I can, I will try to serve God, following the old saying: Servire Deus in Laetitia."[21] Still, this was not an easy path. As in his youth, so in old age, Croce was often subject to bouts of depression. "I need continually to regain courage, to climb back after the plunge into depression and discouragement."[22] Yet a remedy was always close at hand, not in doctor's pills but in the discipline of work, through which Croce found "a renewed serenity" and an "inner calm and dignity." Till the very end of his long life, "going back to my study room" and "sitting again at my desk" always revived Croce's spirits and renewed his energy.[23]

A note in his diary, written sometime later, offers a good example of Croce's feelings in his old age and the beneficial influence of work in calming his nerves. "In the evening I replied to urgent letters, read and took notes. Afterwards I revised in depth the essay written yesterday, making many corrections and additions, and finally went to bed after two o'clock. At night, in the darkness, I feel good, and almost protected from bad news, apprehensions, worries, and nuisances that the day brings me through visits, newspapers, letters, and other means of torment."[24]

The most important political development in Southern Italy during 1944 was the Congress of Bari, held at the end of January. For the first time since 1926, Italian political parties were able to organize a public meeting, freely express their views, and set out their programs. One hundred and twenty delegates, representing the CLN's six parties, took part. Most of them came from the Southern provinces, but a few arrived also from Rome and other cities under German occupation. Oreste Lizzadri of the Socialist Party represented the CLN of Rome and brought to the congress a resolution by that committee and a message from Pietro Nenni, the leader of his party; the resolution was more radical and inflammatory than the message but both contained unrealistic proposals in the conditions of the times. Seventy-seven members of the British Parliament sent their greetings and best wishes, along with some patronizing platitudes. Several British and American newspapermen and radio correspondents covered the congress for the international mass media. Among these Croce had several friends of long standing; with others he had established good relations more recently.[25]

For two months Croce devoted a great deal of energy to the preparation and successful conclusion of the congress. Political leaders held meetings and discussions in various cities on different occasions during which positions were discussed, disagreements smoothed over, and resolutions agreed on. Croce had several conversations with Sforza, and they were able to devise a common strategy. Giulio Rodinò, the leader of the Christian Democrats, urged Croce to tone down his criticism of the king and to avoid associating Prince Umberto with the sins of his father. He failed on the first point but succeeded on the second; Prince Umberto was not mentioned in Croce's speech at the congress. Naples Liberals, to no avail, urged Croce to assume the leadership of the anti-Fascist forces, replacing Sforza. Members of other parties visited Croce, asking for his advice, and even plain instructions, on how to proceed during the congress. Through those meetings and discussions, Croce and his friends found common ground at the congress, where they put to good use their superior political experience and mastery of parliamentary debate. As Croce said in his diary: "We notice a great enthusiasm in the participants in the congress; we hope to proceed with speed and simplicity, with few speeches and without too much rhetorical flourish, and at the end to achieve a common resolution and agreement."[26]

But the Italian government and the Allied authorities did not share this enthusiasm. In fact, congress organizers had to overcome several obstacles before the gathering could take place. During the preceding Christmas, under pressure from the Badoglio government, Allied authorities abruptly cancelled the authorization for a similar meeting to be held in the city of Naples. On that occasion, Croce and Sforza first complained to the local Allied commanders and then sent a letter of protest to Churchill, Roosevelt, and Stalin. The letter, probably written by Sforza, told the three world leaders that their action "seems inconsistent with the resolution of the recent Moscow Conference, which proclaimed that freedom of speech and assembly shall be restored in full measure to the Italian people."[27] As a result of that protest, new promises were made, and then new obstacles were encountered; finally, a gathering of Italian parties was allowed for the new year in the city of Bari. The location was chosen no doubt because it was a smaller city and could be better controlled than the chaotic streets of Naples, but the official explanation mentioned only the distance from the front lines.[28]

Even in January the military authorities, afraid of possible disorder, showed reluctance to grant final permission. A British naval officer, in an official communication to the Admiralty, expressed fear that the Bari congress, dominated by republican elements, would offend the monarchical feelings of Italian sailors and "lead the Italian navy to mutiny, or to scuttle their ships in Taranto." Despite pressure to the contrary from different quarters, in the end Macmillan was able to persuade the British cabinet in London and the Allied generals in Italy that "it would be unwise to withdraw permission now." As usual in his dispatches, Macmillan made astute, if unflattering, remarks, which were useful under the circumstances to obtain his aims. The meeting, he wrote, would no doubt be "uncommonly dull, Croce will open with at least one hour and a half of his melancholy stuff, and I do not believe that there will be any serious disturbances."[29]

After permission was granted, the authorities did little to facilitate the event; quite the opposite, in fact. During the congress, Bari's streets and squares were patrolled by Italian Carabinieri and military police. General Harold Alexander ordered that no Allied officer and no delegate from foreign nations could take part in the congress. Also, for the first day of the proceedings, he limited to eight hundred the number of people who could enter the Picinni theatre, where the congress would take place. For the other days, besides the delegates, no spectators were allowed inside the theatre. No electricity and heating were provided for that large building during the meeting, in a time of very cold weather. Despite prior assurances to the contrary, no direct radio transmission was allowed; only abridged versions of major speeches were broadcast and at unreasonable hours to boot. For instance, Croce's speech, in severely shortened form, went on the air at midnight, and then again at seven in the morning the day after. General Gerald Palmer, the commander of the Allied forces in Bari, made it known that public order would be maintained at all costs and that no political demonstration would be permitted outside the theatre.[30] The aim was obvious, as Croce recognized in his diary: "It is clear that they want to hinder this solemn manifestation, the first to take place after the fall of fascism. The apparatus of troops and Carabinieri, as for an imminent revolt, is enormous, and at the same time ridiculous."[31]

After the opening formalities and the election of a president, the Bari congress began with a speech by Croce, public recognition of his pre-eminent status among the delegates. The speech expressed more than Croce's views; it had been read by his closest friends beforehand, and this process of consultations had led to slight revisions to the initial draft.[32] As usual for Croce, the speech took the form of a lecture, but it was effective and eloquent at the same time, and, contrary to Macmillan's claim, it was only nine pages long, was devoid of "melancholy stuff," and lasted for less than half an hour. The content was appropriate to the occasion, for many delegates were lawyers and well-educated men, able to appreciate historical references and philosophical reasoning, especially if expressed in fine literary style.

Croce had two aims in the speech. On the one hand, he was trying to lift the spirits of Italians and to restore their pride and confidence, looking back to the past for inspiration in the middle of a dreadful present and an uncertain future. On the other, he was addressing public opinion in the Allied nations, in the hope of gaining support and overcoming hostility. The speech, by common agreement of those who were present, was followed with great attention, interrupted with applause, and at the end received a long and standing ovation. In his memoirs years later, Filippo Caracciolo wrote: "The grand old man reads his speech with ease and with clarity. All are listening with great attention. A breath of greatness blows in the entire hall. A long standing ovation greets the end of the speech."[33] Even Lizzadri of the Socialist Party, and a leader of its maximalist wing, was greatly impressed. "In reality, Croce delivered a beautiful speech, and the reference to the king and monarchy was especially good."[34] The historian Agostino Degli Espinosa, who also was present, remarked later that while Croce spoke "many showed commotion and had tears in their eyes." He also was among the few who noted that "more than to the Italians Croce was addressing the winners and he spoke with noble sincerity and with dignity."[35]

The speech contained philosophical and political observations, stressing the relation between authority and freedom and the necessity of both to assure the vitality of society. There were practical reasons to make those theoretical points. Croce wanted, not just to remind the audience of the mistakes of the recent past, but to warn them against allowing radical zeal to prevail over the countervailing forces of moderation and wisdom. In an age when politics, and partisan politics in particular, was acquiring an ideological nature, Croce emphasized that politics is an important aspect of life and of history, but only that – it was a part, not the whole, of human activity.

The speech underlines the drama faced, before and during the war, by men who, like Croce, belonged to the generation born and raised in the ideals of the Risorgimento, when the love of fatherland had informed public life. The Risorgimento had united love of freedom and love of nation, patriotism, and international cooperation. Fascism and imperialism, for their part, had broken that unity and betrayed those ideals. Now, in the present war, old patriots, who had remained faithful to the ideals of the Risorgimento, could no longer wish for the victory of their fatherland, right or wrong, as they had done in the Great War. They were compelled to choose between an Axis military victory, which would inevitably be followed by political enslavement of Italy and Europe under Nazi Germany, or an Italian and German defeat by the Allied nations, as a condition for a return of freedom in Italy and in Germany and peace in Europe. Not surprisingly, then, reflecting on the nature of the present war, Croce defined the conflict as a contrast of different faiths. "Little by little we came to realize that … the present war was not a war between nations but a civil war; even more exactly, that it was not a simple war of economic and political interests, but a war of religion; and because of our religion [of freedom], which had the right to command us, we parted with pain from the desire of an Italian victory." "Even in the middle of bombings, the ruins of our houses and our monuments, and civilian victims, we suffered greatly but did not change our judgment and accepted what was happening as a hard necessity, but a necessity nevertheless."[36] In Germany and in other nations of Europe, other intellectuals found themselves in the same difficult predicament as Croce. Some, like Thomas Mann, followed his example, while others were unable to put other ideals above the nation or to contemplate the defeat of their country as a historical *dura lex*, as a necessary condition for a future resurrection under freedom.

There appears in this speech, for the first time, an idea that, taken out of context, has done harm to Croce's reputation as a politician and also as a historian: "fascism as a parenthesis." In this regard, it needs to be said at the outset that Croce was responding to those British political figures who claimed that fascism was the natural outcome of Italian history and that Mussolini's dictatorship revealed the true character of the Italian people. Such claims were dangerous and harmful in the circumstances of war and the peace negotiations that would follow in due course. Speaking to a political gathering in a difficult time, Croce declared:

> Italy has to be respected and has to be heard. It is true: she has had twenty years of a sad, of a shameful history; we have seen the fatherland of Mazzini and Garibaldi sending its soldiers to fight unjust wars against France and Greece, and even to imitate, in the lands of Yugoslavia, German manners and methods, which are contrary to the Italian tradition and to our disposition. But Italy has had also centuries and millennia of history during which she has made a great contribution to the civilization of the world; and not too far away are the years in which, with the work and industry of her people, she made constant progress in all fields of society under a liberal regime, and more recently, united with sister nations, she has waged a long and victorious war. What is in our history a parenthesis of twenty years?[37]

It is clear that the parenthesis metaphor, like the speech as a whole, had a strategic purpose: to win the Allies' support and soften their enmity towards the Italian people, while also, at the same time, raising the spirits of Croce's compatriots. It certainly was not his intention to offer a new interpretation of modern history; in the midst of the war, there were more pressing issues demanding his attention. In fact, the purpose of the speech was fully appreciated by those who read it, or were present at its delivery, or heard Croce utter the same expression on other occasions. Before writing the speech, he consulted with trusted friends, among them Carlo Sforza, Adolfo Omodeo, and Francesco Flora, none of whom voiced any objection. As Croce wrote in his diary, "I have written the speech for the congress. Sforza, Omodeo, and Flora praised the speech. They approved wholeheartedly everything I said, and were entirely satisfied."[38] Similarly, the historian Degli Espinosa was present in the Picinni theatre that night in January 1944, and, reflecting later on Croce's remarks, stated that "in reality, Croce was speaking less to the Italians than to the Allies, the winners; and he spoke with firm dignity and noble sincerity. On behalf of his own and his friends' anti-fascism, he demanded that Italy had to be respected, because, even if she was Fascist for a time, twenty years were nothing compared to her centuries of civilization." Degli Espinosa also noted the deep emotions that Croce's speech aroused, emotions that were "shared by Italians and British officers alike, and even by those who did not understand a word."[39] There is other testimony to the same effect. When Sandro Pertini, a future president of the republic, heard Croce use the parenthesis metaphor in another 1944 speech, he at once grasped Croce's patriotic intention and afterwards wrote to him expressing his approval. A few years later, in 1947, during the debate in the Constituent Assembly on ratification of the Peace Treaty, Adelchi Attisani of the University of Messina read in the papers Croce's speech and his description of fascism as a parenthesis in Italian history; the next day, Attisani, deeply moved, wrote Croce a letter full of praise.[40] All of them understood the patriotic purpose of that metaphor.

Yet, despite the clear evidence, the expression "a parenthesis of twenty years" has become, in the hands of certain historians and journalists, "Croce's vision of fascism as a parenthesis," that is, an insignificant interlude in Italian history that is barely worthy of notice. Those who make this claim have failed to notice that Croce's statement was an oratorical device, intended to achieve practical aims. In other writings of a more historical nature, Croce described fascism as a moral illness and a repudiation of liberal values in favour of authoritarian ideas, irrational feelings, and a cult that worshipped violence and the role of the strong man. In other words, it represented a crisis of European civilization brought about by past developments in the overall historical process, and was encouraged in its final success by the political divisions and personal rivalries that existed at the time in the Italian parliament. Even in the Bari speech, in fact, Croce described Nazism as a movement "driven by the cupidity of brutal instincts." Moreover, as he had argued in *History of Europe in the Nineteenth Century*, fascism was not an Italian movement only but rather a European phenomenon, which had its origins in intellectual and political developments in Europe after 1870 stemming from Bismarck's policies, the defeat of France and the victory of Prussia, and the ways in which Germany had achieved its unification. For that reason, in his Bari speech, he asked another question: "And then is this parenthesis only Italian history or also European and worldwide history"? In this wider European history, he pointed out, quoting from a recent book by Peter Drucker, responsibilities did not belong to a single country but had to be shared by all. There were differences, of course. There were nations that carried out the program of fascism, and these had to be called "criminals." There were also other nations that tried to appease fascism, and these deserved to be called "fools." "For what happened in the world, the fault belongs to all, with the only difference that the people, now called Allied Nations, were 'fools,' while the Fascists were 'criminals.'" He continued: "Since the old Italian anti-Fascists had neither been fools nor criminals," they were now in a position to demand from the Allies respect and solidarity, not to mention the fulfilment of the promises of "freedom and independence" made by the Allies before and during the war. Croce concluded his speech with an appeal to common ideals. "We have faith that our words and our hopes will be heard and understood by the Allied Nations." The hope was that the Allies would finally overcome "their diffidence with regard to Italian liberal and democratic parties" and stop supporting in Italy, as they had done in North Africa, "conservative elements and semi-fascist forces" in the name of "a misunderstood social conservatism."[41]

The speech also dealt with current political problems. Croce took the occasion, as he put it, "to make a polite criticism of the Allies for their wrong-headed policy in support of the king."[42] Once again, to great applause from the delegates, Croce demanded the abdication of the king and his removal from any position of power. He regarded the king's presence as a corrupting influence in the nation's body politic and an obstacle to a rebirth of freedom. He argued that the king had lost prestige and authority; he had betrayed the oath taken on his accession to the throne; and then he had been associated with the crimes of the dictatorship. Now he had become an obstacle to the formation of an efficient cabinet, since all the leaders of the new democratic parties wanted a clear break with the past. "Until the present king is no longer head of state, we feel that fascism has not come to an end, that it remains attached to us, that it may re-emerge disguised in different forms, that it continues to corrupt and to weaken us, and in this condition we cannot live and breathe freely."[43]

Croce also offered direct advice to the Allies, and an indirect warning to the Italians, that pertained to Europe's post-war future. He expressed the hope that the new political arrangements would be based on liberal ideals, using Italy as an example. "Italy is the first nation of Europe to have been liberated from Nazi-fascism and from German occupation: the other peoples of Europe will look to the political settlement it will obtain with the help of the Allies as an example for their own future life. May the new order be founded on the most complete liberal method, with no more dangers of possible dictatorship, open or disguised." In a subtle way, this part of Croce's speech was also addressed to those Italian politicians who had seen and tasted the bitter fruit of a totalitarian regime and yet were still inclined to authoritarian impulses, or were driven by Jacobin aspirations of renewal, all implying, for their realization, solutions dictated from above and imposed by force on a reluctant population. Croce, of course, preferred to put his trust in a different ideal and a different method. "Let freedom, with discussion and agreement and disagreement among parties ... provide, as only freedom can, true social conservation, and at the same time ... solid progress." Here we have a warning against the impatience of the moment, but also a clear indication that anti-fascism, united against Mussolini's regime, was now divided by different visions of the future.[44]

The main issues of discussion at the congress were the institutional question and the formation of a new government that would include all the anti-Fascist parties. Social problems were also debated and proposals were made for their solution, but demands for the abdication of the king and the choice of a new political leadership remained of paramount importance. After long debate, a compromise was reached. The congress voted for the abdication of the king as the first condition for the creation of a new government of national unity. The final choice between monarchy and republic was postponed until the end of the war, when the Italian people would be called upon to decide the form of the state by a referendum or by a vote of a newly elected Constituent Assembly. An executive committee, or Giunta, was elected and given the mandate to continue the work of the congress; one member from each of the six parties was named to the committee, each enjoying equal rights; Vincenzo Arangio Ruiz, a close friend of Croce and a fellow liberal, was chosen as chairman and Ambassador Caracciolo was appointed as secretary. Croce and Sforza were named spokesmen of the Giunta, in recognition of their international and domestic reputations.[45]

From then on, in dealing with the king and the Allies, Croce and Sforza could justifiably claim to speak for all the other parties. In the days after the congress, both the Giunta and its two spokesmen wrote letters to the foreign ministers of the Allied nations and met with the generals in Italy, apprising them of the conclusions of the congress. Croce and Sforza sent telegrams to British Foreign Secretary Anthony Eden, American Secretary of State Cordell Hull, and Russian Foreign Minister Vyacheslav Molotov. A special message was sent to General Charles de Gaulle of the Free French forces. Croce and Sforza also continued to cultivate good relations with American and British journalists in order to influence public opinion in the Allied nations in Italy's favour. With these actions, the Giunta acquired international status and publicized abroad the views of Italy's democratic parties. Even Togliatti, who later tended to deride the results of the congress, in 1944 had a different opinion, one more in line with reality. "The Giunta is a vital organism that has an international significance not at all negligible."[46]

The accomplishments of the congress were all the more impressive in that they came about in the midst of intense political manoeuvring. At first, on behalf of the Communist Party, the Socialist Party, and the Party of Action, Oreste Lizzadri moved a motion that in practice would have meant the overthrow of the Badoglio government and the abolition of the monarchy. The motion proposed that the congress put the king on trial for his past crimes; proclaim itself as the National Assembly of Liberated Italy; remain in session until the formation of the Constituent Assembly; and form a government with legislative and executive powers to bolster the war effort. As a temporary measure, the motion also demanded that the congress create an executive Giunta in order to carry out the aims of the resolution, to deal with the Allied nations, to provide for the needs of the people, and to recall the congress in Rome after its liberation. In short, the motion envisaged the creation of a body akin to the Committee of Public Safety in the French Revolution.[47]

The radical demands of the three left-wing parties were opposed by the Liberals and the Christian Democrats, almost splitting the congress into two irreconcilable factions. The Jacobin aspirations of the motion presented by the Communists, Socialists, and Actionists ran the risk, in Croce's words, of turning "the congress into a laughing stock before the world."[48] It was the presence and the authority of Croce that saved the day. The villa of one of the Laterza brothers, where Croce was staying, "became the social centre of the congress," with gatherings and discussions lasting until the late hours of the night. It was there that meetings took place and differences were ironed out, mainly between Croce and the young and energetic Michele Cifarelli, a member of the Party of Action but also the chief organizer and secretary of the congress. After a heated discussion that, according to Caracciolo, lasted until 3 a.m., Croce, with the help of Cifarelli, Sforza, Caracciolo, Ruiz, and others, was instrumental in persuading the left-wing parties to withdraw their motion. In the morning, while Croce enjoyed a deserved rest, the text of a new motion, presented by Renato Morelli but drafted or suggested by Croce, was finally accepted by the parties of the left; Adolfo Omodeo supported it on behalf of the Party of Action. The motion proposed the immediate abdication of the king; the postponement of the institutional question until after the war; the creation of a democratic government enjoying full powers and supported by the anti-Fascist parties present at the congress, with the objective of intensifying the war effort and addressing social problems; the preparation of elections for the Constituent Assembly at war's end; and the creation of a Giunta to implement the congress's decisions.

This episode was the first public clash between those who wanted a total break with the past and those who preferred renovation and continuity: a fresh beginning without starting anew on a tabula rasa. The new motion reflected Croce's moderate and realistic position. Once the adherence of the radical elements was assured, Croce then was able to gain the support of the Christian Democrats, overcoming their reluctance to accept the institution of a Giunta.[49]

Following the congress, the speech delivered by Croce at its opening gained wide circulation despite the various obstructions thrown up by Allied and Italian authorities. In contravention of General Alexander's orders, the speech, like those of other political leaders, was recorded in full by agents of the Psychological Warfare Branch (PWB), sent to London, and then broadcast back to Italy by the BBC World Service, where two good friends of Croce, Paolo Treves and Umberto Calosso, were in charge of Italian programming. Old friendships, along with disagreements and political rivalries among Allied figures, played their part in Croce's favour. Inside the PWB, Croce could count on his good relations with Jan Greenless, who was director of Radio Bari and who, before the war, had been director of the British Institute in Naples, housed in Croce's palazzo. Croce's speech was also reported in full the day after its delivery, 29 January, by the newspapers of Bari and Naples, whose editors were old friends of Croce, and probably in other cities where a newspaper was then allowed. The Laterza publishing house was able to print the speech in booklet format, at a small price, and sold several thousand copies. A full documentary on the proceedings of the Bari congress was produced by Italian and Allied staff of an American war-propaganda agency, followed by interviews with Croce and others in Sorrento a few days after the end of the congress. Croce himself reported, relying on his own information, that "the Bari congress had a deep echo throughout Italy." The result of this newfound popularity was evident almost immediately. On their return by car to Sorrento and Naples, Croce and Sforza were surrounded at each stop by small friendly crowds and were warmly applauded, even greeted in some instances with shouts of "Long live the saviours of Italy!"

The congress received good coverage in the international press. In the United States, news on the congress was reported by the Office of War Information, and then reprinted and commented on by local and national media outlets. The historian David Ellwood writes that "the meeting of the Bari congress created a considerable stir in Southern Italy, and in the Anglo-American press, and anxiety among the Allied Military Government."[50] Cecil Sprigge was in Bari at the time; he had several meetings with Croce before and after the congress, and filed accurate reports on its proceedings for Reuters newspapers. His wife, Sylvia, was then still in London working for the *Manchester Guardian*, but she was also active in a committee called Friends of Free Italy. She wrote to Sforza, asking for his and Croce's speeches so the committee could publish them. Sforza sent her the speeches while also providing information about congress proceedings and resolutions.[51]

In various ways, the congress increased international interest in Italy's problems. Through the press and radio reports, the political opinions of the Bari delegates reached members of the American Congress and the British Parliament, where some legislators called for a more supportive attitude towards Italy's democratic parties. In fact, far from the failure implied by some commentators, including Togliatti and, later, certain Marxist historians, a careful reading of Croce's diary and Macmillan's account leaves the strong impression that the Congress of Bari and the initiative of the Giunta had a ripple effect, giving impetus to a movement for change that the Allied authorities could no longer ignore. Macmillan himself admitted as much, using his usual Oxonian understatements. "Although the congress itself had done little harm, the question of the monarchy was by no means quiescent."[52] To discuss the congress resolutions, Sforza had several meetings with General Noel Mason-MacFarlane, head of the Allied Control Commission, and it soon became publicly known that the general, who ran for the British Labour Party in the 1945 election, shared Sforza's views on the institutional question and his position regarding the king was different from Churchill's. For his part, the

French delegate to the ACC, René Massigli, demanded the immediate abdication of the king and requested a formal decision on the subject. Also, General Henry Maitland Wilson, who had replaced Eisenhower as commander-in-chief of the Mediterranean theatre, announced that "he favoured strong action against the king."

Strangely enough, only the Soviet Union continued to support the status quo in Italy. Deputy Foreign Minister Andrey Vyshinsky was in no hurry to remove the king from power, despite the anti-monarchical position of the Italian Communist Party, loudly expressed at the Bari congress by Velio Spano, its leader in Southern Italy before the arrival of Togliatti. But American views carried more weight than Russian ones. In a year of presidential and congressional elections, members of the Senate and the House of Representatives, as well as the media, began to press for the removal of the king and the formation of a new and more representative government in Italy. In order to retain Catholic support, the administration adopted "a more crude diplomacy," as a worried Macmillan put it. "The State Department has suddenly gone mad and sent the most extraordinary instructions to [G. Frederick] Reinhardt [at the ACC], who is acting in [Robert] Murphy's place ... The State department has told Reinhardt ... (a) to tell Massigli that they agree with the French note and that they think that the King should be 'removed' at once and a new government be formed (apparently on a purely revolutionary basis and without legal sanction), and (b) to tell the same thing to Sforza."[53]

Croce's hopes took several more weeks to be realized, but the ground had been prepared. The Congress of Bari, it is fair to say, put in motion a chain of events that could not be resisted. The reactions it generated in Italy and in other nations put pressure on the Allies and on the king, undermining their reluctance to undertake changes. The congress also created a new political actor, the Giunta, which was able to maintain unity among the anti-Fascist parties; its two spokesmen had international standing and their proposals carried weight. Together, the Giunta, Sforza, and Croce, in different ways, compelled the Allies to face a problem and then to seek a solution more in tune with the aspirations of the Italian democratic forces, and more compatible with the ideals proclaimed by the Allied powers themselves, if unpalatable to Churchill.[54]

The Italian anti-Fascist parties may even have contributed to a shift in the balance of power on the Allied side, a development with great importance for the future. At the time, unknown to the Italians, a significant change was taking place in Anglo-American relations in the

Mediterranean theatre. Never enamoured of the British Empire, the United States was beginning to challenge British leadership in Southern Europe; in particular, worried by the increasing influence of the Soviet Union and the Communist parties, American officials started to question the merits of a policy that favoured the conservative elements of Italian society. This development was facilitated by changes that had taken place in the military command of the Alliance. With the departure of Eisenhower to England for the preparation of Operation Overlord, and his replacement by General Wilson, the British political position in the Mediterranean weakened a great deal, as did Macmillan's personal influence. From then on, British proposals would be subject to strong American challenge, even to plain opposition, as never before. Now that a British general had replaced an American one as commander-in-chief in the Mediterranean, the US War Department felt free to join the State Department in demanding a different policy in Italy. With his keen political sense, Macmillan noticed the signs of a new course and reported the changed American position to Churchill, adding to the latter's worries. "The State Department is opposing our policy in Italy as well as elsewhere, and the War Department will not rush naturally to defend a British general."[55] British imperial predominance in the Mediterranean was fast coming to an end under the burden of the war and the impact of growing American influence, a development that created new opportunities and challenges for Italian political leaders that in the future were sometimes exploited adroitly.

5
De Nicola's Negotiations

After the Congress of Bari, the institutional question remained at the forefront of political debate, blocking political progress. The crux of the matter remained the same: how to remove the king so a new government, able to enjoy the support of the anti-Fascist parties, could be formed. The compromise reached by Croce, Sforza, and De Nicola in December 1943 – the retirement of the king coupled with the appointment of a lieutenant general of the realm, followed by a referendum on the institutional question at the end of the war – still seemed the best way forward, but implementing it was fraught with difficulty.

At the December meeting, Prince Umberto had been mentioned as a possibility for the post of lieutenant, but, for a variety of reasons, both Croce and Sforza regarded him as unsuitable. Unlike his wife, a Belgian princess, he had not demonstrated any political independence during the Mussolini years and was known more for his elegance and courteous manners than for his intelligence and political acumen. His selection as lieutenant, then, would not signal a definite break with the past. But early in the new year, during a discussion between Croce and members of the OSS, the name of Umberto was again raised as a possible lieutenant general. Croce then indicated, for the first time, that he had an open mind on the subject. "To this question … I replied that what is important is the removal of the king, the direct and surviving representative of fascism, but for the rest it may be possible to reconsider the situation."[1]

During January and February, meetings about the institutional question continued. De Nicola conducted the main negotiations with the king and those around him. Croce kept discussing the issue with a few fellow liberals, trusted friends, and Allied officers. Sforza remained in touch with the anti-Fascist leaders in Rome and in Northern Italy, and especially with his friends in the Party of Action. He also had several meetings with the ACC's General Mason-MacFarlane, who seemed favourable to the possibility of the king's retirement, or so he let Sforza believe. With meetings taking place in different cities, in a time of difficult communications and among participants with divergent interests, misunderstandings were bound to occur. Still preferring a regency over a lieutenancy, Sforza tended to oscillate between the two solutions, or at least gave the impression of doing so, as was his habit, probably the result of his diplomatic training. When angry disagreements arose between him and De Nicola, Croce acted as peacemaker.

On 10 January 1944 Croce, De Nicola, and Sforza reached a final agreement in principle among themselves, with the details to be ironed out later. De Nicola would meet the king, or more precisely, as he put it in his inimitable way, "would accept an invitation coming directly from King Vittorio Emanuele." At that time he would propose to the king the creation of a lieutenancy, and, if the king insisted on the selection of Umberto for the position, De Nicola and his colleagues would agree. In that case, Croce added, they would "take the necessary guarantees" to avoid "plots and intrigues from the father through the son or those surrounding them."[2]

The Giunta created by the Congress of Bari at the end of January 1944 kept American, British, and Soviet leaders informed of the results of negotiations on the matter of the king while also lobbying for their support. Since both Croce and Sforza did not believe that the king would abdicate in the absence of Allied pressure, they took an extraordinary initiative of their own, possibly at the urging of Sforza, who was often impatient with the slow pace of De Nicola's modus operandi. As spokesmen of the Giunta, Croce and Sforza sent a letter to the three foreign ministers of the Allied powers, Hull, Eden, and Molotov, telling them that "a delegation of the royal powers ... to a lieutenant of the realm was consistent with our political tradition." They also stressed that the proposal was the result "of careful consultation with some of the most distinguished elements in liberated Italy, including high legal authorities and the executive Giunta."[3] The rather verbose letter was probably the work of Sforza. It does not make clear whether the solution being recommended was a lieutenancy or a regency or both. It also made some irrelevant comments expressing Sforza's personal animosity towards the king and Badoglio, comments that would have been better left out of an official communication. Unlike Croce, Sforza was not able to refrain from criticizing Italian politicians in his dealings with Allied officers. It was also redundant, even demeaning perhaps, to stress "the loyalty" and "sincerity" and "lack of ambition" "of the two undersigned." In short, the letter was not well crafted for the purpose it was meant to achieve; in no way did it convey, as was the authors' intention, the "necessity for urgent decisions" in order "to avoid imminent danger."[4]

According to the terms of the armistice, the letter had to be read and approved by the head of the ACC before it could be sent to the foreign ministers. Not surprisingly, Mason-MacFarlane asked Sforza "to add some practical and concrete remarks and proposals." He and Sforza had several meetings on the subject, and, in the end, some points were made clear to the general, if not, perhaps, to the political leaders above him. In their discussions, Sforza warned that "it is necessary to form at once a new cabinet in order to avoid a possible serious danger of two governments, one in Salerno and one in Rome."[5]

The crucial meeting between De Nicola and the king took place on 19 February 1944, several days after the Giunta's letter had been sent to the Allied foreign ministers. After a discussion lasting more than four hours, in Croce's succinct words, "the conclusion was that the king agrees to retire to private life and to name his son as lieutenant." The meeting between the former speaker and the old king, who had known each other in better times, must have been painful, yet the discussion was polite. According to Croce's report, "De Nicola made his case bluntly, pointing out that the road the king had taken and that he did not want to abandon will lead to his personal ruin and to the ruin of the monarchy."[6] In a later account written by De Nicola himself, he related that, in order to persuade the king, he made recourse to legal distinctions involving a king's different responsibilities as a person and as a sovereign, in which the blame of one cannot be attached to the other. But above all he appealed to historical precedent, familiar to the erudite Vittorio Emanuele. "A king, who declares a war and loses it has no choice but to relinquish the throne." The reference to Carlo Alberto and his abdication in 1849 after the defeat in the second war of Italian independence against Austria was unmistakeable, and appropriate to Vittorio Emanuele's own predicament.[7]

During the discussion, De Nicola was subjected not only to the usual royal flattery but also to something resembling bribery. The minister of the royal household, Pietro Acquarone, asked him a loaded question: "If his majesty does not accept your proposal, are you willing to form a new political government and to serve under the king"? Not only did De Nicola reply with a resounding "absolutely not," but he made a veiled threat. "Should his majesty refuse the proposal, the king then could no longer count on his personal service and loyalty; instead he would make public his proposal, the attempt carried out, and the refusal he had received from the king."[8] Overnight, cooler heads prevailed in the royal entourage. On 20 February, during a meeting between De Nicola and Acquarone, the king's decision to abandon the throne was confirmed, and the technicalities for its execution were agreed upon. The proclamation of the king's decision to retire from public life would be written by De Nicola and published in Salerno. But the signing of the royal decree announcing the lieutenancy and the transfer of the royal powers to Umberto would take place in Rome, immediately after the liberation of the capital. With a good grasp of the king's psychology, De Nicola observed, "I did understand the reason of that condition: the king had left Rome as a king and wanted to return still as a king."[9]

Once the agreement had been reached, the king and De Nicola decided on how the news would be communicated to the other actors in the drama: the king would inform Badoglio and the government, and De Nicola would appraise General Mason-MacFarlane of the ACC and Italian political leaders. Croce was among the first to be informed by De Nicola, their meeting taking place in Croce's residence the day after, on 21 February 1944. He quickly approved of the agreement. Though he would have preferred that the king retire immediately rather than wait until Rome's liberation, he was prepared to accept this condition for pragmatic reasons; any further delay in dealing with the institutional question would be damaging to the country's best interests, and besides, with the agreement in hand, it likely would be possible to revisit the issue of timing in the near future. In his conversation with De Nicola, Croce also learned that the king had "expressed high praise for Croce's patriotism ... and loyalty" and for "his attachment to a constitutional monarchy." Clearly, through De Nicola, the king was sending a personal message to Croce. It was known among the royal entourage, and beyond, that Vittorio Emanuele was less than pleased with Badoglio and did not want Sforza, whom he despised, to succeed him as prime minister. In reporting the king's comments, De Nicola, in an indirect way, was thus urging Croce to be ready for a special invitation. He was also reassuring Croce about the king's unchanged feelings towards him, despite his public and repeated criticisms of the monarch.[10]

Armed with Croce's approval of the agreement, the next day, De Nicola discussed the results of his mission with Sforza. Like Croce, Sforza accepted the agreement without raising old reservations or making new difficulties. In fact, according to Croce, not only did Sforza accept the agreement willingly, but he also offered assurances of his help in the future: "[He] is ready to enter the new political combination and to collaborate."[11] At this stage, Sforza probably still entertained the hope that he was going to be the next prime minister after all. There was another reason for his quick acceptance of the agreement. He had been discussing the constitutional subject with trusted friends in Naples, with whom he shared lodgings, and had been impressed by their arguments. They belonged to the moderate wing of the Party of Action and were part of a younger generation not burdened by the baggage of the past. These younger men did not see much difference between a regency and a lieutenancy. For them, the lieutenancy was only a clever way for the king to save face. As such, it was a small price to pay in order to put the institutional question aside and start to deal with the country's pressing economic and social problems. As one of them bluntly told Sforza: "Public opinion is becoming very critical of the opposition ... more delays would damage our reputation and standing among the general public." The ordinary citizen was more concerned with "bread, housing, transport, medicine" than with the institutional question.[12] For his part, Croce had heard similar arguments. He too, at times, must have become tired of all the fruitless discussions on the monarchy's future when other issues remained unaddressed. In his diary, he expressed his relief that De Nicola's negotiations had ended successfully. "Such is the work brought to conclusion by De Nicola with intelligence and wisdom ... and so far it is the only political result that we have achieved in the political field."[13]

A possible solution to the institutional question had been found by Italians, negotiating among themselves. But that question was not solely an Italian affair. Under the terms of the armistice, the consent of the Allies remained essential.

Even before the agreement officially reached the ACC, it met a major obstacle in the form of a speech by Churchill in the House of Commons on 22 February 1944. In that speech Churchill urged that decisions on Italy's future be postponed until the liberation of Rome. But there was more. Churchill also made critical remarks about the personal integrity and political legitimacy of the anti-Fascist leaders, many of whom had suffered jail and persecution under fascism when he himself and other Allied leaders were praising Mussolini. Those remarks reflected his conservative prejudices but also the many frustrations he was experiencing in those times. The military campaign in Italy was going more slowly than anticipated, and, contrary to his wishes, the Mediterranean theatre was becoming of secondary importance. The Americans were taking over the strategic direction of the war. In this context, the future of Italy's monarchy was the last thing he wanted to contemplate. Churchill's policy towards Italy oscillated according to his moods or the necessities of the moment, and was often constrained by short-term realpolitik. Most of the time, he was angry with Italy and the Italians: "Italy has done us great damage, and must be punished and ground down"; "now let the Italians stew in their own juice." Unlike Eden, whose animosity towards Italy verged on racism, Churchill could be generous with Italians, at times. But both of them had no use for Italy as a great power, and had no intention of returning the country to its previous status. In his speech, Churchill tried first to claim the high ground, stressing that the king's government was a lawful one that enjoyed the support of the navy and army, while the new political parties did not yet have constitutional legitimacy. But the political reasons for his opposition to change in the status quo were stated with brutal frankness. "Badoglio will obey our direction far more than any other government"; "a new government will very likely try to wriggle out of the armistice terms."[14] After the war, Macmillan reported the crux of the problem in a very succinct, but sanitized, way in his memoirs. Churchill, he said, had pointed out that "Italian military and naval forces, together with Italian airmen, were now fighting on our side; he was not convinced that any government could immediately be formed which would command the same obedience; when the battle of Rome was over we should be free to discuss the whole political situation."[15]

Churchill's speech created resentment and consternation in Italy among all political parties. The left-wing parties at first proposed a general strike, then, under pressure from the Allies, settled for protest rallies in major cities. In Naples a crowd of more than five thousand people gathered in the main square, where the organizers demanded once again the immediate abdication of the king and the transfer of power to the CLN.[16] Croce himself was as resolute as ever, writing: "The king has on his side the armed forces and the support of Churchill, or even perhaps of Roosevelt, and we lack influence of that nature. But I say: we shall see who is going to win, whether the king with his generals and admirals and the occasional foreign allies, or we with the logic of our request and the coherence of our actions."[17] He and Sforza sent a telegram to Churchill "to prove that he had been badly informed about what he said." The first draft of the telegram, written by Sforza, was highly polemical; however, it was then toned down by Croce before being given to Mason-MacFarlane for transmission to London. The general, in turn, wisely reduced it "to a brief résumé … in which I made all the points you wished to stress." In the original telegram, Sforza offered an effective, if too argumentative, rebuttal of Churchill's main accusations against the anti-Fascist and democratic forces in Italy. In defence of his own record, Sforza could rightly retort that "he was offered by the king on 5 November 1943 the position of prime minister, and had refused only because the king's presence was an obstacle to serious war effort."[18] On this occasion Sforza used his diplomatic skills with adroitness. In his letter accompanying the telegram, he tried to add weight to his argument by mentioning Croce's disappointment: "I found him sorry, almost in despair, for the dangerous phrases of Churchill's speech. Like me, he was more sorry for England's moral reputation than for us." Finally, he stroked the ego of the general with a sure hand. "But I cannot hide from you that if you can succeed in eliminating the impression created by the speech you'll render a service even more to your land's fame than to Italy's. It would be best to avoid a situation in which historians one day will have some reason to say that Great Britain relied gladly in Italy on Fascists and pro-Nazis to carry on a war for freedom."[19]

In agreement with Croce, Sforza wrote several letters also to British and American politicians. Among these were Fiorello La Guardia, then mayor of New York City, and Adolf Berle, who, as undersecretary of the US State Department, was responsible for Italian affairs, among other things. These letters demonstrate Sforza's ability, despite his verbosity, to make clear the main points at stake, as well as his wide range of contacts with Americans of influence. In one letter, Sforza, in good diplomatic fashion, tried to put a wedge between the British and the Americans. "My impression is that General MacFarlane sees the situation much more clearly than General Alexander, who believes in Italian generals [who are] ready now to serve him in order to save their skins but who, in their hearts, hate all of you – a state of affairs that someday may become dangerous. In any case it is already dangerous for the moral reputation of two great nations; how can a British general who acts also on your authority go on relying only on pro-Nazis and pro-Fascists for the four freedom war?"[20]

While Sforza met with Allied officers and wrote to American politicians, Croce used his international prestige to rally public opinion against Churchill's position. For that purpose, he gave an interview to Cecil Sprigge, which was then published in British and American newspapers. In the interview Croce first praised Churchill. "We regard him as a hero, who with great efforts saved England from ruin, and with her the civilization of the world." Croce, as becoming of an Italian historian and Neopolitan scholar, then made a historical comparison with another British hero that England's educated classes would be able to appreciate. In 1799 Nelson, urged on by Lady Hamilton, with whom he was entranced, and with the concurrence of the British cabinet, used the British navy to crush the republicans of Naples and to restore the Bourbon king to the throne, thus inflicting serious damage to the liberal cause and to the reputation of the monarchy itself. "Admiral Nelson … at Trafalgar and at Aboukir saved England and her future against Napoleon, but he also wrote a deplorable page in his life, which still embarrasses his British biographers, when he favoured and helped the horrendous reaction of the Bourbons of Naples against the republican patriots. Now the situation luckily is not so tragic; yet, Churchill with his position, probably against his own intention, is supporting the last remaining authoritarian and Fascist forces in Italy against the liberal and democratic parties. We hope that, once he receives better information, he will change his policy." In the course of the interview Croce also pointed out that Churchill's stance was contrary to Allied interests, because it was causing resentment against the Allies among the Italian people and, at the same time, putting those Italians who supported the Allied cause in an embarrassing position. In rebutting Churchill's arguments, Croce, like Sforza, let the Italian public in on a secret, that matter of the lieutenancy. He probably did so deliberately, to show that the Italian politicians, without outside interference, were able to find reasonable solutions. Again, in making the case against the king, Croce stressed that Vittorio Emanuele, by betraying the Albertine Statute for twenty years, had lost constitutional legitimacy. For the monarchy now to regain the loyalty of the people, "it is necessary [that] a regency, or, as somebody opines, a lieutenancy [be formed] before the entire Italian people will freely decide on the form of the state."[21]

Croce's and Sforza's initiatives had wide resonance in Italy and abroad. Their efforts gained sympathy, sometimes from unexpected sources. Sforza received a friendly letter from two Conservative members of the House of Commons. "We deplore that the prime minister is constantly misinformed about Italy; we know that your line is the only one which may keep Italy in some sort of order. Dissatisfaction about Churchill is growing everywhere; he goes on living on the merits of 1940."[22]

Churchill's speech compelled Croce, Sforza, and De Nicola to have meetings among themselves to decide on their next move. As Croce said in his diary on 23 February, "I am worried by the speech of Churchill, who supports the government of the king, or, as he prefers to say, of Marshal Badoglio, and rejects, or postpones consideration of, the request made by us. Though this will certainly not induce us to change our action, it could induce the king to renege on what he has agreed with De Nicola." But De Nicola soon reassured Croce on that score. He was convinced "that the king would keep his word, and stand firm on the promise made."[23] Once again De Nicola proved right. Because the king, despite Churchill's opposition, kept his commitment, De Nicola could take his next step after days of procrastination that had dismayed Sforza no end, greatly testing his patience.[24]

On 25 February, as he had promised the king, De Nicola met with General Mason-MacFarlane and officially informed him of the agreement reached with Vittorio Emanuele. As Croce reports, De Nicola assured the general, and the many experts he had brought along, that the future democratic cabinet would be much stronger than the present one. The reason was simple: "The royal cabinet has no political power behind it; the new one will be supported by all the six parties of the Committee of National Liberation." For his part, Mason-MacFarlane recognized "the importance of the agreement with the king, his removal from public life, and the position of the lieutenancy." The general made no formal commitment, however. It was not up to him to take a final decision on important matters.[25]

In the course of this meeting, the name of Croce as a possible future prime minister was mentioned again. Evidently, given Churchill's antipathy towards Sforza, British officers in Italy, on their own or under orders from London, were searching for alternative candidates. Many observers in Allied circles were unhappy with the British official policy on Italy, as is evident in the remarks made by journalist Alan Moorehead: "No one can pretend that early attempts to establish a strong government in Italy were a great success. It is true that Count Sforza had more or less ruined his own position in Italy, but no one enjoyed the spectacle of his being tipped ruthlessly overboard on orders from London."[26] With the elimination of Sforza, Croce and De Nicola remained the obvious choices for prime minister. When Mason-MacFarlane raised this matter, De Nicola's reply was prompt: "There are two possibilities: Croce and Sforza; but the first is not willing, and the second faces obstacles, though Croce himself, who would have stronger support among the general population for his moderation, endorses him with determination and wholeheartedly." In his inimitable way, De Nicola was pursuing three aims at once: ruling himself out; defending Sforza's reputation and his ability to be a good prime minister; and promoting Croce as a possible alternative, on account of his moderation and the general support he enjoyed.[27]

That same day, right after De Nicola's meeting with Mason-MacFarlane, Croce received a group of Neopolitan Liberals. They too, dissatisfied with Badoglio and Sforza alike, were searching for an alternative candidate. While De Nicola put forward Croce's name in an indirect way, the Neapolitans were more forthright. As Croce writes in his diary, the reasons for their proposal and for his refusal were made clear. "In the second half of the day, I had a painful discussion with the political men of Naples, who insist that I accept the premiership of the future democratic cabinet instead of Sforza." The Neapolitan politicians explained that Sforza's "aggressive tone and fiery words … have greatly damaged his reputation in public opinion."[28] It was a complaint that Croce had heard before. In January, before the Congress of Bari, a group of Neapolitan friends had warned Croce about Sforza's oratorical flights every time he stood before small crowds. "They notice and lament that Sforza is losing prestige fast, almost day by day; he talks too much, appears everywhere, and makes imprudent statements not expected from a future head of government."[29] They urged Croce "to assume the leadership of the political forces" because he had more common sense and wisdom than Sforza, who "is not able to control his polemical rashness, or to correct the exuberance of his temperament." As he had done previously, Croce refused these new entreaties, in part because of his recognition that he lacked the political qualities necessary for the job. "In reply to their arguments, I firmly declared that I did not possess the experience and ability to govern my country." This time, however, he mentioned another reason, no less important: his unwillingness to betray a long and cherished friendship with a man "who was my colleague in Giolitti's cabinet, and with whom I have been in close relations during his twenty years of exile and misfortune, and who has great faith in me and listens to my advice with great deference." Yet, important as these considerations were, had Croce felt more confident in his political ability, he would have put aside personal feelings and "would have talked frankly and honestly" with Sforza. Friendship was certainly important to him, but national interests and moral considerations always came first.[30]

Whether Croce could have obtained the post of prime minister, had he chosen to put his name forward, is difficult to say. He certainly enjoyed strong support from all the Italian political parties, but he, too, faced reservations among the Allies. This is evident from the account of Filippo Caracciolo. A close confidant of Sforza, a leader of the Party of

Action, and secretary to the Giunta, Caracciolo often was in the middle of important negotiations and had access to confidential information. As a former ambassador and a member of an old aristocratic family, he enjoyed good relations with upper-class British officers. From them he learned that the Allies were favourable to the idea of a lieutenancy but had concerns about the names mentioned for the post of prime minister. "On this subject … I understand that the alternatives suggested by De Nicola, that is Sforza or Croce, are not acceptable to the Allies. Croce is too old and without experience. Against Sforza there are reservations, of which I am not able to grasp the nature and the importance."[31]

The nature of those reservations was frankly, and forcefully, stated by Churchill in his correspondence with President Roosevelt in March 1944. The British prime minister did not draw any distinction between Croce and Sforza: "I have no confidence in either Croce or Sforza for this job. Macmillan tells me that Croce is a dwarf professor about 75 years old who wrote some good books about aesthetics and philosophy. Wyshinsky, who has tried to read the books, says they are even duller than Karl Marx." He then underlined his deep distrust of Sforza, referring to the latter's abandonment of his previous undertaking to support the Badoglio government.[32] The grudge lasted for a long time; at the end of December 1944 Churchill vetoed once again Sforza's appointment as minister of foreign affairs. "On account of his behaviour I have regarded him as a man in whom no trust could be placed."[33] In another telegram, sent to Roosevelt on 15 March 1944, Churchill made clear his preference for the status quo in Italy and his scant sympathy for the democratic parties. "I have consulted with the War Cabinet this morning on the proposal that the British and American governments should accept the six-party programme without further delay … They do not consider that the six-parties are representative in any true sense of the Italian democracy or Italian nation or that they could at the present time replace the existing Italian government which has loyally and effectively worked in our interests."[34]

Unlike Caracciolo, Croce had long grasped the reasons for Churchill's reservations. The Allies, in particular the British, did not want a strong Italian government, preferring instead weak and pliable leaders who were dependent on their support for survival. Reflecting on Churchill's attitude towards Italy while he lay in bed with a broken arm, Croce penned some sad notes on British and Allied policy in Italy. "They have no other interests but to keep Italy under their feet, preventing her from rising and fighting again and from achieving a renewal; and for this reason they support the government of the king and Badoglio, that is, a weak government unable to create for them any obstacle or difficulty, now or in the future."[35] Later Croce would write, but not publish, a short essay on the limits of English liberalism, lamenting its insularity and penchant for narrow-minded self-interest.

Churchill's attitude was only one part of the problem, however. In Southern Italy there were only four old men suitable for the premiership. Two of them, Croce and De Nicola, who enjoyed great reputations and were respected by all, did not want the job. Sforza, who wanted the job, did not enjoy the confidence of the Allies, and at the same time was opposed by the Catholic Church and resented by other parties. Badoglio, who had the job and wanted to keep it, was disliked by the anti-Fascist parties and trusted only by the British. The national leaders in Rome, failing to grasp the strategic importance of Southern Italy, did not send to the South any leader with a national stature, concentrating instead their efforts in the capital and waiting to be liberated by the Allies. This was a mistake that the Communist Party leader Palmiro Togliatti did not make, hence the impact of his presence and the force of his leadership once he arrived in Southern Italy.

6
A Democratic Compromise

Despite Churchill's speech in late February 1944, a possible solution to Italy's political impasse was in sight. The king had decided to retire to private life and had made known his decision to the Allies. Croce and Sforza, after initial reluctance, had accepted the name of Prince Umberto as lieutenant of the realm. It remained to make public the king's decision and, once his retirement took effect, to form a new cabinet.

In March, the political transition received an impetus from an unexpected quarter. Soon after Churchill's speech, even Macmillan began to look with sympathy on the new proposals. In a note of 23 February 1944 sent to the Foreign Office, he wrote: "What strikes me from recent telegrams … is the degree to which the Junta have climbed down. No more talk of Sforza and Croce's baby, the Regency; no more refusal to accept Umberto, and no real demand for forcible abdication of the King. The Allies are relied on to [provide] moral persuasion. This is really a great advance, and I think that the politicians south of the line are very anxious to get everything settled and themselves clearly in office before competitors arise from Rome."[1] There was another development, too, one that weakened Churchill still further and, to Macmillan's consternation, offered evidence of a widening rift in Anglo-American relations. On 13 March 1944 President Roosevelt wrote a letter to Churchill urging the removal of the king from power and expressing support for the Italian democratic parties. Since this was an election year, his stance could be dismissed as mere electioneering. But the president was also expressing long-held views that were in disagreement with British policy.

Not all the players were following the same script, however. Denied membership on the Allied Control Commission, the Soviet Union found other ways to influence Italian affairs. On 14 March it recognized the

Badoglio government and established diplomatic relations with the king. Five days later, Andrej Gromyko, the Soviet ambassador to Washington, presented a memorandum to Secretary of State Cordell Hull in which the Soviet Union demanded that the anti-Fascist parties be included in the Badoglio cabinet in order to settle the conflict between the Giunta and the king's government. The same demand, in the same language, was made by Palmiro Togliatti, leader of the Italian Communist Party, at a press conference in Algiers in mid-March.

These diplomatic moves created worry among the Allies, and hope among the Italians. But they also had an immediate and direct impact on Italian Communists, who suddenly were compelled to change their established policy. The memoirs of Oreste Lizzadri show that there was a direct correlation between the Soviet Union's initiatives and the Italian Communist Party's change of direction even before the return of Togliatti to Italy in late March. In a rally held by the left-wing parties in Naples on 12 March, Velio Spano, then the leader of the Communist Party in Southern Italy, demanded the king's immediate abdication. At another rally a week later in Bari, to Lizzadri's "great surprise," as he wrote in his diary, Spano forgot "all the previous insults hurled against the king, the monarchy, and Badoglio" and instead proposed a government of national unity under the king and led by Badoglio. Questioned by his friend about the sudden change, Spano, during a sleepless night, revealed to Lizzadri the new party policy: "La Svolta," which would shortly be announced by Togliatti, *urbi et orbi.*[2]

The Allies, through diplomatic contacts with Italian Communists, and as recently revealed by MI6 reports of informers and spies from inside the party, were aware of the Soviet manoeuvring that was taking place under their noses. Macmillan noted in his diary that "the large Russian delegation are in constant collaboration with the Communist organization here, which they finance and largely control."[3] In response, Allied and Italian politicians were compelled to take some initiatives of their own. Macmillan understood this necessity better than anyone else in the Allied camp. "The unilateral diplomatic action by the Soviet Government has certainly increased our difficulties in Italy." He also observed that, although the Russian moves "may appear to strengthen the hand of the King and Badoglio ... the very fact that the Junta's cohesion has been weakened will in the long run favour the radical and subversive elements."[4] To prevent such an occurrence, Macmillan advised the British cabinet that the old Churchill policy of "no change until the liberation of Rome" be abandoned in favour of a more flexible posture. "I therefore suggested that we should bring the two sides together and leave them to negotiate." Macmillan was ready to accept the agreement reached by the king and De Nicola, and to leave to the Italians the implementation of that agreement. At the same time, he stressed the limits of any initiative undertaken by Italian politicians: "We can tolerate nothing that impedes the administration of Southern Italy and the conduct of the war."[5]

In the Italian camp, too, there was significant movement. On 16 March, Vittorio Emanuele informed Badoglio and the government of his intention to retire to private life and to name his son as lieutenant of the realm. On 18 March, the CLN in Rome again affirmed its preference for a republic and voted for its assumption of all powers of the state. The sponsor of that motion was the Socialist leader, Pietro Nenni, who had been informed days before, via a clandestine radio broadcast by Lizzadri, of the impending change of position by the Communists, or, as he put it, "our cousins' change of heart." It is difficult to say whether that piece of information prompted Nenni's rash proposition; there is no mention in his diary of Lizzadri's communication. In any case, his radical proposal prompted the CLN's president to resign in protest, while giving rise to concerns among moderate elements in Naples that a radical government in Rome, in competition with Badoglio's cabinet in Salerno, would create new divisions and add more danger to an already troubled situation. The fears of the moderates were also increased by rallies in Southern cities criticizing Churchill's speech of 22 February and demanding the king's abdication.

In the midst of initiatives coming from different quarters, the limits of De Nicola's modus operandi became evident: instead of taking advantage of the pressures being brought to bear, he decided, as a way of affirming his independence, to procrastinate. Throughout his political life, he always patiently waited for the right moment to arrive before acting. On this occasion, left-wing agitation only persuaded him to delay on making public the agreement he had reached with the king. He even resisted a direct request from Vittorio Emanuele himself. He had promised to write the royal proclamation; but, when the king asked for the document, he advised him instead to postpone its publication so as to avoid the impression that he was caving in to the demands of the radicals.[6]

On 14 March Croce met De Nicola in Naples' general hospital, where he was being treated for his broken arm. Physical discomfort aside, he was not in the right frame of mind for a political discussion; the night before, a German air raid had caused great damage to historical buildings of the city and to his own house. Under these conditions, he accepted De Nicola's recommendation of delay without offering a challenge or proposing a different option. "In the afternoon De Nicola came to see me, and he brought with him news so grave about the victims and the destruction of the night before ... in Naples that I was not able to discuss properly with him the political arguments which were the object of our conversation." He added: "In summary, this seems to be the situation. The king insists on having from De Nicola the written formula of the proclamation, with which he will announce his resolution to retire to private life and to name his son as lieutenant. But to De Nicola it seems opportune to postpone this act for a few more weeks, because, in his opinion, after the rally held last week here in Naples, the suspicion could arise that the king's resolution and proclamation was a victory of the three extreme parties, the Socialists, the Communists, and the Party of Action."[7]

Days later, fellow Liberals from Naples proposed to Croce a different course. These were younger men, more attuned to modern politics. They were probably aware of discussions taking place in Naples among other politicians and Allied officers. Naples at the time was the political and intellectual capital of liberated Italy, even if the official seat of government was in Salerno. The most important political leaders lived in Naples, and all the parties had their headquarters in the city. It is not difficult to imagine that these Neapolitan Liberals had been told, or were made to understand, by Allied officers that something new and important was afoot among their left-wing friends. Be that as it may, for good reasons of their own, these young Liberals saw no need to waste more time and to delay an official announcement which was already known to people in high places and probably the object of discussion and speculation in private conversations as well. In a meeting on 27 March, they urged Croce to make public the agreement reached between De Nicola and the king. This time, Croce was in a better frame of mind. He wrote: "I have agreed that it is now not convenient to wait any longer, delays can cause damage and could be even dangerous ... and even if there are unacceptable parts (for instance, waiting until Rome for the beginning of the lieutenancy) we can always reopen the discussion on that point." The next day, in a meeting with De Nicola and Sforza in his villa in Sorrento, Croce urged them to make public the agreement with the king without further delay.[8]

On 23 March 1944 Macmillan sent a memorandum to Churchill and Eden which was destined to change the course of British policy in Italy. The memorandum makes clear that the British were worried by the new diplomatic initiatives of the Russians, or, as Macmillan called them, "the Soviet maneuvers and intrigues." No less worrisome for him was the rift that Italian affairs were causing in the Anglo-American relations. With great clarity, Macmillan listed the reasons for a change of policy and for accepting the new institutional arrangement that De Nicola had devised.

> The advantages of a settlement now are clear. First, it would give us some internal stability until the end of the war and the calling of the National Convention. Second, it would dispose in the comparative calm of the present political conditions of a problem which we shall have to deal soon or later. Third, it would probably result in a more favourable arrangement for the monarchy than may be obtainable later, especially when the weight of opinion of the northern industrial cities begins to make itself felt. Fourthly, it would ease Anglo American relations in this affair. Fifthly, if we can settle matter now, before the full force of the Soviet influence and intrigues has reached its zenith, it will be an advantage ... Finally, if we maintain our attitude of no political change or development before Rome's liberation, we shall be giving a great latitude of manoeuver to the Russians. They will certainly continue to seek advantage at our expenses by representing us as repressing the free development of political life in Italy.[9]

While messages went back and forth between Naples and Sorrento, and between Naples, London, and Washington, "the arrival of a modern Lohengrin," in Bonomi's words, changed the political dynamics completely. On the same day that Croce met with the Neapolitan Liberals, 27 March, Palmiro Togliatti, the leader of the Communist Party, returned to Italy from Russia. In a press interview in Salerno soon after his arrival, and in a speech a few days later to the national council of his party, he formally announced the Italian Communist Party's new position on the institutional question, a policy that has become known as "La Svolta di Salerno" or "The Turn of Salerno." He proposed a government of national unity, composed of the CLN's six parties but serving under the king and led by Badoglio, and leaving the matter of the monarchy's future until the end of the war. Though the new policy had already been publicly announced a few weeks earlier at Togliatti's press conference in Algiers, his willingness to serve under the king and to support a government led by Badoglio, without asking for any concessions in return, was greeted by widespread surprise. In a more general way, and even more important for the future, with the arrival of Togliatti in Naples in 1944, the Italian Communist Party embarked on a new strategic course, less sectarian than the old one but still faithful to the tenets of Marxism-Leninism. This new direction was more in keeping with Italian realities and traditions but still looking to the Soviet Union for inspiration, more open to new ideas but still operating under the rules of "democratic centralism," more accommodating to new members; however, the party remained the standard-bearer of totalitarian ideology.

Togliatti's initiative showed that a remarkable political leader had arrived in Italy. The unity of the anti-Fascist forces was now broken; the Socialist Party and the Party of Action were placed in an awkward position, left with the choice of either abandoning their opposition to the king, and following the Communists' lead, or losing most of their political influence. Without a doubt, Togliatti's intervention was striking in its realism and coherence of purpose. Unlike other politicians in Southern Italy, he had international experience; he had been a leader of the Comintern, and "he knew what nobody else knew," as Pietro Nenni remarked. He also had the leadership ability to transform what he knew into action. His ideas were supported by one of the largest political parties in Italy, and were coordinated with one of the Great Powers and then defended in Allied councils by Soviet representatives. Strictly speaking, Togliatti was not the author of the new policy, as Communist historians have claimed.[10] The policy had already been set out, as we have seen, in Andrei Gromyko's memorandum to Cordell Hull and had undoubtedly been crafted at the highest levels of the USSR, as newly discovered Soviet documents have shown; it was, in many ways, similar to the position of Badoglio and the Allies and had been put forward, though without success, by Italian conservatives in the past. Yet now that same policy acquired a new force and a new meaning. Moreover, Togliatti's initiative came at the right time. Many were eager for a resolution to a crisis of long standing and had grown frustrated with a less accommodating position that had demanded a lot of labour and had borne little fruit so far.[11]

The surprise and consternation sparked by Togliatti's unexpected proposal were reflected in Croce's diary entry of 2 April 1944. "Today … Morelli came and informed me of a sudden change in the political scene, because an Italian Communist by the name of Ercoli arrived from Russia … has summoned a meeting of the Communists, and has urged them and the other parties to collaborate with Badoglio, leaving aside the question of the king's abdication, in order to concentrate all the effort on the war against the Germans; he also has declared that the Communists would collaborate without delay and without conditions." Croce saw immediately the advantage Togliatti's initiative gave to the Italian Communist

Party and to Soviet strategy. "It certainly is a good blow given by the Soviet Union to the Anglo-Americans, because, with the excuse of intensifying the war against the Germans, the Communists will be brought inside the government, allowing them to be the initiators of a new policy which other parties will be compelled to follow." Croce also pointed out the opportunism of the move and the lack of scruples shown by the Communists "about pacts solemnly made." While other parties now would feel forced to follow the new policy, the Communists would not have any compunction about "breaking the pact that united them to the parties of the Committee of National Liberation"; nor would they feel any embarrassment especially towards the Socialists and the Party of Action, "with whom recently they had joined forces in the rally against the speech of Churchill, during which they had demanded the abdication of the king, the exclusion of any members of the House of Savoy, and the proclamation of the republic." Croce also worried about the reaction of the other parties, especially those that had been lukewarm in their opposition to the king. "If the Communists begin to collaborate with Badoglio and the king, what will the other parties do, and in particular the Christian Democratic Party, who also have mass support and do not want to be left out of the government, abandoning the field to the Communists?"[12]

Above all, Togliatti created a sense of urgency among the liberal and democratic forces and also among the Allies. Procrastination had come to an end; the search for a solution to a long-festering problem was now widely viewed as of critical importance. In the last few weeks, especially after breaking his arm, Croce had deferred to De Nicola's counsel; now he resumed his leadership role, and acted with speed and determination. With Sforza's agreement, he changed tactics. Croce wrote in his diary: "We have therefore decided to accelerate what we had already resolved, that is to make public the agreement reached by De Nicola with us Liberals, and the pledge made by the king." The reason for speeding up that announcement was made clear by Croce. He wanted his own solution to be implemented, because he regarded Togliatti's as much inferior. "This way, in place of the proposal made by the Communists, we will substitute our proposal, reached in silence, but which is far superior, because it does not go around but resolves the question of the king's person: besides, now it will be supported by all parties, Communists included." Time was of the essence. "De Nicola has seen Sforza, and tomorrow together they will come here and we will decide what to do next and the initiatives to take."[13] At that meeting, the three men prepared a new document, which would be submitted to the Giunta for its approval.

Croce was not alone in his opposition to Togliatti's initiative. At a meeting of the Giunta on 3 April 1944 – in the absence of Croce and Sforza but not of Togliatti – Adolfo Omodeo, on behalf of the Party of Action, strongly criticized the new Communist position and lamented its destructive effects on political unity. Omodeo reiterated his party's opposition to the king and to Badoglio. Croce wrote in his diary that Omodeo "spoke with force against the proposal of collaboration and the breaking of anti-Fascist unity," adding significantly: "His speech has not been without effect even on Togliatti."[14] Togliatti never showed much consideration for the Party of Action and its leaders, or for its forerunners under the Fascist regime, but the Communist leader, as Croce aptly said, was a "totus politicus" and he never let personal feelings interfere with his political aims. It was not in his interest to run the risk of isolation or to increase the hostility to his proposal, and he may also have been genuinely surprised by the general and vehement opposition to the king and Badoglio. In any event, he was quick to reassure the other parties that "the Communists had taken no concrete steps after their announcements" and "no accord has been made between his party and Badoglio."[15] Two days later, the three moderate parties, encouraged by friends of Croce, had a public meeting of their own in Naples, and at the end of the discussion they took a position more radical than the one proposed by the Communists. With some relish, Croce wrote: "In full agreement they refused a collaboration with the royal government of Badoglio."[16]

In summary, Togliatti's proposal and the reaction to it on the part of the democratic parties gave a new impetus to the political process, compelled the Allies to abandon their opposition to institutional changes, recreated the unity of the anti-Fascist forces, and prevented a direct alliance between Badoglio and Togliatti, if that possibility was ever entertained by the old fox and his unexpected new ally. Croce's comment at this point is quite appropriate: "The fault for what happened, or was going to happen, belongs on the whole to the Anglo-American politicians, to Churchill, to Eden and Roosevelt, who for several months have rejected our reasonable and well-reasoned proposals, and opposed the requests of Italian liberals and democrats for the king's abdication in order to form a democratic government."[17]

On 6 April, to reach a final agreement and to sanction an official resolution, the Giunta and its two spokesmen met in Sorrento, at Croce's villa, out of respect for his age and his continuing convalescence. To underscore the significance of the event, several journalists of the Italian and international press were present. Also there was Togliatti, who had replaced the hapless Spano as the Communist representative on the Giunta's executive. On this occasion at least, the Communist leader showed much deference to Croce. In the end, the Giunta considered a document – drafted by Croce and discussed beforehand among Croce, De Nicola, and Sforza – which declared that the proposed lieutenancy would be the equivalent of an abdication, and that it should begin immediately after the royal proclamation, without waiting for the liberation of Rome as the king desired.[18] Since this document is not well known, it deserves to be quoted at length:

> There is, and there has always been, consensus among us, despite appearances, concerning the necessity of forming without delay a government consisting of all the anti-Fascist parties for the material and moral reconstruction of the nation, and for a vigorous contribution to the war against the Germans. The Congress of Bari put aside the question of the form of the state, about which the Italian people shall have a free choice at the end of the war. It dealt with the other questions that arose from the continuing presence of Vittorio Emanuele III as head of state; and voted for the removal of the king by means of abdication. Afterwards, Carlo Sforza and I discussed the issue with Enrico De Nicola; he then assured us that our aim could be equally achieved by the institute of a lieutenancy, which, though not mentioned in the Albertine Statute, has many precedents in our constitutional history; on our part we decided not to remain rigid on a point of mere form. Asked by us, Enrico De Nicola took upon himself the task to express to the king in person the complex reasons that had compelled him to formulate his proposal, and he informed us without delay about the result of his mission; he told us that the king had resolved to name, on the day of the liberation of Rome, the Prince of Piedmont as lieutenant general of the realm, until the final decision of the Italian people; but the king also assured us that he was ready to make such an announcement right away. You will recognize, with us, that the highly patriotic work done by Enrico De Nicola removes the obstacle before us. Only the wish of the king to transfer the powers to the lieutenant in Rome leaves us with some perplexities still. And we wish that on this point, and on all the rest, you express your opinion. If the parties that you represent will maintain a strong and loyal unity, we will form a government that will have sufficient moral authority to save our country.[19]

The account of that meeting in Croce's diary, and in a letter to Bonomi sometime later, is very short and mentions the main points only. From other sources we know that the debate was lively, appropriate to the subject and to the strong personalities involved. But in the end, after much discussion, unanimous agreement was reached, as Croce had hoped. "The meeting, despite the reservations of some, approved of our work and voted that the lieutenancy be instituted right away, without waiting for the liberation of Rome." In Croce's diary, there are some interesting comments on Togliatti's participation. He apparently caught Croce's interest more than others. "Togliatti has been among the first to approve the result that we have obtained, and has not raised any difficulty or objection." In another diary entry written soon afterwards, Croce expressed his surprise that Togliatti was being so moderate. "Togliatti came to the meeting, and has been most reasonable, and willing to accept our proposal as the new basis of policy. *Mah.*"[20] Mah, indeed! With that typical Italian utterance, full of popular wisdom, Croce expressed all his surprise and wariness.

The minutes taken by Caracciolo show that, during the meeting, Croce's proposal and Togliatti's initiative became intermingled, with speakers using one to support the other. This tactic clearly fit the needs of the non-Communist representatives, who cited Togliatti's arguments to defend their backing of Croce's proposal. Only the members of the Socialist Party and the Party of Action raised strong objections, but without reaching the breaking point. They also pointed to some conflict between the new proposals and the resolutions passed at the Congress of Bari. But their arguments did not prevail. In the end, the lieutenancy came to be equated with abdication, and the Giunta recognized "the necessity and urgency of the formation of a new cabinet," "praised the initiatives of De Nicola and Croce," and expressed the hope that "these initiatives may bring a quick and full solution to the present Italian crisis without waiting for the liberation of Rome." On the last point, Togliatti's position underlined his strategic sense and negotiating style: "We need to preserve our unity, and to keep in mind the urgency with which the Italian crisis has to be resolved. The time when the king will depart from the scene is important, but it is after all a question of formality, and the Communists are not interested in questions of forms. What does interest us is obtaining a political guarantee, a formal promise by the Crown for the convocation of the Constituent Assembly."[21]

With the consent given to Croce's and De Nicola's negotiations, the Giunta removed one of the major obstacles to the creation of a new cabinet and put in motion a chain of events leading to a new political course for the country. Indeed, with that vote at Sorrento, the Giunta had effected a significant political turn of its own. Failing to recognize that fact risks attributing the "Svolta" exclusively to the leadership and initiative of Togliatti. Truly, the "Sorrento resolutions," as that meeting should more properly be defined, mark the end of a stalemate and the rediscovery of national purpose for the common good – in other words, a new beginning.

Many books have been written on the "Svolta of Salerno," praising or criticizing the outcome, and the debate continues with unabated intensity. On the subject of Togliatti's role, Leo Valiani, a leader of the Party of Action, a historian, and a protagonist in the events of that time, in 1960 offered the following equitable assessment:

> Despite his miscalculations and lack of knowledge of the political situation, shortcomings that Croce or Sforza could have pointed out to him, if only he had met with them before his announcements, the leader of the Communist Party found himself ... in a more moderate position, momentarily more favourable to the monarchy than that of the old Liberal leaders, who had realized the incompatibility of anti-Fascist democracy with Vittorio Emanuele's continuance on the throne. Despite its problematic features – the breaking of anti-Fascist solidarity, and the reversal of prior Communist Party positions – Togliatti's initiative contributed to propelling history in the direction favoured by the great liberal figures of anti-fascism.[22]

The achievements of the Sorrento meeting were significant, even if obstacles remained. As Croce wrote: "This way we have made a step forward; but what will follow is full of uncertainties and dangers. We will try to persuade the Allied authorities, and especially the British, not to create any more obstacles to our work, to the detriment of our interests and theirs."[23] To persuade the Allies was not an easy task, as Croce had recognized a few days before. "I have observed that the British and the Americans, who deal with political affairs of Italy, are slow to understand them. And even now they did not realize what was very clear to all of us, that the new Communist policy of collaboration was mainly against the Anglo-Americans."[24]

Liberal politicians had certainly scored a success, but, even so, they also had cause for worry. With the arrival of Togliatti, the Communist Party had assumed the leadership of the left-wing forces in Southern Italy and in particular had underlined the weak position of the Socialists, as reflected in the vacillations of poor Lizzadri, who in the end, inside and outside the meetings of the Giunta, without clear direction from his party in Rome or from Nenni, felt compelled to follow the Communist line despite his misgivings. The Communists gained new prestige and increased their influence among different strata of society; their membership began to grow by leaps and bounds, soon reaching one hundred thousand. This generated a sense of foreboding in political circles. With his usual perspicacity, Macmillan was among the first to recognize the new danger. "The communist position," he wrote, "makes the liberal and moderate parties very uncomfortable." The Allies, no less than the Italians, were deeply concerned by the growing influence of the Communist Party, as well as by the financial support the party was receiving from the Soviet agents operating in Italy.[25] These concerns were echoed in the political conversations at Croce's villa. There, he made, not for the first time, an interesting comparison between fascism and communism, expressing his fears about the new threat to freedom and liberal ideals:

> We are always talking about the effect produced by the Communists' attempt to take the direction of the political affairs here in Naples; we also talked about the crowd of people that are rushing to join that party: civil servants, army officers, former Fascists, misfits, etc.; we fear a new fascism for Italy ... if communism is bolshevism and is implemented by a totalitarian regime ... we should remember that Mussolini imitated the Russian example, employing its political methods but coming to terms with the economic interests ... The terrible thing is that after we longed so much for freedom during twenty years and for the expansion of moral forces that freedom allows, after we suffered pain and shame for its loss, now with a tortuous turn of events we could lose freedom again.[26]

After the war, many intellectuals, even those with a liberal background, would succumb to the charms of Togliatti and to the allure of the Soviet Union; some even came to view communism as an evolution of liberalism, in a more vigorous and coherent form. Croce was not one of them; he never entertained any doubt about the dictatorial nature of the Soviet regime, nor did he suffer any illusions that communism might evolve in a liberal direction, as he explained in his *History of Europe in the Nineteenth Century*, published in English in 1933. Even when he accepted the necessity and opportunity of collaboration, Croce maintained an attitude of wariness, expressed in the classical maxim *timeo Danaos et dona ferentes* (beware of Greeks bearing gifts).[27]

At the beginning of April 1944, a political breakthrough finally had been achieved. The road was now open to the formation of a government of national unity. All the Italian political parties were in agreement, despite some grumbling; the plan was also endorsed by the Allies, who now began to apply pressure on all the players in order to speed up negotiations and reach a quick conclusion.[28]

Two main problems remained. The first concerned the timing of the king's retirement; the second had to do with the name of the next prime minister. The first issue was a personal decision on the part of the old king. Italians and Allies agreed that he should retire immediately, without waiting for the liberation of Rome. Croce was in favour of this solution to the very end, and he let the king know his preference with a personal message, "moved only by the desire not to poison or complicate any further the questions under negotiation."[29] But, despite advice and pleas from Italian politicians and strong pressure from Allied officers, the king stood his ground. He would leave the public scene only after the liberation of Rome. That stance was unwise: in the end it brought more personal humiliations and allowed the Allies to interfere in a strictly Italian affair. It also greatly damaged the prestige of his son and split the moderate forces once more.

The choice of a new prime minister generated an equal amount of discussion and acrimony among Italian politicians. But, in fact, that question was resolved in a definite way, despite some American reservations, in a series of telegrams and exchanges between Macmillan and Churchill. It was finalized by the newly minted Allied Advisory Council (AAC)[30] on 8 April, when its members, now including Soviet representatives, met to discuss the latest developments in the Italian political situation. In the middle of the discussion, Macmillan was shown a telegram from Churchill approving his plan and also giving precise and blunt instructions. "I am very glad to receive your news. You have evidently handled the situation with remarkable skill. I approve your proposed plan of action. I do not mind very much whether the King retires now or waits till Rome is taken, as long as Umberto is created Lieutenant and Badoglio remains the head of the Government. Do all you can to keep Sforza out of any office of real power."[31] With that telegram, the choice of prime minister was made, and the fate of Sforza was sealed, his ambition thwarted by Churchill's pique. After reading the telegram, Macmillan cut the discussion short and "supported by Murphy, and everybody else, moved my motion," which incorporated the suggestions he had forwarded to Churchill previously. Then the council adopted a resolution, for transmission to the commander-in-chief of the Mediterranean sector:

a) Welcoming the development leading to the formation of a broad-based government;
b) Stating it to be in the Allied interest that Badoglio should continue in such government to hold the office of prime minister and foreign secretary;
c) Emphasizing that the new government must be made to declare its willingness to assume all the obligations of the old government;
d) Insisting that whatever arrangement is entered between the new government and the king must be regarded as binding until such time as the whole Italian people can be consulted on the institutional issue at the end of the war.[32]

Churchill's telegram and Macmillan's resolution showed the limits of Italian sovereignty but also offered a compromise: the king could go, but Badoglio had to stay. It was a difficult choice for many, but one necessary to move forward. Croce became instrumental in making that choice possible. The day after, on 9 April 1944, he was notified of the decision taken by the AAC and came to know the British position, or rather their "Imperial preferences." That day he had a meeting with his old friend and SOE officer Max Salvadori. There is no doubt that Salvadori was on an official mission. Croce wrote that "in the afternoon came Max Salvadori … who informed me that the British representatives in Naples recognize that they had made a big mistake in supporting the king and opposing our requests, and that they are now in a grave situation regarding the Communist danger that has been developing. For this reason, they are willing to put pressure on the king, demanding that he retire now, name a lieutenant, and order the formation of a ministry composed by all parties." That was the good news; then came the bitter pill: "But they want to keep Badoglio as prime minister because they have signed the armistice with him. If we accept Badoglio, the obstacle to the formation of a new ministry would be removed, and it would then be possible to achieve the solution advocated by us within three or four days."

During their conversation, Salvadori likely told Croce that, in the opinion of Churchill and Macmillan, "Sforza should not be either prime minister or foreign secretary." By Croce's account, it would seem that at this point he and Salvadori were joined by Sforza and Tarchiani. It was an uncomfortable situation for all of them, and in particular for Sforza. To make the latter's defeat more palatable, Croce sugar-coated his arguments. He tried to persuade Sforza that "he should no longer oppose the permanence of Badoglio as prime minister, once he was surrounded by ministers of other parties" – especially given the probability that, once in Rome, "Badoglio would have to surrender his place to another head of government." Also, "after six months of fruitless negotiations," it was important to avoid "the accusation that another refusal on his part had made the desired change impossible," a charge already in circulation in the press and among the general public. Tarchiani supported Croce's arguments, adding that the time had come "to accept political necessities"; with direct reference to Sforza's conundrum, he also stressed that "sometimes it is necessary to be ready to lose one's popularity." Naturally enough, Sforza was reluctant to make that sacrifice. At first, he stated bluntly "his repugnance to collaborating with Badoglio." He suggested that it would be best to maintain their opposition, to wait a little longer, hoping that soon the Allies would agree to the replacement of Badoglio. But, in the end, as often happened, Sforza succumbed to Croce's reasoning, or as Croce put it, "Sforza accepted as just the points of my observations." Once the accord was reached among the three of them, "Salvadori agreed to refer our conclusion to the Allied authorities, to travel to Salerno, to see their representatives, and afterwards to let us know how things stand."[33]

Sforza was not the only one reluctant to serve under Badoglio: all the leaders of the anti-Fascist parties in Southern Italy were unhappy with Badoglio's continuance as head of government. And so, once again, Croce came under strong pressure to put his name forward for the post of prime minister. Several times before he had refused that same invitation. This time the call came from an unexpected party, with whom he had often been engaged in heated disagreement. The effort was sponsored, inside and outside the meetings of the Giunta, by members of the Party of Action, supported by the Socialist Party. On 19 April, Croce had a stormy meeting with Omodeo, Tarchiani, and Craveri, his son-in-law. All three were members of the Party of Action and were of a republican persuasion, but were probably concerned with the split that existed in their party on the institutional question. Unlike Badoglio, Croce would enjoy the confidence of all the factions of the party. "And all three … subjected me to an assault, urging with force that I accept the premiership of the government, which Sforza cannot assume, and thus take the place of Badoglio." In making their case, they seemed to be grasping at straws: after hearing a junior British officer criticize the old marshal recently, it was clear to them that "the Allies are no longer supporting Badoglio, and he can easily be replaced." Even this three-pronged assault did not succeed. "Naturally, I rejected the offer ... emphatically, even shouting."[34]

After the shouting match, in a calmer manner, Croce explained the reasons why at that stage it would not be wise to antagonize the Allies. In his peroration he even put forward some reasons why Badoglio was a good choice. He enjoyed the support of the Allies and had their confidence; he was a good soldier – an important qualification in a time of war, especially since he was in the process of reorganizing the army; and finally, he was in the middle of negotiating better conditions for Italy, trying to change its co-belligerent status into a regular alliance. On this occasion, Croce was really speaking only as a good lawyer would, in an effort to remove obstacles in the way of an agreement. Still, his claims had some merit.

The next day, undeterred by Croce's clear refusal, a member of the Party of Action, in a meeting of the Giunta, made a last attempt. He presented a motion urging the Giunta to propose Croce as the next prime minister, replacing Badoglio. This time, Croce was not even asked his opinion on the matter, and, after a brief discussion, the other members of the Giunta voted against the motion. Togliatti bluntly stated his position again: "The Communist party ... has no reservation about Badoglio."[35]

Another surprise was in store. On 12 April Vittorio Emanuele announced over the radio to the Italian people his "final and irrevocable retirement from public life" and stated that his son, Umberto, would become lieutenant general of the realm once Rome was liberated by the Allies.[36] Italian legal experts had drafted the original proclamation. Croce had seen the message in advance and was asked for comments. He suggested some small changes and, in the interests of greater clarity, he proposed a significant one: "The king shall keep the lieutenancy during the time of war and until the day on which the whole Italian people can decide on the form of the state." But under pressure from the Allied authorities, now eager to get him out of the way, the king was compelled to delete this change and replace it with a statement dictated by Macmillan. In the process, the lieutenancy, by its nature and purpose a temporary arrangement, became a permanent institution. Without realizing the consequences, the Allies, in their haste and arrogance, had imposed a virtual abdication. In practical terms, Umberto had become a lieutenant of a king who was no longer a king, having permanently retired to private life. The result was an awkward constitutional mess that, luckily, hardly anyone noticed or bothered to mention, then or later. When Croce read the revised proclamation in the newspapers, he was surprised, even shocked. "Not only does it not contain the modifications that I had suggested and had been requested by me, but the formula itself of the proclamation is different than the one I had seen, and it is now strangely illogical, because the king establishes a lieutenancy sine die, and declares that he is retiring to private life permanently. So, of whom will the lieutenant be a lieutenant? Of a king who is no longer king? And if the lieutenant becomes incapacitated, or dies, or resigns? Who will name a new lieutenant of the king, who is no longer a king?" Rather than dwell on the contradictions fashioned by "so-called experts," Croce decided to ignore them. "In conclusion, I cannot make out what happened. Anyway, faced with the fact, perhaps it is not worth the trouble trying to understand it, since it cannot be changed or remedied."[37]

After the royal proclamation, the negotiations for a new cabinet began in earnest. Croce played a leading role in these talks, which lasted more than three weeks; in some instances, his influence was decisive. Sforza had several discussions with Allied officers. Party leaders had negotiations among themselves, jostling for position and advantage. Badoglio met with all the leaders, making promises to all. But Croce sent and received emissaries to other parties and remained at the centre of the deliberations. The most important decisions were reached at his villa in Sorrento, where all party leaders went for meetings and discussions. Years later, in a speech to Parliament, he said that he was the "the principal agent" in the formation of the new government.[9] His role was facilitated by the Giunta's refusal to negotiate as a whole; instead it allowed each party to deal separately with Badoglio. That decision marked the return of parties in the political life of Italy and in the formation of governments. But in the conditions of the times it also enhanced Croce's leadership. Even Togliatti recognized Croce's contribution: "I have to say that in order to overcome the obstacles encountered in that month of April for the formation of the new Badoglio government ... Croce's collaboration was the most important ... He was the most intelligent of our adversaries, and for this reason, perhaps, it was less difficult to establish a collaboration."[38]

Croce met several times with Badoglio to negotiate a program and to choose, or to approve, names for the various cabinet positions. In the first meeting they established a good working relationship, reinforced later by reciprocal admiration. "I had to be on guard," Croce wrote, "because I was taken by feelings of sympathy for this old soldier, who, notwithstanding his faults and errors, freed Italy from Mussolini on July 25th, and then faced great dangers and even an attempt against his life." In subsequent encounters, without much difficulty, they found agreement on several subjects. "We agreed that the government has to be completely new, with the exception of a few military and technical collaborators, not compromised with fascism."[39] Both recognized that it was essential to bring public finances under control and to keep a wary eye on future Socialist and Communist ministers. For his part, Croce asked for the creation of a commission to oversee the purge of Fascist elements from the state, a request that Badoglio accepted. Badoglio himself summarized well the priorities of the new government, which included agreements made with the Allies. "The new ministry had to deal first of all with the war, the purge, transportation and communication, the supply of foodstuffs, and ordinary administration, refraining, however, from political, economic and social reforms, which are postponed to the time when Italy, fully liberated, will have again free elections and a parliament."[40] In one of their first meetings, Badoglio invited Croce to be part of his new cabinet. As Croce wrote in his diary, because of age, health, and personal inclination, he was "not willing to assume the administrative responsibilities of a cabinet post," and so Badoglio asked him to become a minister without portfolio. Croce agreed.[41]

During the negotiations, Croce had formal meetings with official members of the ACC. But the most important and difficult meetings were with Italian leaders. In all of them there were resentments and scruples to be surmounted. Croce had to use his authority and influence to persuade others to accept Badoglio's leadership. Only because Croce acted with patience and tenacity, and played the role, as he put it, "of adviser, persuader, and mediator," was a final settlement achieved.[42]

Croce's most delicate discussions were with a disappointed Sforza, "who disliked the idea of serving under Badoglio." Sforza probably never completely realized the full force of the British veto over the choice of prime minister and the bitter nature of Churchill's opposition to his ambitions. He tended to give undue weight to the personal assurances of his American friends, confusing diplomatic pleasantries with solid political guarantees. Armed with those promises, he continued to hope that it would be possible to replace Badoglio either with himself or with somebody else in the near future. Even when he "was resigned to accept the king until Rome" and Badoglio as prime minister, he thought that he might be made minister of the interior, the most important post in the cabinet. Once holding that powerful position, Sforza assured Croce, with some confidence, that he would be able "to offer direction to the whole government in the interest of all of us against Badoglio and the

Communists." But, eventually, Croce was able to overcome Sforza's reluctance, persuading him to join the cabinet "as minister without portfolio beside me."[43]

Croce was also able to persuade the Party of Action, or at least its more moderate wing, not to remain out of the new government in splendid isolation but "to collaborate with Badoglio." Having obtained their collaboration, then Croce went to battle for the interests of the Party of Action itself. It was Croce who was responsible for Adolfo Omodeo's selection as minister of education against the opposition of the Christian Democrats, the wishes of Badoglio, and the indifference of Togliatti. In a recent speech, Omodeo had made harsh criticisms of the Catholic Church and "violent and sarcastic accusations against Catholics in general." For that reason, Giulio Rodinò, the leader of the Christian Democrats in Southern Italy, "demanded Omodeo's exclusion from the government as minister of education," "in the name of his party and of the ecclesiastic authorities." The Christian Democrats always had a special longing for the ministry of education and later it would become one of their ministerial fiefdoms; but on this occasion they were compelled to retreat. Croce recounted that "I remained firm and refused his request; I could not allow the interference of the church's authorities in the formation of the government, a matter that concerns only national interests." Apart from the question of principle involved, Croce's support for Omodeo was also based on other solid grounds. "Omodeo has shown himself to have the qualities necessary to be a good minister of education" and, besides, "he was the only capable man that the Party of Action could offer." Croce's confidence in Omodeo was well placed. To reassure Catholics in Italy and abroad, at a time when international support was necessary, one of the first acts of Omodeo as minister was to issue a directive to continue Catholic instruction in Italian elementary schools as before.[44]

Against a smear campaign orchestrated by the Communist Party, Croce persuaded Badoglio to accept Renato Morelli, a lawyer and a former employee of Naples' biggest bank, as undersecretary to the cabinet. That way, Croce had a trusted friend in a strategic position. Morelli played the role of special messenger between Salerno and Sorrento, carrying messages and documents from Badoglio to Croce and vice versa.[45] Croce did not always have his way. Sometimes Badoglio refused his suggestions, whether for personal or political reasons. Other times he switched names to positions different than the ones suggested by Croce. Probably owing to Togliatti's pressure, and against Croce's advice, Badoglio assigned to the left-wing parties both economic ministries, so a Socialist became minister of industry and a Communist minister of agriculture. Both Croce and Badoglio, however, agreed that each party was entitled to equal representation in the cabinet, repeating the rule adopted in the CLN council and in the Giunta. There were difficult moments that required special efforts by both sides to prevent the negotiations from collapsing. At one crucial meeting with Badoglio, a nervous Croce was compelled, as he confessed to his diary, "to rely on my good sense alone, to avoid the danger of failure." But, despite Croce's anxieties, things worked out. On 18 April, Badoglio was at his charming best when, Croce wrote, "in a little more than an hour we devised a first list of the new cabinet."[46]

Comparing the first draft list with the final outcome, the most glaring difference concerns the number of ministers without portfolio. The original draft had only three such ministers – Croce, Sforza, and Rodinò (all three had been ministers in Giolitti's last cabinet in 1920–1) – but the final list had five. There was a story behind the change, suggesting other dealings and more meetings than those reported in Croce's diary. Croce wrote: "Badoglio asked me to be minister without portfolio ... on account of my age and my health ... I should have been the only one in that office; then we added Sforza, whom the Allied authorities did not want as minister of foreign affairs ... later we also added Rodinò, who preferred a less burdensome position; then the Socialists demanded one of their own beside us, the lawyer Pietro Mancini, who is still a young man; and finally, the Communists had Togliatti, who is even younger."[47] As a result, parity among the parties was maintained and the presence of the major leaders was assured; in fact, it was Croce who, according to his account, demanded the inclusion of Togliatti. The five ministers without portfolio became the inner circle of the cabinet, meeting to discuss important issues and to establish priorities. In the enlarged group, Croce held a position of prominence. But, had he remained the only minister without portfolio, as originally proposed by Badoglio, the new cabinet would have acquired a different significance and become known as the Badoglio-Croce government, thus enhancing the position of the Liberals and strengthening the ties with the traditions of liberal Italy.

Finally, on 21 April, as Croce recounted, "Badoglio could announce to the press the formation of a new cabinet." It was a historic moment: "Thus finally we assured the formation of the first democratic ministry after the fall of fascism." The protagonists had reason to be pleased with the results of their efforts, and these feelings were shared by the press and the general public. As Croce recognized in his diary: "In general, the discontent of the last days has now been succeeded by a sense of relief and general satisfaction." The task had been hard, the conditions less than propitious. If the talks had collapsed, "a great discredit would have befallen the reputation of Italy." But, with patience and some skill, failure had been avoided. "Truly the formation of such a cabinet was very difficult and painful and even illogical, because we had to create a political organism out of six parties that are different, unequal, and antagonistic, but had to be treated as equal, giving to each one an equal number of representatives and positions." At this point, Croce thought of Machiavelli: "Fortune has helped us in this first step. Let us hope it will help us in the future."[48]

In this atmosphere of general satisfaction, almost no one bothered to mention De Nicola. Only Croce saw fit to thank him personally for his contribution. "With Renato Morelli and Alfredo Parente I paid a dutiful visit to De Nicola, thanking him for his work of capital importance, without which the new ministry would have lacked the necessary premise." De Nicola had played a significant role during the negotiations. He had several meetings with the king and Badoglio, with Croce and Sforza, with other party leaders, and finally with Allied authorities, always offering useful advice. In his diplomatic way, he probably told Sforza painful truths about his political prospects. Croce had long ago recognized De Nicola's political acumen and had tried to involve him directly in the cabinet as a minister and in the past had even offered him the leadership of the Liberal Party. Yet, notwithstanding the universal respect in which he was held, the Actionists refused to grant to his party a cabinet post, and so the small democratic party was excluded from the government.

Despite his disappointment, De Nicola gave a positive appraisal of the new government. "He told me," Croce said, "that the cabinet we have just formed is the best we could do under the circumstances, despite the irrational and mechanical way with which it had to be assembled."[49]

De Nicola's assessment has merits. The formation of Badoglio's new cabinet influenced the future course of Italian history. It established the guidelines that any future Italian government had to follow for the duration of the war. Italy's limited sovereignty and its status as a defeated nation were reconfirmed, but the collaboration between the monarchy and the forces of the anti-fascism recreated a sense of national unity that had been lacking since the disaster of September 1943.

At the same time, the laborious negotiations that led to the government's creation underlined both the strengths and weaknesses of the political parties. The presence of the Communist Party inside the government created novel problems, then and later. But at least Italy escaped the fate of Greece, where the Communists' exclusion from government led to civil war. Whatever its ultimate goals, the Italian Communist Party committed itself to the creation of a democratic society, not to a Soviet-style revolution. Even more important, the Christian Democrats now acquired a central position in Italian political affairs. This was evident in the meetings of the Giunta and in the negotiations for the new cabinet. Their influence was recognized by everyone, and no solution was ever devised without their input and support. Togliatti was the first to appreciate their strength and acted accordingly, proposing an alliance between the Catholic masses and the working class. Finally, the formation of the Badoglio cabinet revealed the weak position of the Socialist Party and its sense of inferiority vis-à-vis the Communists, reflected in the contrast between the indecision of Lizzadri and the determination of Togliatti. The Communists had better leadership, a stronger organization, more financial resources, and, last but not least, the support of one of the Great Powers.

The Turn of Salerno embarrassed the Socialist Party but isolated the Party of Action. Its proposals ignored completely the constraints imposed by the war and the presence of the Allied powers in Italy, not to mention the mood of the Italian people. The party was also deeply divided at the national and local levels. The split of 1944 foreshadowed the divisions of two years later that finally destroyed the party. Carlo Rosselli's dream of achieving a synthesis between liberalism and socialism was never realized, the victim of its eclectic nature, as Croce had pointed out a long time ago. The Liberal forces showed their weakness also, and their divisions. It is difficult to imagine the successful formation of the new Badoglio cabinet without Croce's leadership. But, despite Croce's prestige, the Liberals did not regain the prominence that they had enjoyed before the advent of fascism under Giolitti. During the negotiations for the new cabinet, and also in the meetings of the Giunta, the Liberal Party acquired the reputation of a small party, one rich in personalities but without a strong following among the general public. Once the fiction of equality inside the CLN ended, the Liberals could not match the organizational clout of the mass parties and would be reduced to minority status.[50]

7
A Government of National Unity

On the morning of 24 April, the new government held its first meeting in Salerno, then the temporary capital. In the afternoon, in the nearby city of Ravello, where Vittorio Emanuele had established his residence, the full cabinet met the king for the official swearing-in ceremony. Finally, after long negotiations, the government of national unity was properly constituted and could begin work. In its short life, the cabinet usually worked well, according to Croce and Togliatti. Badoglio proved to be a good chairman, able to get things done and to keep meetings under control.

But, not surprisingly, animosities remained. Even in the first meeting, in the midst of a terrible war, a great amount of time was spent on the oath of office that ministers, by tradition, were required to take before assuming their responsibilities. In the past, each minister had to read an oath that promised loyalty to the king and to the House of Savoy. Since that oath was now unpalatable to several members, new words had to be found. After much discussion, Alberto Tarchiani, a member of the Party of Action, proposed an acceptable compromise. In the meeting with the king, as agreed, Badoglio read a short statement asserting the political independence of each member and their desire to come together for the common good. The king replied with appropriate words of his own, praising the unity of the cabinet in a difficult time. These formalities dispatched, as Croce writes, each minister then "signed the papers of the oath" necessary to assume ministerial responsibilities.[1]

Once the new cabinet started its work, Croce became the chief adviser to Badoglio. The two of them usually met before cabinet meetings, and Croce was asked his opinion about the most important issues. He was briefed about the international position of Italy, its relations with the

Allies, and the state of the armed forces. As a sign of Croce's pre-eminence in the cabinet, Badoglio allowed him to read the terms of the Long Armistice, then known only to a few people. Nobody else in the cabinet had seen the full text of the armistice, unless, as is probable, Togliatti had been given a copy or a summary by the Russians. As Croce writes in his diary, at the beginning of May, "Morelli brought important documents, and among these there was also the text of the armistice, which Badoglio did not communicate to other ministers."[2]

It was Croce who wrote the program of the third Badoglio government to avoid a long debate without reference to a written text. The document was discussed with the other ministers without portfolios, then brought before the full cabinet and finally accepted with only minor changes. Much work had gone into the whole process. As Croce reported the event in his diary, the crucial meeting took place at his villa in Sorrento on 26 April 1944. "Sforza came first and then the other ministers without portfolio, Rodinò, Togliatti, and Mancini, together with Morelli, the undersecretary to the cabinet. For more than four hours we read, reread, and discussed the program, adding a few short phrases, deleting some others, and changing a few words here and there, but in the substance my writing remained intact."[3]

The program, published the next day, laid out Croce's and Badoglio's priorities, or what the new government regarded as "the vital and urgent problems of the hour," chief among them "the continuation of the war effort against the Germans, increasing the food supply and enhancing hygienic measures for the population, and the beginning of the painful but necessary purge." For the new government, the "supreme object" was "the war of liberation of Italian lands, now invaded, in which the foreign enemy is united with what is left of the old and nefarious regime." To fulfil that priority, the government was going to increase the Italian contribution to the war effort, "augmenting the number of our soldiers fighting beside the Allies." The government also "will regard as its duty to help in any way possible the efforts of the heroic patriots in Northern Italy, who, despite their different origins, are today all united to free Italy and defeat Hitler's Germany." The second priority was the "epurazione," or purge, designed "to remove from public life and the civil service those dangerous elements" who "had played an active part in the old regime, and still retain the same aims, intentions, and attitudes." That undertaking, for Croce, had to be done not out of a desire for vengeance – on the contrary, "all of us want to forgive and forget" and wish "to heal the wounds and recreate harmony among Italians" – but for reasons of safety, so the country "will not fall again, even in different guise, under the ways of life of which we have experienced horror and shame." Furthermore, the purge had to be done expeditiously. The work was already under way, "but the government will make sure that the program, guided by certain and just rules, is brought to conclusion with speed and energy in the shortest time possible."

While the government intended to give priority to the war effort, it would not ignore the country's social problems. The government promised "to resume industrial activity, support food production, fight against speculation, increase internal commerce by repairing roads, bridges, and buildings, and try as well to obtain the necessary supplies from foreign powers." The cabinet also wanted to bring some order to the chaotic administration of the state, so government decrees could come again under institutional scrutiny in order to create a modicum of ministerial responsibility. Croce gave particular importance to another proposal. "In consultation with the local branches of the Committee of National Liberation," he recommended the creation of a Consulta, "a small consultative body, symbol of Parliament, which now is lacking, to which periodically the government will report on its work." Croce was asked by the cabinet to formulate the criteria for the Consulta. To that end, he sought the advice of young jurists from Naples, many of whom would later have brilliant careers in the courts or in Parliament. A plan was put together in a short time and then accepted by the full cabinet. The same proposal, with minor modifications, was approved again and enacted several months later by the next Bonomi government, and Sforza was appointed as the body's president.[4]

Besides the actions to be taken, the program listed the important issues that could not be addressed now "because they do not belong to this hour." Among these was "first of all, the institutional form of the state, which will find its solution when, with the country liberated and the war ended, the Italian people will be called to vote in free elections and by universal suffrage will elect a constituent and legislative assembly." Thus, for the first time, in an official document, the Italian government had promised the election of a constituent assembly under universal suffrage. No less important was another matter. The government pledged not to introduce radical reforms in the organization of the state and in the structure of society. As Croce put it, "reforms of the political system and of the economic order cannot be undertaken or concluded when the war is still raging, and Italy is divided into two parts, the most important and the biggest still occupied by the enemy."[5]

These statements regarding the maintenance of the political and economic status quo were factors that made possible the formation of the government of national unity. The pledges made by Italian politicians were based on the conditions dictated by the Allies for the formation of a new cabinet under Badoglio. As such, they bound not only the present government but any future one until a peace treaty would be signed and a constituent assembly elected. In a way, they were an addendum to the Long Armistice, and a significant one indeed.

Croce's interventions in cabinet discussions reflected the priorities set out in the government's program. In particular, he continued to advocate greater participation in the war effort alongside the Allies. Once again he encouraged the idea of a volunteer unit, possibly led by a veteran officer of the First World War. He urged Badoglio to raise the question with the Allied authorities, despite the failures of the past. "About the volunteer corps, I observed to Badoglio that even if it comes to nothing because of the Allies' opposition, it is still opportune and useful that he should approve the idea, and offer the proposal, to make evident their unwillingness to allow increased Italian participation in the war."[6] During the first days of the battle for the liberation of Rome, the Italian troops at the front were kept away from the fighting. To add insult to injury, the Allied command even declined the offer of ten well-armed Italian battalions for combat duty. Tarchiani, Sforza, and Croce sent a letter of protest to Badoglio, and even threatened to resign if the humiliating situation were not corrected. "It is distressing to observe that troops of every nationality are engaged in the fight, except our own. So then we may be accused later of having done nothing for the liberation of Rome and of our country, with negative moral and diplomatic consequences as a result." Afterwards, Badoglio raised the question with the Allied general in command of the operation and was told that Italian troops would take part in the liberation of Rome.[7]

There were pressing needs that had to be addressed immediately. During those months, many works of art and historical documents were lost, destroyed by bombs or sometimes burnt by vengeful German officers. Croce made special pleas to American generals on the subject, and, thanks to his efforts, the books of the National Library of Naples were returned safely in a speedy manner. A more controversial matter involved monuments built during the Mussolini regime to celebrate fascism's achievements or its leader's stature; many of these were now being destroyed at random and out of spite, not by foreign soldiers but by Italian civilians eager to burnish their anti-Fascist credentials. During

Mussolini's dictatorship, Croce had denied that fascism had any artistic creativity or literary merit. But in 1944 he proposed a decree, which the cabinet approved, to preserve objects "that have artistic value, or monuments that have historical importance, or even things that stand as a curiosity of the past regime."[8] Later, on his recommendation, Carlo Antoni, a scholar of German culture active in the Resistance, and a friend of Croce's, was asked to document, while memories were still fresh, all the atrocities committed against people and buildings by German soldiers during their occupation of Italy. In a short time, a useful report was produced that was then buried in the archives, where it has remained to this day, almost completely forgotten.

The Badoglio government discussed the question of the purge on various occasions. The purge had various political and economic aspects. First of all, it involved the banishment from public life of old Fascist leaders and the removal from the civil service of those individuals who had occupied high positions in the apparatus of the old regime "who were greatly compromised with fascism," or who "could be reputed to be dangerous" to the new democratic order. Second, it concerned the punishment of Fascist leaders for crimes committed against the country and its liberal institutions before and during Mussolini's dictatorship. Finally, it had to deal with the trials, and eventual punishment, of those businessmen who had realized illicit profits during the regime or had accumulated a great amount of wealth during the war through questionable means. The purge had all the makings of a difficult issue; it was subject to conflicting interests and complicated by political passions, individual resentments, and partisan calculations. Even historical judgments on the origin and nature of fascism played a large part in shaping the discussion and decisions, especially by those who regarded fascism as an expression of the financial and economic interests of the bourgeoisie. The final outcome years later left everyone dissatisfied, with accusations and reproaches directed against the politicians of the time. But the nature of the problem itself did not permit clear-cut solutions. The way Mussolini had achieved, exercised, and in the end lost power made it difficult to separate the wheat from the chaff. Several cases were self-evident, but many more fell into a grey area. Sometimes the purge gave rise to farcical situations. Mussolini's dictatorship had lasted more than twenty years, and during that time few people had been known to be openly anti-Fascist; as a result, decisions to purge certain Fascists were often made by those who themselves had been Fascist until the fall of Mussolini or who had ordered or carried out the persecution of anti-Fascists.

In the instruments of surrender, the Italian government had agreed to purge and remove Fascist elements from the apparatus of the state. Now the Allies were adamant in demanding the elimination of Fascist leaders and the removal of old generals from positions of command. But frequently they used those requests to put pressure on the Italian government in order to achieve their own aims, which were not always disinterested; in fact, they made exceptions when it suited them, favouring elements of the old regime who were amenable to their designs. Meanwhile, each Italian party had its own particular position, reflecting its political ideals and electoral considerations. For that reason, proposals ranged from the punishment of single individuals to a general cleansing of Italian society. For some, the purge was the occasion for public atonement, to expiate the sins of the past and to create a new, virtuous society. Others had a different set of priorities. Many sensible politicians, however, recognized the need for retribution for past crimes, but were also mindful of the need to avoid further disruption of the administration of the state and giving rise to an atmosphere of fear and uncertainty among civil servants and the general public.[9]

On the "vexata questio," Croce wrote a short essay that assumed the form of an open letter to his fellow Liberals. The essay, which had a wide circulation and generated a great deal of discussion in the press, makes evident that Croce was concerned with the overwrought passions that the issue was generating. Written under the weight of "grave thoughts and fears," it was an exercise in persuasion and a call for moderation and generosity. Its tone was calm and rational, devoid of the inflammatory rhetoric that was so common during those months.

For Croce, the purge, though painful, was "inevitable and also necessary." He indicated the criteria required to guide the purge and the aims that the operation needed to achieve. First of all, the purge "had to avoid the impulse of vendetta, which is a stupid and nasty thing, harmful more to those who harbour it than to those who suffer its consequences." What was equally important was avoiding another impulse, one that often is borne out of a generous disposition and can drive a person to a dangerous goal: "to do justice," that is, not to punish a specific crime as defined by the Criminal Code but "to punish the violation of the moral law." As Croce pointed out, "this task was reserved to God, and certainly does not pertain to the power of common mortals over other men." The aim of the purge had to be more modest: "The end we have to reach in this work is only to make our society better, or a little better, than the preceding one, as far as we are able."

To achieve that aim it was necessary "to remove from the active participation in public life those who, for what they have done and said in the past, can still be regarded as dangerous to the apparatus of freedom and to the peaceful and orderly society that we wish dearly to build." Also, it was important "to remove from public life those who have held positions of great responsibility in the old regime … even if they are no longer dangerous, because their permanence in high offices would offend public opinion, and, even worse, would offer a bad example of past crimes gone unpunished, or, in the cases of turncoats, of impudence rewarded." As a general rule, "in this undertaking of cleansing and removal, we need to be strict with peoples who held high offices, but we should be lenient with the great multitude of those who occupied the lower ranks or were employed in humble positions." Unless guilty of specific crimes, special indulgence had to be applied to "those who served the old regime for economic reasons, or out of fear, or because moved by vainglory, ignorance, or lack of intelligence and discernment." Moreover, even for those who had enjoyed high positions, sometimes special considerations were to come into play before a decision of removal was taken. "Even an occupation of high office was not enough for a guilty verdict." Unlike others who favoured a general condemnation applied to special categories and ranks of the Fascist Party or to positions and job classifications in the bureaucracy, Croce believed that the process must proceed "case by case" and be "conducted with an open mind, generosity of heart, and the severity of a judge." In conclusion, the purge was "a painful and even hateful job … certainly necessary but in many ways thankless." Those who were going to be charged with the undertaking had a difficult task, indeed: "They had to show wisdom and generosity, moderation and energy at the same time."[10]

Whenever in the following months he was required to intervene on the subject internally within the government or in dealings with the Allied authorities, Croce followed these principles of moderation. In cabinet meetings and discussions, he advised that the task "had to be completed in short time, bringing to conclusion a painful period of Italian life." To that end, "he proposed and the cabinet accepted that after a year no more charges should be laid." On the punishment of "Fascist crimes," those committed against the institutions of the state when in fact the alleged "crimes" were legal under the existing legislation of the time, the cabinet had to decide whether or not to apply justice retroactively. On different occasions, Croce expressed strong views "against any trace of retroactivity as contrary to a fundamental principle of law."

Also, he opposed the retroactivity principle because, under it, the death penalty would have to be applied in several instances. Eventually, a compromise proposed by Sforza was agreed on. The Fascist leaders who had promoted and directed the armed insurrection in October 1922 or the coup d'état in January 1925 were subject to life sentences. Those who had committed crimes in the consolidation of the Fascist regime or were guilty of high treason after 1926, when the regime had reintroduced the death penalty in the Italian legal system, could be sentenced to life or condemned to death.[11]

The decree discussed and approved in 1944 had a very short life; it was revised and greatly changed a few months later by the next government. The aim was always the same for those who had a Jacobin mentality: to make the purge and its prosecution more far-reaching. In fact, frequent changes to the rules, and the replacement of commission personnel, made the issue more tangled than ever and the stated aim more difficult, or impossible, to achieve. The entire process became a bureaucratic nightmare, until two years later, when Togliatti, as minister of justice, in agreement with De Gasperi, the prime minister, cut the Gordonian knot and put an end to the purge with a sweeping amnesty. That decision had the merit at least of putting a divisive issue to rest, but Croce regarded it as "scandalous." The eager prosecutors, and their political sponsors, should have remembered the old saying that "those who try to grab all in the end lose all," as Pietro Nenni conceded in his memoirs.[12]

The purge was not the only question on which Croce and Togliatti had different views. At the end of May, the cabinet discussed whether to increase farmers' rents or leave them unchanged. In the conditions of the time, there were good economic reasons for an increase, since, owing to inflation, the purchasing power of money was much less than before the war, when the rates had been set. At the same time, there were powerful political reasons to leave rents unchanged until calmer times had returned. The first solution favoured the landlords, while the second gave an advantage to the peasants, or, in many cases, to the tenants and leaseholders, who often employed peasants for work on the land. During the cabinet discussion, "the only time I spoke on an agrarian question," Croce proposed a modest increase, while the minister of agriculture, a Communist lawyer, opposed it, defending the status quo ante bellum. Croce's proposal was then rejected by the cabinet. That discussion gave Togliatti the opportunity, years later, to joke with malicious pleasure about "the agrarian interests" and "the philosophy of a southern landlord," that is, Croce himself. "Alas, the good old Don Benedetto ...

who usually dozed in those torrid days in Salerno during the cabinet meetings, instantly became wide awake when agrarian contracts were discussed, proof that, even in his case, the immediate economic interests of group and class took precedence over all other considerations."[12]

Croce was indeed a rural landlord in Southern Italy, and political adversaries with a Marxist inclination could therefore easily claim that his position was nothing more than an expression of class interest. Croce was aware of that possibility; months before, he had written to the editors of a Communist periodical: "I advised my Communist colleagues that it is true that I possess or administer lands that, some twenty years ago, I donated to my daughters, but I am among the provident administrators, who are paid rents in kind and not in money."[13] Despite Croce's disclaimer, Togliatti's anecdote is often repeated to underline Croce's agrarian interests. Hardly anyone has noticed that in the end the same Communist minister of agriculture, Fausto Gullo, went one step further than Croce. As Croce wrote with some amusement, "the funny part is that my modest proposal ... a year later, when I no longer belonged to the cabinet, was adopted by Mr Gullo, who had opposed it before; he increased the rents much more than I proposed, and in some cases made the increase even retroactive!"[14] Under the new proposal the pre-war rents were adjusted to reflect the monetary value of post-war products. As a result, there was no longer any difference between payment in cash or in kind.

Croce also played a role in shaping Italian foreign relations. On his own initiative, sometimes at the request of Badoglio, he had several meetings with the ambassadors of the Allied powers. Having read the secret terms of the Long Armistice, and privy to secret information supplied by Badoglio, Croce could talk to British and American diplomats with knowledge and authority, demanding specific changes. The goal was always the same: to alleviate the harsh conditions of the armistice and to warn the Allied authorities about new dangers. For example, Croce was among the first to voice fear about the present conditions and future status of Trieste and the Istrian peninsula, "which Tito has occupied, and where now he is killing even Italian partisans who happen to be there or are going there."[15]

Badoglio asked Croce to write something about "the hatred that now surrounds Italy in the world and how Italians have to deal with that feeling." In response, Croce wrote a short essay on the subject that he later read at the opening of the Liberal Party congress in Naples at the beginning of June 1944. As on other occasions, he did not direct his remarks only to the Allies; instead, he urged Italians to work hard to repair the damage done by fascism and Mussolini's wars, and to make special efforts to regain the respect of other nations that Italy previously enjoyed. He also advised Italian leaders "to talk frankly to the forces that now hold the destiny of the world" in order "to dispel resentments, suspicions, and vindictive feelings." For their part, the Allies had to avoid "mortifying" Italy because "Europe cannot do without the spiritual force of Italy, its moderation and common sense."[16]

On Badoglio's instructions, the undersecretary of foreign affairs, Renato Prunas, gave Croce a detailed report on the precarious diplomatic position of Italy. "He clarified in all particulars the difficult international condition of Italy, and the painful treatment imposed by the Anglo-Americans, and our efforts to ameliorate the situation, so far without much effect ... especially because of British ill will and their secret political aims." The undersecretary also stressed that the situation was made more difficult "by the lack of understanding, even by the dullness, of the Allied representatives, who, according to terms of the armistice, now are in charge of our affairs."[17]

The Allies' lack of understanding of Italian affairs is often mentioned in Croce's diary, sometimes with amusement, more often with sadness. In his dealings with foreign dignitaries, in high or low positions, Croce usually kept his feelings under control and rarely showed impatience, but he was always direct and forthright. In April 1944 he met two Russian ambassadors, just arrived in Southern Italy, "with whom I talked for about an hour and a half, telling them everything that was important and that they should know." As was their wont, Stalin's emissaries did not reciprocate Croce's openness: "They discussed things in a generic and banal way."[18] Croce was on more solid ground with the new British ambassador, Noel Charles, who, at least on one occasion, "answered my observations with intelligence and a benevolent disposition. He does recognize the grave dangers to which Italy is exposed; he also hopes that the situation will soon improve and Italy will achieve the status of ally." On this point the ambassador did not reflect his government's position. But he was closer to official policy on another topic. The ambassador assured Croce that "Rome would be spared from bombardment," because "the allies had no plans to occupy the city militarily."[19] On that issue, Italian entreaties were not the only considerations for the Great Powers. The Allies had no intention of alienating the Vatican; Roosevelt in particular wanted to avoid antagonizing Catholic voters just before the presidential elections. In a long conversation with Alexander Kirk, the new American ambassador, Croce urged that Rome be spared military occupation. Unlike his hermetic Soviet colleagues, Kirk spoke openly and freely, giving all sorts of assurances. Croce seemed impressed by this unusual candour. But, on this occasion, Sforza was closer to the mark; in a letter to Croce, he observed that Kirk tended to deal in "moralist platitudes."[20]

It is difficult to establish the real effects of these meetings and discussions. They certainly did not do any harm and probably produced some benefit. One can fairly assume that, by echoing the views then being expressed by Macmillan, they had at least an indirect influence on future events. In a memorandum written in May 1944, Macmillan urged Eden and the British Foreign Office to soften their attitude towards Italy. "I have been convinced for some time that England cannot continue with a purely negative policy on Italian affairs. We cannot merely drift along in the hope that something will turn up." He set out two alternatives, either to follow a policy based on "the grievances and emotions of the recent years" or "to consider calmly our own interests and the broader needs of Western civilization." He preferred the latter option. "I strongly feel that we should have a positive policy based upon the desire to rescue the Italian people and help them to preserve their social, economic and religious life, and thus prevent them, perhaps, from falling into the hands of the extreme communist movement on the one hand or the fascist reaction on the other." This was bound to happen, Macmillan concluded, "if the people feel that the liberal government has failed to deliver the goods."[21]

Croce's relations with the monarchy remained strained. Yet, despite his recent criticisms of the king, when the new cabinet met in Ravello for the official swearing-in ceremony, he found the old monarch particularly cordial. During their conversation, "he told me that in the villa … where he was now staying, he had found several books of mine, and was reading especially those of a historical and biographical nature."[22] A few days later, this time at his own villa in Sorrento, Croce had a long and friendly discussion with Prince Umberto. Recently designated to assume royal functions and to succeed his father, the prince was asking the country's political leaders for their opinions and advice. Croce urged Umberto to change his advisers, "choosing men who are in agreement with the democratic parties … and to assume a new political attitude, less passive than before and more attuned to the new and changed times." In his diary, Croce noted that he was "uncertain about the power of intellect, the passion, and political vigour of the prince."[23] This negative assessment explains in part his previous reluctance to accept the prince as his father's successor.

A few days later, Croce's doubts were confirmed. The prince, following the advice of his entourage, gave an interview to *The Times* of London which displayed stark evidence of his lack of political judgment. As Croce reported in his diary, "much scandal has been generated by an interview given to *The Times* by the Prince of Piedmont, in which, among other things, he asserted that Italy declared war on England and France because such a war was wanted by Mussolini, but also because the whole Italian population was in agreement with the decision, so much so that there was no voice of opposition and no one demanded the recall of Parliament." Of course, under the Fascist regime, political disagreement was impossible; there was no free press or a free Parliament. The power to call Parliament into session rested with Mussolini, so Parliament neither debated nor approved a declaration of war. As Croce wrote, according to the Albertine Statute, the power to declare war rested with the Crown, and so only the king could have blocked Mussolini's desire for war. Croce was greatly dismayed by the prince's statements, because, as he put it, "that interview ... can do great harm to Italy." The prince's comments were in fact used by Eden and other British politicians to justify a hard line against Italy. Croce spoke to Badoglio and had the question brought before the full cabinet. There, Croce led the discussion and proposed a motion which rejected "any imputation of responsibility to the Italian people for the Fascist wars." The motion also reminded the prince that "it is not in the democratic and constitutional tradition that members of the Crown make political declarations not previously agreed on with the government in power." Finally, Badoglio was ordered to provide the prince with new advisers.[24]

Croce also tried to repair the damage done in Britain. He turned again to his old friend, Cecil Sprigge, and gave him an interview that was also published by *The Times* and Italian newspapers and then broadcast on radio. In the interview, he rejected the prince's arguments and assertions, noting that, when the war was declared in Italy, there was not general approval, as claimed by the prince, but "a widespread sense of horror ... and national shame." Unlike Churchill, who had blamed Mussolini alone for the war, Croce maintained that "the responsibility for that war falls both on Mussolini and on the king." He did not mince words. "The monarch has violated, or allowed to be violated, the constitution with his hypocritical attitude and justifications ... To throw on the Italian people his own fault and his own mistake is not a worthy thing." The controversy caused Croce great distress: "Old monarchist that I am, I feel pain on seeing the royalists themselves destroying the monarchical idea, and ask myself if this is not the fulfilment of a historical fate." Indeed, since 1922, the Fates and Furies had joined forces to lead the House of Savoy down the road to perdition.[25]

Over the next few years Croce's opinion of the prince appears to have greatly improved. "Having had occasion to see the prince, when he was lieutenant of the realm, for political conversations in 1945 and in the first months of 1946, I noticed his ever-increasing political experience, his ability to ask serious questions, to listen carefully, his feeling of personal responsibility and constitutional correctness. All things that he lacked until then, because he had been kept away from public business ... by his father."[26]

There was a sad epilogue. A few days before the liberation of Rome, and in preparation for the transfer of the royal powers to Umberto, the king sent his minister of the royal household to Croce with two requests. The first concerned the king's strong desire to surrender his duties in Rome and to inaugurate the lieutenancy there. That way, from his point of view, the circle would be complete: he had left the capital as a king and had returned as a king. Croce understood the sentimental value of that request and saw, at this stage, no political reason to deny it. In agreement with Badoglio, he brought the question before the cabinet, and, after a long and heated discussion, his motion was carried, ten to six voting in favour. The king's second request shows the monarch's high regard for Croce, but it also revealed that "the relations between Vittorio Emanuele and Badoglio were less than cordial." To this Croce added, "The king also recommended that I assume the leadership of Italy's government, because he believes that I alone have the qualities necessary for that difficult job ... *Utinam!* – (If only that were true!)" – was his response.[27] When the long-delayed liberation of Rome finally came, the Allied authorities summarily denied the king's request. The proclamation of lieutenancy was issued under duress and amid some confusion in Ravello. Soon afterwards, the king went into exile in Egypt, where he enjoyed the hospitality of King Faruk and where he died a few years later without the presence of his family. A long reign, which had begun with great hopes under the banner of a liberal Italy and reached its apogee in the Great War, ended in bitterness, loneliness, and tragedy.

The third Badoglio cabinet, the first democratic government of the new Italy, did not last long but fulfilled an important function. It ended the division between the Crown and organized political parties, and reunited the North and South, whose division had resulted from the events of September 1943. The new cabinet was recognized by the CLN branches in Rome and Milan. It was supported by all the political parties, by the armed forces, and by the partisans of the Resistance. Last but not least, it was accepted by all the Allied powers. The creation of that government showed that the future political life of Italy rested on compromise and cooperation; there would be a continuity of the state and not a dramatic rupture with the past and its traditions. The future would be one of moderate change, not revolution.

Both Croce and Togliatti praised the role of Badoglio in his latest incarnation as a leader of a democratic government. In May 1944 Croce wrote in his diary: "Relations in the cabinet are good, the discussions are fruitful, and they lead to decisions." A few months later, in a public speech, he added: "Marshal Badoglio chaired the government with fairness and deference towards all the ministers, and on some rare occasions, he even showed a courteous but firm resolve."[28] Twenty years later, Togliatti concurred with Croce's assessment. "My opinion is that, despite the confusions and the difficulties of the time, the Badoglio government, with the participation of all the anti-Fascist parties, had a great influence on the future development of our country."[29] The old fox had charmed even Allied officers, according to Alan Moorehead. "Badoglio was a sympathetic figure in those days, a handsome old man with charm and wit … he talked logically and freely … he had patriarchal dignity."[30]

8
Rome's Liberation

On 4 June 1944 Rome was finally liberated by the US Fifth Army, with a small contingent of the Italian army taking part in the operation. Both the American and Italian soldiers were received with jubilation by the Roman people.

Over the following days, in quick succession, the king retired to private life and Prince Umberto became lieutenant general of the realm; in Salerno, Badoglio, after some hesitation, offered his resignation to the prince and was asked immediately to form a new cabinet that "would include the participation of the political leaders who are now in Rome."[1] The day after, Umberto, Badoglio, Croce, and a group of senior ministers were hurriedly flown to Rome to meet with the leaders of the CLN. Once there, under the supervision of General Mason-MacFarlane of the ACC, both groups met in a small room of a noisy hotel occupied by Allied officers, who paid no attention to the Italians' presence. The place itself was tainted with bad memories; in that hotel and in the same room, Mussolini in 1922 had formed his first government after the March on Rome.

In the Allies' plan, Badoglio's visit to Rome was a mere formality without much importance; no negotiations were envisaged. The meeting between the two delegations was to be brief; Badoglio would offer a small shuffle of his cabinet, replacing and adding a few ministers as he saw fit. Then the new and old ministers would be flown back to Salerno. In Macmillan's words, "a political crisis had to be avoided at all cost" … "Political leaders are to have twenty-four hours to make contact with their colleagues, and form a new cabinet in the essentials."[2] In his opening remarks at the meeting, Mason-MacFarlane was even more precise: the proceedings had to be concluded by 7:00 p.m. that evening.[3]

Croce shared Macmillan's view. Like Macmillan, Croce wanted only small changes in the cabinet to meet the aspirations of "the Romans" and to accommodate the inclusion of major political figures. He hoped that the political leaders in Rome would accept, and even appreciate, the work that their compatriots in Salerno had been able to accomplish, and would propose only minor changes. Aware of the radicalism of the Party of Action's leaders, and fearful of their impatience, he had sent a message to Rome, which was then printed in several newspaper articles, as a warning against unrealistic expectations. The message expressed satisfaction "with the deserved success" against the Germans, pleasure for the liberation of Italy's capital, and pride for "the heroic and stubborn struggle of our patriots" in other parts of Italy. Deep personal feelings were evident as well. "Soon we can share the joy of meeting again; finally, we will be able to talk with you, brothers and friends; and together we shall lament our painful and common losses."

The article's political message was subtle. Croce was telling his Roman friends that in Southern Italy the anti-Fascist politicians "had not remained inactive or idle ... We have taken advantage of the favourable conditions provided by our prior liberation from the Germans." To avoid misunderstanding, he reassured them that they were inspired by common ideals: "We felt it our duty to do what you found impossible, and to work according to your ideas and feelings, which were also ours, as we had come to know." To make his point more cogent, and to dispel "perplexities" or plain ignorance, he listed the achievements of the Badoglio government. "You will therefore find that the difficult and painful question of the king's person has been resolved and a lieutenancy has been created in his place, a development that can be accompanied by further guarantees. You will find a democratic ministry formed by representatives of all the anti-Fascist parties, and made up of people not only from Southern Italy but also from other regions: a cabinet that certainly can be reorganized and improved but that at the moment governs and administers." To prove that the new cabinet was not a monarchical entity and was different from the previous Badoglio administrations, Croce pointed out the concrete actions undertaken by the new ministry, actions that were in accordance with aspirations common to all of the anti-Fascist parties. The government was carrying out "effective military participation of Italy beside the Allied Powers, a rigorous purge of Fascist elements from the civil service and from public life, a reorganization of political institutions, and the establishment of a consultative assembly where the government will explain what it is doing and where it can ask for advice." Croce was aware of the conflicts that could arise once the two groups met in Rome; he suspected that in Rome some politicians would reopen troublesome questions already settled in Salerno. To forestall such debates he called for a rational approach: in the conditions created by the war and the presence of foreign armies, Italians, whether in Salerno or in Rome, faced severe constraints. "But I am sure that when you have learned all the facts, you will recognize that we had no other choice, because politics is done, and is judged, according to the reality as it exists, rather than, as some contend, in accordance with desires and imagination."[4] In other words, there is no place for wishful thinking in politics.

As it turned out, though, Croce's appeals were ignored. Pietro Nenni, the fiery leader of the Socialist Party, expressed the opinion of all the Roman leaders: "A Badoglio government cannot be regarded as an anti-Fascist government." None of the CLN leaders in Rome had forgiven or forgotten Badoglio's long complicity with fascism or his ruinous behaviour after the armistice in September 1943. For those reasons, they had no intention of serving under Badoglio. Nor were they interested in learning the hard facts of the new reality as they existed in Southern Italy. They had lived for months in hiding in Rome, facing daily dangers; once returned to freedom, they were eager to advance their own proposals, and confident of their acceptance. Unaware of, or indifferent to, agreements reached in Salerno, they proposed to Umberto, perhaps with his own prior approval, that a new government be formed under a different leader, the former premier, Ivanoe Bonomi, then president of the CLN.

Once so dramatically chosen, Bonomi proceeded with his usual calmness to appoint a cabinet in which most of the old ministers, apart from Croce and Togliatti, were replaced with politicians of other parties. Admittedly, two of Croce's closest Liberal friends, Alessandro Casati and Marcello Soleri, were appointed to the key posts of minister of war and minister of the treasury respectively, and in the inner cabinet, which acted as an advisory body to the prime minister, the leader of the Christian Democrats, Alcide De Gasperi, replaced the wise but old Giulio Rodinò. Giuseppe Saragat, one of the Socialist Party's rising stars, edged out the lacklustre Socialist Pietro Mancini. Nonetheless, Croce was not pleased. He lamented especially the replacement of Omodeo and Tarchiani by two other Actionists, whom he judged less competent. More fundamentally, he resented the behaviour of "the Romans" and regarded the transfer of power from Badoglio to Bonomi as a mistake;

in his opinion, impatience and ignorance had led to a foolhardy initiative, bound to produce more harm than good.[5] In a sense, he proved prescient. While the equality of the six parties in the new government was reaffirmed, with each party having the same number of representatives in both the inner and full cabinets, in effect the mood changed. Competition replaced cooperation, blocs formed, and divisions along ideological lines increased. The prime minister, rather than leading, was compelled to mediate among competing factions. Muddling through became the order of the day, which suited Bonomi's character.

A few months later, Croce gave a critical assessment of this turn of events:

> The unity among the anti-Fascist parties began to crack and weaken in the second coalition government of June 1944, soon after the liberation of Rome ... It is enough to say that the influential and worthy men who emerged from the catacombs and from hiding were not able to enter into an agreement, as would have been desirable, with those who came from Southern Italy, who had had the luck to breathe the air of freedom for nine months, and who, moreover, had acquired the experience and the practice of the rather new methods of government, made necessary by the terms of the armistice and by the delicate relations with the authorities of the Allied powers. Not only did they not show any desire to examine and to discuss the program agreed on and put into effect by the former government, or to modify it, if necessary, but they did not even ask for any information about it. An impulse of feeling, though generous, prompted them to start from scratch, to begin everything anew again, throwing away even that which did not need to be redone, and which, instead, would have been better to continue building on still.[6]

In May 1945, after the liberation of Northern Italy, while yet another government crisis was looming on the horizon, Croce returned to the developments that had followed the liberation of Rome. In an interview with Reuters, he claimed that mistakes were made at that time which should not be repeated. He urged the new proponents of radicalism to remember that the formation of the Bonomi government "was complicated by preconceptions, and marred by passions and claims which were unfounded and dangerous." He continued:

> Once Rome was liberated, our anti-Fascist friends, who had regained freedom after nine months of hiding, unaware of the difficulties that we had

> met and overcome in Salerno, thought that everything had to be redone anew, and in a radical and quick way. To no avail, I tried to recommend calm and prudence [but] in twenty-four hours they put together a new cabinet, which they proclaimed to be the first Italian democratic government, as if we in Salerno had formed, or allowed to be formed, an aristocratic and reactionary one! The result of their actions was ... the Allies' veto of the new government, which lasted for more than a week, [and] finally the admonition that it was necessary to receive the approval of the Allied powers before the cabinet could take office: approval that we in Salerno did not ask for and were not reminded to seek – thus, our dignity was respected, as I can testify from direct experience since I was the principal agent in the government's creation.[7]

As Croce said, the happiness of "the Romans" was short-lived, for the new cabinet had a rocky start. From London the old lion roared his displeasure, and the life of the new government came to a standstill. As Macmillan put it in his diary: "Churchill was furious that Badoglio had been supplanted" – all the more so since he had learned the news from the morning papers.[8] Soon after, Churchill sent a telegram to Roosevelt protesting the audacity of "a group of hungry and old politicians [who were] ... unrepresentative and without a popular mandate." The outburst was unfair, insulting the reputation of men who had suffered jail or persecution for years and had faced the danger of death or deportation for the last nine months. Churchill's view also contradicted his earlier promise of "no change before Rome"; now he wanted no change before the end of the war and the liberation of Northern Italy, if ever. To protect the status quo, he tried to undo what the Italians had done, and what the Allied officers and General Mason-MacFarlane of the ACC had allowed to happen amid divisions of their own: in Salerno the British supported Badoglio while in Rome the Americans backed Bonomi. Churchill wanted to restore Badoglio to power, and in this effort he was able to enlist the support of an amused Stalin; but he met the opposition of the American president, who already was unhappy with British supremacy in the Mediterranean. Yet, even so, as a result of Churchill's hostility, the Italian government remained in a state of limbo for several days, as Macmillan had to admit: "General [Henry Maitland] Wilson, the Supreme Allied Commander in the Mediterranean, in accordance with the terms of the armistice, was withholding consent to its formal assumption of power until it gave guarantees of cooperation with the Allies."[9] Herbert Matthews of the *New York Times* was more specific: "Churchill was furious. He held up the Allies' approval of the cabinet for eight days, much to the discouragement of the Italians and of those who were anxious to see a genuinely antifascist, liberal government in Italy. The British Prime Minister was afraid that a new set of men would not abide by the very onerous armistice terms, which Badoglio had signed."[10]

Bonomi and his ministers were astounded by the British response. In Croce's words, "surprised by the sudden and unforeseen blow," they reacted in confusion and disarray, showing "neither light nor strength." For the unfortunate situation that had been created, Croce blamed the Italians and the Allies in equal measure. Like Churchill, he was upset "by the quick elimination of Badoglio and by the attitude of extremism that had preceded and followed it." Yet at the same time he resented Churchill's intervention. In contrast to Sforza, who regarded "the little accident as useful" since it had provided a good lesson of realism "to the newcomers," and unlike others who considered the event as insignificant, Croce, "mindful of the Italian reputation at stake," regarded Churchill's response as a national offence. In a private meeting with Bonomi, he advised the new prime minister to act immediately, without waiting for full cabinet approval, "and launch on his own initiative an energetic protest, though couched in diplomatic and respectful language, against the Allied powers, complaining of the incoherent and offensive way in which they behaved, and which showed they were partly to blame."[11]

Croce also wrote a longer letter to the cabinet stating his position on the subject and indicating the proper way to proceed.

> My advice as I have already personally told Bonomi, is that we should not accept with passivity the decision of the Allied powers; rather, we should make a firm and dignified protest, though written in respectful terms, to be presented to General MacFarlane, so he can transmit it to the three Allied governments, from which that act has originated. It is true that by the armistice agreements they can interfere in our affairs; but it is also true, and reasonable to expect, that such actions should be done in a logical way, and not in an incoherent and offensive manner. Moreover, the crisis happened under the supervision of General MacFarlane, who urged us to proceed rapidly and demanded that the new cabinet be moved immediately from Rome to Salerno and that it start its business and be entrusted with the transfer of power at once. To order suddenly that all this be suspended, and that the former cabinet, which has already resigned, resume office temporarily, places the old and the new ministers in a grave and painful situation, but also upsets the feelings of all Italians … I also add that, even if approval

> [of the new cabinet] comes soon, the protest seems to me to be equally necessary and even a matter of duty.[12]

Prodded by Croce, the cabinet debated and approved his suggestions and then Bonomi wrote a letter of protest to the Allied authorities.

But, in the end, the resolution of the crisis was the result of forces more powerful than Italian protests. American intervention and Macmillan's advice persuaded Churchill and the Foreign Office to approve the Bonomi cabinet. It took several days for reason to prevail, as Macmillan had predicted it would. "I think the Prime Minister will climb down, because I don't think there is anything that can be done, nor would be wise to do."[13] Macmillan gave two reasons for accepting the new course. "First, the Bonomi Government is probably an improvement on the Badoglio Government." Second, and much more important, there was no need to strain further Anglo-American relations by unduly antagonizing the United States over the Italian question when weightier military plans were under discussion between the Allies, who had to decide whether to exploit to the full the Italian campaign or send more troops to southern France in support of Operation Overlord.[14] In due time, that advice was accepted, and a diplomatic subterfuge was found to justify the delay. As Macmillan wrote in his diary, "the Foreign Office appear to have adopted my suggestion that the Allied Government should use the Advisory Council as the excuse for the delay and ask for specific statements in writing that all the members of the new Government have seen the obligations entered into by the late Government – short terms, long terms [armistice], etc. – and are prepared to accept them; also a statement in writing that the institutional questions will not be raised without the permission of the Allies."[15] Finally, repeating verbatim Macmillan's advice, on 18 June 1944 General Wilson "authorized the new Government to take office, after complying with the conditions: (i) written statement from Bonomi that he accepts the short and long armistice terms and other engagements of the Italian Government, and that all the members of the Government are acquainted with them and accept them, (ii) that the question of the monarchy will not be raised again without the permission of the Allies."[16]

The solution devised by Macmillan was humiliating for Italy and for the government, but Bonomi and his colleagues had no choice but to comply. It was a very inauspicious beginning for the new cabinet. From the vantage point of international law, not much had changed: what was a discreet understanding between political parties in Salerno became a public imposition in Rome, reaffirming Italy's political status as a defeated nation, subject to limited sovereignty. Croce's comment is sad but appropriate. In Salerno, the Badoglio government "did not have to wait for special approval; its formation and its work were accepted immediately and even praised." But, as Croce adds, evidently with the actions of the Romans in mind, "then we acted with dignity and prudence and with some ability."[17]

At the end of June, the Allies inflicted another humiliation on the Italian government. They demanded the cabinet's acceptance of the publication of the Long Armistice, which at the time, officially at least, was still a secret document. This was a violation of the agreement reached in Malta between Badoglio and Eisenhower. Though he had been dismissed abruptly by the CLN leaders in Rome, Badoglio came out in support of the government, reminding the Allies of their original promise.

Bonomi called a meeting of his senior ministers. The meeting was a mere formality, for he had already come to believe that publication of the Long Armistice was the right thing to do, as Croce reports in his diary: "He was already disposed to comply, to say yes, to make no opposition, and to ask no questions." He was not alone in this position of compliance. "The others agreed with him; using sophistical reasoning and pious illusions, they argued that the publication of the armistice terms would help us, because it would arouse the indignation of the American people, and this would compel the American administration and the Allies to change the conditions of the armistice and to take a new attitude in our favour." For Croce, however, the publication of the armistice terms "would be, at this time, a hostile act, offensive and humiliating to Italy, that will reduce further the authority and the prestige of the present government."[18] But the result was a foregone conclusion. A disappointed Croce wrote: "In the meeting of the ministers without portfolio that took place at my villa in Sorrento, the vote was six against one, that is, I was the only one who proposed to reject the request, and to ask, instead, that the Allied authorities explain the reasons for their demand and for the violation of the agreement made with Badoglio and further to explain the advantages they expected to achieve."[19]

Then still more humiliations were inflicted on the government. Without any apparent reason but vexation, the British again vetoed the appointment of Sforza as minister of foreign affairs. This time even Bonomi felt compelled to protest and to defend Sforza's reputation and loyalty. To add insult to injury, the British also insisted upon the reinstatement in their previous positions of two former ministers who enjoyed their confidence. Once more, Croce voiced his opposition in cabinet. "I tried to make him [Bonomi] understand that should he submit to this request, he would compromise the dignity and the authority of his ministry ... I also pointed out that to accept among us these two new ministers, imposed by the British, from whom they have begged help and support, is shameful and intolerable." All agreed with Croce, but Bonomi, not a fighter by nature, did not press the issue.[20] And so the new government, born with naive confidence, began its life under a reasserted Allied tutelage. Suddenly challenged, or even outsmarted, the British imposed new burdens on the Italians, using and abusing their position of power without fostering either the interests of Italy or their own.[21]

In the new government, Croce was unhappy from the beginning. He had had a bad impression of the new political atmosphere since his arrival in Rome; thereafter, hardly anything pleased him. He was immediately perturbed by the radicalism of some leaders, "especially the foolhardy rashness of thoughtless persons" and "the extremism adopted in certain speeches and acts." He disapproved of the way in which the cabinet was put together. "The composition of the ministry had been an indecent show, taking place among crowds and amid the noise and conversations of hotel rooms, with groups plotting against groups, with [Meuccio] Ruini moving from one group to another, adding or withdrawing names from the ministerial list, and Bonomi completely dominated by him."[22] He did not like the final composition of the cabinet; in his opinion, ministers had been chosen more for partisan reasons than for personal ability. "This way, we have ended up with a ministry inferior to the one we formed in Naples." He did not approve of the removal from office "of men who are useful and very expert." He mentioned the Christian Democrat Rodinò in particular, an old friend. He regretted the replacement of Tarchiani and Omodeo with other members of the Party of Action who did not have the same experience and ability. Judged too moderate by their radical friends in Rome, those two members had been replaced as a punishment for their actions in Naples. It was an improvident and foolish move. As Croce said, "with Omodeo, the Party of the Action ... lost a minister who had the prospect and the temperament to reform and renew the Italian school system, and they have fired him when he had just initiated his work."[23] Above all, Croce was dismayed, even surprised, by the weakness shown by Bonomi in choosing his ministers, in dealing with the other parties, and in reacting to the Allies' impositions. "Bonomi has shown himself to be a very weak man: honest, intelligent, expert in the state's administration, but always ready to yield to the more audacious and to the more arrogant; pro bono pacis, as he often repeats."[24] Croce's opinion was not limited to his diary. In a private meeting with Bonomi, he lamented "his weakness in dealing with the political parties, and his unwillingness to use the power of his position and his office in imposing his own choices."[25]

When the government began to carry out its business, Croce's uneasiness increased. Highly disciplined in all his activities, he could not approve of the way in which Bonomi ran cabinet meetings: the agenda was either not known in advance or was not followed, and as a result "the discussion was chaotic" and lasted too long. Wasting time was always a capital sin for Croce, whether in private or public affairs. In his eyes, Bonomi had another shortcoming too: he did not like to make decisions. "Bonomi does not put the questions discussed to a vote, and then accept the decision of the majority; he wants to reach an agreement at all costs." Sometimes, to reach an agreement, recourse was made to verbal sophistry. This happened when the cabinet discussed the most important decree proposed by the Bonomi government, one providing for the election of the Constituent Assembly and addressing the institutional question. Croce wrote that "about the future Constituent Assembly and the Referendum, which some parties want to precede it, we have adopted a contradictory formula that is subject to a double interpretation." He pointed out that shortcoming to Meuccio Ruini, at the time Bonomi's right-hand man. His reply was rather astonishing, given the importance of the issue: "This way we will leave both contending parties happy."[26]

Despite Croce's criticisms, Bonomi displayed political dexterity in preserving his coalition under competing pressures. The crafty formula he devised for addressing the institutional question, though repellent to Croce's logic, had the merit of being acceptable to the left-wing parties, which demanded that the matter of monarchy versus republic be settled by a majority vote of the Constituent Assembly, and by the moderate parties, which wanted it to be decided directly by the Italian people through a general election. Delaying tactics can be useful, especially in presence of sharp ideological conflicts, as a means to avoid a rupture, to overcome an impasse, and to move forward, in the hope that time will soften differences or lessen the urgency of the issue in dispute. With some luck, this happened in Italy in 1944, when, in the end, both sides agreed to settle the institutional question by referendum, each believing itself to have a better chance of achieving victory.

In the new environment there were many issues that annoyed Croce, compelling him to take a stand in opposition. He had no use for the cabinet's practice of reopening questions that had already been addressed and settled by the Badoglio government. In one cabinet meeting, Bonomi proposed to rewrite the purge decrees enacted by Badoglio in Salerno, hoping to make them more stringent and punitive. The new proposals were indeed more comprehensive, but also more cumbersome, difficult to enforce, and open to abuse. With the support of Togliatti, Croce opposed that move as counter-productive, to put it mildly. "I was enraged, and reminded Bonomi that those decrees had required a great deal of work and discussion, and were examined truly point by point by us, and then received the approval of the Allies; a revision of them now would mean a waste of time and a loss of two months." Instead of drafting a new decree, Croce urged Bonomi to name a new commissioner in charge of the purge, replacing the fired Omodeo, so work could start again in earnest on the implementation of the old law.[27]

Then there was a more mundane, but still important, issue: the price of bread. Once again, as before the advent of fascism, the Italian government had to decide whether to abolish the state-mandated price of bread, kept low for social reasons, which was draining the resources of the treasury and, while pleasing the urban population, was upsetting the farmers, who hoped to gain a higher price in the free market. Croce urged Bonomi, unsuccessfully, to follow the example of Giolitti, who had faced and resolved the same problem in the 1920s, when both of them had been members of the cabinet. With his bold decision to lift controls on the price of bread and let the market decide, Giolitti had restored the national budget and brought a degree of stability to national finances. Bonomi, as usual, dithered, unwilling to face the criticisms of the left-wing parties and the trade unions; instead, he created a committee to study the problem further, hoping, perhaps, for a bumper crop to arrive.[28] Croce's conclusion was severe: "Bonomi gives continual proof of his weakness. His character is now even weaker than in 1922, when fascism was becoming widespread" and Bonomi was prime minister or minister of defence.[29]

In the new cabinet, Croce was the voice of moderation, but sometimes he was more uncompromising than others, especially when issues of public morality were involved. It was Croce, almost alone, who urged the purge commission to take a hard look into the past behaviour of the senators, because "almost all of them were accomplices of fascism, and a few had even been spies in the payroll of the police."[30] On another occasion, the fate of a general with a poor military record was at stake. Instead of a leave of absence and then retirement with full pension, as proposed by Bonomi and supported by others, Croce demanded harsher punishment, because the general had failed to carry out his duty in September 1943 and had passively acquiesced to German demands. "The general had left the units under his command without orders and had allowed his soldiers to be disarmed by the Germans." Because "he had given proof of great irresolution and inability," the general, Croce argued, deserved not a pension but a discharge with dishonour.[31]

On 15 July the Italian government moved from Salerno to Rome. That same day, Croce offered his resignation from the cabinet. The reasons were both personal and political. As he wrote in his resignation letter, once the seat of government was relocated to the capital, frequent travelling from Sorrento or Naples to Rome made it impossible for him to continue in his ministerial position. It was also impossible to transfer his residence to Rome permanently, on account of his "advanced years" and "family conditions" and also because he was "very tired and fatigued."[32] However, in another letter, written soon after the formation of the Bonomi government but not then acted upon in view of the controversy with the Allies, Croce set out different reasons. Here, Croce wrote that "I cannot give the same support to the second democratic cabinet as I gave to the first one, which we formed in Naples." In his mind, the political leaders in Rome "had not appreciated our work in Naples, and in particular my own contributions." There were more profound reasons as well. The prevailing atmosphere inside the cabinet had changed and new attitudes had emerged. In the Badoglio cabinet, Croce enjoyed respect, almost reverence; he had a place of supremacy. His advice was sought and usually accepted and valued. In Rome, power returned fully to political parties, and political action was guided principally by ideological considerations. Party interest became more pronounced, and at times even paramount. Croce still enjoyed great respect, but now he was viewed mainly as the president of the Liberal Party.

Other things had changed too. Croce's political relations with Sforza had deteriorated; their friendship remained, but often they found themselves in disagreement. His new Liberal colleagues did not always share his positions, and sometimes had different perspective on issues or showed more deference to Bonomi. Inside the cabinet, he had a bitter feud with Togliatti, who, in an editorial published in the Communist periodical *Rinascita*, of which he was the founder and editor, had called into question Croce's anti-Fascist credentials and intellectual and moral integrity. On that occasion, Croce probably felt that Bonomi and his other friends and colleagues had not come to his defence in a strong enough fashion, as the unfounded accusations demanded and cabinet solidarity required.

For a variety of reasons, then, Croce felt uncomfortable in the new environment, as he plainly said in his diary. "I do not feel that I can exercise that authority that I enjoyed with Badoglio and also with my other colleagues."[33] On another occasion, when some controversial decisions had been taken, he was even more blunt. "Red with shame for the things seen and heard this morning, I felt some comfort thinking that soon I will no longer validate with my name … this wretched political line that we are following."[34]

At the time of his resignation, Croce was in a sad mood, troubled by the host of serious problems afflicting the country. His sadness was shared by other political leaders of his generation, those raised in the values of the Risorgimento. That era was now coming to an end; new mass parties had emerged or returned to the fore; new political leaders had arrived. The Risorgimento was no longer the inspiration for their policies; they had other points of reference. De Nicola advised Croce to give his resignation letter a political connotation, stressing less the personal motives and more the public issues. "De Nicola," Croce wrote, "understands well the political reasons for my disgust and for my resignation." Both agreed that "the conditions of Italy are very grave. Young leaders have not learned the lessons of the Fascist era, and that era's long duration has caused those of political experience to die or to decay mentally, because they were compelled to inactivity or to resort to empty talk and lamentations concerning the present and the future, their hopes and their fears."[35]

A few days later, he had another painful meeting with Vittorio Emanuele Orlando, the old premier who had guided Italy to victory in 1918. Orlando, too, "recognized that Mussolini had destroyed the entire political class, which had been formed in the previous sixty years of freedom; furthermore, he had broken the tradition of that elite, leaving behind a generation either without education or badly educated." Croce's diary entry about this meeting deserves to be quoted in full, both for the feelings it reveals and for the insight it provides into the outlook of the old Liberal leaders. "The conversation with Orlando yesterday has left a painful echo in my mind. I realize that I love Italy more than ever, and suffer very much in thinking about her fate and her future. We have been defeated and conquered, and this we should never forget. But even the vanquished have a dignity to preserve, and even the vanquished have or need to find means to defend themselves … especially amid the contrasting interests of the world; and it is possible to work in favour of Italy in the middle of those conflicts; even to restrain the hostility, the oppressiveness, and the cupidity of the British; it can be done, but it requires men of steady arm and sharp eye, which is not the case of poor Bonomi."[36] The difficult situation required the genius and the temper of a Cavour; but, given the conflicting pressures and precarious conditions of the times, the most even a Cavour, perhaps, could do was to muddle through the chaos, albeit with dignity and self-respect.[37]

Even after his resignation from cabinet, Croce played an important role in the affairs of the country. He continued to receive a steady stream of visitors from all walks of life, Italians in the majority but also foreigners. He was kept informed about national affairs and international events by political leaders, members of the cabinet, and civil servants. He gave several interviews to Italian newspapers and to Allied war correspondents. He held meetings and had conversations with Allied officers and ambassadors.

His villa in Sorrento remained a centre of political activity, but sometimes it must have resembled a social welfare office. An entry in his diary for September 1944 is revealing in this regard: "Today the usual visits of persons who seek my assistance or interest and whom I try to help as best as I can. But to help them all, I should have a proper office with secretaries and documentation and filing cabinets." A subsequent remark is interesting for the light it sheds on his life under the Fascist regime: "And to think that for a period of twenty years, nobody came to ask for my assistance, as if I were dead: I took advantage of that tranquillity to study and to write. Now, instead, I can hardly do any literary work at all."[38]

Affairs of a different nature demanded his attention also. With a librarian and an archivist, he discussed how to save or to retrieve the books of Naples' national library and the documents of the national archives taken to Northern Italy by Mussolini. Croce was among the first to see the long list of secret documents collected over the years by the police and read by Mussolini with keen interest – and later explored, with great profit, by Renzo De Felice in his monumental biography of the dictator.

The purge proved to be a headache both inside and outside the cabinet. Often Croce saw first-hand the troubles that the purge could cause for certain individuals and their families. He wrote: "I have doubts and fears about the purge, and since January I have advised [the government] to proceed with prudence and generosity."[39] He tried to help a mother of three whose husband had been suddenly jailed for something that he had done twenty years before and that was now of little political or legal significance. An old woman, in dire straits, complained about the firing of her son-in-law from his high school teaching job; according to the purge commission, he was guilty of having been a member of the Fascist Party – at a time when membership in the party was a condition of employment for all. With some indignation, Croce wisely wrote to the minister of education: "It is not our duty to increase the pains and the difficulties of common people."[40]

While the purge was sometimes an excuse for personal revenge, it could also offer an opportunity to repay acts of kindness. After the fall of Mussolini and the end of the war, there were quite a few cases in which anti-Fascists came to the aid of someone who had helped them during the years of the dictatorship. Croce himself did quite a few of these good deeds. Once, at the urging of Mario Vinciguerra, a true anti-Fascist hero, Croce wrote a letter in favour of Mario Missiroli. Missiroli was a famous and brilliant journalist and a man of charm and wide culture but unfortunately also an inveterate turncoat at every change in the political winds. Still, he was not without some redeeming qualities, as Croce recognized. "Despite his penchant for sophistry, which leads him to defend what should not be defended, let alone justified, he is not in reality a bad man, and during the Fascist regime he maintained some dignity and tried to help old friends in difficulty; at the time of Giolitti's death he was the only one who dared to write something worthwhile in favour of the old premier."[41]

The purge could be exploited for political advantage, a temptation hard to resist by individuals with a Jacobin outlook or inquisitorial inclinations. This danger was evident in a case in Naples. Croce's Liberal friends in that city told him about "the horrors that a commissar, sent by the purge committee, is perpetrating in Naples in violation of all the legal norms; he orders arrests and searches against statutory guarantees and contrary to all dispositions of the law; the result is that nobody feels any longer free or secure from being arrested, searched, and put in jail by the police because of the whims of an individual. That commissar is a Communist from Calabria, a very rude and rough fellow but happy to create turmoil and disorder, hoping or dreaming to foster the social conditions favourable to a revolution." Only the direct intervention of the prime minister could stop such dreadful nonsense, and Croce tried that avenue, though without much confidence. "I promised to collect information, and then to write to Bonomi, who is, after all, personally in charge of the so-called purge."[42]

Inside or outside of government, Croce's personal authority remained undiminished, in Italy and abroad. From the United States, Croce received a cordial letter from Albert Einstein, whom he had met in Berlin in 1931. Einstein expressed his pleasure over Croce's involvement in political activity, because "you are among the few ... who enjoys the confidence of all."[43] When in October 1944 Italy sent its first envoys to the United States to discuss economic matters and to negotiate a financial loan, Raffaele Mattioli, the head of the two-man mission, asked Croce for a letter of reference to present to President Roosevelt. With his typical sardonic humour, Mattioli wanted from his old friend "a letter of yours which says that we are two men of good will and common sense, not completely unaware of things of this world (and a little of the other), and also possessing some technical ability."[44] Croce gladly agreed, such was his regard for Mattioli. In his letter, he assured Roosevelt that, "as man of studies and a member of prestigious American learned societies," he could vouch for the reputations of the Italian envoys; "they are among the most respected chief executives of Italian banks ... and as such experts on the questions they are coming to negotiate; even better, they are men of good will and common sense, very learned and very intelligent, with whom the exchange of ideas and the discussions would be mutually beneficial to both parties, and will produce, I am sure, good fruits."[45] The Mattioli mission was successful indeed, not only for the financial agreements it negotiated, but also for breaking the ice between the two countries and for laying the groundwork for better relations in the future, as Roosevelt himself noted in his reply to Croce.[46]

Croce, as president of the Liberal Party, met regularly with the Liberal leaders of Rome, Naples, and other cities. With them he discussed affairs of state but also problems of the party. In those months, a movement was under way to unite the Liberals and Liberal-Democrats; efforts were also being made to launch a Liberal newspaper in Rome and Naples. Both enterprises came to a successful conclusion thanks to Croce's direct intervention. The newspaper in particular was for a few years a very successful operation. Under the direction of Mario Pannunzio, it became one of the liveliest journals of post-war Italy and at times reached a circulation of more than 100,000, larger than that of the Socialist *Avanti!* at 42,000 and of the Communist *L'Unità* at 40,000.[47] Croce was a regular contributor to the newspaper, writing short, pointed articles on a variety of subjects. The paper and its editor soon became famous for engaging in a battle in defence of liberal ideals against authoritarian proposals, whether coming from the right or from the left, from the Vatican or from the Kremlin. The paper also was among the first to denounce the political violence, verbal or physical, sponsored or tolerated by the Communist Party, or undertaken by individual militants of the party in the name of anti-fascism or for personal reasons, a tendency that was especially pronounced in Central Italy and in particular in the so-called Red Triangle of Emilia. With equal persistence, the paper reported the ethnic cleansing perpetrated against the Italian population by Tito's partisans in Dalmatia, Istria, and the city of Trieste.

Sometimes Croce's meetings dealt with social problems of the times. "A delegation of Liberals from Salerno came here to Sorrento, and told me of the bad conditions in that province, where violence and robberies are rather common, and the Fascist mentality still persists, under different names and manners."[48] He heard similar complaints from a bishop of a different city. On this occasion it fell to a lay philosopher to comfort a man of the cloth, an occurrence that happened several times in Croce's life. News of violence and the persistence of Fascist behaviour under different guises and colours are recurrent themes in Croce's diary and in other writings.[49] Not all discussions in Croce's villa were concerned with national problems, however; some had a local flavour. He reported that a delegation of Liberal faithful from Benevento went, or were encouraged to go, to Sorrento with the goal of pleading the case of a favourite son, Raffaele De Caro, whom they recommended for a cabinet post.[50]

On another occasion, Croce met men of a different calibre who were engaged in underground activities in the North. At the end of the year, a delegation of the Committee of National Liberation for Upper Italy (CLNAI) came to Rome to discuss reciprocal assistance, in financial and military matters, between the Allies and the Resistance. The delegation was met with indifference on the part of the government and party leaders and was left to carry out its negotiations with the Allies on its own. But after the negotiations were over, three of the four members of the team, Ferruccio Parri, Alfredo Pizzoni, and Edgardo Sogno, had a long and cordial meeting with Croce in Rome.[51] Afterwards, Croce sent a message in the form of a short essay to the partisans in the North, addressed not only to "Liberal patriots" but "to all of you who are in that part of Italy not yet liberated, and are fighting together for the honour and the liberty of our fatherland even through you are moved by different ideals."[52] Croce viewed the Resistance as an expression of the whole Italian people, even if it had been organized by different political parties. "In that period ... whether Liberals, Catholics, Socialists, or even Communists, we all shared a common feeling: the fundamental need of freedom." Later, when the Communist Party and the Party of Action, for political and partisan reasons, began to emphasize their own contributions to the Resistance and downplay the participation of others, talking about "our martyrs," Croce, closer to historical truth, claimed instead that "those martyrs had died for mankind, not for a party" and "now belonged to the pantheon of the nation."[53] After the war, the memorial tablets that he was asked to write, whether they commemorated common people or party leaders, stressed that same point.[54]

Even when he was out of government, Croce's opinions were sought by Allied correspondents; a visit to Sorrento was an obligatory stop for those who wanted a fair understanding of Italian problems or a quick course on Italian history. During these sessions, unlike in the past, Croce became annoyed or irritated when the interviewer's ignorance of Italy was all too evident. Once, when the correspondent turned out to lack the "most elementary knowledge" of Italian history and politics, Croce, in a sharp tone, told him that "rather than write, it would be more advisable to read" about Italy, and then gave him a list of English authors for that purpose, to which the confident young man paid no attention.[55]

With old acquaintances, Croce was more patient, using these occasions to foster the interests of Italy or to call attention to the problems of the present. In an interview with two American newspapermen, he lamented the contradictions of the Allies' attitude towards Italy. They asked the Italians to increase their war effort, as a condition of improving its standing, but then denied the army the military equipment it needed.[56] In another interview, also with an American reporter, Croce again appealed for a change in the political status of Italy: "Italy has to be given back her dignity." To that end, he called for revision of the armistice terms. He pointed out that the financial arrangements and the economic conditions imposed on Italy were creating inflation, social unrest, and general poverty: "That armistice has weakened Italy and will lead to her ruin." He appealed to the wisdom of the governments and to the generosity of the Allied peoples, asking for a new, more compassionate policy aimed at alleviating the suffering of the Italian people.[57] On the same subject, Croce had a long conversation with Max Salvadori, who was in a position to report his views to higher authorities. Again he lamented "the harmful intrusion of the Allies in the administration of Italian affairs, made on the basis of the armistice terms."[58] As a son of a British mother and an Italian father, and a former Italian citizen and graduate of Italian universities, Salvadori was among the very few British officers truly familiar with the country. Unfortunately, he was convinced that everything he wrote went straight into a wastepaper basket.

Whenever Croce had conversations with Allied diplomats, the aim was always the same: to improve the conditions of Italy and to create goodwill. Usually his interlocutors paid polite attention to his arguments, but sometimes the result could be hilarious. Once he met the British ambassador to talk about foreign affairs and Allied policy towards Italy, "but the conversation with [Noel] Charles failed; he ... jumped from one argument to another, and never stopped even saying things that an ambassador should not say. After moments of surprise, I realized that he was, as often the British and the Americans are, bene potus; in fact, he drank much during and after dinner, but he probably came already drunk from home."[59]

In September 1944 Croce gave a speech in Rome which dealt mainly with foreign policy and Italian relations with the Allied powers. The entire Italian government was present, together with Allied officers and ambassadors. In that speech Croce gave expression to a feeling that remains present in the Italian consciousness today. It concerns the perception that Italians have of the Second World War. "The unspoken point about Italy's relationship with the rest of the world is that Italy, though defeated according to the laws of war, does not feel conquered, and she is not willing to be included among the peoples defeated, but instead affirms her right to be with the victors." It is not difficult to recognize the origin of that feeling. The new leaders of Italy regarded the war not so much as a traditional struggle among nations, waged to conquer territories or to rectify borders, but as a civil war among European peoples fought for contrasting ideals. Almost all the new Italian leaders had been anti-Fascist when Mussolini was admired in Europe and in the world, even by those who now were waging a war against him. Many of them had suffered persecution. Now they saw their sufferings vindicated. With some reason, then, they saw the Allies' victory as also their own. It was natural for them to feel part of the Grand Alliance. They could even claim to have anticipated the success of that alliance with their years of opposition and struggle. The Allies had a different perception, however. Their countries, too, had suffered because of Italian policy. For three years, their soldiers had met Italian soldiers on the field of battle. They had entered the war against Italy not because Italy was a Fascist nation but because Italy had declared war on them, without provocation, at a time when they faced great danger. Now that Italy had been defeated, some thought that it was time for revenge; all found it difficult to distinguish between Fascists and anti-Fascists, or between Mussolini and his successors.

In his speech, Croce answered with clarity a question often raised by the British press and by the political leaders of the Allied nations: "What does Italy want?" For Croce, Italy certainly wanted material assistance, to begin the work of reconstruction, and to alleviate the suffering of its people; Italy also hoped to maintain its territorial integrity. But, most of all, "Italy wants to be recognized as an ally, and to participate in the councils charged with building the new Europe." Equally important was Italy's desire "to abolish soon or to change profoundly the terms of the armistice that harm and weaken the Italian government in all its undertakings." The revision of the armistice was necessary so that Italy could be ruled by Italians, and no longer be subject to rules, or whims, of foreigners, who were often ignorant of the country's present reality or traditions.[60]

The speech was widely reported in the Italian and international press. The *New York Times* described Croce's words as "the expression of every thinking Italian." Sandro Pertini, decades later a president of the republic but in 1944 a Socialist Party leader in Northern Italy, wrote to Croce to confess "my profound emotions during the speech." He praised Croce for his courage and for his ideas, noting, "Yesterday you appeared as a courageous fighter of freedom." He added: "You deserved the gratitude of the fatherland. With the strength of your thought, with the passion of your Italian heart, you have raised Italy from the abyss in which it was thrown by Fascist folly, and have placed her beside the free nations who want to be master of their own destiny. Every Italian should be grateful to you."[61]

During the summer and fall of 1944, the Allied powers' policy towards Italy slowly shifted in a more positive direction under American pressure. In this gradual evolution, Croce's efforts no doubt played a part. His writings, press interviews, and public speeches kept the Italian question alive before national and international public opinion, and offered arguments to columnists and politicians in the Allied nations willing to challenge current policy. The movement for change, and the debates that generated it, are reflected in Macmillan's diaries and also in the advice he tendered to the British cabinet. His position was the result of his observations on the ground, of meetings he had in Italy, and of reports and memoranda he received from Allied and Italian sources all over the country. He pointed out the contradictions of British policy and advocated a different course, more generous and no longer dominated by old grievances or mistrust of new leaders. "We accepted Italy into a position different than that of a beaten enemy, we have invented and, to some extent, benefited from the doctrine of co-belligerency, and, from the larger aspect, prosperity like peace is indivisible." Macmillan reiterated the top priority of Allied policy in Italy: "It is essential that law and order be maintained." But Macmillan, unlike others, was aware of the great issues at the stake: a new policy was needed in order to preserve the fruits of victory, both for Italy and for the Allies. "The problems that face Italy are serious enough … It will need all the patience, courage and devotion that British and American administrators can give if we are to preserve Italy from total collapse to anarchy, revolution and despair. To fail to make the effort because of our grievances against Italy, however justified, would be 'propter vitam vivendi perdere causas' – to have won the war and lost the peace."[62]

9
From Bonomi to Bonomi

The result of a precarious and rushed compromise, the Bonomi cabinet was weak and divided. In its short life, barely five months, the government passed only one significant law, which committed it to calling a Constituent Assembly and to addressing the institutional question at the end of the war. In foreign policy, Bonomi was able to improve relations with the Allies; he had a cordial meeting with Churchill and established regular diplomatic relations with the United Kingdom and the United States. More provinces were returned to Italian control. But, in other respects, the internal situation was still dire. The ACC continued to interfere in Italian political affairs, at both the national and provincial levels, and to print its own paper money, which the Italian government was required to redeem. The cities, the countryside, and roadsides were rife with criminal activity. Social problems remained acute. Transportation was dangerous and unreliable. Food was inadequate, medicine scarce. Inflation was rampant and the black market flourished. In the midst of all of this, the government was plagued by internal dissension. In Salerno a compromise had been achieved between the six parties and the monarchy, and between the Italians and the Allies. Also in Salerno, a truce had been established among the parties themselves, which agreed to serve under Badoglio on a basis of equality. These arrangements involved the postponement until the end of the war not only of the institutional question but also of the reforms of Italy's social and economic structures desired, and often demanded, by the radical parties. In Rome, some parties chafed under those restrictions and tried to regain their freedom of action as if a war was not in progress. Frequent clashes were the result.[1]

In an interview with Reuters, Croce explained the nature and the origin of these divisions and the dangers they posed. In his opinion, there was then a fundamental conflict in Italy as a result of the war and the weakening of the state's authority. "There are among us restless parties in perennial agitation," he said, who "are proposing, with unreasonable hopes, radical changes, which are as vague as they are vast." He pointed out another worrisome development: "Among us a kind of political extremism is becoming common and widespread, united with unconscious tendencies to dictatorship." There was a great deal of impatience in those months, with demands for quick solutions and no respect for the rule of law or due process. But, naturally, there were countervailing forces too. "Among us there are also parties that are mindful of freedom and want to assure the protection of liberty for all, and also want to preserve, until the time when it would be possible to change them, what remains of the lawful institutions and the legal forms of the state."[2] Government was hampered by frequent dissension between these two groups. On major issues, the cabinet was evenly split; on one side were the moderate parties, the Liberals, the Christian Democrats, and Bonomi's own Labour Party, however small in size; on the opposite side were the more radical parties – the Socialists, the Actionists, and the Communists.

The government confronted several troublesome issues. One stemmed from, as Croce put it, "the way the purge and the punishment of fascism was proceeding." This law had just been revised under the leadership of Sforza. But it was still cumbersome and open to abuse. It also gave the Allies a way of interfering in Italian internal affairs, through favouritism or political blackmail. But, above all, the rigid application of the law hindered the functioning of the state. The moderate parties wanted to limit the purge to those who had been in a position of power, those who had been part of the ruling elite, and those who had been guilty of the most serious crimes. The radical parties, and especially the Socialists and Actionists, wanted a broader application of the law. They viewed the purge as a golden opportunity to achieve a moral overhaul of Italian society by removing from positions of influence and power those leading politicians, business leaders, military officers, and highly placed bureaucrats who had played key roles during the Fascist regime. Some went even further: their aim was to punish the bourgeoisie as a class, in conformity with their theory of fascism as an expression of bourgeois self-interest. With that kind of surgical operation, fascism would be cut from its economic roots and would never be able to return, Italy would solve its old structural problems, and the economy would be free from the exploitation of monopolies.

Croce had a different perspective. He feared not the resurgence of fascism but the continuation of the old regime's authoritarian mentality and the spread of Jacobin zeal. The "ethical state," promoted by Gentile and put in place by Mussolini, had collapsed under the destruction of the war and could never be revived. But the fall of fascism was followed by the emergence, or re-emergence, of political parties that wanted to impose from above their world view on others. For Croce, these were the real dangers to Italy's democratic future – not generals, admirals, business tycoons, or deputy ministers of the past regime, who, by professional habit and personal interest, were accustomed to take orders from the political masters of the moment. Writing to Sforza, Croce complained that too much importance was given to the purge of civil servants and military personnel, to the detriment of other issues. "It is necessary to discover their responsibilities, and to punish them with severity." But one had to remember that "in reality they are poor devils, simple employees, fearful of losing the stipends and perks of employment, unable to devise a political program, and to sustain the intellectual effort and the courage that it requires." Sforza, by contrast, was deeply concerned with "a conspiracy of generals." Croce told him that, "by emphasizing too much this point," he was neglecting "all the other very grave and very dangerous problems and misfortunes of Italy that certainly do not depend on the conduct of generals."[3]

Another matter of contention concerned the power and functions of the Committee of National Liberation. For the Liberals and Christian Democrats, the CLN branches were temporary organizations that had to be replaced by traditional organs of the state as soon as military conflict and related emergencies ended. Moderates feared the radical influence of the Communists in these bodies, which might evolve into something resembling local soviets or Jacobin clubs. The left-wing parties instead wanted the committees to continue, and even to extend their activities. In their scheme, the committees had to become the organizing centres of the new democracy, assuring the participation of the masses in the life of the state. In short, "they had to assume the direction of public life," as Croce feared. For the Liberals and the Christian Democrats, this would be an usurpation of the people's will. Only political parties were the true expression of the people, and the legitimate representative of their interests, and political power had to come by free election and popular vote.[4]

Besides these differences, there was also, boiling under them, a legal and constitutional issue that involved the question of legitimacy and sovereignty: whether the source of power rested with the CLN or emanated from the Crown, or from the Crown in cooperation with the six parties that formed the CLN. For Croce, and Togliatti, the issue had been settled already with the formation of the third Badoglio cabinet in Salerno. On that occasion, the CLN's six parties had entered into an agreement with the monarchy and with the Allies to postpone the institutional question until the end of the war. In Southern Italy, the Socialists and Actionists had agreed to that compromise with some reluctance, and after the liberation of Rome their new leaders tended to reopen the issue at every opportunity. The favourite slogan of the Socialist leader, Pietro Nenni, was "all the power to the CLN."

Conflict on these issues reached the breaking point in November 1944, when the commissioner responsible for the purge demanded the dismissal of several admirals and high-ranking civil servants. In response, the cabinet split in two; the three-left wing parties sided with the commissioner, while the three moderate parties opposed the request and were supported by Bonomi. Unable to reach a compromise, the prime minister then resigned. This only exacerbated the disagreements. The Socialists and the Actionists insisted that Bonomi should offer his resignation to the CLN and that the CLN itself should name his successor. This way the primacy of the CLN over the Crown would be established once and for all. In Croce's words, the CLN would become the new state, "taking the place of the existing state, and leaving the latter as an empty shell." Bonomi, instead, presented his resignation to the lieutenant, or the Crown, from whom he had received his mandate in the first place. In so doing, he reaffirmed the compromise of Salerno and indicated that the ultimate source of legality and legitimacy rested with the Crown, or the Crown and the CLN. An important constitutional point was made and the continuity of the state was reaffirmed. As Croce put it succinctly: "The only good result of this crisis was the upholding of the legal foundations of the Italian state."[5]

Months before the crisis came to a head, Bonomi himself had resolved to shuffle his cabinet. At the beginning of July 1944, Croce had learned that "Bonomi ... recognized the weakness of his government and the necessity of a shuffle."[6] During the summer months, Croce and other moderate leaders became deeply concerned about what they called the "deceits" of the Socialist and Communist parties, inside and outside government, and resolved "to take a firm and resolute stand against them."[7]

Bonomi shared the same view, or so it seemed. In September, he assured Croce that "his own program corresponds with my advice and desires." Later, he told Croce of his plan to correct the situation by dismissing "incompetent" ministers and reducing the number of ministers without portfolio. "He has it in mind to speak clearly, at the next meeting, to the Socialist and the Communist ministers and to show them a new determination; he wants to give to his cabinet a better shape, especially now that the liberation of Northern Italy has been postponed; he aims to get rid of incompetent ministers, and finally to reduce the number of ministers without portfolio."[8] According to Croce's diary, during the fall, in private conversation, an agreement was reached between the two of them. Bonomi was to form a new cabinet, supported by all the six parties of the CLN, but he would reserve to himself the right to choose the ministers. Should his proposal fail, he was willing to form a government supported only by the three moderate parties. In either case, to strengthen his future government, he would create an inner cabinet, "with a group of three ministers without portfolio, made up of Croce, De Nicola, and Orlando." For his part, Croce persuaded De Nicola and Orlando to accept this proposal; to assure the success of the operation, he was even willing to rejoin the cabinet himself.[9] Had this solution succeeded, it would have marked the Liberals' return in force to political power. But the negotiations collapsed, in part because of Bonomi's insensitivity to the feelings of De Nicola and Orlando, who were brittle personalities in the best of circumstances.

Bonomi resigned on 25 November 1944; the crisis had lasted two weeks. Subsequently, he was returned to power, but he was supported only by four of the six parties: the three moderate parties plus the Communists. The Socialists and the Actionists remained outside the cabinet. They had been defeated in their attempt to replace Bonomi with a different leader, to move government policy in a more radical direction, and to shift the balance of power from the Crown to the CLN. There were other new developments. The Liberal Party continued to be represented in the cabinet, but it was denied the post of deputy premier that it had held before; there were now two deputy premiers, De Gasperi and Togliatti.[10] Both Croce and the Socialist leader, Nenni, had suffered a disappointment. The reason was the same for each of them: the shrewdness of the Communist Party leader. The final outcome was not without elements of drama. Along the way, there had been expected proposals that never materialized, and sudden withdrawals, broken promises, and personal betrayals, all recounted in Croce's diary, which for this period often reads like the plot of a mystery novel. He frequently expressed his resentment of the constant double-dealing. "So much falsity!" "How many intrigues!"[11] At the end of one day, he confided to his diary: "After four hours spent in these discussions, I returned home dejected and exhausted ... like a donkey well beaten."[12]

In the beginning, the Socialist and the Actionists, forgetful of past events, foolishly proposed Sforza as prime minister and minister of foreign affairs. The idea was immediately dismissed by the ACC and by British Foreign Secretary Anthony Eden, who declared in the House of Commons that "Count Sforza had worked against the Bonomi government and therefore his record is not one to give us confidence."[13] Eden's intervention created a rift in Anglo-American relations, leading the US secretary of state "to administer a public rebuke to His Majesty's Government." In response, Churchill, "much hurt" and "astonished at the acerbity of the State Department's communiqué to the public," felt compelled to raise the matter with Roosevelt. It was one of the most heated exchanges in their secret wartime correspondence. Not only did Churchill not obtain any satisfaction, but he was bluntly reminded by the president, ever ready to clip British hautiness, that "Italy is an area of combined Anglo-American responsibility" and that Eden's "move was made prior to any consultations with us in any quarter, and it is quite contrary to the policy which we have tried to follow in Italy since the Moscow conference of last year." The president left no doubt about the American position: "The composition of the Italian Government was purely an Italian affair."[14] It was left to Croce to defend Sforza's honour, and particularly his anti-Fascist record, before the British public. In an interview with Cecil Sprigge, he advised British politicians "to avoid words ... which cause pain and create a sense of injustice and discomfort in all who had had faith in England, and now wish friendly and peaceful relations among the peoples of Europe, enjoying equal dignity after the atrocities of the war."[15] Sforza himself cut short a quarrel embarrassing to all concerned, withdrawing his name from consideration.

The crisis, and its final outcome, provided still more evidence of Togliatti's political brilliance, to say nothing of opportunism. The negotiations showed anew that the unity pact between the Communists and Socialists was a source of strength for the former and an albatross for the latter. Togliatti invoked the pact when it was useful to his party and ignored it when it was not. He first reaffirmed the Communists' alliance with the Socialists while attacking the Actionists, who were aligned with the Socialists in the crisis. At one point, in a semi-secret meeting, he proposed a new government made up of Christian Democrats, Socialists, and Communists, with Alcide De Gasperi, leader of the Christian Democrats, as prime minister and also minister of the interior, the most important positions in the cabinet. With that move, he revealed his long-term objective, which remained a constant in Communist Party strategy, in all its permutations: an alliance, or a "Historical Compromise," as it was called later, between the Catholic masses and the working class organized by the Communists. With frankness, he told a surprised Croce: "You know that one of our aims is to make an alliance with the Catholics in order to undertake social reforms."[16] But the proposal, in Croce's words, "lasted l'espace d'un matin." Some of the Christian Democrats, then and later, were tempted by the idea of an anti-capitalistic coalition, but De Gasperi rejected it, fearing the dangers it posed. Croce, however, believed that it was the Vatican that wielded the decisive veto, regarding the initiative as something unnatural and even blasphemous.

During the negotiations De Gasperi acted with great circumspection and displayed skill and ability, even craftiness when necessary. He was always deferential to Croce, ready to give reasonable explanations for his actions or changes of direction. But Croce's final comment about him and the Christian Democrats was unequivocal: "De Gasperi was not fully loyal to the Liberal Party ... We worked together in the crisis of November, though we were less than pleased with their [the Christian Democrats'] behaviour during the crisis and especially at the end."[17] In fact, Croce and De Gasperi were pursuing different strategies, one certainly more linear and the other undoubtedly more realistic. De Gasperi wanted to place his party at the centre of the political spectrum, as an indispensable element for any coalition. A formal alliance with only the left-wing parties or the moderate ones would have hindered the achievement of that goal. De Gasperi and the Christian Democrats wanted to curb the influence of the left-wing parties and shared the moderate position of Croce and the Liberals. But De Gasperi, unlike Croce, was not ready or willing, at that stage, to face the united opposition of the three left-wing wing parties. Such opposition would have made it difficult for any government to deal with the social agitation then convulsing the country and, even more worrisome, to control the partisans of Northern Italy at the end of the war.

Given the radicalism of the Socialist Party and the moderate position of Togliatti, De Gasperi and the Christian Democrats found it convenient to accept the presence of Communists in the government. At first the possibility of the Communists' inclusion seemed remote. In fact, for a while the Socialists and Communists marched together, as the unity pact between the two parties demanded, and Togliatti seemed to support fully Nenni's radical demands. But it was only a tactical position, and Croce saw right through it, predicting that the Communists "would break the pact with the Socialists if they see the possibility of a coalition of the three moderate parties and the danger of remaining out of the government. To remain out of power is contrary to their strategy, by order of Stalin it is said; this is also clear because, inside the government and with the help of the government, they are succeeding in achieving a penetration of the state's administration that for now is their main policy, and, it has to be recognized, a very successful one."[18] The prediction proved accurate. When the three moderate parties were ready to form a government by themselves, or at least threatened to do so, Togliatti refused to follow Nenni into the wilderness and eagerly accepted Bonomi's offer to join the new cabinet – to the amazement of Nenni, the Party of Action, and some modern historians.[19]

During the negotiations, Bonomi's behaviour was far from straightforward. At the beginning of the crisis, Bonomi told Croce that he was prepared to form a new government supported only by the three moderate parties. "He gave the assurance of not wanting to fall back to the vicious circle of his first ministry."[20] But in a meeting with Macmillan he enunciated a different policy. "Bonomi spoke quite sensibly. He spoke of his intentions to make some changes in the government; to introduce a sort of inner cabinet … he wants to keep the Socialists and the Communists in the Government at all costs, in order that they may share the burden of responsibility during the difficult winter." He made a good impression on Macmillan. "I think he is quite a good man, with some subtlety and shrewdness, and more firmness perhaps than he is generally credited with."[21] That subtlety was bound to produce some unwelcome surprises for Croce. In the middle of the crisis, Bonomi wrote a clever letter, too clever for his own good perhaps, to De Gasperi, Nenni, and Togliatti, demanding an immediate reply. He explained to them that he wanted the cooperation of their parties and hoped that "at least two of you" would agree to become his deputy premiers, "in order to share with me the responsibility of the government's political direction, as the representatives of the larger movements of the Italian people."[22] Nenni refused Bonomi's invitation outright but De Gasperi and Togliatti accepted. As Croce had foreseen, faced with the possibility of remaining out of government, without any qualms Togliatti broke his party's alliance with the Socialists.

As a result of Bonomi's manoeuvres, the Liberal Party suffered a grievous diminution of influence. Croce was annoyed by the sleight of hand that resulted in the Liberals being shut out of the deputy premiership. In a private conversation with Bonomi, he lamented his lack of candour and broken promises. In his diary, he was even more blunt: "Bonomi is always the same Bonomi, whom I have known and observed in action since 1921; to put together his cabinet he has violated all the agreements undertaken and even the rules of good manners. He is an honest man, but his weakness mars his honesty."[23] Croce also compared Bonomi's past and present political behaviour. When he was in power in the 1920s, he had facilitated – through his frequent vacillations – the victory of fascism. Now, showing the same lack of judgment and energy, he had embraced the Communists, creating another danger to the future of liberal institutions. "So Bonomi, in order to form his cabinet, has facilitated the alliance of the Communists with the Catholics, or at least he has increased their hopes."[24]

Yet, despite Croce's caustic comments about Bonomi, the Liberals ultimately supported his new government, "not because of the man, whose deficiency and weakness we recognize, but for what, in this political moment, he has come to represent." The possibility of social upheaval, or even military intervention, left no other option. Croce's fears were spelled out in his diary: "We cannot allow Italy to enter into a situation that would be, under a different name, neo-fascism – republican, socialistic, and revolutionary but in practice impotent – and that would end with a government of the Allies."[25]

Not all of Croce's judgments about Bonomi's new government were negative. In an interview with a British newspaper, he rebutted criticisms often heard in the Allied press, telling his English audience that "the Italians deserve not blame but rather praise for having, with patience and prudence, solved legally a conflict that in other countries has generated uprisings and armed conflicts." He was even pleased that the government had acquired an opposition; the Socialists and the Actionists could scrutinize government policy and hold ministers accountable. He had kind words for the Socialist leader, Pietro Nenni, "in whose heart I feel the beat of an old Italian democrat and republican, who loves Italy as much as we all do, and is solicitous of our renaissance after so much ruin."[26]

Yet Croce's disappointment remained. After the cabinet had been formed, he wrote a long lamentation in his diary: "I remained awake until the last hours of the night, tormented by the doubt that I did not do all I could to avoid the 'diminutio,' the diminished status of the Liberal

Party. I have decided to write in the morning a letter that explains and narrates the events, and have it published in the Liberal papers."[27] That letter, however, revealed that Croce himself was partly responsible for the outcome of the negotiations: he had not been willing to thwart the formation of a new cabinet, fearing that this might harm the interests both of the Liberal Party and of the country itself.[28] Yet his sense of responsibility, for his party and his country, was only one part of the problem. His diary makes it clear that he did not enjoy negotiations. He was not cut out for the wheeling and dealing of multi-party discussions; he did not have the stamina, or the stomach, for nocturnal meetings and under-the-table scheming. He did not like to waste time in his own undertakings, and resented any waste of energy in long and fruitless talks; he much preferred to seek solutions through discussions and majority votes. He could be discreet during conversations and never betrayed a personal confidence, but in political affairs he tended, by natural inclination, to speak his mind and be direct, avoiding equivocation, and to accept assurances at their face value. In short, he was not a good negotiator for his party. He was firm, even obstinate, on questions of principle or when issues of great import were at stake. But he was not partisan enough when dealing with the more mundane interests of his party. Whatever the problem, he was quite ready to accept a person of another party to deal with it, provided he had the right qualifications. "A party is not a sect or a mafia association … whenever I happen to believe that it would be useful to our country, I will propose and support persons of a different party for offices in which I believe they could do a better job than anybody else. I could not behave differently."[29] These were good intentions, but other leaders and other parties operated more pragmatically, and under different principles.

Finally, there was a logistical difficulty. Croce lived in Naples and Sorrento and the centre of political activity was Rome. As a result, despite the amount of correspondence back and forth between those cities, there were delays in the flow of information and problems of coordination. This intrinsic weakness, along with the Liberal Party's organizational shortcomings, was recognized at the time by Leone Cattani, the party's young and energetic new secretary. In a speech during the summer, he lamented that "our policy, in the CLN first and in the government later, had been inadequate to our historical reputation and to the tradition that we represent … The cause of such deficiency had been the lack of contact between the party and its representatives … The formation of the government, and the agreements reached before and the actions that followed later, happened without efficient and meaningful contact with the organs of the party."[30]

From his involvement in the negotiations for the Bonomi second cabinet, Croce drew important conclusions, all set out in a diary entry. One was that "Italy has an absolute necessity to push forward new leaders in the political arena, men who are neither too young nor too old, because with the old survivors of liberal Italy, it is not possible to create new life."[31] The old leaders, of whom he was one, had passed their prime. In the present crisis they had shown, once again, their shortcomings. "Bonomi is Bonomi," lacking determination and subject to indecision and weakness of character. Sforza tended to act with rashness and without due consideration, living "in a sort of delirium of himself." Orlando was still energetic despite old age "but seems not fully attuned with modern times"; besides, he was surrounded by poor advisers. De Nicola, though "more able than the rest of us," was allergic to "the conflicts of politics." Then there was Croce himself, continually urged to assume a role of leadership, "who has devoted all his life to the study of philosophy and literature, and never entertained the idea of having to govern his country – a role for which, in any case, he lacked qualifications, apart from common sense."[32] In this diary entry he made no mention of Francesco Saverio Nitti, a friend of his youth, with whom he always maintained cordial relations. But there are critical remarks about his political activities elsewhere in the diary. There is no doubt that Croce associated Nitti, too, with the failings of the other old Liberal leaders.

These political figures were men of intelligence and learning, and over the years they had acquired a great deal of political experience and administrative knowledge. But they lacked the basic qualities of leadership and the resolute determination required of the man of action, especially in dangerous times. They belonged to another era, when politics was dominated by members of the elite and personal relations were permeated with deference. In the age of mass parties, inspired by ideology, they were not able, or willing, to accept the discipline of party politics, preferring to retain their independence. They also found it difficult, often impossible, to reach and to maintain agreements among themselves, let alone to play second fiddle to somebody else, especially to one of their own. Before and after the advent of Mussolini, their vacillations were fatal to the Italian parliamentary system, and even to liberalism itself. After the Second World War, their divisions and irresolution accelerated the demise of the Liberal Party as a leading political force.

Years ago, Arnaldo Ciani offered an astute analysis of the Liberal Party's weakness after the war. The party did not have a solid organization covering the whole country and remained a movement of the elite centred in the cities. The party also did not have a well-defined economic program; its proposals sounded abstract and conservative, seemed far removed from the social needs of the time, and had little resonance with the common people. The old stalwarts of the Giolittian era had serious limitations: their culture was aristocratic, lacked the common touch, and ignored the techniques of political propaganda and mass communication so important in the modern era. They were skilled parliamentarians, displaying great flair and eloquence, but were not able or willing to fight their battles in the public domain. As for the new generation, they, too, did not possess the tough qualities and the driving ambition necessary to lead a modern party; they also lacked an understanding of the aspirations of the masses. For all these reasons, the party never produced a popular leader, let alone a charismatic one, able to command wide appeal among the general population, or even the rank and file. The Liberal Party had in Croce only a prophet. To be sure, he commanded intellectual authority, showed common sense, and was able to offer good ideas, but these attributes proved unequal to the task of creating a mass political party.[33]

After the crisis was over, before he left Rome and returned to Sorrento, Croce had a last meeting with the lieutenant. In the course of their conversation, "I pointed out to him the mistakes of Bonomi and the weakness of his cabinet, so he could be aware and … be ready in the future for another occasion [of this kind] … In case of another government crisis, Bonomi should not be given the task of forming a new cabinet again. But there should be another leader able to take over on short notice, Orlando for instance … or, if one is ready to take such a grave step, De Gasperi of the Catholic party."[34] Those last few words show the persistent animosity, even the mistrust, between the old Liberals, belonging to the Risorgimento tradition, and the modern leaders of the Christian Democrats. It took a while, for some much longer than for others, to forget the wounds of the past and find common ground in the face of new challenges and dangers.

Early on, despite his misgivings about Catholic politicians, Croce had detected in De Gasperi a "serious man" capable of assuming the leadership of the moderate forces and uniting them in defence of freedom and in pursuit of social progress. During the Fascist regime, Croce had met De Gasperi for secret talks, in the Vatican library, where he was employed as a simple clerk and where he kept in touch with many anti-Fascist politicians and promising young men, the future prime minister Giulio

Andreotti among them. Later, Croce came to admire De Gasperi's political realism and moderation, and he was not alone in this regard. The Roosevelt administration also was receiving favourable reports on De Gasperi. Myron Taylor, Roosevelt's special envoy to the Vatican during the war, had been told during confidential conversations with the pope and his top officials that "De Gasperi was an intelligent man ... learned, serious, active, and even fair-minded."[35] No other Italian politician could claim such credentials before American authorities. A year later, after a short meeting in Milan, Leo Valiani came to the same conclusion about De Gasperi. He saw a new leader "with a strong sense of the state" who was "destined to lead the country for the next five years."[36]

As minister of foreign affairs in the new cabinet, De Gasperi had regular meetings with Allied authorities and soon acquired their trust and confidence. He became the Allies' point of reference in Italian affairs, and a mutual affinity of interests and outlook began to take shape, more with the Americans, admittedly, than with the British. A man of great personal integrity, in private and public life, possessing strong political beliefs and a deep religious faith, De Gasperi was also endowed with clarity of vision, determination of purpose, and a strong attachment to liberty and democratic institutions.[37] But, unlike Liberal leaders, he was also the leader of a mass party, the Christian Democrats, who had a national organization with offices in every city and town of the country, in the North and in the South, among the peasants, the workers, and the middle class. Eighty years after the papal denunciation of the errors of liberalism in its famous "Syllabus," it was the Christian Democrats, not the Liberals, who were going to be entrusted with the protection of the Risorgimento heritage, or what remained of it after fascism. A Liberal could not feel too many qualms over that – only, perhaps, some regrets.

10
The Northern Wind

In Northern Italy, on 25 April 1945, the forces of the Resistance mounted a general insurrection against the German occupation. Many of the major cities, even entire regions, were liberated by Italian partisans, and the CLNAI assumed the functions of government. Then, in May, the war finally came to an end, leaving ruin and desolation but also hopes for a new beginning, captured in the term "Il vento del Nord." Croce himself was swept up in this general feeling. On 26 April he wrote in his diary: "In the afternoon, great relief for the rapid liberation of Northern Italy from the Germans by the action of the partisans and the patriots, and without the threatened and feared destruction. This is a great benefit for Italy, and important also for moral reasons. There are days when the heart swells and beats faster, but the mind becomes thoughtful for the great work that lies ahead, for all of us."[1]

Yet there were also grounds for concern. The number of partisans had hugely increased in the last months of the war, and after the end of hostilities many of them – Communists and Christian Democrats alike – refused to surrender their arms to the Italian or Allied authorities as required by previous agreements. Violence became widespread in the cities and in the countryside; often, bands of armed men robbed the defenceless or took the law into their own hands for different reasons, pursuing private vendettas or political agendas. There were times when moderates feared the advent of a Jacobin democracy or a Soviet revolution, whether by accident or by design. Like others of his background, Croce was apprehensive about the future, and he repeatedly expressed his fears in his diary. In September 1945 he wrote: "In the evening I had a conversation with Tamagna, a friend of Max Ascoli, who has just returned from a sort of inquiry in Northern Italy. He told me that there the political parties can hardly keep their own members under control, because among the population there is a great clash and almost the beginning of a civil war between those who belong to the extreme right and those who have joined the extreme left, both unconsciously nostalgic or even eager for a new fascism, either for the heritage of the old regime or for the situation of the 1920–1922 period."[2]

That summer, worried by the political chaos and the prevailing atmosphere of violence, Leone Cattani, the secretary of the Liberal Party, wrote to the other parties. He complained that in many places freedom of expression was denied to members of the moderate parties; he also pointed out that great quantities of arms were being hidden for political reasons and that violence and intimidation were often used against political opponents "who are not Fascist."[3] Croce, for his part, kept stressing the value of freedom. In a message to the Liberal partisans of Northern Italy, a few weeks before the liberation, he pointed out the ongoing threats to freedom, the first stemming from "the indifference of the many." He added, "Against freedom all over the world there are, in open opposition or waiting in devious ambush, forces that want to destroy it, or to replace it with a different dictatorship but substantially the same as the one we have known."[4] In a speech in Florence in June, Croce called attention "to the danger of the hour." He defended the principle of freedom "as an ideal that belongs to all" and as "a fundamental good, superior to any other." This ideal needed to be protected, especially against those who wanted to instal a so-called true democracy and harboured "intentions of violence, oppression and even dictatorship" in order to achieve that goal.[5] This was a direct reference to the Communist Party.

Many moderates feared a possible uprising by the Communists, supported by the partisan formations under their control. Croce sought reassurances from the Allies should that happen. In a meeting in March, he asked Macmillan if, "in case the Russians should support their agents in Italy, England would give us her support in our struggle to avoid a totalitarian regime, that is, a new tyranny under a different name." Macmillan did not answer directly but, befitting a diplomat and a politician, sounded sympathetic and understanding. His noncommittal reply, however, clearly reveals that the division of Europe into two parts had already taken place. "He told me that Stalin was not a Communist but a practical man, and he will keep his promise; though he has had a free hand in Bulgaria and Romania, he has allowed England to do what needed to be done in Greece, without any intervention, even in an indirect way."[6] Macmillan reported the same meeting in more casual terms, leaving aside the political situation in Eastern Europe and the Balkans. "Now very old and talkative, but with a great deal of wit and mischievous humour ... Croce was very amusing after luncheon in his chaff of the Communists and their philosophy."[7] In June, Croce had a meeting with Noel Charles, the British ambassador, who was less guarded. "He ... was very cordial with me, even deferential. We discussed various arguments, and talked also about the present crisis. He told me that the British do not intend to withdraw their troops from Italy, and hope that the Americans (though they are very eager to return to America) will not withdraw theirs either, until after the elections, in order to assure a free vote. Public order will be kept by the Italian police and the Carabinieri, but for good measure the Allies will be there too."[8]

Soon after the liberation of Northern Italy, calls for a new political course increased in Milan and found a strong champion in Rome. At the beginning of May, Pietro Nenni, the leader of the Socialist Party, put forward his name as the next prime minister and demanded the creation of a new government with a different program, more dynamic than that of Bonomi and more in tune with the public's aspirations. A few days later a CLNAI delegation from Milan, which had led the insurrection in Northern Italy, arrived in Rome and demanded the formation of a new cabinet, supported by all six parties of the CLN. The Northern leaders proposed a radical program, reasonable in some parts but clearly inspired by the left-wing parties, that, if implemented, would have changed profoundly the structure of Italian society, and that ignored previous agreements with the Allies and was bound to prompt their intervention in Italian political affairs.[9]

Even Croce recognized that, after the liberation of the North and the reunification of Italy, the formation of a new cabinet "was not only necessary but beneficial." "After twenty months of separation between the two parts of Italy," it was necessary to bridge "the different experiences and the different work done, the different thoughts and hopes entertained."[10] In Croce's mind, the formation of a new cabinet should be the occasion for South and North to find common ground. It was essential that the political negotiations should not be "complicated and troubled by preconceptions, by preconceived ideas, by passions, and by unfounded and dangerous demands." Once again, as after the liberation of Rome, his was the voice of moderation. Croce was in favour of some adjustments, but he did not want a completely new program, as if everything done in the past had been wrong or useless. Above all, he did not wish to repeat the mistakes made after the liberation of Rome, when "our anti-Fascist friends, who came out after nine months of hiding, unaware of the difficulties encountered and overcome by us [in Salerno], thought that everything had to be redone completely, and in twenty-four hours formed a new cabinet, despite my advice for prudence and calm." The result, as we have seen, was that the Bonomi cabinet was initially vetoed by Churchill and then, after that obstacle had been overcome, it had to suffer the humiliation of waiting a considerable time for the Allies' approval.[11]

There were other points of divergence between the two camps. While the Northern leaders demanded radical reforms and proposed a new government of national unity but clearly under the leadership of the left-wing parties, Croce believed that the next cabinet should be supported by all six parties of the CLN but not lean left or right until the next general elections determined the composition of the future Parliament. The government, before those elections were held, should maintain the equality of the six parties, continue to require unanimity for all decisions, and follow the same program as before, albeit with some adjustments. In making this case, Croce was calling attention to an important point, often forgotten then and later. In the absence of a regular Parliament, the government had the right to pass decrees that had the force of law. In this way, a group of parties, without the consent of the population, could impose a social and political revolution on the country, which could then be presented to the next Parliament as a done deal. For that reason, Croce opposed radical reforms; instead, he felt the new government should concentrate its efforts on those problems that demanded immediate attention, fell clearly within its jurisdiction, and did not require the agreement of the Allies. Specifically, it should "restore order to the administrative functioning of the state, increase the supply of food, assure public safety ... continue and bring to an end the purge of Fascist elements, and, finally, prepare the electoral law for the elections of the Constituent Assembly, in cooperation with the Consulta ... that had been promised for a long time and only recently instituted."[12]

Croce's position was pragmatic and realistic given the constraints imposed by the Allied occupation and by the terms of the armistice. The Allied armies still maintained control of Northern and Central Italy; only at the end of the year were those regions returned to direct Italian administration. The approval of the ACC was required for any political change or economic reform. Furthermore, the agreement signed between the Allies and the CLNAI in December 1944 demanded the disarmament and the disbandment of all partisan groups soon after the liberation and the end of the war. The head of the ACC reminded Italian politicians that the existing political arrangements had to be respected by all until the next general elections. For good measure, he also made clear that the ministers of military departments needed the commission's approval before they could assume their functions. Finally, Italian political leaders were told that they required the permission of Allied authorities to travel to Northern Italy, and that they had to promise to make no political speeches once there. Nenni, a born orator who was never one to shun a microphone or a platform in the presence of a crowd, was not able to respect that rule; at the end of his first public speech in the North, he was promptly arrested and jailed, his short imprisonment coming to an end once he apologized. Thereafter, for the rest of his trip, he made no more public speeches.[13] Togliatti, more prudent, did not fall into the same trap. Before a crowd of faithful, he simply claimed that sometimes silence can be more eloquent than speech-making.

On 12 May 1945 Bonomi resigned as prime minister, and Prince Umberto, as lieutenant of the realm, began the political consultations necessary for the formation of a new government. These negotiations, accompanied by the usual manoeuvring, lasted for more than six weeks, generating criticism and disappointment. The task was difficult. Any new cabinet had to enjoy the Allies' approval and the support of the six parties, and it had to be capable of assuring law and order and at the same time of channelling the high hopes created by the liberation of the North. The stakes were high indeed. The man chosen to lead the new government would acquire considerable prestige, which would likely translate into political success for his party at the next general election. Initially, the choice was between Pietro Nenni, the leader of the Socialist Party, and Alcide De Gasperi, the head of the Christian Democrats. Both claimed, with good reason, to enjoy the support of the population. For a while, Orlando seemed to have a fair chance as a compromise candidate, one able to reconcile the different positions and to assure the unity of all parties. After long negotiations, and some posturing, another candidate was proposed by the CLNAI. A veteran of the Great War, Ferruccio Parri had been one of the main organizers of the Resistance in Northern Italy, and he was by far its most popular leader, known to all as "Maurizio." He was now a member of the Party of Action but enjoyed general admiration, even affection, among the partisan groups and the general public for his personal integrity and courage; he seemed to embody the hopes and ideals that had inspired the Resistance. Few noticed that he had no political experience or administrative expertise.[14]

Once in Rome, Parri, to acquire "a clear vision of the situation before accepting the premiership," had meetings with all the party leaders. He had also a cordial conversation with Croce, during which the latter "spoke frankly, telling him the truth, without turning to cunning devices or subterfuges." Croce set out the differences among the various parties and the issues in dispute. "I gave an account of what had happened in the last two weeks, and told him the reasons for the suggestion of Orlando as premier." Then he came to the crux of the matter. "I explained that the crisis above all else revolves around this point: Socialists, Communists, and the so-called Party of Action want to control, surreptitiously, through the premier's office, the ministry of the interior and the preparation of the electoral law for the Constituent Assembly, in order to be in a position to overwhelm the other parties at the polls and then to realize or impose a republic of a Communist or Socialist nature. The other parties want to avoid this, and for that reason the Liberals ask to have the ministry of the interior for themselves, because the Liberal Party, more than the other parties, can protect the democratic rights of all." During their conversation, Parri's arguments produced a good impression on Croce; the two men shared the same goals and recognized especially the importance of forming a government soon for national and international reasons. Talking afterwards to his friends, Croce had kind words for Parri: "I believe that he is a conscientious man, not at all ambitious, or weak or easily influenced and swayed." Later that year, in a private conversation with a mutual friend, Croce confessed, "I have the greatest respect for Parri, as a hero and as one of the purest men … for his years of opposition to the Fascist regime and for his untiring effort in organizing the partisan struggle."[15]

At this time Croce was no longer a member of the cabinet but, as president of the Liberal Party, still exerted considerable influence. His diary is one of the best sources on the changing positions of the various parties, the ideas of the different leaders, and their shifting alliances. It also sheds light on Croce's political views and objectives. During the negotiations, Croce and the Liberal Party tenaciously pursued a few aims above all. They wanted to restore public safety and avoid radical measures. They also wished to reduce the powers of the CLN branches and, in their place, to accelerate the return of the normal organs of the state. Croce in particular stressed the equality of the six parties, inside the committee and the government, and condemned any attempt to create a bloc of parties with supreme power, let alone a government dominated by a single party.

Contrary to conventional wisdom, Croce was then well disposed towards the Socialists and in favour of an alliance between them and the Liberals. He had friendly meetings with the various leaders of the Socialist Party, including Rodolfo Morandi, Sandro Pertini, Giuseppe Romita, Ignazio Silone, and, especially, Giuseppe Saragat, the future leader of Social Democrats. Croce wrote that Saragat "was in full agreement with me on a future collaboration between liberalism, the pure liberalism open to all reforms ... and socialism, [which] ... rejects all dictatorial aspirations and ... undertakes once again a separation from communism, from which, in the course of its history, it already has been separated several times."[16]

In a meeting of the Liberal Party executive, Croce stated that "the Liberals should lean towards a collaboration with the Socialists, rather than with the Catholics or Christian Democrats, who are more distant from us than the Socialists; besides, they are untrustworthy allies, as they showed during the last crisis."[17] Later, he made his differences with De Gasperi clear. De Gasperi "was resolute, even violent against a Nenni premiership" and proposed instead that he himself assume that position. "I have been reserved but let him understand that we Liberals see Nenni's candidacy in a different light."[18]

At the beginning of June, Croce "had a long and friendly conversation" with Nenni in Naples. During that meeting, besides discussing the political problems of the moment, Croce indulged in historical and philosophical considerations, as was his habit on such occasions. "In summary, I told him this: as a general premise, not only do we not have anything against it, but we would welcome a form of collaboration with socialism. In this collaboration, the Liberal Party would demand the observance of liberal methods as an absolute condition, but it would be open to socialistic requests, and would put them into practice in a gradual way, and in a manner consonant with civil progress." Croce then touched on the history and relations of the two movements. "The affinity between liberalism and socialism was established by their common origin in modern thought; their division in the past was caused by materialistic and dictatorial Marxism, and in the present by Russian pseudocommunism." He noted that "speaking personally, I do not believe that the Liberal Party would oppose in principle a Socialist premiership." He then listed the three difficulties that stood in the way of Nenni's personal and political ambitions and that made a collaboration with the moderate parties difficult. First, there was the probable opposition of the Allies, and in particular the British, to a new cabinet led by a leader of the Socialist Party. The second difficulty was the personality of Nenni himself, with his penchant for fiery oratory and radical slogans, or as Croce put it, "his polemical violence and extremism, which frightens many people when they hear his name." Finally, the greatest obstacle to a collaboration between socialism and liberalism was the pact that then existed between the Socialist and Communist parties, which Nenni was not willing to break, or even to ignore, as Togliatti had done recently, when it was convenient to do so in the interests of his party. That pact created uneasiness among the moderate forces, and their apprehensions were increased by the rapid growth of the Communist Party.

In that meeting Croce stressed again that there was a fundamental difference between socialism and communism. "The two movements are by their nature different and antagonistic, and one will have to absorb or eliminate the other, as is shown by events from 1900 to this day. But which of the two will prevail? Communism, ideologically and morally inferior to socialism, now has in its favour the support of victorious Russia and widespread 'arrivismo' or unscrupulous ambition, which threatens Italy with a new fascism; also, it fascinates people with the myth of equality and happiness on earth, and for that reason it is politically very strong and greatly dangerous; it could undertake a coup d'état, which, once effected, would be very difficult to undo."[19] Croce's musings reveal that "the Communist Question," which has tormented the life of the republic, was already taking shape and throwing a dark shadow over Italian politics.

To Croce's arguments, Nenni offered his own. He was confident that "in the present union between socialism and communism, the first would prevail over the second." He promised to tone down his oratory and use more temperate language in his speeches. Lastly, he was certain that "the British democrats," meaning the Labour Party, would not oppose a Socialist premier in Italy.[20] None of these claims would prove to be true. But, for a while at least, Nenni tried to follow one piece of Croce's advice. According to Liberal Party secretary Leone Cattani, during the negotiations for a new government, Nenni, to improve his chances, suddenly showed "a new sweetness" and "tried to build bridges in all directions" Unlike Togliatti, who equivocated on the matter, he defended Italian sovereignty over Trieste, then claimed by Tito with the support of the Soviet Union. He was ready to accept the Liberal demand that the political prefects appointed by the CLNAI be gradually replaced by state officials. He wanted to solve the institutional question by a popular vote and not by a revolution. And he had no intention of touching, let alone abolishing, the Concordat between Italy and the Vatican, negotiated by Mussolini in 1929.[21] But Nenni did not make the concession that Liberals most wanted: he was unwilling to turn his back on his alliance with the Communist Party. Without that initiative, Nenni lost an opportunity to place the Socialist Party at the centre of the political system. In the judgment of Leo Valiani, Nenni failed to realize that a great deal of the Socialists' popularity after the war stemmed from the belief that they, much more than other parties, could assure social progress, political freedom, and law and order at the same time.[22]

During the negotiations for a new cabinet, Croce made a decision with momentous consequences. On other occasions, as we have seen, Croce had refused to become premier himself; this time, he twice rejected the possibility that a leader of the Liberal Party become the next head of government. With that decision, the Liberal Party left the leadership of national affairs to its rivals, sealing its future as a small party.

The reasons given by Croce for this decision are interesting but unconvincing. He refused to take into consideration an idea that Valiani recognized as realistic, had the Liberals not made several mistakes or been less frightened by Jacobin terminology, or, one may add, had Croce been more politically audacious and more confident in the abilities of Liberal leaders.[23] Valiani thought that Niccolò Carandini and Manlio Brosio were possible Liberal candidates for the premiership. Croce did not mention either man in his account of the negotiations, though one can imagine his reservations. Elsewhere in his diary he offered praise for but also expressions of disappointment with Carandini and Brosio.

At one point, during a meeting of the full CLN, the Socialist and the Communist representatives proposed a new cabinet under the leadership of a member of the Liberal Party, supported by their parties but without the participation of their own top leaders, Nenni and Togliatti. Croce's fear in this case was that, unencumbered by official responsibility, Nenni and Togliatti would be free to lead social agitation in the country, thus undermining the government's authority. "For my part, by instinct, I have always refused the offers of Nenni and others to give the premiership to a man of the Liberal Party, and now the reasons for my refusal appear clear to me." "In short, they want a weak government, in order to dominate it until the elections and to overcome it through the elections, and then to establish, according to the occasion, either a Jacobin social republic or a bolshevism of commissars in the Russian manner."[24] A few days later, another possibility appeared. Some members of the Liberal Party executive proposed Marcello Soleri, the present and future minister of the treasury, and a former Giolitti minister in the 1920s, as prime minister. Croce's comment in response is typical of a man afraid of receiving a poisonous gift. "About this proposal I am perplexed, and regard it as worrisome and dangerous for Italy, for our party, and for … the liberal future of Italy; my perplexity arises from the old saying 'I fear the Greeks even when they bring gifts,' because this idea is not fully our own but was first proposed to me by the Socialists and by the Communists."[25] The explanation is unpersuasive – unless, of course, Croce had doubts about the suitability of Soleri for such an onerous job. No longer in his prime, the old Liberal stalwart was then in poor health, and in fact he was to die a few months later, his loss lamented by all.

Croce's position was likely rooted in his apprehensions about the Communist movement and its leader. In his meetings with Togliatti, the conversations remained cold, formal, and lacking in trust. Both men knew that they had little in common and were drawn together only by the exigencies of the moment.[26] Croce's distrust of communism and Communist leaders surfaced even in a meeting with Giorgio Amendola, then a rising star in the Communist Party and the son of an old friend of Croce, the Liberal leader Giovanni Amendola. "In the evening, Giorgio Amendola came for a visit; he was very affectionate and full of memories of the times when he used to frequent our house. He also spoke with wisdom, showing common sense and political moderation. But I am never sure of a Communist's sincerity, though this time I had a great desire to believe in it."[27]

Croce was not without doubts concerning the wisdom of his political decisions. "We need to await the future developments; but I wonder if, at a certain point, following the decision of the party's majority, it would not be more convenient that I stand aside, leaving the responsibility to men younger than I am, who may have the political sense and boldness that I am lacking. I went to bed very tired; I slept very soundly at first, but I woke up too early and then remained awake for the rest of the night."[28] Changes were occurring in Croce's life. He still enjoyed good health and his mind was as sharp as ever, but age was catching up with him. Herbert Matthews of the *New York Times*, before returning to the United States, paid a visit to Croce in Naples in 1945. He saw a very different Croce than the one he had met in Capri a few months before. "This was an old, tired and unhappy man … He felt profoundly that this was no longer his world, and that work was his only consolation."[29] More than political activity, always regarded as a momentary and painful necessity, work for Croce meant thinking, reading, and writing. That was his true world, where he found peace and consolation. Politics was something different, done out of a sense of duty but without enthusiasm.

After long negotiations, Parri was chosen as the new prime minister on 21 June 1945. The Northern leaders had succeeded in imposing one of their own as leader of the new government. De Gasperi, Nenni, and Togliatti agreed to serve in the new cabinet, in which they held positions of great responsibility. The Liberals were satisfied with the government program. Parri accepted their position on the need to limit the powers of CLN branches, and other bones of contention were addressed satisfactorily or patched over for the time being. More than a permanent solution, the new cabinet was a temporary compromise among the big parties. Many had come to the conclusion that Parri was the best man to channel the passions created by the Resistance and to avoid a clash between Rome and Milan. Despite obvious setbacks, the Liberals could claim some success. As Croce wrote, "in the present conditions, the Liberal Party has obtained all it wished for in order to defend … the good of Italy."[30] At least, the Liberals had avoided the "shift to the left" that Northern leaders and radical parties were demanding. Moreover, the Liberal Party could take satisfaction in the fact that, not only was the equality of the six parties inside the cabinet reaffirmed, but it held significant positions in the new government. Marcello Soleri was reappointed to the treasury, Vincenzo Arangio Ruiz was named minister of education, and Manlio Brosio became deputy premier and also deputy to Parri in the all-important post of minister of the interior, responsible for maintaining law and order.

Croce's account in his diary of the events leading to this outcome helps to explain why the new government had such a short life. Parri was accepted as prime minister because no one dared to oppose the Northerners but also because, as Croce writes, "the moral authority of Parri and his prestige did not permit opposition, though there were doubts about his lack of experience in government and administrative affairs."[31] In particular, "the Socialists and the Communists … applauded and accepted Parri's candidacy … out of reverence for his person and respect for the Northern demands, not because they really wanted him, given his lack of government experience." Croce also noted that the two left-wing parties had the same long-term goal regarding Parri. "There is no doubt that the Socialists and the Communists wanted to undermine him, using for their own purposes the open opposition of the Liberals, or the hidden reservations of the Christian Democrats." In the end, Croce had the clear impression that the big parties, for different reasons, hoped that

Parri would fail. "It is natural that they did not want the solution of the crisis to increase the prestige of the Party of Action."[32] These comments foreshadowed the demise of Parri and the future troubles of the Party of Action; hard pressed by the mass parties, Parri's cabinet and his party, full of noble intentions, ultimately collapsed under their own contradictions, leaving behind long-lasting recriminations and deep regrets.

During this time, Croce was involved in two polemical disputes, both concerning the heritage of the Risorgimento and the traditions of liberal Italy. In one instance, the selection of the minister of education gave rise again to a bitter quarrel between Croce and the Christian Democrats. During the negotiations, De Gasperi's party demanded that position for itself; Croce immediately and forcefully expressed his opposition. His stand almost spelled the end of Parri's ambitions. At first, the other parties supported Croce and rejected the Christian Democrats' "arrogant demand and offensive tone." But in the end, to prevent the negotiations from collapsing, the same parties announced their readiness to accept the Christian Democrats' request. Left alone, Croce stood his ground with stubborn resolution, as he always did when fundamental principles were at stake. He regarded the ministry of education as "of supreme importance to us Liberals," adding: "That position should not go to a representative of a sectarian party and, for that reason, neither a Catholic nor a Communist [should hold it]."[33]

The reason was simple but fundamental, at least in Croce's mind. Beyond the partisan interests of the moment, the Liberal Party had to defend the freedom of education, the secular character of public schools, and the separation of church and state – three principles that, in many ways, were part of the heritage of the Risorgimento. In name, then, of those ideals, Croce would not accept that "a member of the Christian Democratic Party, a party inspired, if indirectly, by the Catholic Church, should become minister of education." That ministry required someone who had an open mind and was immune to dogmatic principles. "The Liberal Party could never concede that point, even if it had to break the coalition of the six parties; never could it allow the year 1945 to become memorable for this very grave act; if it had permitted the Christian Democrats, that is the Catholic Church ... to take possession of the ministry of education ... it would have been totally discredited and its president ... personally disgraced."[34]

Parri's short government is known also for an exchange between the premier himself and Croce that took place at the end of September 1945. At stake in that debate was not a political program, as some have claimed, but once again the heritage of the Risorgimento; the question was, and is, whether that period of Italian history deserves a positive or negative assessment. Croce's arguments on this occasion are usually misrepresented, as if his intention was to undermine the government's authority and Parri's leadership. In fact, at the beginning of his speech, Croce praised Parri's role in the Resistance. "My admiration, my gratitude as an Italian, for Parri's actions in the heroic and tenacious struggle against the Fascists and the Germans is so great and so sincere that it does not impede but rather demands that I speak to rebut frankly a historical assertion which he made yesterday and which created not so much a scandal as a surprise. He said that even before fascism, Italy did not have democratic governments."

As he had done in the past in his *History of Italy*, and in 1942 with one of his most eloquent essays, "Soliloquy of an Old Philosopher," Croce defended the achievements of liberal Italy. Referring to "the debt which all of Italy today has towards that past" and the duty of all "to defend the Italy created by our forefathers of the Risorgimento," he declared that Italy, from 1860 to 1922, contrary to Parri's assertion, "was one of the most democratic countries in Europe, and her development was an uninterrupted and often accelerated ascension towards democracy." In those years, Italy shed the shameful and miserable conditions of the past; barefoot and ill-fed crowds disappeared from city streets; the Italian people enjoyed better health than before, became more literate, acquired the status of citizens, and achieved almost universal suffrage. Italian workers created their own associations, established trade unions and cooperatives, obtained the right to strike, founded the Socialist Party, and sent their own members to Parliament, where after the war they became the largest political party.

Croce also made a theoretical point that encapsulates his political beliefs. He claimed that, during the Risorgimento, Italy became a democracy firmly founded on liberal principles. This was only natural because, "without democracy, liberalism languishes ... and democracy ... without the observance of the liberal method and system, corrupts and perverts itself and opens the door to dictatorship and tyranny." For Croce, liberalism and democracy went together, one reinforcing the other. To stress the point, Croce cited himself as an example. "Those, like me, who grew up in that liberal and democratic blossoming of Italy, will never forget that their highest achievements were the result of that system of Italian life which made it easy ... to mature without constraints of any sort, to wander in the wide world of universal culture, to learn from all, Italian or foreigner, and from different schools, to profess and to uphold what one believed to be the truth." Here Croce had a political aim in mind; after twenty years of dictatorial rule and in the midst of new totalitarian movements, he was promoting the spirit of freedom and the liberal ideals that had animated the time of his youth and early adulthood. "Even now I wish that Italy would return, certainly not to the state and condition of that time, because terrible and great events have since occurred, and conditions are new and different and difficult problems are confronting us, but to the manner and the spirit of those days, which after all is the eternal path of true human life: to be free among a free people, as Faust once said."

In the last part of his speech, Croce lauded the government's program, as presented by Parri, "because those proposals tend to restore Italy economically, administratively, and morally, and leave the political questions to the next Parliament, which the Italian people will elect in the near future, and to the free discussion of the press in the present." In Parri's proposals, in fact, Croce saw continuity with the program of the Badoglio government. "This line was followed by the first democratic government, formed in Salerno, in April 1944 … the later deviation from that line, on several occasions and at various points, has not been fruitful; and public opinion has shown frequent signs of impatience and disapproval." Croce ended by noting that the Parri government's pledge to restore law and order was wise and bound to produce good results. "I would like to add, in order to reinforce Parri's promise to restore public order and to increase the means for its defence, that public order is not only a necessary condition for the preparation of the next general election, but is also a condition that the Allied powers, their citizens, and their businessmen justly demand from us in return for their economic aid; furthermore it is essential for the confidence it creates in the general population, businessmen and working people alike."[35]

Croce's speech was greeted warmly. In his reply, Parri qualified and toned down his assertions about Italian history. The Socialists joined in the applause, but the Actionists and Communists remained silent. Those who take their inspiration from Piero Gobetti and Antonio Gramsci regard the Risorgimento, for different reasons, as a failed revolution, a movement without heroes, even an incubator of fascism. For Croce, in contrast, as he wrote in his *History of Europe*, the creation of a free, independent, and united Italy was a crowning achievement of the liberal movements of the nineteenth century, a fruitful synthesis of conservation and progress, moderation and boldness, and as such deserving of admiration and praise.[36]

11
The Advent of De Gasperi

The choice of Parri as premier was greeted positively, especially among the Northern Resistance forces. The beginning of his government was indeed promising and many thought that he was the right man for the times, able to channel the general aspiration for an end to violence and the impetus for a new political order. But disappointment soon set in. His strengths were widely recognized: he was a man of integrity and courage and an expert in military matters. Yet, under the burden of his new responsibilities, Parri's shortcomings were no less evident; he was "completely devoid of political qualities," he was a monotonous public speaker, he had no administrative experience, he was unwilling to delegate, and, to compound the last failing, he tended to procrastinate and often remained immersed in minutiae.[1] More important, Parri's government was not able to improve the political situation or to restore law and order. The bureaucracy was generally ignored or badly used, and it, in turn, assumed an attitude of non-cooperation; as a result, the authority of the state suffered. At the same time, private initiative was discouraged. Many industries remained under the control of political commissars and workers' councils. The trade unions acquired powers and functions that were beyond their normal scope, and sometimes they exploited their influence for political advantage.[2]

The Liberal Party, in tandem with the Christian Democrats, took on the role of opposition. Its leaders talked of broken promises, accusing Parri of steering the government in a direction different from that agreed on at its inception. For instance, contrary to his commitment to rein in the CLN branches, Parri, once in office, allowed these committees to increase in number, membership, and power. As we have seen, Croce and other Liberals worried that the committees, which had been useful after the fall of Mussolini and during the German occupation, could now usurp the more legitimate functions of political parties as "Communists, Socialists, and Actionists" turned them into "soviets."[3] Another concern was the purge of Fascist elements, which was extended to new categories both in the civil service and in the private sector. Despite Nenni's best intentions as minister responsible for the purge, its result was disarray in public administration and fear among the economic elite that deeply affected industrial production and financial investment.[4] At the same time, Parri had promised to refrain from party politics, but, once in government, he continued to participate in the affairs of his own party, the Party of Action, much to the annoyance of the Liberals, the Christian Democrats, and the Allies. He tended to favour the left-wing parties and often acted as the leader of the left bloc. In any labour dispute, using the slogan "from the anti-Fascist revolution to a democratic revolution," he took the side of the trade unions. More worrisome still for the Liberals, Parri claimed "to derive his powers directly" from the forces of the Resistance and to be responsible only to them. The end result was that the cabinet became divided, and the lack of cabinet solidarity sometimes involved the office of the prime minister itself. Parri, as minister of the interior, was responsible for maintaining public order, but Manlio Brosio, his deputy in both functions, criticized the inefficiency of the police forces and levelled strong accusations against the various CLN branches whose creation Parri himself had encouraged.

It would be wrong to blame Parri for all the country's difficulties. The problems were complex and the means available to address them scarce or non-existent. Any other government would have had to operate under the strictures of the armistice, which greatly curtailed its freedom of action. To complicate matters, the same armistice allowed Allied officers to meddle in Italian internal affairs even though they lacked adequate knowledge of the country's challenges. To hamper government action still further, the six parties were divided in two equal blocs, and inside those blocs each party had its own priorities and preferences.[5]

Criticism of Parri began to appear in Croce's diary soon after the government took office. During an official visit of the prime minister to Naples, Croce noted: "Parri seems a good man but without practical experience and knowledge."[6] Later he came to regard "Parri's continuance in power as dangerous to Italy." In some ways, Croce said, the present situation could be compared to the turmoil of the 1920s, which had preceded the advent of fascism and had opened the door to Mussolini's adventures; he stressed, "we Liberals should not repeat the mistakes" of that time.[7] He also noted, with increasing worry, the international implications of Parri's actions. Relations between the prime minister and the Allied authorities had deteriorated; often, members of the ACC preferred to deal with De Gasperi, the minister of foreign affairs, bypassing Parri, the prime minister, creating an uncomfortable situation for all. In the middle of August, Croce had a meeting with Alberto Tarchiani, the new Italian ambassador to Washington and an old friend of Parri. Both agreed that American assistance was necessary for the reconstruction of Italy. They also agreed that, to receive economic help from the Americans, political stability and democratic legality were critical. "It is necessary that Italy avoid revolutionary disorders and not fall under the control of the extreme parties."[8]

In a speech to the National Council of the Liberal Party, Croce strongly criticized the government's actions and once again demanded that consideration of radical reforms be postponed until after the general election; in the interim, the focus instead should be on the essential problems that affected the everyday life of the population. He also argued that the government should respect the old principle of equality among the six CLN parties, on which had rested the legality and legitimacy of every government since the compromise of 1944. In Croce's view, Parri had violated that principle by favouring the creation of a left-wing bloc. "The union of the six parties does not admit the prevalence of a single party or another group, but demands a suspension of partisan tendencies by all parties." That requirement meant that the key task for a new government was "how to re-establish the peaceful and fruitful collaboration of the six parties that symbolically represent a parliamentary majority."[9] In a letter to the CLN's six parties, Leone Cattani, Liberal Party secretary, reiterated Croce's criticism. He lamented the disarray of Parri's government, "devoid of unity of action … weakened by discordant positions on essential questions … uncertain in financial and economic affairs … slow and unable to achieve a democratic normalization of the country." Like Croce, Cattani called for "a return to the spirit of unity that had characterized the six parties during the struggle against fascism and the German occupation, instead of the virulent partisanship that lately had poisoned the atmosphere of national life." To that end, he proposed a new cabinet able to assure public order and to prepare for the next elections in a spirit of freedom, "so they could be held under the principles of legality and equality, without violence but respecting the rights of all."[10]

By the end of the fall of 1945, differences inside the cabinet had reached the breaking point. Unable to change the government's policies, the Liberals, with the full agreement of the Christian Democrats, took the initiative and demanded Parri's resignation, threatening also to withdraw from the CLN. Despite the usual rituals that characterized these occasions, the Liberals and the other parties quickly settled on a new prime minister, selecting Alcide De Gasperi, head of the Christian Democrats, in December. For the first time in the history of modern Italy, the leader of a religiously affiliated party became head of government. De Gasperi enjoyed widespread admiration, among Italians and the Allies alike, for his personal and political qualities. The Liberals in particular respected "his sincere democratic spirit, and his sense of responsibility, shown in defence of national interests and the good name of Italy."[11] Even when he was displeased by the behaviour of his party, Croce always remained on good terms with De Gasperi himself. In his diary he described him as "a serious man" who "offers sound assurances," praise not given to any other leader. Leo Valiani agreed with this assessment. He wrote that, during the meeting in Milan just after the liberation between the leaders of the Northern Resistance and the political leaders of Rome, "De Gasperi ... was not much different from the leaders of the left-wing parties. He was favourable to a vast purge, nationalizations, workers' control over industry, and agrarian reform. But then he also talked about something else. He spoke about the need for the government to be above political factions, to strive for the restoration of the state, the prestige of the state, respect for the law, and the force of the law."[12]

Some commentators, especially those identifying with the Party of Action, have considered the demise of Parri and the advent of De Gasperi as a turning point. They view the end of Parri's government as another episode in the long line of lost opportunities that has marked the history of Italy from the Risorgimento – if not the Renaissance and Reformation – to the Resistance and the republic.[13] In his recent biography of De Gasperi, the historian Piero Craveri debunks that argument, noting that, under Parri's administration, many problems came to the fore and none found a solution. For him, the choice between Parri and De Gasperi did not imply "an alternative ... between revolution and restoration, but between a spurious notion of revolution and a classical conception of democracy" in which "the state remains above the parties, as a guarantor of the democratic life of the country." Far from the beginning, then, of a political regression, the advent of De Gasperi was "the necessary premise for a profound renovation of Italian public life."[14]

After De Gasperi agreed to be the next prime minister, negotiations among the parties for the formation of the new cabinet began – with all the usual elements of comedy, surprise, and even drama. To increase the authority and prestige of the government, Croce and De Gasperi urged the inclusion in the cabinet of independent figures. "Orlando said that he was willing to participate, but only on the condition that [Francesco Saverio] Nitti participated." However, Nitti, a former prime minister never known for modesty, wanted to remain outside the government "because he was working for a great party of national unity," a statement that amused Croce, who was used to such utterances from his old friend. Predictably, because Orlando and Nitti refused to participate, "Bonomi too did not want to be part of the ministry." Croce's disappointment was understandable. "So the enlargement of the cabinet with independent figures failed on account of the refusal of these men."[15] In one of their conversations, Croce told Orlando that he was making the same mistake he had made after the Great War, when, unable to overcome personal animosities, he refused to join forces with Giolitti "in order to fight and to destroy fascism." Croce's final comment on the matter is apt: "I do not believe that senility is affecting Orlando; it is probably the contrary; he has not changed; this is the same Orlando of the old days."[16]

The Liberals had initiated their opposition to Parri and then demanded his resignation in agreement with De Gasperi's Christian Democrats. But De Gasperi, apparently unbeknownst to the Liberals, had also reached an understanding with the Socialists, or at least with their leader, Nenni, with whom he had established a close friendship. At first the Liberals had demanded the post of minister of the interior in order to assure public order, but eventually they accepted De Gasperi's candidate, Giuseppe Romita, a Socialist, regarded by Croce as "honest and moderate." Yet Croce also complained that the Christian Democrats were not "very faithful" allies.[17] In other respects, agreement was harder to reach. At one point during the negotiations, the Liberals, showing little flexibility, ran the risk of remaining outside the cabinet. The other parties were reluctant to accept their demands as the basis for the next government program. To gain time, De Gasperi, during a late-night meeting, feigned illness. Then Prince Umberto made hurried phone calls, threatening intervention. Letters of clarification were written, nocturnal meetings held. Demands were toned down and at length an agreement was reached, general exhaustion playing a not inconsiderable role. In the end the Liberals obtained the three ministries that they demanded: public works, treasury, and war. With those portfolios, Croce said, "the Liberals will have three strong men in the cabinet" and be in a position to control the armed forces, the national economy, and the reconstruction of the country.[18] Even more important, the new government accepted, with minor modifications, the ten-point program proposed by the Liberals and presented by Cattani, their secretary general and main negotiator, who probably on this occasion filled a role bigger than that of Croce himself. The list may be summarized as follows:

1) reaffirm cabinet solidarity and ministerial unity in internal and foreign affairs, especially "in defence of national interests";
2) reassert "the authority of the state and respect for law and public order";
3) pacify society, as a pre-condition for elections;
4) replace all politically appointed local officials;
5) complete the purge by the end of February 1946;
6) abolish all the special courts created after the end of the war;
7) assure freedom of work and abolish all the special privileges granted to the trade unions;
8) respect the independence of the courts;
9) protect freedom of expression, including on the part of the press and radio; and
10) prepare the ground for municipal elections and undertake "quick preparation" for Constituent Assembly elections.[19]

Croce was pleased with what his party had accomplished. "The crisis has been resolved satisfactorily. We obtained good results."[20] The Liberals had achieved a change of government and entrusted the new cabinet to a leader who enjoyed their confidence; they had set a new direction to the country's political affairs; and their party's position in cabinet had been strengthened. Another source of satisfaction was that the original constitutional compromise, which was based on the consent of the Crown, the CLN, and the six parties of the CLN acting on an equal basis, had been reaffirmed. Parri's claim to derive his authority from the forces of the Resistance alone was rejected. The road to a Jacobin democracy, or at least to dangerous experiments, had been closed. But the Liberals paid a high price for their success. They had achieved a tactical victory and suffered a strategic defeat. During the negotiations, the Liberal Party split on fundamental issues. The left wing of the party was not pleased with the fall of Parri and the rise of De Gasperi, preferring instead a continuation of Parri's leadership with minor changes and adjustments. The party's leaders in Northern Italy did not share Croce's fears about the municipal and provincial CLN branches. Unlike Croce, they regarded those committees not as soviets in the making but as necessary instruments for the renovation of Italian society after twenty years of fascism.[21]

Even more important for the future of their party, the Liberals were outmanoeuvred by De Gasperi. In the negotiations, the Liberals went on the attack, with Cattani defending his party's position with determination, "like a mule," in Nenni's words. De Gasperi assumed an air of moderation and at opportune moments offered compromises, achieving in the process a pivotal position for himself and for his party. When the dust settled, the Christian Democrats found themselves at the centre of the Italian political system, where they remained for the next fifty years. Under De Gasperi's leadership, the Christian Democratic Party was able to portray itself as a party open to reforms but willing to assure law and order, and ready to defend the interests of the middle class and industrialists without ignoring the needs of the workers and peasants. De Gasperi had adroitly placed his party where Croce wanted the Liberals to be.[22]

The Liberal Party became divided into left and right factions, conservatives and progressives, monarchists and republicans, no longer content with the centrist position advocated and maintained by Croce. From then on, the Liberals were identified with the forces of conservatism, as if they were aiming to return to the past. No longer able to claim the high ground, pushed away from the vital centre, and without a young political leader of recognized national stature, the Liberal Party would never again play a leading role in a political crisis. The Christian Democrats' growing influence cut the ground from under them and reduced their potential for expansion.

Croce was aware of this but unable to do much about it. He did not possess the personal stamina and partisan spirit required to guide his party out of its predicament. At the beginning of December 1945, when there was the possibility of a government without the Liberals, Croce made a revealing entry in his diary. "Tonight I meditated on the possibility that we leave the coalition of the six parties and assume the role of the opposition; and I also meditated on the method that we need to follow, once in opposition, in order to avoid an influx in our party of cheering followers, who would like to change the nature of our party."[23]

The "cheering followers" were the members of a new political movement, called Uomo Qualunque (Common Man), and the readers of a weekly periodical of the same name. The periodical first and the movement a little later had been founded by a brilliant populist, Guglielmo Giannini, a mediocre playwright but an effective public speaker from Naples. In a short while the movement came to enjoy great success, especially in Southern Italy. The periodical in its heyday reached a circulation of almost a million, far outdistancing its rivals. It directed its criticism and relentless polemics against anti-Fascist leaders in general and the left-wing parties in particular. Common Man, both the movement and the periodical, attracted those people, rich or poor, who were dissatisfied with government policy and the conditions of the times, but its most enthusiastic supporters were among the middle class and the state bureaucracy, which had become disgruntled and fearful for the future. It also offered a temporary refuge to the remaining political elite of the Fascist regime, especially at the local level, until they founded their own party.

By reason of their libertarian attitudes, individualistic ethos, and distrust of an invasive state, the "Qualunquisti," as they were called, were both allies and rivals of the Liberals. On the surface, both parties shared the same concerns. But deep down, they were divided by fundamental values, and the differences far outnumbered the similarities. With a long history behind them and a well-grounded ideology at the core of their policies, the Liberals were a centrist governing party with a vocation for problem solving. By contrast, Qualunquismo, a protest movement born out of the current difficulties, was not based on a coherent political program, let alone a philosophical system. Its adherents were good at repeating slogans, even better at hurling insults, but they were less successful at offering solutions, not to mention well thought out proposals; their platform contained half-baked ideas that resembled little more than querulous complaints. Lower taxes, smaller government, an administrative state, politicians replaced by accountants and technicians: such ideas did not make a coherent, substantive political program.[24] Stylistically, too, the Qualunquisti were cut from a different cloth. Their language had little in common with that of the leading Liberal politicians; in the press and especially on the hustings they appealed less to reason and more to feelings, sometimes to gut instincts. Giannini's speeches and writings were plain and direct, and sometimes coarse, a far cry from Croce's classical prose and rational argumentation.[25]

Croce had a meeting with Guglielmo Giannini at the end of October 1945, when the Liberals already had reached agreement with the Christian Democrats to replace Parri. "After supper, came Giannini ... who asked me that the Liberal Party accept within its ranks the hundreds of thousands of his readers and followers." For an ambitious political leader, the offer was attractive and hard to refuse, and indeed, in different times, Giannini would be courted by both the right and the left. But philosophers, or at least some of them, march to a different drummer. "I told him that this was not possible, because we are a political organism, and his movement is only a crowd." Giannini, as Croce reports, "was a little disappointed." In his diary, Croce made astute observations on Giannini's personality: "a man naive and sentimental, and at the same time with a sad disposition, who dislikes men of politics and war, because he lost his only son in the war ... in an airplane accident." With good foresight, Croce also cast doubt on the future of the movement, "despite the unexpected immense success of today, which is anyway not solid ... I told him that perhaps it could happen that looking back, in a few months, he will see none of his followers, who will have disappeared as fast as they had gathered around him."[26]

Rejected by Croce, Giannini devoted his energy to his own movement, which, as Croce predicted, lasted only a few more years, with ever-dwindling numbers of followers. But the Liberals had forfeited a golden opportunity to bring into their fold a gifted leader and "thousands of his followers and readers," who had the ability to galvanize the middle class and to appeal to the "common man" by speaking their own language; with their plain parlance and common touch, they perhaps could have helped the Liberal Party overcome its elitist reputation. But Croce never contemplated turning the Liberal Party into a mass movement. He much preferred a small but influential party with a coherent program to a big party with contradictory policies trying to appease divergent interests. By temperament and education, he could have hardly tolerated, let alone approved of, demagogical posturing, unfounded accusations, and scurrilous innuendoes. Concerned with the clarity of ideas and the logic of arguments, he felt no attraction to a rabble-rouser like Giannini. In contrast, "a serious man," like De Gasperi, was seen as a congenial partner.

Croce, like other Liberals, had probably reached the conclusion that an alliance between the Liberals and the Christian Democrats was necessary to face the challenges posed by the growth of the Communist Party. Only the party affiliated with the Catholic Church had a mass organization able to match, even surpass, the Communists' strength. On the same day as his meeting with Giannini, Croce had a long discussion with De Gasperi that revealed a deep affinity between the two men. "De Gasperi, Morelli and Cattani came for supper, and after supper for more than two hours we discussed from every angle the problems of the Constituent Assembly, the referendum, the monarchy and the republic."[27]

To reach an agreement with the Christian Democrats was not an easy task for the Liberals and for Croce in particular. There were old grudges to be overcome, and also recent disagreements to be forgotten. Many meetings between the old rivals were needed. A propitious encounter took place at the beginning of December during the negotiations for the replacement of Parri. On that occasion Croce had a long conversation with Monsignor Giovanni Battista Montini, the future Pope Paul VI and then a key figure in the entourage of Pope Pius XII as one of the two acting (*sostituto*) secretaries of state. In his younger years, during the Fascist regime, Montini, as spiritual adviser to the Catholic University Federation, had a great influence on young men who later became prominent Christian Democrats, such as Aldo Moro. Moreover, after the war he became a strong ally of De Gasperi and had sharp differences with the so-called Roman Party, a group of prelates who had reservations about De Gasperi's liberal orientation and urged the Christian Democrats to adopt a conservative, even reactionary program.

The meeting between Croce and Montini was arranged by common friends, and no doubt with a political purpose in mind. In Croce's words:

> I went to the house of Marquise Giovanni Visconti Venosta for a diplomatic tea, and I had a long conversation with Monsignor Montini ... I told him that certainly liberalism and the Catholic Church do not coincide, because for liberals freedom is an absolute and for the church instead it is relative, to be used or abandoned according to the particular or superior interests of the church. But if the confluence or cooperation of Liberals with the church in defence of the liberal regime has happened to date only episodically and sporadically and in a weak and fleeting way, it seems to me that now we are entering an age that demands an enduring alliance, because liberalism and Catholicism have before them and confront the same enemy, the materialistic and totalitarian and dictatorial bolshevik regime, which threatens Western civilization and its principles. On this it seems that Montini was in agreement with me.[28]

The two men discussed the current political crisis and the disagreements between the Liberals and the Christian Democrats that had emerged during the cabinet negotiations. "I also told him the facts and the reasons for the difficulties of reaching agreements with the Christian

Democrats, who are not fully reliable as allies. Without challenging my observations, he assured me that the church does not interfere in the political affairs of that party. I believe that to be true, and that has been confirmed to me by other sources."[29] No doubt the task of De Gasperi was made easier as a result of that conversation, not only in his dealings with the Liberals but also in his relations with the Vatican.

Before the fall of Parri, in the middle of October, Croce had another important meeting, this time with Giuseppe Saragat, then the Italian ambassador to France but also the leader of the social-democratic wing of the Socialist Party. After the end of the war, the Socialists were embroiled in a bitter feud between their filo-Communist and democratic factions, the "fusionisti" and the "autonomisti," as they were called. The quarrel was a repetition of the old clash between the maximalists and reformists that had paralysed the Socialist Party after the Great War and had been fatal to liberalism, socialism, and the country as a whole but propitious to Mussolini. At the October 1945 meeting, Saragat told Croce about the three-way split in the Socialist Party between those who urged an outright union with the Communists; those, like Nenni, who wanted only a close alliance with them; and those, like Saragat, "who are the intellectual and learned elements of the party, and who want to preserve the character and history of socialism, which is essentially liberal." Croce wrote: "This clash is very important for us Liberals ... because a separation of the Socialists from the Communists could make possible future political alliances in the interest of our country and of our common Western civilization. Alliance or certain agreements are possible with the Socialists, many of whose proposals we accept ... and whose other ideas we can discuss ... But the same is not possible with the Communists because of insurmountable moral and intellectual differences, and also for historical reasons that pertain to the past and to the present, especially now that Communism had become synonymous with bolshevism, Stalinism, and Russian expansionism."[30] Using the power of reason and "the arms of criticism," Croce and Saragat saw the oppressive nature of Soviet communism and its incompatibility with freedom. Others had to wait many years before the collapse of the Soviet Union allowed them to reach the same conclusion.

During the fall of 1945, a new government had been formed, a new leader had emerged, and future alliances were slowly taking shape. A political realignment was under way; the pretence of equality among the six CLN parties was coming to an end. After the war and the liberation of Northern Italy, only three parties acquired a mass following, surpassing all the others, and began to dominate the political landscape. Within a year, the Liberal Party and the Party of Action would be relegated to a marginal position, destined to have an ever-diminishing impact. Sadly, with their decline, the ideals of the Risorgimento faded away and a liberal-democratic alternative to fascism and communism never materialized, remaining only a dream.

12
Election and Referendum

On 2 June 1946 Italy witnessed its first free national election since 1921, this time for the new Constituent Assembly; simultaneously, a referendum on the institutional question was held. Together, the election and the referendum, both conducted under universal adult suffrage, marked the end of one era and the beginning of another. The referendum in particular had historic significance. For the first time, the Italian people, men and women, had the chance to choose the form of their state.

In preparation for the election, the Liberal Party held a national congress in late April 1946. There, Croce delivered one of his most important political speeches, which sheds light on the opposition waged by Liberals during the Fascist regime. He reminded his audience that Liberals under fascism had not disappeared but had maintained a substantial subterranean presence. During Mussolini's dictatorship, "the Liberal Party, which no longer had legal status, and for that reason had neither an office nor the possibility of meetings, nevertheless continued to exist from one end of Italy to the other through personal relations, reciprocal visits, the hospitality of friendly homes, the agreements we reached inside them, and also thanks to the support which we received from young people, who joined with us and remained immune to the allure of fascism and were not frightened by its intimidation."[1]

In his speech, Croce expounded on philosophical concepts and political ideas that were by now familiar to his listeners. "It bothered me to write that speech," he later said, "because I was compelled to repeat things already said before. But this is the nature of politics; unlike the studies which nourish and renew the mind, politics enslaves the mind, turning it into its own phonograph."[2] Once again Croce stressed the difference between political and economic liberalism, or *liberismo*, a term denoting the market economy or the capitalistic organization of economic activity. Croce regarded liberalism as an overarching philosophy of life, one that has freedom as its supreme ideal and that relies on individual initiative and personal responsibility. His liberalism could accept state intervention in economic affairs as long as such intervention increases human freedom and assures better production and distribution of goods and services. However, he expressed his reluctance to enunciate a full economic program. Instead, he urged Liberal economists and experts to study individual problems and then present their proposals for discussion inside and outside the party. For his part, he was in favour of reforms that addressed the needs of the people and of changing times, provided they were undertaken not for ideological reasons but because they were "able to assure the continuous civil and social progress of our country."[3]

In accordance with those statements, the congress passed a motion calling for the abolition of all monopolies, in both the private and public sectors, in order to increase competition and eliminate unfair privileges. In labour relations, it proposed measures for social assistance in favour of workers, the control of inflation, the elimination of unemployment, and the reform of agrarian contracts. Despite the Liberals' opposition to nationalization, their program was open to substantial reforms and certainly was not a blind defence of conservative or reactionary interests, as their adversaries claimed.

During the congress, Croce suffered some disappointments. On the institutional question, he advised the party to remain neutral in the referendum, allowing members to vote according to their individual preferences. Instead, the congress voted by a large majority to support the monarchy, though allowing each member to vote according to his conscience. The same position was reaffirmed at a meeting of the party's National Council in May. In the end, despite Croce's best efforts, the Liberal Party suffered a split on this issue that destroyed many old friendships and weakened its appeal among the electorate.[4] A group of left-wing Liberals, who favoured the republican cause, abandoned the party and joined other movements more attuned to their ideals.

The congress did contribute to unity of a different sort. Bonomi, Nitti, and Orlando proposed an alliance of all liberal and democratic forces for the next general election. After long discussion, the Liberals came out in support of this idea, and the new alliance took the name of National Democratic Union (UDN). This was the first attempt after the war to unite all liberal-democratic forces in a single body positioned between the Christian Democrats and the Socialist and Communist parties.

Negotiations for the creation of the new union had begun some time before in Rome, mainly through the work of Bonomi. In mid-March 1946 Croce received a letter from Bonomi appraising him of the progress of his initiative:

> I wish to inform you, though Morelli has kept you abreast of our work, that the union of the liberal-democratic political forces has made good progress. Both Nitti and Orlando see the opportunity to unite in a National Union (perhaps National Democratic Union) all those elements who are willing to join a program of order and freedom. Among the first to join the future union should be the Liberal Party, the Labour Party, and Nitti's Reconstruction Union, and then other minor movements. With the first three the talks have proceeded well. The union also should remain open to the many independent elements, who until now have not yet joined any party. Then we should launch a manifesto ... Our friend De Nicola is also with us. I wish to know your thoughts.[5]

In Croce's diary the union is mentioned for the first time three days later, on 19 March, when a meeting with Bonomi, De Nicola, and others took place in his house. "We discussed the alliance of the Liberal Party with the Labour Party and with others. This alliance should include Orlando, Nitti, and, we hope, De Nicola, who despite the urgings of all, and mine in particular, has no intention of participating ... Bonomi will continue the discussions and the negotiations in Rome with Orlando and Nitti."[6]

Living in Naples, Croce sometimes felt left out of the initiative. "I am sorry not to be well informed about the negotiations going on in Rome for an alliance of the democratic parties."[7] But, despite his distance from the centre of action, he acted as a sort of clearing house for suggestions and proposals coming from Rome or elsewhere. As always in this period, when political questions were involved, he consulted with De Nicola and then incorporated his advice into his own response. He also travelled to Rome when his presence was deemed necessary to overcome an impasse or to speed up negotiations, even to smooth ruffled feathers, which was not an easy task when so many prima donnas were involved. He met with Bonomi to discuss the choice of candidates for the election, and was instrumental in obtaining the inclusion in the UDN's national list of candidates the names of Luigi Einaudi and Niccolò Carandini; the latter was then the Italian ambassador to London but also the man who Croce hoped would soon be his successor as president of the Liberal Party – a hope that, to his disappointment, never materialized.[8]

Croce's diary and the correspondence of three former premiers, Orlando, Bonomi, and Nitti, illuminate their thinking on the purpose of the new political alliance. For all of them, a union of democratic parties was required to confront the threat of totalitarianism posed by both the old right and the new left. This alliance was needed to defend the heritage of the Risorgimento and to be open to reforms. It would need to be the champion of a new constitution based on freedom and able to assure the security of a free people. More specifically, for Bonomi, the new grouping must unite "the elements that are willing to embrace a program of freedom and order" and welcome those who belonged to similar parties or to no party at all. Orlando was more precise; the union had to attract "those who are not Communists, or Socialists, or Christian Democrats." Nitti had a different focus; the alliance had to avoid being cast as a conservative movement and had to propose social reforms that met the challenges of the times.[9]

In a letter to the three men, Croce asked that "liberal" be placed beside "democratic" in the new organization's name. The peculiar request shows that Croce had become strongly attached, not only to the ideals of liberalism, but the very sound of the word "liberal." In this attachment, which likely stemmed from the relentless propaganda campaign waged by the Fascist regime against liberals and liberalism, he was in a minority even among his peers, as we learn from his letter. He wrote:

> I pray that you will not leave alone in the name the word "democratic," which it seems to me is of little significance, because nowadays it is used "as a sort of competition" even by priests and bolsheviks, and often it is used against us liberals. The use of that word by us could sound, therefore, as a rather servile flattery paid to extreme parties. I would like to add, as you as scholars and experts in political science already know, that liberalism and democracy are like the famous Siamese brothers, two persons with a single circulating blood system. By choosing, then, "liberal democratic," we will remain faithful to the theoretical truth, which is known and dear to us, and also to the empirical truth, because we are two parties which are joining forces for common goals and common work … [At the same time] I see that in the newspapers the expression "liberal-democratic concentration" has appeared … [and] spontaneous expressions are always the best. I hope that you will see no difficulty with this.[10]

Despite Croce's wishes, the word "liberal" was not included in the name of the union. But the writing of the body's manifesto was entrusted to Croce by general agreement. The manifesto was published at the beginning of April; it bore the signatures of the four old Liberal figures, but immediately the real author became known and the document was referred as "Croce's Manifesto" in the press. Before writing it, Croce received several suggestions from his friends in Rome. For Orlando, the manifesto had to avoid generic propositions: "We need to make categorical and vibrant proposals, suitable to the historical moment and able to reach immediately the minds and hearts of the masses." It "had to stress a few points, those that have a real, true, and immediate gravity and importance." For Bonomi, the manifesto had to be "concise," yet it also needed to promise a future founded on freedom and appeal to independent-minded people, especially to those not yet committed to any other party. Nitti urged that the manifesto be "clear, simple, and short," so it could be understood by the general population, and to that end it had to be "without equivocal expressions." Above all, it must not "be regarded as a reactionary document."[11]

When Croce wrote the manifesto, he was going through a period of emotional distress; he was worried by the illness that was threatening the life of Adolfo Omodeo, his longtime friend and collaborator. "Today, more bad news about Omodeo, whose condition, after a brief improvement, has worsened again. For that reason, I was deeply depressed when Morelli arrived from Rome bringing three letters from Orlando, Nitti, and Bonomi, who asked me to write our manifesto ... First, I had a moment of rebellion, more so since the document had to be ready by tomorrow morning, so Morelli could take it to Rome with him. Then I agreed, thinking that by having to overcome this difficulty, I would overcome my anguish. So I began to think and to write the manifesto during the evening and by midnight it was ready."[12] In the morning, Croce showed the document to De Nicola for his comments before sending it to Rome. "De Nicola came, together with [Giovanni] Porzio, and the manifesto was read and amended with a few changes."[13]

Croce's manifesto was clearly written, even eloquent in parts, but it was not a stirring document written with the "general population" in mind, as Orlando had recommended, nor was it as "short and concise" as Bonomi and Nitti had wished. Three pages long, it did not resemble a typical piece of party propaganda full of promises. But it made a few important points clear. The UDN's ties with the Risorgimento were reaffirmed and its anti-Fascist nature emphasized. Croce urged other smaller movements to join the new body, putting aside old differences "in the name of liberty." On the institutional question, the manifesto advised voters to follow their convictions. Reassurance was given to the Catholic Church and its followers. In the new constitutional order, whether it took the form of monarchy or republic, "state and church will live in freedom and in religious peace." The manifesto did not offer a clear economic and social program, though it promised to grapple in a fair way "with the problems of reconstruction" and "with the reforms of economic organizations." Its strongest words were in defence of freedom. The UDN promised "to defend and to protect in the strongest way the freedom of all Italians," and finally there was the old liberal battle cry directed against totalitarianism of all stripes: "It is necessary to guarantee all freedoms, from the political to the religious."[14]

The presence of a renowned philosopher at the helm of a political organization brought both advantages and disadvantages. As noted earlier, Croce's philosophical system and theory of liberalism had little to say about those institutions that ensure and promote the viability and vitality of a free society and democratic government. Similarly, in the manifesto of the UDN, and also in other writings of this period, Croce stressed the value of freedom as the guiding principle of political activity, but he remained vague on economic and social matters. It was an obvious gap, exploited by his adversaries then and later; Croce himself was aware of that shortcoming, as he confessed in a candid letter to a young and promising scholar, Enzo Santarelli, then following a liberal orientation but later embracing Marxism. He was ready to address the concept of freedom and to elucidate its implications in practical and theoretical terms. But, when it came to concrete economic problems and their solutions, he preferred to rely on the expertise of others.

> Why? For a very simple reason. Because I am prepared and competent to render services in the first field, but I am not fully competent in the second. [To offer prescriptions in the latter,] I would have to acquire not only a different experience and a different habit, but also a different animus and passion. And it is not possible to make these changes when one is eighty years old, either because one has no desire to live another life, or one will not have enough time to acquire the necessary competence. On the other hand, if I should formulate economic proposals, I would not like to do so in the same manner as other parties, that is, in vague, equivocal, demagogical [terms], knowing that they are a mere pretence and serve only to gain applause and attract votes.

In his letter to Santarelli, Croce also explained the origin of his frame of mind. "I am in agreement with you that my elaboration of freedom has been shaped and inspired by the resistance to Fascist oppression. For that reason, I believe that such a resistance is still necessary today, because freedom is in many parts of the world denied and under threat; especially in Italy, which finds itself in the midst of new totalitarian ideas (progressive democracy Russian-style, which equals absolutism and anti-freedom) and the survival of old ones, the defence of freedom requires vigilance and firmness."[15]

Croce's arguments were philosophically sound and logical but they flew in the face of the fact that political movements and electoral competition follow particular rules, ones which should not be neglected if a party and its leader hope to attract popular interest and support. Modern politicians are well aware of these conventions. Today, political speeches are researched and produced by ghostwriters and then revised by public relations experts. This process would have been anathema to Croce, regarded as a scarlet letter "on the candid stole worn by Philosophy," as he once put it.

The election campaign began with a disappointment. Croce failed to persuade De Nicola to run for office. First he received non-committal responses but then came a final refusal in writing: "I am very sorry not to be able to obey your order."[16] Though he was not surprised, Croce's disappointment is evident in his diary.

> I made a visit to De Nicola, together with Astarita and Porzio, in order to compel him, as he had promised, to run in the next elections as a Liberal candidate in the constituency of Naples, or in any other constituency, convinced as we are that once in the Constituent Assembly he would certainly be chosen as speaker by different parties. But his desire to avoid annoyances of any sort, of not wanting to be bothered by criticism, foolish polemics, and malicious gossip, proved an insurmountable obstacle. I used all sorts of arguments to overcome his objections and refusal, which is really worthy of criticism in the dangerous conditions prevailing now in Italy. The only result I obtained was a promise to think further about the proposal, and then to write his final response tomorrow: that is, he will repeat his refusal in writing.[17]

The election was held under proportional representation; adult men and women voters, twenty-one years and older, were able to elect 556 members to the Constituent Assembly. Of course, the rules of proportional representation are a little more complicated than the first-past-the-post electoral system. In the Italian system, there was a national list determined within the guidelines of proportional representation. The country as a whole was divided into regional or provincial ridings, each having a number of seats based on its population. In these ridings, each party was represented by a list of candidates. Electors first cast their ballots for the party of their choice, then could mark their preference for a number of candidates within that party's list. Finally, the major party leaders were able to run in three different ridings, choosing one if elected in all three or two of them. Victory rewarded the mass parties, those that were well funded and organized and that were willing to employ the tools of modern propaganda.

The electoral results were not what the UDN's leaders expected. Popular participation was high, more than 90 per cent. The Christian Democrats finished in first place, with 35.2 per cent of the votes cast and 207 deputies elected, allowing De Gasperi to remain prime minister for the next eight years; they were followed by the Socialists with 20.7 per cent and 115 deputies, and by the Communists with 18.9 per cent and 104 deputies. All the other parties received single-digit support. The UDN obtained only 6.8 per cent of the popular vote and elected 41 members to the Constituent Assembly. It fared poorly in Central and Northern Italy, where it garnered only 2 or 3 per cent of the vote even though many of its candidates were well-known professionals or had been outstanding figures in the Resistance. It did much better in the South, where it received more than 15 per cent of the vote, coming second only to the Christian Democrats. In these parts of Italy, the influence of the old political leaders remained strong with rich and poor alike.

Despite the disappointing results, the outcome still offered a good basis from which to grow; the UDN was the fourth party in the Assembly, and it had expert parliamentarians and leaders with national reputations. But it was not to be. Immediately after the election, the UDN split into its original factions, in the midst of the usual recriminations. The majority of the elected members remained with the Liberal Party, but the three former premiers went their separate ways, unable to submit to any kind of collegial discipline.[18]

Croce was elected to the Constituent Assembly, but his personal showing was not stellar and much overshadowed by the spectacular results scored, in number of votes, by De Gasperi, Nenni, and Togliatti. He ran on the national list, and his name was present also in the provincial lists of Naples, Rome, and Milan. He was elected on the national list and was also successful in the provincial list of Naples; but in his own city, Naples, he came fourth, and in Rome and Milan he received only a few thousand votes, not enough to reach the threshold for election. Both in the national and regional lists he came well behind candidates who lacked his stature but who, unlike him, had worked hard in the campaign. Croce's participation in the election was limited and sporadic; he took part in only a few public meetings, mainly to support old friends. At one of these rallies, he spoke just a few words, in order to rebut "a Catholic orator's assertions against liberals." In the diary there is no mention of the UDN split; he probably regarded the event with equanimity. In the past he had not shown great interest in the establishment of a big party, let alone a mass movement. During the Liberal Party's April congress, he had made a statement that captured well his main goals as a party leader. "I agree with Carandini that what is most important is not to increase the rank and file of the party but to maintain the coherence of ideas and purpose, and to wait for the propitious hour."[19] Unfortunately, the propitious hour never arrived for the Liberal Party.

The defeat of the Liberal forces in the elections of 1946 has attracted a great deal of attention from historians. Recently, Fabio Grassi Orsini has pointed out that intimidation played a role of some importance during the campaign. In many parts of Central and Northern Italy but also in Apulia in Southern Italy, Liberal candidates were often not allowed to speak and in several cases were even victims of violence. Most of the time, the violence was perpetrated by former Communist partisans, who generally acted on their own initiative but whose conduct in some instances was tolerated by their local party, which then protected them after the fact. More often than not, this violence went unpunished. Police investigations ended without charges for lack of supporting evidence, creating a sense of apprehension among law-abiding citizens.[20]

Before and during the elections, many people interpreted the violence – together with the huge rallies and frequent demonstrations, replete with fiery and threatening language, organized by the radical movements – as the beginning of a social and political revolution led by the Communist Party. To avoid that outcome, the middle and upper classes began to look for a party that could defend the traditional ways of life, maintain law and order, and protect private property and individual freedom. The Christian Democrats, supported by the Catholic Church, were able to speak to these voters and alleviate their fears, presenting their party as the only bulwark against bolshevism. The Liberals did not have the organization, the manpower, or the financial resources to match the Christian Democrats' strength, confidence, and drive.[21]

Other scholars, including Pietro Scoppola, have seen in the decline of the Liberal elite and the success of the three big parties the beginning of a new era, the "Republic of Parties," to use Scoppola's apt expression. A tectonic shift was under way in politics after the war and a new paradigm was emerging. With the introduction of universal suffrage and proportional representation, many voters abandoned the old parties, and the Liberals in particular, and flocked to rivals with superior organization based on mass participation.

In the republic after the war, following the example of the Fascist Party, mass parties were highly structured institutions – like modern corporations – employing thousands of militants. These parties provided social services and fellowship, sometimes in competition with the state or even with the church, and acted as instruments not only of political participation but also of social mobility through career opportunities. The Liberal Party, meanwhile, steadfastly remained an elitist movement, relying on individual figures to carry its message. This had been a strength in liberal Italy, when the political class was small, the franchise limited, and party affiliation fairly loose. Then, during elections, a few banquets, enlivened by speeches, were enough to maintain the allegiance of the faithful. When mass parties began to dominate the political system, the Liberals failed to respond in kind, and it showed at the ballot box.

In the changed environment, the old elite could hardly maintain the support of its traditional clientele, let alone reach or inspire the new voters brought into the political arena by universal suffrage. The Liberal Party's weaknesses were already manifest before the advent of fascism but were accentuated after the Second World War. By temperament, education, and training, the Liberal leaders, young or old, did not have the wherewithal to organize and lead a mass party; they could not accept the tough discipline and the personal and professional sacrifices demanded by such organizations and much preferred to remain independent-minded, though politically ineffectual.[22]

If the election left Croce disappointed, he was not much heartened by the results of the referendum either. The referendum put him in an awkward position. For him, the choice between monarchy and republic was, at bottom, a question not of rational considerations but of feelings. He was a monarchist and naturally wanted the retention of the monarchy. But he soon disappointed the followers of the king when, as president of the Liberal Party, he advised the party at its April congress to remain neutral on the institutional question, allowing its members to vote according to their conscience. Unlike other monarchists, he saw other priorities that were even more important for the future of freedom and democracy. According to Croce, in the aftermath of the election and referendum, Liberals had two duties above all: first, they had to accept and defend the result of the referendum; and second, whether monarchy or republic was chosen, they had to endow the new state with those institutions that protect the freedom of the individual and the rights of citizens. His main concern was the fate of liberty, since events in recent years, both in Italy and in the rest of Europe, had shown that "freedom can be protected and respected by a monarchy or by a republic, and can be overcome or suppressed under one or the other." With Europe already divided in two opposite blocs, Italy's election and referendum would be "taking place under grave difficulties and in conditions adverse to freedom."[23]

Weeks before the election and referendum, Croce made known his preference on the institutional question with a short note to a Neapolitan newspaper, declaring that he was unwilling "to pass as a cunning man" who "hides his own thoughts."[24] He saw no necessity for a radical change, and no reason for a new form of state. For him, and for others of his generation who shared his disposition, the monarchy was a useful symbol in uncertain times, assuring historical continuity, national unity, and political stability. It was difficult, almost impossible, to break the ties with "an old house that was gloriously and politically tied to the Risorgimento of Italy."[25]

On several occasions in his diary, Croce confessed his apprehension for the future of the House of Savoy. "I do not know if the monarchy can survive in Italy; but for my part I will not join the many people, often former royalists, who show no respect to a royal house that for centuries ruled over an Italian province, and later guided the whole of Italy on the road to unity, independence, and freedom."[26] When Prince Umberto, after the sudden abdication of his father, became king at the beginning of May, there was much rejoicing among the faithful that a dashing younger man, unencumbered by the heavy burden of the past, was now the Crown's standard bearer. But for Croce, the changed status of the prince left the monarchy's future in the same precarious condition as before; his mood did not change and his doubts remained. "I received an affectionate telegram from the prince lieutenant, in the act of assuming the Crown because of his father's abdication. I confess to feeling great pain for this young man, with whom almost certainly will come to an end a very ancient house, whose destiny has been connected politically and even poetically with the Risorgimento."[27] For the future of the monarchy, Croce placed his trust in the wisdom of people or, perhaps, in the hands of fate. Comments written in 1945 after a meeting with Prince Umberto show a reluctance to be wholeheartedly involved in the campaign for the retention of the monarchy, let alone to assume a position of leadership in that fight. He wrote that on this "young prince … who displays effort and good will in the performance of his duties … [there] hangs a sad destiny, to be, perhaps, the last head of a reigning house that is the oldest in Europe among all the other monarchies, and that has had its glories and virtues, and at the end unified Italy as an independent and liberal nation." Croce expressed his impotence to alter the course of history. "But this pain that I feel does not transform itself into a plan of action for which the conditions are lacking and unlikely to arise."[28]

Croce's position on the monarchy was not without contradictions. In the recent past, he had harsh words for the old king, accusing him of being partly responsible for fascism and demanding his abdication for that reason. At first, Croce had not been greatly impressed by Prince Umberto's intelligence or ability; his opinion of him later improved, but the first impression lingered. Cordiality in their personal relations never turned into admiration. Yet, from the beginning, he recognized the monarchy's symbolic function and the important ties with the traditions of the Risorgimento that the retention of the monarchy would sustain. "I have always made a distinction between the person and the institution, and always expressed my conviction that, for Italy, it was convenient to keep the figure of the king as a symbol of national unity and political stability."[29]

Croce set out the reasons for his stand in a letter to Carlo Sforza, a count who then was campaigning for the republican cause with particular fervour, as often happens with disgruntled aristocrats. At the end of the letter, Croce's political priorities and real concerns are stated with force.

> Dear Carlo. What to say? I, who, in October 1943, worked with you in an attempt to preserve the monarchy by means of a regency (do you remember our meeting in Naples with Badoglio?) do not believe that the personal faults of the royal family are enough by themselves to resolve the institutional question. Then, our design enjoyed general support, and the opposition came mainly from the old king, who even later preferred the lieutenancy to abdication. Now the question is put to a popular vote,

> and I feel myself and I will become one of the people, unus de populo; that is, I will vote according to my feelings, but I will put no pressure on anybody else, and will use instead great discretion; because, in this case, it is not a question of science or morality, but one in which feelings and hopes prevail, and, by necessity, those are different in each individual. The majority will decide; and then all of us will have to show discipline and obey the result, whatever it is going to be, avoiding foolish recriminations and rash conflicts.[30]

On 2 June, with these forebodings, Croce cast his vote for the monarchy. By a fair margin, the republic won and the monarchy lost. In total, 23,400,000 ballots were cast; of those, 54.3 per cent were for the republic and 45.7 per cent for the monarchy – roughly 12 million for one and 10 million for the other. The results revealed a dangerous split between the North and the South. In the Central and Northern provinces, a large majority had favoured the republic but in the Southern regions, including Rome, the monarchy had received even bigger majorities. In Lombardy the republic obtained 64.1 per cent of the votes and in Tuscany 71.6 per cent; in contrast, in Sicily, 64.7 per cent of voters chose the monarchy and in Naples the number was even higher, 76.5 per cent.

As many had feared, recriminations arose as soon as the ballots began to be counted; when the final result became known, they were immediately challenged, with even some high-placed Liberals stoking the fire. The victory of the republic was marred by riots in Naples and other places in the South where the vote was decisively in favour of the monarchy. The government inflamed the situation by sending two army battalions, composed of former partisans from the North, into Naples. Law and order was restored in due course, but not without several dead and wounded and considerable damage to property. The fact that a greater tragedy was avoided had less to do with the use of force than with the intervention of Croce and De Nicola. In an act full of symbolic associations, the two old Liberals appeared beside the local prefect and the commanding general and appealed to the people of Naples for an end to violence. Their loyalty to the republic and acceptance of the popular verdict – echoed by all other Liberal leaders – discouraged further challenges to the legality of the referendum result and did much to assure the vitality of the new state. Their intervention was, perhaps, one of the most valuable contributions to the reconstruction of Italy after the ruin and divisions brought about by the war.[31]

A note in Croce's diary reads as an elegy for the end of the monarchy and a stout defence of those who had not voted for the republic. "The referendum has divided Italy in two parts that almost stand in equilibrium ... By a great margin, Naples gave a majority vote to the monarchy. The feeling that moved those who supported the monarchy has been spontaneous and tied to tradition and to good and generous intentions. Those who mention the usual vulgarities and talk of reaction, of fascism, of votes bought and sold, etc. ... slander without reason these intelligent and sensitive people."[32]

After the election and referendum, Umberto went into exile and spent the rest of his life in Oporto, Portugal, the same city where his ancestor Carlo Alberto had lived after his own misfortune. His reign had lasted for barely a month, hence his sobriquet as the King of May. Within a short time, the king's cause lost political force, but a small movement of diehards remained, never posing a danger to the republic, the number of followers ever dwindling. Only the quarrels and the romantic affairs of the royal family's younger generations, for a while, remained of interest to the general public, finding a place, and eager readers, in the gossip columns of glossy magazines.

13
The Constituent Assembly

Following the election and referendum, Croce's mood was dark. "With the elections of June 2, a very difficult period has opened for Italy, and there are many problems to be solved."[1] Omodeo's death made his anguish sharper. "The irreparable loss" of his old friend led him "to burst into tears." Waking up "around four o'clock in the morning," he meditated "painfully on the future of Italy, of Europe and the world ... But afterwards, at the end, the conclusion has been the same, one that I have repeated to myself before in the course of events: that life is courage, it is confidence, it is work. And outside of this, there is no other good and no other refuge."[2]

Two of the Constituent Assembly's principal tasks over the years 1946–7 were electing a president and drafting a constitution for the new republic. With regard to the presidency, everyone agreed that the person selected had to be an outstanding leader, able to unite a deeply divided nation and be respected by all; ideally too, in the interests of national harmony, the new president should be from the South since the prime minister and the speaker of the Assembly were Northerners. Not many men met those qualifications; the field was restricted to the few surviving leaders of liberal Italy. The name of Orlando was soon put forward by the Christian Democrats, and was just as quickly withdrawn in the face of opposition from the Socialists and Communists. Croce, for his part, informed De Gasperi that he would vote for the former premier without hesitation, "since he is older than I am, and he has also been head of government."[3]

After the failure of Orlando's candidacy, Croce's name was mentioned in various quarters. His prestige was then unmatched, both in Italy and abroad. He enjoyed support and respect in the North and in the South, among republicans and royalists, Liberals and Socialists. Before the Liberals made any move, in fact, his name was officially proposed by the Socialist Party's executive. The news was brought to Croce's house by Liberal friends returning from Rome. "In the afternoon came [Giovanni] Cassandro, [Renato] Morelli, and [Alfredo] Parente. Discussions and information about the proposal of Nenni, who has launched my name as president of the Italian republic. Tomorrow [Sandro] Pertini and [Ignazio] Silone should come to deliver the letter, which demands my assent to the candidacy: but the content of the letter has already been anticipated by Morelli."[4] Liberals and Socialists were then divided by political and economic issues, but personal relations between Croce and the most important Socialist leaders had always been respectful. The letter that Nenni, leader of the Socialist Party, wrote to Croce on this occasion reflects those feelings of admiration. "We would be happy to give our votes to you, mindful as we are of the high interests of our country, and in the knowledge that today, before the world, nobody better than you can represent Italy, and can at the same time assure with more loyalty the life of the Italian republic."[5] Croce was pressured to accept the offer. De Nicola, in particular, first sent a message through a common friend, then made a visit to Croce's house to issue a personal appeal, urging him "under the sheer force of logical argumentation" to accept the Socialist offer because a refusal would be in the circumstances "a dereliction of duty before history!" Croce resisted with logical arguments of his own. At the end of the meeting, Croce commented astutely on De Nicola's psychology and his unusual modus operandi, with which he was already very familiar. "It seems to me that De Nicola kept urging me so strongly to accept the offer in order to save himself from that heavy office."[6]

Simultaneously, negotiations for filling the presidency were under way in different quarters, and sometimes at cross purposes. While Croce was meeting with De Nicola, the prefect of Naples arrived to inquire about De Nicola's intentions on behalf of the minister of the interior, who happened to be Giuseppe Romita, a prominent Socialist but belonging to a party faction different from that of Nenni. Instead of the expected acceptance, the envoy was given a clear refusal, which he relayed to Rome by a telegram dictated by De Nicola himself.

Croce refused without hesitation the Socialists' offer, noting in his reply to Nenni that he lacked the necessary qualifications for the high office.[7] He made the same point in his diary. "I know myself and know what I can do, and what I cannot do,"[8] one entry read. Two days later he returned to the same theme, and with even more force. "Really I could not accept: I do not feel fit and qualified for that position, in which I could waste energy and time, worrying about the good that I could not do, and the bad I could not prevent." He also answered another argument widely used by those who were supporting his candidacy. "I … know that it is foolish, and even unbecoming, to think that it is possible to save Italy from the terrible consequences of defeat caused by fascism through my literary and intellectual prestige."[9]

Croce's refusal was a wise decision for several reasons. By temperament he was not really suited for the position of president; at that stage of his life – he was now eighty – he no longer had the physical stamina required to carry out the functions associated with the office. There was, moreover, another consideration of far greater import. At the time, a Croce candidacy for the post of president risked reopening old wounds on the vexed subject of relations between church and state. Given his reputation and the tenets of his philosophy, Croce's election as president of the new republic could be interpreted, against his wishes, as a challenge to the spiritual authority of the pope. There was fear inside the Curia that, under Croce's guidance, the republic could become a counterpoise to the authority of the Vatican, as the monarchy had been in the past. The Christian Democrats, pressured by the Vatican and emboldened by their electoral success, made known their reluctance to support a Croce candidacy. "The Christian Democrats are against me," Croce wrote, "because, asinine and shameless as they are, they say that I am an atheist philosopher and in Rome there is the Vicar of Christ."[10] As usually happened in such cases, the unexpected attack generated an immediate reaction, and Croce for a fleeting moment entertained the temptation of accepting the challenge. "I, truly, having been assured of the united votes of the Communists, Socialists, Liberals, and other democratic elements, could engage in the fight with the certainty of victory, more so since the Christian Democrats, cautious and fearful as they are, would not dare to challenge the bulk of Italian public opinion. And truly I would like to teach a lesson to these shameless bigots."[11] The temptation did not last long. After giving vent to his indignation, his original position was reaffirmed. "But I cannot; I really do not feel fit and suitable for that office."[12]

With that decision, Croce avoided some unpleasant surprises, for his calculations regarding support for his candidacy were not realistic. The Christian Democrats, though cautious, were not timid in exploiting their new position of strength, and in any fight they were sure to find the necessary allies and votes, even in unsuspected places. Despite promises made in public or in private conversations, it is doubtful that Croce could count on the support of the majority in the Assembly. The parties he had mentioned as being in his corner all had their own political priorities, and none was willing to damage its political prospects by taking avoidable risks. The Socialists themselves were not firm in their support of Croce; they were negotiating a coalition government with the Christian Democrats and were eager to make compromises in order to reach that goal. Nor did the Communists have any intention of embarking on a collision course with the Catholics for the sake of a liberal philosopher known for his criticism of their ideology and political program. Togliatti's strategic aim, to which he remained faithful through thick and thin to the end, was to achieve an alliance with the Catholic masses, and he was not inclined to rekindle the old battles of the Risorgimento dear to the bourgeoisie. Far from being willing to place Croce on a pedestal, Togliatti, after his return from Russia, was bent on undermining his reputation as a necessary step in laying the foundation of the Communist Party's cultural hegemony. Finally, the unwillingness of many democratic elements to defend secular principles, even when they were blatantly violated, soon became all too clear. When the Constituent Assembly, a few months later, debated the incorporation of the Lateran Pacts into the constitution, thus transforming an international treaty between two states – Italy and the Vatican – into a fundamental law of the country, the Communists and others joined the Christian Democrats to vote in favour, while Croce and Nenni took the opposite position and suffered a resounding defeat.

At the end of June 1946, by a huge majority, the Constituent Assembly elected Enrico De Nicola as the first president of the republic, or, in the official terminology, as provisional head of state. His election was not without elements of suspense. On learning of De Nicola's refusal, one of the political leaders in Rome wisely advised the others to ignore it and to proceed with the election as planned, thus forcing De Nicola's hand with a fait accompli. The tactic worked beautifully, to everybody's great relief. The day after the Assembly's vote, De Nicola paid a courtesy visit to Croce, who wrote: "I had taken a few notes for a new work when suddenly De Nicola appeared; he was very moved by the votes he had received by all parties, and this made it impossible for him to refuse the nomination. We talked for quite a while and with reciprocal affection. He was put in a position from which he could not refuse. Indeed, had he refused, the impression would have been bad in Italy and abroad. But, above all else, I admired the spirit with which he accepted his new destiny."[13]

The presence of De Nicola in Croce's house soon became known in Naples, and during their discussions photographers and newspapermen turned up and took pictures of the two old sages standing side by side, asking questions of both. The next day, their stories filled the front pages of the local and national papers. It was a good omen. The monarchy had received huge support in Southern Italy, and now the two most important political figures in the South, known previously for their support of the royal cause, appeared together, showing loyalty to the republic. The public significance of their act could not be mistaken: in the history of Italy, a page had been turned – the monarchy was gone and the king could not return. The message sent to those who had voted for the monarchy was clear: the state was in good hands and it was time to put the past behind and look to the future with confidence.

De Nicola's election as head of the state proved beneficial to the life of the republic. With his constitutional scruples, juridical knowledge, and political experience, he helped to place the new constitutional order on solid foundations. In a more general way, the appointment of an old Liberal politician to the presidency fostered national unity, healing the wounds created by the referendum. No less important, his presence reestablished links with the traditions of liberal Italy that proved useful during the hard work of reconstruction after the trauma of the war and Mussolini's dictatorship.

With the matter of the presidency settled, the Constituent Assembly turned its attention to the drafting of a constitution. Italy's earlier constitution, the Albertine Statute – based on the Belgian constitution of 1831 – had guided the country from 1861 and remained in place even during the Fascist regime, never formally changed but continually violated. In the end, the substantial differences between that constitution and the one that would replace it in 1946 reflected the desire of anti-Fascists to surround the democratic system with strong safeguards – so that what had happened once could not happen again, as Togliatti put it. The new constitution certainly achieved that goal, preventing a repetition of authoritarianism in the future. Yet, after twenty years of dictatorship, the efforts of the Assembly produced a long, rigid, and prescriptive constitution without the elasticity of the old document.[14]

In the Assembly's deliberations on this matter, the Christian Democrats were driven in large part by their worry that the Marxist parties, then operating under the spell of Stalinism and still aspiring, if only in the long run, for a proletarian revolution, might emerge victorious at the next election. "The greatest worry of De Gasperi was the fear that the Communist Party in the future could obtain the majority of votes," according to Giuseppe Dossetti, a Christian Democrat and one of the architects of the constitution. To forestall the possibility of a Soviet-style revolution in Italy, the Christian Democrats put in place an elaborate combination of checks and balances. Leo Valiani quipped that the Christian Democrats and the Communists were afraid that in the future one could be outlawed by the other. This mutual distrust, in the words of Dossetti, created "a labyrinth" that presented obstacles to the government's functions, hindering the executive powers "with excessive guarantees" and impeding the emergence of "the centrality of the executive," unlike the evolution undergone by more robust Western democracies, where the prime minister's office has become the locus of government power.[15] The Communists initially regarded some aspects of the constitutional labyrinth as bizarre, "bizzarie," to use Togliatti's word, but on being ousted from government in mid-1947, they embraced them with a new-found enthusiasm.

The Christian Democrats' fears were at the basis of the second part of the constitution, that dealing with the institutions and functions of government. New structures and apparatuses were created that broke the unity of the state and reduced the power of the central government, providing safeguards against authoritarian temptations or Jacobin aspirations. The constitution established a Parliament, made of two chambers with equal powers, in order to delay government bills; a constitutional court to guarantee the legitimacy of laws; a judicial council to assure the independence of the courts and to appoint judges at all levels; and regional governments to bring power closer to the people and to curtail the powers of the central cabinet, an objective also furthered by the constitution's provision for popular referenda. Finally, the constitution reserved to the president of the republic the right to withhold, or delay, a law passed by Parliament, and also the prerogative to approve a bill before it was presented to Parliament for debate. In this fashion, the constitution created a modern democracy, founded on free elections and political parties, while enshrining parliamentary supremacy, limiting the powers of the executive branch, and restricting the authority of the prime minister. In the Italian system of governance, the prime minister, or the cabinet, even with a large majority, does not enjoy the power and authority that pertains, by law and by tradition, to a British or Canadian prime minister under the Westminster system. The prime minister is only primus inter pares; he has the duty "to promote" and to "coordinate," even to "direct," the policy of the cabinet, but lacks the means to give force to that duty, let alone to impose his will or his priorities. He does not have the sole authority to choose his ministers, nor can he dismiss them at his pleasure; he cannot call elections at his discretion, and does not control the agenda of Parliament or the legislative process, which rests with the speaker and the house leaders. This imbalance among the organs of the state has been recognized by leading scholars and politicians alike, such as Giovanni Sartori and Giorgio Napolitano. The latter noted: "The constitution of 1948 certainly emphasized the prerogative of Parliament, but neglected the requirements of the executive. This way the needs of stability and the efficiency of political activity remained of secondary importance, creating a weak government."[16]

The hopes for a more equitable and inclusive society are reflected in the first part of the constitution, which deals with the fundamental principles of the republic and with the rights and duties of the citizens. Here, liberal and socialist ideas are certainly present, but these are overshadowed by elements of Catholic social teachings. In an attempt to bring the masses into the state, the framers of the Italian constitution spelled out the rights not only of individuals but also of classes while at the same time placing traditional liberties alongside more modern ones. The aim was not simply to revive the liberal state but to give shape to a democratic society and to inject substance into the concept of popular sovereignty. The constitution recognizes political freedom and assures the rights of the individual living in a free society; it establishes the equality of men and women before the law, and ends discrimination based on class, gender, religion, and economic conditions; it recognizes private property and the role of the market economy, but it also demands that economic activity exercise a social function, putting public welfare above private gain; it stresses the right to equal opportunity for all, but also the right of workers to full employment and education, so that they can enjoy full citizenship; it mandates the promotion of public health, the protection of the environment, and the preservation of Italy's artistic heritage; it repudiates war as a way of resolving conflicts among nations; and, finally, it demands the removal of social and economic obstacles that create an impediment to the fulfilment and enjoyment of the rights granted. In short, the clauses of this section are the blueprint of a modern welfare state.[17]

The Italian constitution was not the work of an outstanding jurist but rather the result of political parties cooperating towards a single goal. The social philosophy expressed in the first part in particular shows that the constitution was the outcome, in the main, of a compromise between the Christian Democrats on the one side and the Socialists and Communists on the other – the three parties that dominated the Constituent Assembly, having received more than 80 per cent of the popular vote in the general election, and that were then united in a coalition government under the leadership of Alcide De Gasperi, the leader of the Christian Democrats. Yet, in the drafting of the constitution, the Christian Democrats were in a much stronger position than the left-wing parties. To achieve their aims, they could make an alliance or enter into agreements with the Communists or with smaller parties of the right, or with both, when it was necessary or convenient. The frequency of this practice made some members uncomfortable. Croce, for one, was neither pleased nor amused by the way some decisions were reached. In January 1948, a few months after the Liberals had rejoined the government alongside the Christian Democrats, sending the Communists and the Socialists into opposition, he confided to his diary: "Much discomfort for the deplorable things that happen in the Constituent Assembly, especially for the reciprocal concessions between the Christian Democrats and the Communists in favour of their parties, who are supposed to be adversaries; there have been agreements ... [that are] shameless and such as to compromise the political and moral life of Italy."[18]

To expedite the drafting of a constitutional text, the Assembly created a special committee of seventy-five members, the best and brightest of each party. That committee was then further divided into subcommittees, each dealing with a specific section of the constitution. In all of these committees, the Christian Democrats, more than other parties, were represented by astute politicians, well-trained lawyers, and, in some cases, outstanding scholars. Above all, they could count on a group of bright young professors, trained in jurisprudence and freshly graduated or teaching at various faculties of the Catholic University of Milan, which was known to have been, over the years, the breeding ground of many anti-Fascists, a few heretics even, but hardly any Liberals. These *professorini* displayed keen zeal and sharp pugnacity of purpose, acting under the able leadership of Dossetti. (Dossetti later quit politics, became a monk, and was chosen as a *peritus* – or adviser – to the Second Vatican Council; he, along with two other of his original colleagues, is now a candidate for sainthood.) They probably made the most important contribution to the final shape of the constitution, especially in drafting the articles of the first section. No other group was so well organized, coherent, and determined. They, however, were not the only Catholic actors in the framing of the constitution. All the Christian Democrat members on the various committees, at each turning point or difficult decision, could count on the full support of the party, the wise guidance of the prime minister, and the advice and, sometimes, direction of the Vatican. (Monsignor Giovanni Montini, the future Pope Paul VI, and Monsignor Angelo Dell'Acqua were particularly influential; they have to be considered to be among the protagonists of the Italian constitution.)[19]

The participation of the Liberals in the drafting of the new constitution reflected their diminished status. But their contribution was far greater than their small numbers warranted. Liberal ideas are evident in the clauses that assure freedom of expression, protect the rights of the individual, curtail the use of arbitrary powers, guarantee the independence of the courts, and bestow a parliamentary structure to the overall architecture of the state. Moreover, within the committees the Liberals tended to act as individual members rather than as a group subject to party discipline; this in general weakened their position but sometimes could increase their chances of success, especially when a proposal came from someone whose reputation carried weight and who could argue his case effectively. Luigi Einaudi was instrumental in drafting the articles that guarantee freedom of education, assure freedom of scientific research, and impose budgetary restraint on government spending. Two other Liberal leaders played important roles. Meuccio Ruini was formally a member of the Labour Party, but he belonged to the liberal tradition and shared the heritage of the Risorgimento. As chairman of the Committee of 75 and one of the subcommittees, he was influential in the drafting of the whole constitution; possessing unmatched familiarity with the machinery of the old liberal state and abundant conciliatory skills, he could be regarded as the James Madison of the Italian constitution. Last but not least, Enrico De Nicola, as the new president of the republic, often had meetings with members of the various committees; he was a fine jurist of wide learning and experience, well qualified to give advice or to suggest solutions.[20]

None of the surviving political leaders of liberal Italy took part in the workings of the various committees. They limited their contribution to delivering speeches during the sittings of the full Assembly and during the general debates on single articles, when, notwithstanding the cogency of their arguments, it was more difficult to effect changes or to influence final outcomes. The drafting of the constitution was thus deprived of the benefit of their considerable political and administrative experience, as Togliatti himself recognized. After twenty years of dictatorship, in the new Assembly there was a dearth of practical knowledge about the inner workings of the state, particularly the interrelations among its different organs, and the functions of government. Often members of the younger generation were carried away by general ideas and partisan enthusiasm, without giving due consideration to the wider juridical and social implications of a proposal. Croce was once an amused witness to such a spectacle. "I heard a long speech by a Christian Democrat, rumoured to be a convert from communism or socialism, who now lives an ascetic life in a convent and teaches law at the University of Florence: a very bizarre speech it was indeed, full of childish arguments and strange comparisons, ending with an invocation of the Virgin Mary and a large sign of the cross."[21] Yet a much younger Andreotti, barely out of university, was deeply impressed by the same performance. "In the Assembly there was a beautiful speech by Giorgio La Pira in favour of the constitution's draft: a lesson of sociology and high politics at the same time. When he concluded the speech, invoking the help of God and the assistance of the Virgin Mary, a shiver of excitement passed through the Assembly."[22]

In general, the old Liberal leaders felt out of place in the new environment dominated by the discipline of mass parties. Not the least of their failings was that they sometimes tended to indulge in recriminations over the past and often were polemical in defending their achievements. Croce, for instance, had to use all his influence to avoid a public spat between Orlando and Nitti about their relations with the Vatican and their own contribution to the solution of the "Roman Question" before it was finally solved with the Lateran Pacts in 1929.[23]

There were, however, happy exceptions, at least once in a while. Orlando gave a long and critical appraisal of the draft of the constitution: at eighty-six years of age, he delivered a remarkable speech, full of political wisdom and juridical doctrine, which lasted for more than two hours without ever losing the attention of the Assembly. A few of his suggestions were accepted in the final revised text; most importantly, as a result of his intervention, the proposal for a national assembly, with undefined powers, sitting occasionally alongside the Chamber of Deputies and the Senate, was abandoned. But no attempt was made to remedy other shortcomings he had pointed out: the generic and badly defined powers given to the president of the republic; the dysfunctional relationship between Parliament and government; and the weakness of the executive branch. Above all, no heed was given to his warning about the inconvenience, even the danger, of "the totalitarianism of the Assembly." For Orlando, the excessive concentration of power in the legislative branch would require, in order for the government to carry out the nation's business, either a powerful leader supported by a large majority or, "more likely, as is the case today, a government through personal agreements among the leaders of a coalition." This practice, according to Orlando, would create a strange beast: "a directorate government, characterized by a plurality of leaders, not bound by the unity of direction that is proper to the unity of the state."[24]

Yet, exceptions such as this notwithstanding, it seems clear from Croce's diary and his correspondence that after the war, facing new problems and more pressing needs, Liberal politicians were no longer willing to fight old battles. In particular, they did not have the energy or the enthusiasm to defend, let alone to fight for, the traditional principles that had assured the separation of church and state during the Risorgimento and that are essential to the maintenance of a secular modern society. Some Liberals were simply not ready or willing to challenge the demands of the Vatican, afraid of losing the support of local church authorities or of offending the sensibilities of their Catholic voters. Others, however, had plainly become indifferent to the old issues, and were more concerned with the defence of private property rights and the danger of communism. Only a few shared Croce's fighting resolve and constant vigilance in protecting the Risorgimento's ideals.

Croce's diary leaves no doubts about his worries during the constitutional debates. "I am very uneasy about the many uncertainties among Liberals, when it comes to religious and secular questions," he once wrote.[25] Unlike some of his colleagues, "afraid to face the blackmail of the priests at the next elections," Croce girded his loins for the struggles ahead in the old-fashioned way: "I read again the writings of Celsus against the Christians, in order to acquire a new vigour in the great old polemic."[26] Unlike others, he recognized the church's right to full freedom of expression, but it was a right to be exercised in an open and direct way, not through political intermediaries. In the constitution there are several clauses that were imposed by the Christian Democrats and reflected direct demands made by the Vatican. The sectarian nature of those items should have been unpalatable to all Liberals, young or old. For his part, an offended Croce was not willing "to let pass without a fight the absurd and anti-juridical demands of the Christian Democrats."[27] He also tried to strengthen the resolve of other Liberals, as we learn from a diary entry in April 1947: "I spoke firmly to Morelli so that it is known among members of the party that if new deviations from the secular nature of our party should happen again, I will resign as president." He went on to say, "I repeated the same warning to Cassandro," then the secretary of the Liberal Party, "who shortly sent a telegram to [Epicarmo] Corbino," the chairman of the Liberal parliamentary group in the Assembly.[28] But Croce's warnings and threats failed; "electoral worries" in many instances led to different choices. To his dismay, in meetings in Naples and in Rome of members of the party's executive, he learned that only a few colleagues shared his views and were ready to give battle, cost what it might at the polls. "The majority of Liberals are not willing to oppose the bad and offensive articles imposed by the Christian Democrats at the request of the Vatican: this is, indeed, an improper imposition of the church that a Catholic like Manzoni or like Cavour would not have tolerated."[29]

In those meetings, as on other occasions, he made clear his opposition and also his willingness to make his criticism public. "I told them that I am ready to speak against those articles, and to defend the liberal concept of a constitution, which cannot be the expression of a single party but instead has to protect all of them."[30] It was at Croce's direct request that the Liberal leaders in the Assembly proposed an amendment against financial support to religious schools. The proposal passed with a slim majority against the vehement opposition of the Christian Democrats and the lukewarm support of the Communists. Croce was pleased, as he noted in a letter to his friend Luigi Russo. "I send instructions and telegrams to Rome on the question of financial support to religious schools, urging all to remain vigilant; though we were abandoned by our unreliable Communist allies and their chief, [Concetto] Marchesi, a happy proposal by Corbino prevented the Christian Democrats from achieving their aim and running away with the stolen goods."[31]

But celebrations were short-lived for Liberals in those months, and significant victories few and far between. When the Constituent Assembly debated the inclusion of the Lateran Pacts in the constitution, Croce's criticism received approval from different quarters, including Socialists and Actionists. But then, out of the blue, an unholy alliance between the Christian Democrats and the Communists carried the day, Togliatti defending the deal "with a subtle and sullen speech, full of threats," as Croce put it. In newspapers and private letters, Croce could only condemn "the shameful scandal" and protest "against the badly devised and insidious articles" and their "anti-juridical nature and political vacuity."[32] He also lamented the offence done to the tradition of liberal Italy and the *vulnus* inflicted on the body politic of the new republic. "This is a shameful insolence, done by priests. This way Italy, already oppressed by foreign powers, which have taken away from us lands, borders, colonies, arms, and have destroyed our material and spiritual wealth, now Italy, the returned slave of foreigners, has to endure also the priestly yoke; foreigners and priests, the two different enemies of her sorrowful and yet glorious history. With those articles of the Lateran Pacts, the pope declares himself, in temporal matters, superior to the Italian state, and at the same time prevents the state from legislating in some of its own jurisdictions."[33]

After the elections, Croce would remain president of the Liberal Party for a few more months, but his participation in national politics decreased markedly. He attended the Constituent Assembly only a few times and on special occasions. His direct contribution to the drafting of the constitution was limited to personal advice to his friends and to the members of the Liberal Party. At one time he even expressed the desire to resign from the Assembly, making room for someone younger and more energetic. Urged by friends, including De Nicola, to stay on, he did so but, out of scruples, returned his remuneration to the Assembly's administration.[34] Age was dictating a slower pace. Also, Croce disliked travelling from Naples to Rome, a journey prone to accidents and delays in those days, which he undertook only when strictly necessary and always with the assistance of devoted friends. And so he probably was not present when the Assembly, in December 1947, adopted the new constitution by an overwhelming majority.

Croce seldom spoke before the Assembly. One of the few times he did so was in March 1947, on the reading of the constitution's initial draft. On that occasion, dealing with an unfamiliar subject, he did not deliver a great speech, according to historian Paolo Pombeni, an authority on the constitutional debates. Still, Croce was among the first to raise troubling questions about the novelties proposed, while pointing out glaring shortcomings of the new constitution. He was listened to with great deference by friends and foes alike; parts of his speech had wide resonance inside and outside the Assembly, discussed in the press and on the radio in Italy and abroad. But Croce expressed a minority position and was unable to change the outcome in any significant way, though he did have a marginal influence in determining the document's final wording. After he had lamented the poor language of some of the articles, a literary committee was struck that included one of his friends, Pietro Pancrazi, a fine writer from Tuscany. As a result of Pancrazi's work, the final text is more fluent and elegant than the first draft, but the substance remained, of course, unchanged.[35]

In his speech on the constitution, Croce expressed several reservations and pointed out some shortcomings and contradictions. Besides questioning the style of the document, he also lamented the way in which it had been produced, noting "the lack of coherence and harmony of the present design." Unlike the Albertine Statute, which was the work of a single author, the constitutional draft under consideration was the fruit of committees, "but," Croce said, "the effort had not produced a happy result." Not only had there been too many authors, but, even more worrisome, they had lacked a common purpose. "They did not share an overarching and unifying principle" and "they did not pursue the same practical and political aims." Inside the committees, "each one of the three larger parties' representatives tried to bring water to his own mill." Several articles, Croce pointed out, were the fruit of "negotiations undertaken by members of the big parties; these have resulted in agreements that incorporated the requests of each one, in a more or less satisfactory way, often bad rather than good; but the compromises have neglected the technical requirements that the occasion and the task demanded." Instead of fashioning a blueprint for an ideal society that reflected their parties' ideological program, the aim of the constitution's framers should have been much simpler and limited in scope but at the same time more attuned to the requirements and nature of such a document. The need was "to give to the Italian people a body of juridical norms that assure and guarantee to all persons, regardless of political opinion, economic class and social conditions, the protection of the law, and the exercise of freedom." Even in a speech on legal matters, Croce made a philosophical point that he had been emphasizing for some time and on various occasions. He reminded the honourable members, and the critics of his political creed, that freedom is not an empty formula, but rather that "the exercise of freedom as a logical consequence, as times change and civilization grows, is always accompanied by social justice, with which freedom is entwined."[36]

While Croce saw in the constitution "several incoherences and contradictions," and deplored a few compromises, "either barren of or pregnant with future dangers," he focused his special criticism on two specific items, both keenly desired by the Christian Democrats and finally endorsed, after some qualms, by the Communist Party, led by Togliatti, in his hope of preserving the current coalition and even, perhaps, turning that coalition into a lasting collaboration. One was the incorporation of the Lateran Pacts of 1929 in the constitution. Croce reminded the Assembly that, once before, he had spoken against the Lateran Pacts, declaring that "I was the only one, in 1929, to speak in the Senate against the Lateran Pacts; but even then I made clear that I was not against the idea of a reconciliation between church and state; my repugnance and opposition were directed against that particular kind of reconciliation, realized not with a free Italy but with an enslaved one, and through the man who had enslaved her and was doing so not to achieve religious peace but to increase his prestige and to strengthen his tyranny." Now, in 1947, after the fall of fascism, Croce posed a rhetorical question that was troubling the minds of many people, inside and outside the Assembly: "What do the constitution of a state and a treaty between two states have in common?" He strongly opposed "the strange inclusion in the constitution" of a "treaty between two states" and described that inclusion as "a strident logical error and a juridical scandal" and also "an offence to the legal tradition of Italy." For Croce, this measure was typical of the many questionable compromises achieved between political parties on controversial issues. The inclusion of the Lateran Pacts in the constitution gave the Vatican veto power over some matters that were strictly under the purview of the national government alone in other countries.[37]

The other issue that aroused Croce's ire was the creation of regional governments, which in the future, he said, would change the old centralized structure of the Italian state, based on the Napoleonic Civil Code, giving it almost a federal flavour. In this case, his criticism was shared not only by Nenni and Nitti but also, for once, by Togliatti. Perhaps, Croce granted, it was necessary to decentralize services and to give more autonomy to municipal and provincial authorities, in order to meet the changed conditions and to satisfy certain special local traditions. But he saw no need to introduce radical changes, and he believed that it was a mistake to create novel institutions just for the sake of change. "This sudden frenzy and rapid destruction of the organization and administration of the state ... this creation of untried and complicated regional institutions is a frightening undertaking ... like a walk along an unknown road."

At the end of his speech, with an evident feeling of nostalgia, Croce praised the Albertine Statute, which had furnished the underpinnings of liberal Italy's achievements. "I am a son of that age, for under the beneficial blessings of freedom I grew and learned ... And I believe that it is the duty of sons to defend the work and honour of their fathers." With Croce's words, while a new constitution was being born, the old statute received an honourable burial. "The Statute of 1848 provided the framework for the splendid progress of Italy in every field of activity for more than seventy years." It worked well because "it was a flexible instrument, not a rigid one like the present proposed constitution ... and it allowed in an incremental way, as social and cultural conditions changed, the right of workers to strike and the enlargement of the franchise," among other positive features.[38]

When the Constituent Assembly adopted, by a large majority, the proposed draft of the constitution and began the debate on individual clauses, Croce often expressed his disappointment. In a diary entry at the end of March 1947, he wrote:

> It is the first time that I am not pleased with the Liberal Party ... Many members of the party, contrary to the arguments set out in my speech ... and despite the incoherence and the juridical impropriety of several articles of the constitutional project, have voted in favour of the text wanted by the Christian Democrats, that is by the pope, which is an insolence and a shameful imposition. Some have been impelled to do so perhaps by religious scruples, but others by electoral preoccupations. On the other hand, the bad example came from the top: Orlando, Nitti, and Bonomi voted in favour at the end, after they had spoken against it. Only a few remained firm, and among these especially the honourable [Americo] Crispo, who ... during the general discussion defended my position with great logic and vigour.[39]

Croce's speech and his diary contain astute comments on the constitution. Some of his criticisms were confirmed by future events; some of his fears did not materialize after all. The institution of regional governments, when it was realized after some delay, weakened further the unity of the state and the authority of the central government and increased animosity among regions. Nor did the new institution, contrary to what its proponents had promised, bring the administration closer to the public. Instead, a plethora of laws was passed and another layer of civil servants was added to an already bloated bureaucracy, complicating the delivery of services and often squandering scarce resources and increasing the opportunities for corruption.

On the other hand, the inclusion of the Lateran Pacts in the constitution provided some privileges to the Catholic Church, but it did not create a sectarian state. Even under the long tenure of Christian Democrat governments, Italy remained a secular society and, despite the odd skirmish between church and state, freedom of expression and religion retained the full protection of the law. Over the years, the influence and practice of religion steadily declined; divorce and abortion laws were enacted and then confirmed with huge majorities by popular referenda. In 1984 the government and Vatican agreed on a liberal revision of the Concordat. But a clear separation of church and state has proven to be elusive. Perhaps it is even an impossible dream, given the fundamental role played by the Catholic Church in the long history of the Italian nation and the presence of the Vatican and the pope in the heart of Rome, not to mention the feelings of the Italian people.

14
The Peace Treaty of 1947

Besides the constitution, the other issue that deeply concerned Croce in 1946–7 was the ratification of the Peace Treaty between Italy and the Allies. The treaty had first been discussed at the London Conference in 1945; negotiations continued during 1946 at the Peace Conference in Paris and later in New York among the foreign ministers of the Allies. Finally, the Peace Treaty between the Allied Powers and the Associated Nations and Italy was signed in Paris in February 1947.

The treaty was not the result of negotiations between Italy and the Allies; it was instead the outcome of compromises and rivalries among the Great Powers, each pursuing its own interests or supporting the claims of its allies. The agreement, so laboriously achieved, was then imposed on Italy without discussion or the possibility of modification. The treaty was a punitive document full of hostility towards Italy and the Italian people. The aim of the Allied powers was to reduce Italy to military impotence and economic dependence. In particular, Great Britain and France wanted a Mediterranean without an Italian navy and the region devoid of any Italian political influence. For Croce, the treaty was a product of egoistical nationalism, another sign of the European malaise that had led to the birth and triumph of fascism and the spread of imperialism.

The treaty declared Italy responsible for starting a war of aggression as an ally of Germany and Japan. To add salt to the wound, it reminded the Italian anti-Fascist leaders that the regime of Mussolini had collapsed as a result of the Allies' victories and their invasion of Italy. In the final document, as at each conference that led to it, Italy was treated as a defeated nation which had already surrendered unconditionally. The subsequent status of co-belligerent, negotiated by Badoglio, made no difference and had no practical consequence. The Italian contribution to the resistance against Germany was mentioned but given no effectual consideration. Promises made during the war were ignored or forgotten. During the international meetings, Italy was isolated and remained without friends; no champion of its interests emerged among the Great Powers. Only the United States showed some sympathy at times, but it rarely challenged seriously the claims of other nations. The Italian representatives, usually old anti-Fascists, always spoke in a cold and hostile atmosphere, and their pleas were summarily rejected.

The treaty has to be regarded as an old-fashioned piece of diplomacy, myopic and narrow-minded. It looked to the past and ignored the future. It burdened the fledgling Italian democracy with heavy demands, harming its development. The new republic was made to pay for the sins of the monarchy. Anti-Fascists had to assume responsibility for the crimes of Mussolini. The harsh terms of the treaty offered ammunition to the new Fascist movement, allowing it to launch baseless accusations against the anti-Fascist leaders while ignoring Mussolini's policies and forgetting his responsibilities and the atrocities of fascism. Fortunately for Italy, however, the treaty became obsolete almost as soon as it was signed. The rivalry between East and West was already evident, and soon after ratification Italy was invited to join the Western European Organization and the North Atlantic Treaty Organization (NATO) by its former enemies. Leon Blum, the French Socialist leader, expressed well the nature of the treaty: it was a treaty against the enemy of yesterday, not with the ally of tomorrow.[1]

As a result of the war and the imposition of the Peace Treaty, Italy suffered painful territorial losses and saw its international status greatly diminished and its sovereignty impaired. The country surrendered all its colonies, both those conquered with great fanfare under Mussolini's regime and those acquired earlier by liberal Italy in Africa and in the Aegean Sea. This was a blessing in disguise, allowing Italy to avoid the troubles soon experienced by France and Great Britain as they faced liberation movements in their own colonies. But in 1947, when hardly any European leader saw the need for, let alone the duty of, decolonization, it was regarded in Italy as an act of punishment, pure and simple.

On its eastern border, with the exception of Trieste, Italy lost all the lands gained in the Great War. During and after the Second World War, ethnic cleansing took place in Istria and Dalmatia. Thousands of Italians were killed by Tito's partisans, and others were harassed, persecuted, and compelled to emigrate; as a result, more than 350,000 Italians left those old Venetian lands in a painful exodus. The Free Territory of Trieste was created under Allied administration. That solution poisoned for years the relations between Italy and Yugoslavia, and between Italy and Great Britain, which appointed the administration's chairman. Only in 1954 was Trieste returned fully to Italy, and relations between Italy and Yugoslavia immediately improved, with mutual economic advantages.

France failed to obtain the Aosta Valley, thanks to American opposition, but demanded – and obtained – modification of Italy's western border, which had remained unchanged for more than two hundred years. Those small, but strategic, changes along the region of the Alps made the border no longer defensible. Moreover, with the possession of the villages of Briga and Tenda and their hydro-power plants, France acquired control of the electrical supply of Turin and Genoa, the industrial centre of Italy. With a callous gesture, France also demanded the "return" of the historical archives of the province of Savoy and the city of Nice that had been ceded by Piedmont to France in 1860 as part of the alliance between Cavour and Napoleon III.

Only the border between Italy and Austria remained unchanged, and that was mainly because the Soviet Union strongly opposed the modifications in favour of Austria that were proposed by France and Great Britain. Left to their own devices, Austria and Italy reached an accommodation: the German-speaking minority in the South Tyrol was given considerable autonomy and the region received a great deal of economic assistance.

The terms of the Peace Treaty reduced Italy to military impotence, leaving it unable to defend its own borders, let alone pose a threat to other nations. The Italian army became almost a police force; strict limits were placed on the number of soldiers, tanks, and heavy guns. The existing fleet was divided among the Allies, and so was the merchant marine. In future, Italy was to be prohibited from building submarines, battleships, aircraft carriers, and long-range fighter planes. The Allies also saw fit to protect their future commercial interests: Italy could not buy any military aircraft built in Germany or Japan. Fortifications on all the borders had to be destroyed; naval bases on the mainland and in the islands were to be dismantled. The Allies also demanded from Italy a promise that it would not build or experiment with an atomic bomb.

The economic clauses of the treaty were equally harsh. Italy had to pay $360 million to various nations as reparation for war damages. At the same time, it could not claim any reparation from other nations. In an act of generosity, France, Britain, and the United States forfeited their share of reparations, but Italy had to pay the expenses for the repatriation of its own prisoners of war in Allied hands. Italy and Italian citizens could not request compensation for damage done by the Allies. On the other hand, Italy had to accept and redeem all the money printed and used in Italy by the Allies, a policy that led to high inflation.

The treaty also affected future policy and interfered with internal matters. Italy could not prosecute citizens who had expressed sympathy with the Allied cause, worked for the Allied powers, or spied for them. At the same time, Italy had to release to the Allies those Italian generals who were regarded as war criminals or were accused by other nations of crimes against humanity. The treaty had some contradictions. Italy was asked "to assure freedom of expression to all her citizens … regardless of political opinion." But it should not allow the revival of a fascist party. Finally, underlining the unilateral nature of the document, a clause stipulated that the treaty had to be signed by Italy but that it would enter into force with its ratification by the Allied powers, even without Italy's signature.[2]

After the war, Croce paid close attention to foreign policy issues. In the spring of 1945, he had protested against Italy's exclusion from the San Francisco Conference, which had been called to establish the United Nations. For the occasion he wrote a letter to *The Times* of London and granted an interview to Reuters. He told British and American readers that the exclusion of Italy from that gathering was a simple act of revenge, certainly not a contribution to a new era of international cooperation or to a more peaceful world. For Croce, the exclusion was a useless and gratuitous offence to the pride of a sister nation. Above all, it ignored the Italian contribution to the Allied cause on land and sea and through the efforts of heroic partisans and "thousands of men and soldiers employed by the Allies behind the front lines." Croce concluded his argument by invoking Talleyrand: "To exclude Italy from the San Francisco Conference, besides opening a wound in Italian national feeling, would be something worse than a crime; it would be a political mistake."[3]

In September 1945 the foreign ministers of the five Great Powers met in London to discuss the terms of the treaty with Italy. In the House of Commons and in the press, British politicians debated the issue at length, arguing whether the peace with Italy should be punitive or whether it should follow a more constructive path. As a contribution to the discussion, Croce sent a letter to the *Manchester Guardian*, using the good offices of his old friends Cecil and Sylvia Sprigge. He urged the British people to reject "sentiments of conquest and spoliation" and to oppose a treaty that would render Italy "mutilated, humiliated, crushed, and reduced to impotence." He appealed to British politicians to avoid a harsh peace, because Great Britain in the future would have no reason to fear new threats from a democratic Italy; instead, both countries should make a special effort to re-establish the cordial relations between them that had existed before fascism.[4] At this time, Croce also wrote an essay in which he recognized a bitter truth often mentioned in the international press: Italy indeed owed a debt to the Allies for having regained its freedom with their intervention, and for not having been able to get rid of Mussolini through its own efforts alone. Yet, while "debts have to be repaid however acquired," it was also true that "debtors may deal with honest and reasonable creditors, or may meet greedy and ruthless usurers; and it is in the interest of the Allies not to be numbered among the latter."[5]

After the London Conference ended and the stringent terms of the future treaty between the Allies and Italy became known, Croce wrote a letter of protest to an Italian newspaper. In this piece, he noted first of all the difference between the promises made in the past by the Allies and their new attitude in the present. "In truth, the present policy of the Allied Powers towards Italy, when it is compared with the promises and declarations made before and during the war ... generates a sense of injustice. All of them, big and small, or almost all of them, like howling dogs, want to devour a piece of Italy's body, not only our colonies but our national territory, and parts of our scarce economic resources." At that point, Croce made an astute observation: "What is now happening is a political fact, the eternal and ever-recurring reality of war with its cunning and lies, with the ensuing cry of 'vae victis' and with the usual unrestrained ambition and unbridled desires." He pointed out the origin of that brutal fact, and the consequences it had produced. "The accursed fascism opened the doors to the feral and plundering instincts of man." Now the disease had spread and become general, and even the victors were no longer able "to put obstacles in the way of the greed of their countries and the nationalistic and imperialistic egotism of their own public opinion." Against that general trend, Croce urged Italians "to protect and to defend" with determination the national interest, but at the same time he invited them to build a better society, in which it would be possible "to cultivate and to nourish a sentiment of moderation and humanity, and to follow the ideal of freedom, and the intelligence that enlightens it."[6]

For Croce, and others of his generation, England was still the hegemonic power and key to the solution of European problems. For that reason, during and after the war, he tried to mollify Britain's hostility by talking to British correspondents in Italy. In August 1946 he had a conversation with Cecil Sprigge. Naturally enough, Sprigge tried "to justify the United Kingdom's policy and the treatment to which she is subjecting Italy"; to this, Croce replied: "Great Britain feels the inferior status to which in the present she has been reduced in many ways, and she is frightened by the future, and this fear gives rise to her indecent and foolish policies against Italy."[7]

When the terms of the Peace Treaty were finalized, after several international meetings, Croce gave an interview to a Brazilian newspaper. In that interview, he lamented that, as a result of the war and the policies of Mussolini, Italy had returned to the situation of five centuries ago, when it suffered foreign invasions and its states came under the domination of European powers. He also mentioned a more recent fact that Allied nations tended to forget. During the Fascist regime, when Mussolini faced opposition – both open and covert – in Italy, he was admired by foreign leaders "as a model and as an example." Tongue-in-cheek, Croce continued: "The names of those admirers are known, men who now sit among the victors and dare to speak of morality and the justice and punishment that have to be meted out to Italy." For Croce, the proposed terms of the Peace Treaty, coming after the destruction suffered by Italy during the war, meant "the final and total dispossession of any military force and possibility of defence, and the opening of her borders to the power of her neighbours." The terms of the treaty were not only a negation of promises made during the war, they were also a violation of the common interests of European civilization, "interests that demands a limit to the oppression, destruction, and humiliation of defeated peoples, who are necessary components of that civilization." On that score, Croce reminded the Allied powers that their policy after the war was fomenting "suspicions and envy and hatred among the peoples of Europe, between the victors and the vanquished," so much so that the victors were still feared but no longer "admired as great leaders, nor as benefactors of mankind." Once again, Croce lamented that the Peace Treaty ignored the Italian contribution to the war against Germany. But he also advised Italians to avoid regrets and to work harder in order to repair what "had been built with a century of hard work by the generations of the Risorgimento."[8]

On 1 October 1946 the Paris Conference ended and the terms of the Peace Treaty became known. The news generated a great deal of discussion in Italy and soul-searching among political leaders. In January 1947

Croce met with Nenni, the Socialist leader who was then serving as minister of foreign affairs. His advice was that Italy should either ratify the treaty without protest or reject it outright in defence of national dignity. Croce favoured the second option and was ready to face, as he put it, rather too optimistically, "the little dangers that could be the result of that decision" because the historical and moral advantages "for those who look to the future would be far greater than those dangers." Croce was certainly aware that the Allied powers could put the treaty into effect even without Italian ratification and could also "undertake retaliation." He did not advise active resistance to that possibility but made some practical suggestions to blunt at least some of the most unpleasant consequences. "I believe that the government, with some special laws and administrative regulations, could facilitate the execution of the treaty's clauses." But the government of Italy "should never accept or approve the full treaty, with its spirit of vendetta and punishment." Whether Croce's suggestion could have been acted upon, it is hard to say. A policy of defiance required unity of purpose among Italian political parties and a readiness to accept more sacrifices in a time of hardship. Those two conditions were greatly lacking in Italy at the time.

At the end of their conversation, Croce raised two other points that, no doubt, strongly appealed to Nenni's patriotic feelings and democratic preoccupations. For Croce, the treaty had to be rejected for its long-term moral implications but also for a more immediate political reason. If the country's leaders humiliated themselves by accepting the treaty, not only would they earn the opprobrium of "future generations," but "in the present they would be lending support to the shameless propaganda of old and new Fascists, who already are accusing all of us of having, through our hatred of fascism, ruined Italy and favoured Italy's defeat in the war." Such an argument, Croce observed, "finds an echo among the crowd" and "appeals to those who conveniently seek a scapegoat rather than the truth in historical events, and are always ready to blame others and to spare themselves, trying to escape their own responsibilities." Nostalgic admirers of the Fascist regime, then or later, chose to forget the simple truth that, as Croce put it, "the defeat had been prepared by the folly, the rashness, and the gross ignorance of Mussolini," who had sent the Italian army "to Africa, Greece, and Russia to fight with inadequate resources ... against more powerful and richer nations."[9]

As soon as the terms of the Peace Treaty were finalized, representatives of the Allied powers tried to make the bitter pill more palatable by promising, in private conversations, possible revisions once the treaty was ratified. Some Italians gave undue weight to those promises while others hoped to find new support in the British Labour Party or among the French Socialists. The old philosopher, schooled in the teachings of Machiavelli and Marx, was not impressed. After meeting with Niccolò Carandini, then the Italian ambassador to London, a fellow Liberal, and the man Croce had urged to assume the leadership of the Liberal Party, Croce wrote: "He defends and even supports the British policy towards Italy, and regards this attitude as helpful and friendly. I pointed out that it is not a question of what the British say in private conversations, but of what they do in their treaties. It seems to me that Carandini does not see the difference, and so allows himself to be deceived."[10]

Those who put great store in the Allies' goodwill had a point, however: revisions to the treaty were indeed soon made, when, as a result of changes in the international situation, Italy's contribution to European defence was deemed necessary. But Croce never vacillated in his opposition to the treaty, nor did his resentment against the Great Powers' leaders ever wane. The treaty is always mentioned in his diary with a "feeling of sadness for the attitude towards Italy of the so-called victors and peacemakers of the world."[11] A typical entry reads as follows: "I began to think about the speech that I will give in the Constituent Assembly on the Peace Treaty, or, better, against the approval of that treaty. It is a painful task, because it compels me to relive the pain and feel the shame of the past, and especially the shameful folly of the British, who, out of vengeance and blind egotism, want to destroy and obliterate a sister nation, which played a role no less significant than that of Great Britain in the creation of European civilization."[12]

The Peace Treaty came before the Constituent Assembly for ratification in July 1947. Ratification of international treaties was one of the very few matters that required a vote of the Assembly, other than the approval of a new constitution and the passage of an electoral law. In all other areas, the government, enjoying the confidence of the Assembly, had the power to carry on the nation's business by orders-in-council. With respect to the treaty, the Constituent Assembly faced a difficult task. All parties, in different ways, were disappointed with a treaty imposed without negotiations and dictated to Italy after the Allies had reached agreements among themselves. The choice before Italian politicians was stark: refuse the imposition and face the consequences; or forget the injustice and accept the diktat, and then start working for a new era of cooperation among European nations, thus creating the conditions for revisions to the treaty in the near future. This was the policy suggested by De Gasperi, Sforza, Einaudi, and others. Croce and other old figures of liberal Italy favoured rejection of the treaty. They were joined by a few members of the younger generation, who also felt compelled to defend the dignity of their nation. Leo Valiani was among this group; he spoke and voted against the treaty, in particular lamenting the loss of Istria and Fiume, the city where he was born to Jewish parents. He and others feared that the humiliation inflicted on Italy by the Allies would cast a shadow over the republic's future, repeating the experience of the Weimar Republic after the Treaty of Versailles, not to mention the advent of fascism in Italy. In Croce's case, contrary to some claims, he opposed the treaty's ratification not for nationalistic reasons or because of the loss of Italian colonies. Nationalism was foreign to his political outlook. Deep down, he longed for a return to traditional patriotism and to the kind of European cooperation that had existed before 1914. He was afraid that the approval of the treaty would inflict a grievous wound on the fibre of the nation and weaken the pride that is necessary to sustain free institutions and economic recovery or social reforms.[13]

Before the ratification debates, Croce had meetings with other political leaders; he also received several petitions from Italian individuals and organizations in Trieste and Istria, urging him to draw attention to their plight. He discussed with Orlando "the shameful and abominable treaty," and the former premier, who had guided Italy to victory in the Great War, agreed that the honourable thing for them to do was to vote against ratification. For Orlando, there was simply "no necessity and no utility" that demanded ratification of the treaty, with the accompanying "ignominy" such an act would involve.[14] Orlando had expressed that position in a speech delivered at the inaugural session of the Constituent Assembly. With his mastery of jurisprudence and familiarity with European political tradition, he appreciated more than others the legal and moral implications at stake. "The treaty regarded, and still regards, Italians as enemies," a concept that "turned those Italians who had fought beside the Allies ... into traitors and mercenaries, because they had fought beside the enemy."[15]

Don Luigi Sturzo, the former head of the Popular Party, who had just returned from the United States after twenty years of exile, wrote to Croce urging him to oppose ratification. "Even in this latest unhappy period of our political life, I believe that the ratification of the treaty is not necessary in relation to the results of the Paris Peace Conference, and also it is dangerous to national and European interests. It is highly desirable that in the Constituent Assembly somebody explain the equivocations and the misunderstanding surrounding the ratification even with regard to international relations."[16]

Croce discussed the treaty several times even with De Nicola, the new head of state. In one of those meetings, when he expressed a desire to resign from the Assembly on account of his age, the president urged him to postpone the decision. "De Nicola told me that it is my imperative duty to remain as member of the Assembly until I have spoken against the treaty and its ratification." In another meeting, at the beginning of July 1947, Croce showed De Nicola the text of his speech against the treaty. "I let him read my speech, and he approved it in full, advising only a few small changes, in order to make clear that my judgment expressed the feeling of the Assembly, and even of those members who do not agree with my position."[17]

During the ratification debate in the Constituent Assembly, the discussion in the country and in the press was lively and heated. Croce took advantage of that popular interest and wrote two newspaper articles on the topic of the treaty. He invited readers to remember the issues at stake and the dilemma faced by the nation: "To ratify or not to ratify the Peace Treaty is a political act that concerns the health and the future of the country." Such an issue demanded a display of courage, "because nations grow with acts of courage, not with cautious and fearful actions."[18]

The same ideas had been expressed by Croce at the National Council of the Liberal Party a few months before. In that gathering, he told fellow Liberals that "the Peace Treaty raises serious and grave questions." As he put it: "All are jumping to prey upon Italy whenever possible, regarding the country as 'res nullius,' open to plunder and destruction." He continued: "Our borders are changed and redrawn by foreigners ... we have been thrown back to the condition of a few centuries ago." For these reasons, he felt, Italy's response should be unequivocal. "The supreme guiding principle, for me, should be this: to defend and to protect the interests of Italy as much as possible, but above all else to save fully the dignity of Italy." To make his point more cogent, Croce called attention to the sad events then taking place. "Only a person who has abandoned his dignity can remain indifferent to what it is happening against us, seeing our ruin and witnessing the exodus of Italians from the city of Pola, which reminds us of the saddest days of our history, days that we never imagined could reappear in front of our eyes, not only as Italians but even as civilized men."[19]

Croce's speech against the Peaty Treaty on 24 July 1947 was his second major intervention in the Constituent Assembly, the first, on the constitution, having occurred the preceding March. His intervention took place immediately after Carlo Sforza, the new minister of foreign affairs, had outlined the government's position with realism, foresight, and resignation: ratify the treaty under duress while protesting against its unjust nature, call for revisions to the document, and, in the meantime, follow a policy of cooperation with other European nations. By universal consent of those present, Croce's speech was one of his best. His audience realized the solemnity of the occasion, and, since Croce spoke without the benefit of a public address system, many gathered around him to better hear his words. The speech resembled a scholarly essay but was also a fine piece of oratory; the prose was eloquent, the tone austere, and the message suffused with "a feeling of piercing pain," as a witness remembered.

As usual in Croce's public speeches, there were theoretical observations. The speech, in fact, contained reflections on the nature of war and its relation to law and morality. Croce declared his opposition to the institution of the international tribunal to try military and political leaders of Germany and other defeated nations. "War is an eternal law of the world, and it takes place outside of any juridical order." Generals deserved praise or blame for the victories they achieved or for the defeats they suffered, for the glory or shame they brought to their nations and to their peoples. The creation of an international tribunal had no foundation in law but was an expression of the arrogance of victorious powers and reflected their own interests. Much better was, as Croce put it, "the old practice, devoid of hypocrisy," according to which the leaders of a defeated enemy were put to death, "thus bringing the war to an end." He explained: "Julius Caesar did not send before a tribunal, ordinary or extraordinary, the heroic Vercingetorix, after his noble surrender, but, moved by vendetta or believing his life dangerous to the security of Rome, brought him to Rome behind his triumphal chariot, afterwards sent him to jail, and then ordered his killing by strangulation." For Croce, the war had been the result of historical forces and of the actions undertaken by various parties, each of which bore a different responsibility. Now there was a need for a common expiation: what was required was not a spirit of vendetta, disguised as justice, but the collaboration of all nations to heal the wounds caused by the conflict and to avoid the recurrence of aggression.

Croce also made historical judgments. As he had already said on other recent occasions, fascism was but a short period in the long history of Italy. Moreover, Italian fascism had been an imitation of the nationalism and imperialism preached and practised by other nations. It had triumphed first in Italy, owing to the moral chaos, political divisions, and social strains caused by the Great War. But fascism soon spread to other nations, and Mussolini had received praise from leaders of the Allied powers. Croce offered a rebuttal to the claims of some British and American commentators; Italy never had imperial aspirations after the fall of the Roman Empire. Liberal Italy had tried to maintain European peace through alliances, and those alliances had a defensive nature. In the past, Italy made a significant contribution to European civilization. In the present, it should be placed in a position to participate fully, on a basis of equality, in the recovery of Europe.

Approaching his main argument, Croce recognized that Italy had suffered a military defeat: an admission not often made by other Italians, then or later. "We Italians have lost a war, and all of us have lost it, even those who opposed it, even those who were persecuted by the Fascist regime that declared it, even those who died for their opposition to that regime. … The shameful war, engaging our fatherland, engaged us also, without exception, because we cannot separate ourselves from our fatherland, from its victories or from its defeats, for better or for worse." In the course of his speech, Croce gave several reasons for rejecting the Peace Treaty. First of all, there was a moral reason why the treaty should not be approved: "The treaty is a document contrary to the truth." Italians should not accept "the spirit that is present in the treaty." The treaty was not only the notification of what the victors intended "to take away from us"; more important, it contained "a moral judgment and the sentence of a punishment that Italy had to suffer in order to be able to join the victors in their superior place." Second, the treaty did not deserve to be approved because of the process that had led to it. The treaty had been imposed as a diktat to Italy after Italians had been excluded from the peace negotiations. Moreover, the Allies had reneged on the promises that they had made during the war. In fact, the Allied powers had sacrificed "the destiny of Italy in order to satisfy their discordant aims and appetites." The treaty was not an example "of collaboration among nations," or a way "to impede the recurrence of war." Far from generating a spirit of cooperation, the treaty was already creating recriminations among nations.

The treaty had to be rejected because of what it would mean for the future of Italy. The army would be reduced to a police force and would be unable to withstand a foreign invasion. The Allies already "had divided among themselves the fleet that fought beside you and for you." The destruction of fortifications at the borders and the dismantling of naval bases on the coasts would reduce the country to military impotence. The treaty deprived Italy of its colonies and, more important, "transferred parts of the Italian population to other countries, in violation of the Atlantic Charter." It imposed heavy reparations that would cripple the Italian economy and burden the Italian people, violated the sovereignty of Italy over its own population, and opened the door to foreign intervention in internal affairs. The treaty made it impossible for Italy to contribute to the construction of a new Europe. It should not be approved because it was also contrary to the vital interests of the entire continent.

In the last part of his speech, Croce addressed the possible consequences of a rejection of the treaty. A vote against ratification would not produce any change in Allied policy, "because the document is written in such a way that its clauses will be put into execution even without Italy's approval." He rejected the argument of those who disliked the treaty but urged its approval "as a pure formality," following which Italy could start working for changes, as the Allies themselves were advising and promising. Croce warned that the Allies' promises had been found wanting in the past; the treaty itself was the negation of promises made during the war. Rather than relying on the future benevolence of the Allied powers, "we need to rely on ourselves." He recognized that, in the precarious conditions then prevailing, Italy was not in a position to resist the impositions of the Allies; but, even if it had to accept their demands under duress, it should not offer a formal approval of the treaty. "It is impossible to compel the Italian people to declare beautiful something that they feel is ugly." For Croce, then, the path of action was clear: the treaty deserved "a resounding no." Despite future difficulties, the country's priority was now "to preserve national dignity … which is worthy to be defended, accepting sacrifices and dangers."[20]

Croce's stand can be regarded as one of the last cries of the patriotism rooted in the Risorgimento. The patriots of the Risorgimento certainly would have understood his position and appreciated his advice. And his speech still resonates with those who share those ideals. More than a call to resistance, it was a protest against injustice, a lament over an adverse, dreadful fate. Like the chorus in a Greek tragedy, Croce gave voice, and literary dignity, to a suffering nation, hence the speech's enduring appeal and historical value.

Croce's speech made a great impression on the Assembly, but it did not affect the final vote. Many shared his feelings but were not ready to accept his stern advice. As Croce wrote in his diary, "my speech was followed with great attention, but in the end it received the applause of only a few. Truly there was no place for applause in a matter so important and so painful. But the attitude of the Assembly has been too cautious, much more than was to be expected in a decision that concerns the honour and the future of the nation."[21] As with his remarks on the constitution, Croce's speech on the treaty was debated in the Italian press and mentioned in international papers. It was translated into French and English and published in France, England, Switzerland, and probably also in the United States. The Laterza publishing house printed the speech in a booklet which had a large circulation in Italy. Later, Luigi Russo included it in his new periodical, *Belfagor*, warmly approving of Croce's position: "I myself corrected the proofs of your beautiful speech. Today it is even of greater interest, if yet more painful."[22] Croce received letters of support from common people and from old friends. One of them, a university teacher, expressed well the general impression made by the speech: "I have read, more than once, your speech in the Constituent Assembly against the ratification of the Peace Treaty, and felt an intense emotion … Those high and firm words … express the deep and genuine voice of the wounded nation … As an Italian I wish to express to you my personal gratitude."[23]

Croce's position was mentioned by other speakers during the ratification debate in the Assembly. Among these, Luigi Einaudi best expressed the pro-ratification position and the difficult choice it required. The day after Croce spoke, Einaudi took the floor: "Like all of you, I heard with emotion and then read with profound admiration the historical judgment that Benedetto Croce delivered on the ratification of the Peace Treaty. Should the author decide to add another chapter to his *History of Italy*, that speech would provide a worthy conclusion to that great work." He described Croce's speech as "a solemn historical judgment on a treaty imposed on us by the will of others." With great perception, he noted that Croce's remarks "conclude an era in the history of Italy." For Einaudi, the war and its aftermath had brought to an end the epoch of the national state with full sovereignty and unrestrained claims on its own people and often against other countries. Without denying for a moment the injustices inflicted on Italy by the Allies, Einaudi argued, more realistically than Croce, for the ratification of the treaty. For him, ratification was the only way to put an end to an unhappy and tragic past and embark on the journey to a better future. "For this reason, with a heart that bleeds for the violated Alps, I will vote in favour of the treaty's ratification, as the necessary means to rejoin the international community, and at the same time with the aim of working with tenacity for the creation of a new union among the European nations."[24]

Later in July, at the end of the great debate, the Peace Treaty was ratified by a large majority. The Communists abstained and the Socialists left the chamber during the vote; neither of them ever suggested a rejection of the treaty. Only a small minority voted against ratification. Croce, Orlando, and Valiani were among them.

In a few years, the hopes of De Gasperi, Sforza, and Einaudi were realized. It did not happen without some difficulties and delays, but eventually the most offensive clauses of the treaty were revised or modified. Italy rejoined the international community, became a member of the United Nations, played a leading role in the European Union, and was an important part of the NATO alliance. In due course, Manlio Brosio, a former Liberal leader, became secretary-general of NATO, and an Italian admiral headed its naval forces in the Mediterranean, replacing a British admiral no less. The leaders of republican Italy deserve full credit for these achievements, especially since they occurred in the context of frequent opposition at home and hostility abroad.[25]

Yet, despite Italy's post-war success on the European stage, the war greatly weakened the reputation of the country, both in the international community and among its own people. Rosario Romeo, the leading biographer of Cavour, has argued persuasively that the war and Italy's defeat led to a decline of patriotism, a weakening of national pride, and, even more troubling, "a profound and secret lack of confidence among various strata of society and the ruling elite in the ability of Italy to reach the level of the more advanced countries."[26]

15
A New Course

Even as the Constituent Assembly debated the momentous issues of the constitution and the treaty with the Allies, political manoeuvring continued. As already recounted, after the general election of 1946, the coalition of six parties that had created the Committee of National Liberation and ruled Italy from 1944 came to an end. The election resulted in victory for the three mass parties: the Christian Democrats, the Socialist Party, and the Communist Party, in order of number of seats won. The Liberal Party and the Party of Action were the losers: reduced to minority status, they were destined soon to disappear or to play a marginal role in the country's political life. Alcide De Gasperi, as the leader of the majority party, formed a new government with the Socialists and the Communists that came to be called the "tripartite" coalition, despite the presence in the cabinet also of the much smaller Republican Party. Without ever losing his reservations about their intentions, the Christian Democratic leader wanted to involve the left-wing parties in the reconstruction of the country, the drafting of a new constitution, and the negotiation and ratification of a treaty with the Allied powers. But, without shared ideals and common interests, the collaboration proved difficult; the three parties could not agree on a coherent economic program, nor were they able to devise and carry out a common policy in national and international affairs.[1]

Croce had opposed the tripartite coalition from the beginning. He voiced his position at the National Council of the Liberal Party in January 1947: "A government cannot be formed on the basis of various and contrasting interests of parties ... trying to please in turn each one of them with small concessions." That formula had produced bad results in the past, and in the future "things will go from bad to worse." To avoid that fate, it was necessary to embark on a different path; a new government was needed in order "to face the great menace that comes from anti-liberal and dictatorial parties, which today, and not only in Italy, have power in government." "It will be impossible to govern," he said, "if we do not return to the system of a government inspired and directed by a clear program, which in turn compels the other parties to wage a clear opposition in order to gain, with their criticism, the right of succession."[2] But, during the following months, despite the Liberals' opposition to the tripartite coalition, relations between De Gasperi and the Liberal leadership remained close, consultations taking place often, both formally and informally. In February 1947, after De Gasperi had greatly reduced the influence and the number of Socialists and Communists in his cabinet, Croce and De Gasperi had a friendly conversation in which they "discussed the political situation and the way he had composed his new cabinet."[3] No doubt, the discussion concerned not only the present but also the future. Long before the final showdown came, several documents reveal that both the Liberals and the Christian Democrats were suspicious of the Communist Party, resented its ties with the Soviet Union, and feared its ultimate objectives.

In 1947 there were several developments that affected political events in Italy and changed relations among the parties, further undermining the government's cohesion and effectiveness. Relations between the United States and the Soviet Union deteriorated, and the Cold War began in earnest; in March the Truman Doctrine – which pledged US assistance to countries threatened by communism – was proclaimed, and in June the Marshall Plan for the economic reconstruction of Europe was announced. As a result, the continent was divided in two antagonistic camps. In Belgium and in France, the Communists were expelled from government. In Eastern Europe, the Soviet Union imposed the hegemony of the Communist parties and the creation of "popular democracies." Finally, in September, the Cominform was created to coordinate the activities of Communist parties internationally and to assure Stalinist orthodoxy. In Italy a series of incidents further weakened the government and created the conditions for a new political direction. In January 1947 the Socialist Party split between a reformist wing and a maximalist one; the first demanded independence from the Communists and a foreign policy favourable to the Western powers, while the second was in favour of a "unity of action" with the Communist Party and a foreign policy of neutrality towards the United States and the Soviet Union. The split weakened the Socialist Party and stunted its growth, and increased the appeal of the Communist Party, which now became the strongest party of the left.

In the past, collaboration with the Communist Party had been regarded as a temporary necessity by De Gasperi, but it never was popular among the great majority of Christian Democrat voters, and it was opposed by almost all of the Catholic clergy. Now, the Vatican began to speak out with greater frequency against Stalin's policies in Eastern Europe and to demand an alliance of democratic forces against the danger of international communism. Those calls found a sympathetic echo among the middle class and the Catholic electorate. Both were frightened by frequent acts of public violence, often politically motivated, undertaken by Communist militants or by organizations under their control. Those fears, exacerbated by the weak and inadequate response of the police, soon found expression at the ballot box. In local elections in the fall of 1946 and the spring of 1947, anti-Communist movements on the right gained ground, eroding the position of the Christian Democrats. Blaming the losses on the party's alliance with the Communist Party, the rank and file began to demand a change of course.

In these difficult circumstances, De Gasperi acted with great caution. Through his numerous contacts in Italy and abroad, he was one of the first to appreciate the Truman administration's willingness to contain Soviet expansion. As a minister of foreign affairs, he already had established strong links with Allied authorities; on a trip to the United States in January 1947, he gained the full confidence of American leaders. Once the cabinet and the Assembly had approved the Peace Treaty, and the Communists had voted for the inclusion of the Lateran Pacts in the new constitution, De Gasperi moved with determination, overcoming even some opposition within his own party.[4] In May, after laborious negotiations among the parties and meetings between their leaders, he was able to form a new cabinet, his fourth in less than two years. For the first time since the fall of Mussolini, Italy had a government based on a single party, the Christian Democrats, though supported in the Assembly by the Liberal Party and by the Common Man movement.

Besides Christian Democrats, the new cabinet also included several independent figures, members of the Liberal establishment who enjoyed great professional respect and popular support. Some had played important roles in the Northern Resistance; all of them had the confidence of the middle class and the trust of the business community. The most significant member of the group was Luigi Einaudi, an economist of international renown, for many years a correspondent for *The Economist* magazine, and then governor of the Bank of Italy. He became deputy premier and budget minister; in the latter capacity, he was in charge of Italy's economic policy. But, as well as his economic competence and academic credentials, "Einaudi possessed, in the opinion of a leading economist, Federico Caffè, the ability to inspire confidence and the gift of generating hope, essential in difficult times, when one demands sacrifices to obtain ideal goals."[5]

May 1947 was the last time that the Liberal Party played an important role in Italy's political affairs, even if it was no longer the leading player. During the negotiations for a new cabinet, the Liberals made things easier for the Christian Democrat leader in two ways: first, they refused to serve in any government in which the Communist Party was present; and then, in the end, they supported the new government but did not demand a formal coalition through direct participation in the cabinet. With that second move, De Gasperi was given a stronger hand in choosing his ministers and keeping at bay requests from the Common Man movement for cabinet seats. And so, instead of a coalition between the Christian Democrats and the right-wing parties, the new government took on a single-party complexion. This formula was likely more palatable to the Young Turks of the Christian Democratic Party, who had little use for the Liberal Party and Italy's liberal heritage. It also seems that, during the negotiations, the Liberal leaders, especially Croce, acted more with the national interest than party considerations in mind. Later on, a price would be paid for that position at the polls.

The important negotiations had taken place in Rome. Living in Naples, Croce was not present at crucial meetings. But he was kept informed about the main events, and he sent letters to Rome giving advice and instructions. In two instances, his intervention was perhaps decisive. The first involved overcoming Einaudi's reluctance to join the cabinet, something that was essential to the success of De Gasperi's – and Croce's – plans. In his diary account of this matter Croce's sense of urgency is plain: "Before seven in the morning, while I was still in bed, Renato Morelli arrived, and he was very upset because of Einaudi's reluctance to be part of De Gasperi's cabinet; this would risk prolonging the crisis and increasing the obstacles to its solution. Immediately I grabbed the telephone and entered into communication with Einaudi, urging him, even imploring him, to accept the invitation, because his refusal could cause the ruin of the country, as well as damage the reputation of the Liberal Party."[6]

Einaudi had his own good reasons for not rushing to a quick decision. But Croce's pressing call, "la tremenda telefonata," as Einaudi described their conversation, helped to remove his doubts. Afterwards, De Gasperi and Einaudi were able to reach an agreement concerning the government's economic program and his position in the cabinet. Not without some resistance from the majority party, Einaudi was allowed to create his own team inside the government, choosing like-minded ministers for key economic portfolios. Later, from his privileged position in the cabinet and as governor of the Bank of Italy, Einaudi was able to give coherent direction to the government's economic policy and financial investments. Outside the cabinet, Einaudi found a valuable ally in Donato Menichella, his deputy and later his successor at the Bank of Italy. An outstanding civil servant with unequalled knowledge of the industrial and financial system, Menichella was involved with all of the most important government economic committees, influencing their decisions with his expert advice. Both men recognized that sound public finances were in the national interest in order to bring down high inflation and build the economy. When the end of negotiations for a new cabinet appeared in sight, Croce's relief was evident in his diary: "Later, from Rome, Cassandro communicated to us that Einaudi's disposition had become more favourable. At midnight, I was told of his acceptance. I did some reading and wrote letters; but I was compelled to accept several visits, despite the fact that I was tired from the tension that had lasted the whole day."[7]

During those hectic weeks, Croce also helped to calm the nerves of De Nicola. In the middle of the political turmoil, De Nicola suddenly announced his resignation as president, giving as an excuse the prorogation of the Constituent Assembly and his poor health. On the urging of mutual friends, Croce immediately paid a visit to him and pleaded that he remain in office at least until a new government was in place. A few days later, in an interview with a Brazilian paper, Croce publicly came to the president's defence, stating that the resignation was dictated not by political motivations but by personal matters and difficulty sustaining a lifestyle that "was contrary to his temperament." No doubt there was some truth in that statement, but other observers, perhaps closer to the mark, did see politics at work. De Nicola was sensitive to his position of neutrality and wanted to maintain the independence of his office. He probably did not fully approve of De Gasperi's new cabinet, or at least his methods in creating it. Certainly, he was opposed to the dismissal of the current cabinet without a parliamentary debate and before a confidence motion had been voted upon. In the end, having made his point, De

Nicola, as on other occasions, needed the support and understanding of a trusted friend in order to reconsider his position. When he accepted Croce's gentle advice, his decision was greeted with general relief.[8]

During the final days of the negotiations, Croce was in Rome. He took part in the talks and voted for the new government on a confidence motion in the Constituent Assembly. His speech on that occasion, written in a hurry early in the morning, only hours before its delivery, was not among his best efforts; yet, because it did not resemble an essay, as most of his other speeches did, it was likely more effective politically. At the beginning of his remarks, Croce reaffirmed the differences between the Liberals and the Christian Democrats, noting that on several occasions he had criticized the latter's subservient attitude towards the Vatican's demands and their vague promises made and then forgotten in past negotiations. More recently, he had opposed the alliance of the Christian Democrats with the Marxist parties, describing "the tripartite coalition as ruinous to our country," and had called the Christian Democrats "accomplices of bolshevism." Now, however, the situation had changed. "The Liberal Party votes its confidence in the new government, and in doing so, needless to say, it remains faithful to the ideals that guide its actions, and that are in contrast with those of the Christian Democrats on some substantial points." The reason for the party's decision was to be found in the country's precarious state. "It is evident that before a person can be a Liberal or a Christian Democrat, it is necessary that he be alive; and Italy could not cultivate either ideal if she dies, that is, if she falls into the moral, economic, and political ruin that at present is threatening her." To avoid that peril, old adversaries had to come together, putting aside their differences, because a dramatic choice confronted them: "The duty to save our country is now paramount, and compels us to give our vote to a Christian Democrat government, since this government has accepted that duty as its main object and principal policy."

Croce also refuted a criticism made both by the Marxist parties and by well-known Christian Democrats on the left wing of their party. The essence of that criticism was that De Gasperi had embraced a regressive policy, supported by right-wing parties that represented the reactionary forces of Italian society. Croce repeated what he had stated in other writings of a more philosophical nature. In a time of great ideological debate involving differences on fundamental ideals, it was important to remember that the issue at stake was nothing less than "the future of freedom." Croce told the Assembly, and more specifically the Marxist parties, that, for Liberals, or at least those who followed Croce's and

Einaudi's teachings, "liberty was not one thing among other things, but ... a religious principle that has no need of social qualification, because that principle has in itself the impulse to elevate all men and to place them in a condition to achieve and enjoy ever-increasing justice." To reinforce his argument, Croce referred his audience to the body of literature written by liberal authors about social questions. At the time there was much discussion in Italy and Europe about the Beveridge Report, which, in its support of extensive social welfare measures, inspired much of the British Labour Party's program after the war. Much debated then, too, were the theories of William Ropke on the social market economy – "Rhine capitalism," it was later called – of post-war Germany. Croce stated: "I will not make a list of writers and titles of books, written by British, American, and Swiss authors, who in recent years have shown how, following liberal principles, one can, and indeed should, solve the injustices and shortcomings of the economic system; nor will I remind you that an Italian philosopher, [Croce], has made a fundamental distinction between liberalism, which is a moral and religious principle, and economic laissez-faire or 'liberismo,' which is a practical method and as such has great and beneficial efficacy, but also its own limits, according to places and circumstances, and cannot exclude, in an absolute way, the intervention of the state in economic affairs." To those who assessed a position or program as progressive or conservative according to the seating arrangement of the Assembly, without making reference to historical events and the present situation, Croce had this to say: "The abstract discussion about 'right' and 'left' does not show ... where ... one may find, from time to time, the reality of freedom and the justice that flows from it."

Turning from theoretical considerations to more mundane matters, Croce strongly criticized any effort to draw a direct connection between past issues and present positions. On the institutional question, for instance, Croce, Einaudi, and De Nicola had voted for the monarchy but at the same time had publicly stated their support of the results of the referendum. Now, both in the Constituent Assembly and in the press, several leaders of the left-wing parties were alleging that the new government, supported by the Liberals, posed a danger to the republic and formed perhaps the first step in a return to the monarchy. For Croce, that claim was baseless, "clearly the result of unfounded fear and exaggerated suspicion." He declared: "We liberals, who openly defended the royal institution and voted for the monarchy ... always stated that we would accept and respect the electoral response, as we have done till now and will continue to do in the future, because … for us Italy is now a republic, to be served with devotion."[9]

In his speech, Croce directly challenged Togliatti, "who often gives me the pleasure of narrating a 'fictional life' of myself." With that ironical understatement Croce referred to the relentless attacks against his philosophy and politics by the Communist Party and its intellectual sympathizers, often former pupils of Gentile.[10] Without abandoning his friendly tone, but using solid arguments, Croce also rejected a novel constitutional theory, insidious in its consequences, that was put forth then, and repeated later, by the Communist leader and his successors. In his speech on the confidence motion, Togliatti had accused De Gasperi of having broken the anti-Fascist pact that had existed among the parties of the Committee of National Liberation. For Togliatti, the violation of that pact deprived the new government, or any future government for that matter, of political legitimacy. The veiled but clear implication was that in Italy a government, to be democratic and legitimate, had to be anti-Fascist and had to include the left-wing parties. Moreover, only the participation of the Communist Party, which more than others had fought in the past against fascism and now led the working class, could lend a truly anti-Fascist and democratic character to any government. On this point, Croce reminded Togliatti that he too had once supported the participation of the Communist Party in a government of national unity, "of which I was the demiurge." That had happened in a time of war, when Italy faced a political emergency that demanded the union of all parties before an election could be held. "But all of that belongs to the past, from which we are now separated by the recent election, which made illogical and unnecessary a mechanical composition of ministerial cabinets among different and opposing parties, especially since the experience had shown that the old method produces only a government of impotence." Croce argued that the new government was the natural result of the 1946 elections. In a liberal and democratic system, only the popular vote gives legitimacy to a government, and a parliamentary majority provides the right to govern. No single party can claim a privileged position allowing it alone to enjoy legitimacy. "The results of the election demand a return to the constitutional practice of a majority that governs and of a minority that wages its opposition democratically, hoping with its actions to become one day the majority. This is the great gain that we have obtained by this difficult crisis."

Togliatti's peculiar constitutional theory became a rallying cry of Communist propaganda, then and later, and was even supported by some prominent scholars, as evident in a letter from Croce to Luigi Russo, who did not approve of the new government and lamented the demise of the tripartite coalition. In reply to Russo, Croce offered an unequivocal defence of the new cabinet. "To regard as an abuse of power the government of a parliamentary majority, sanctioned by a popular vote, and to talk of dictatorship and a return to fascism is pure folly, because that is the normal way in all the parliaments of the world, according to the British model." In that letter to Russo, Croce made a keen observation: "The Communists and the Socialists do not want to fight the Christian Democrats but rather want to share the banquet and the spoils with them, causing in the process the ruin of Italy by imposing wrong-headed policies or by impeding the adoption of the right solutions. A good example is the Communist [Mauro] Scoccimarro, the former minister of finance, who did not take a single lira from the rich but has allowed the devaluation of our money in order to reduce Italy to a pulp, ready for a soviet coup."[11]

The collaboration between the Liberals and the Christian Democrats after the war showed that both had learned the lessons of the past. In the 1920s disagreements between the Liberals and the Popular Party and the antipathy between Giolitti and Sturzo had facilitated the victory of Mussolini. After the Second World War, facing a new common enemy, the heirs of both Giolitti and Sturzo buried old animosities and united against the Communist danger, sparing Italians the fate of Eastern Europe. But differences remained, and sometimes resurfaced. The Liberals were no longer anti-clerical, nor were they eager to revive old quarrels; in general, they remained faithful to the basic tenets of liberalism, fundamental among which were individual rights and the separation of church and state. The Christian Democrats were, despite their name, a secular party, a party composed of Catholics rather than a Catholic party, yet on some occasions its leaders were willing to comply with the church's demands, especially on questions involving public education, marriage, or sexual morality. On one of these occasions, Croce spoke and voted against a government bill. "I promised to give support to a motion of censure against the minister of education, [Guido] Gonella, who does not hesitate to commit abuses of power. I took that decision since I wanted to make very clear the position of our party: we support De Gasperi's cabinet against the anti-parliamentarian pretences of the Communists, the Socialists and their allies; furthermore, we support the economic and financial policy of the government, but we are not their allies in all their actions, and above all we do not want to be accomplices in their abuses."[12]

Croce expressed the same position to Luigi Russo, in the process giving a restrictive significance to the new government. "We Liberals are not formally members of the cabinet, but we have allowed Einaudi, as an economic expert, to be a minister of the government with the sole aim of saving Italy from economic and financial ruin, which would be a disaster for all of us and for all the parties." He continued: "Because our agreement with the Christian Democrats concerns only one point, namely the recovery of the economy, and because we also intend to preserve our independence in all the rest, I supported a motion of censure, presented by the former members of the Party of Action, and contributed to its victory." But, despite momentary disagreements, the convergence between the Liberals and the Christian Democrats endured for some time, and the friendship and mutual respect between Croce, Einaudi, and De Gasperi became stronger since their political closeness was based on shared ideals. During the events of May 1947, in particular, Croce admired De Gasperi's "prudence and courage," especially commendable in a time of "fear and conformism."[13]

The fourth De Gasperi cabinet must be regarded as a watershed in the history of Italy after the war. The Christian Democrats assumed the pre-eminent position in the Italian political system and acted as the fulcrum of any government for the next fifty years. The government finally adopted a coherent economic policy of reconstruction and began the creation of a welfare state at the same time. Foreign policy took on a clear Western orientation and resisted neutralist temptations. Law and order were defended against personal violence, social agitation, and political intimidation, though sometimes legal limits were overstepped in the process.

New documents have led to a better assessment of the events of May 1947. No longer can it be said that the demise of the tripartite coalition and the birth of the new government were brought about by US intervention. Fabio Grassi Orsini has shown that international conditions played a role and were a contributing factor, but much more important were the conditions in Italy itself: public disorder, political violence, economic difficulty, and fear of communism. Equally important was the leadership of De Gasperi: his determination overcame the reluctance and fears of other Christian Democrats, persuading them to set their party on a new journey in uncharted waters.[14]

It is now difficult to disagree with the conclusions of Piero Craveri, one of the most eminent historians of modern Italy, in his recent biography of De Gasperi.[15] In his view, shared more or less by other historians, including Pietro Scoppola, the new cabinet was not a government of the right but rather a meeting of "national forces." The old Liberal elite and the new leaders of the Christian Democrats found unity in the common endeavour to create a modern democracy. In many respects, the social and economic program of the new government was a continuation of that of its predecessor. Several ministers carried on and retained their old positions. Some of the independent Liberal ministers had been courted or consulted before by the left-wing parties. Menichella was held in high esteem by Nenni. Togliatti himself was not against the return of Liberals to the cabinet. And finally, the industrialists, far from adoring Einaudi, resented his opposition to their privileges and monopolistic practices. The new government, and the others that followed it, preserved the fundamental structure of the Italian economy as it had developed over the last fifty years, first under liberal Italy and then under fascism: a system characterized by a mixture of free initiative and government intervention, private enterprises and public corporations. The main difference was that the Marxist parties lost hold of the levers of power and were relegated to the opposition, where they were to remain for a long time – with the approval of the Italian people, as shown in the electoral results.

16
The Elections of 1948

The elections of 18 April 1948 were a dramatic event in the history of modern Italy. Their results assured the predominance of the Christian Democrats in the Italian political system and crushed the revolutionary aspirations of the Marxist parties. At stake was the future of the Italian democracy and the nature of Italian society, the shape of the country's institutions and also its place in the world. On the one side stood the Christian Democrats, allied with the small liberal and democratic parties; on the other were the Socialist and Communist parties, united in a Popular Front, with Garibaldi's face as their emblem. Many at home and abroad realized that a great event was taking place, affecting not only the welfare of Italy but also the security of Western Europe. The parties mobilized all their resources, huge rallies were organized in big and small cities, fiery speeches were made in the public squares, militants zealously carried out their assigned tasks, leaflets were distributed by the millions. The United States, the Soviet Union, and the Vatican intervened in the campaign, both openly and covertly. The pope called on the faithful "to be with Christ or against Christ," a call that was then repeated in pulpits all over the country. It the end, the electoral campaign assumed the tone of a crusade, and the contest became one between good and evil, freedom and dictatorship, West and East.

Yet, important as these appeals and efforts were, they tended to reinforce existing feelings rather than change them. As Robert Ventresca has shown, after living for twenty years under Mussolini's dictatorship, the great majority of the Italian people had no desire to embrace another radical adventure, driven by the same illusions and producing in the end, perhaps, the same results. In the wake of wartime destruction, the prospect of progress within the bounds of law, order, and good government was more persuasive and reassuring than the allure of social revolution. After the elections, an era of unprecedented economic progress and social change dawned, altering forever an ancient landscape and traditional customs that had remained unchanged for centuries.[1]

Croce's diary contains only a few, brief references to the elections, but these reflect the prevailing atmosphere in the country. "I have not added any note to the diary in these days, out of laziness, or, better, overcome by the confusion of the present situation, which involves political life as well as the personal and family lives of everyone and prevents me from undertaking any regular and well-planned work." On the same page is this observation: "Anxiety for the results of the elections has gripped all of us; though on our side there is hope and faith, everybody feels the gravity of the hour, because these are not normal elections, which concern only the fate of Italy, but rather have become a point on which today is centred the great contrast and the terrible fight between the two groups of the world's powers."[2]

Because it was "a choice of civilizations," to quote the Socialist Giuseppe Saragat, the elections were fought with particular intensity, both sides appealing to lofty ideals but also resorting to unorthodox means and unfair tactics. The campaign depressed Croce; he resented political propaganda based on emotions rather than reason, and he was dismayed by the charges and counter-charges hurled wantonly by parties against their adversaries, who were now treated as enemies. He especially condemned "the bad faith of the Communists, which is now their usual approach." But Croce's most pointed criticisms were aimed at the personal conduct "of some shameless so-called Communist intellectuals." Close to election day, he wrote of his "disgust for the persistent lies that are heard nowadays."[3]

While Croce did not participate directly in the electoral campaign, he was not entirely absent from it. By now, his political involvement had been greatly reduced, but his contribution to the philosophical debates at the heart of politics remained constant and undiminished. In cultural affairs, Croce, even in old age, was often at the centre of controversies. He sent a steady stream of articles to liberal newspapers; he also wrote longer essays or book reviews for his own periodical, *La Critica*, which continued to be published regularly though under a slightly different name (*Quaderni della Critica*) and in a different format.

Under Mussolini's dictatorship he had defended the values of the Risorgimento and liberal ideals; under the republic, he continued to uphold the tenets of a liberal society against old adversaries and new threats. After the war, Croce, unlike many other politicians, no longer feared a resurgence of fascism. For him, fascism had run its historical course; history, exacting a terrible price, had brought that movement to an inglorious end. The new Fascist Party, or Movimento Sociale as it was called, and the right-wing organizations that emerged from the ashes of the defunct regime were regarded as a nuisance rather than an actual danger, no longer posing a real threat to the country's democratic institutions. The real threats came from different sources. The power and influence of the Vatican demanded special vigilance. With the Christian Democrats in power, Croce continued to defend the separation of church and state and the interests of public schools. He resented the confessional temptations of Catholic politicians and fought against the interference of the Vatican in Italian political affairs. In particular, despite the political alliance between the Liberal Party and the Christian Democrats and his personal friendship with De Gasperi, Croce felt compelled, when the occasion arose, to protest publicly against the partisan way in which a Christian Democrat was running the ministry of education. In one instance he accused the minister of neglecting the interests of public schools and focusing instead on the needs of Catholic institutions; more specifically, he pointed out that the minister had turned Italian public schools into "a Catholic fiefdom," dispensing "favours" and committing "abuses" in the exercise of his authority. Croce's interventions in support of secular society are frequent in this period. But once he confessed that in old age, after so many battles won and lost, he no longer enjoyed "fighting with priests," who "do not avoid even calumnies, believing that these serve the ecclesiastic authority."[4]

More frequent and certainly more intense was the polemical contest with the Communists. After the war, Croce saw in the Communist Party and in Marxist and Leninist philosophy a new danger to the freedom of Italy and a more pressing challenge to liberal ideals. In a letter to an old friend, who was a candidate for the Popular Front though he had been a staunch Liberal in the past, Croce confessed that he feared the advent of "a new dictatorship, much worse than the Fascist one"; because, after all, the Fascists "were donkeys and buffoons" but the Communists "are logical and programmatic."[5] He wrote several essays on Marxism, criticizing the main points of the doctrine and rejecting the new interpretations offered, with the enthusiasm of neophytes, by philosophers recently converted to dialectical materialism. In his writings and speeches, he relied not only on his own philosophy and experiences but also on news and reports brought to his attention by friends and acquaintances who had travelled to Eastern Europe and had seen firsthand the results of Stalin's policy and the consequences of Soviet domination. He pointed out that the Soviet Union was following the path of imperial Russia, and that its expansion was a threat to the freedom and independence of European peoples. Long before others, he expressed the view that the Soviet Union under Stalin, far from being the promised land described by its admirers, was an authoritarian state run by a political elite and a technocratic bureaucracy that enjoyed special privileges denied to the working class.[6]

Inspired by Marxism and Leninism, the Italian Communist Party offered its militants a total conception of life and a new vision of history. After the war, under the active leadership of Togliatti, the party's intellectuals undertook a systematic revision of modern Italian history and literature, putting forth, especially after the publication of Gramsci's *Notebooks*, an interpretation of the Risorgimento as a failed revolution that reflected the shortcomings of the Italian bourgeoisie and the failure of democratic leaders belonging to the Mazzinian tradition to fashion an alliance between peasants and workers. It was part of a comprehensive rewriting of history, with the aim of achieving cultural hegemony in every field and of assuring a solid foundation for the party's providential mission. This enterprise involved not only Marxist intellectuals but also the political leaders of the party at every level, whether in Rome or in the provinces. Its scope became evident even in a marginal event, the centennial celebrations of 1848 organized by the city of Turin. At the time, the city was under the administration of the Communist Party and had as its mayor a well-known leader of the party, Celeste Negarville. He already had embarked, despite protests, on a campaign to change the toponymy of the city, erasing from streets and squares old names tied to the House of Savoy and replacing them with new names associated with the Resistance and the Communist movement. Well in advance of the 1848 centennial celebrations, the mayor created an organizing committee for the event. It soon became apparent that the committee was dominated by Communist intellectuals and by scholars well disposed towards the general aims of the party. As a result, the program for the celebrations acquired a partisan bent, reflecting more the party line than the reality of the historical events of 1848. The program did not mention the achievements of the Risorgimento or the contribution to Italian unification by the House of Savoy. The lofty aim of the committee was to move away from "the sterile rehearsals of dynastic claims." The best approach, the committee thought, was to celebrate not the proclamation of the Albertine Statute, or the first war of Italian independence, but the publication of Marx's Communist Manifesto and the social agitation that took place in Italy and the rest of Europe in 1848. Already offended by their exclusion from the planned celebrations, Liberals in Turin reacted forcefully. They accused the Communist administration and the committee of wanting "to promote a historical revisionism" bound to substitute "new distortions" for the "old Fascist fables." More to the point, these Liberals believed, the Communists wanted to exploit the celebrations and the events of 1848 as propaganda for the elections of 1948. Outgunned in Turin, the editors of the city's two leading papers turned to Croce for help, asking him to write a protest against the committee's plans.

In response, Croce wrote two small but sharp pieces in the form of letters to the editor. These letters reminded readers that Marx's Communist Manifesto was published in London and remained almost unknown in Italy and other parts of Europe for a long time. Then Croce went to the substance of the controversy:

> If in France the political revolution became entangled with a social revolution, in Italy the revolution was fully political and national, and the rare proletarian revolts did not acquire any great importance. In the history of Italy, 1848 is the year in which Giuseppe Mazzini harvested the fruits of the education that he had given to the new generations through the 'Young Italy' movement; the year in which one of the oldest and most respected royal houses of Europe, the House of Savoy, united its past with the future of Italy, through the nexus of liberty and independence; and finally the year in which Piedmont realized through war and diplomacy the centuries-old dream of the brave Italians.[7]

Croce's intervention created quite a stir in Turin and in other parts of Italy, turning a local dispute into a national debate. With haste but without much success, the president of the committee offered assurances of "his cultural impartiality" and of "the academic competence of the participants." For their part, the Communists deployed their best weapons in a well-orchestrated rebuttal to Croce's criticism. One after the other, local dignitaries, national leaders, well-known intellectuals, veterans of the Resistance, and finally a mother of heroic partisans spoke out. Abandoning his institutional neutrality, even the president of the Constituent Assembly, Umberto Terracini, saw fit to intervene, displaying his usual politeness, wide learning, and well-known casuistry. All of them, with different degrees of subtlety, ignored the facts in dispute and instead made comments on Croce's political views and cultural preferences, questioning even his authority and his integrity. More with sadness than with resentment, Croce replied that, in place of arguments based on logic and history, his critics had made recourse "to a series of diversions."[8]

The Turin controversy was emblematic of wider cultural trends in Italy as a whole. After the war, there was a sudden revival of Marxism accompanied by widespread admiration for the Soviet Union and for Stalin in particular. Many university teachers who had been Fascists or followers of Gentile became Marxists or joined the Communist Party. Even a few liberal intellectuals looked with sympathy on Togliatti's party, whether because they supported its social program or because they viewed its presence as a counter-balance to the power and influence of the Catholic Church. During the elections of 1948, the Popular Front was able to obtain the support of many well-known writers and academics, and, to ensure that this support endured, the Communist Party sponsored the creation of the Alliance for the Defence of Culture. An alliance manifesto gathered more than four thousand signatures among famous artists, scholars, movie stars, and athletes. Among the intellectuals who signed the document, a number were old friends of Croce. He condemned their involvement with the Alliance in no uncertain terms: "I wrote two polemical letters to newspapers against the position taken, whether willingly or not, by the so-called intellectuals in favour of bolshevism and the new menacing totalitarianism."[9]

Once again, as during fascism, Italian culture split into two factions, with one camp supporting freedom and the other succumbing to the allure of radical solutions and of authoritarianism. In reaction to the activity of the Communist Alliance, liberal intellectuals organized a cultural conference with the title "Europe: Culture and Freedom." Some months later, they created the Italian Association for the Freedom of Culture, which had chapters in major Italian cities and ties with similar organizations in other Western nations. The association, which for a while at least enjoyed American support, including covert assistance from the CIA, promoted a great deal of cultural activity. In 1948 Gaetano De Sanctis, a distinguished classical scholar, devout Catholic, staunch Liberal, and one of the few university teachers who in 1931 had refused to take the oath of allegiance to fascism, a decision that cost him his teaching position, wrote a manifesto for the conference (later adopted by the association). Croce wrote in his diary: "On March 1948, I signed a manifesto announcing a conference of intellectuals to be held after the elections. The whole manifesto was written by Gaetano De Sanctis, but the central part is a transcription and elaboration of notes sent by me."[10]

In the manifesto and in the newspapers, Croce drew a fundamental distinction between politics and culture, that is, between the duties that belong to citizens in their making of political choices and those duties that pertain to intellectuals in their cultural activities. The two realms must remain separate. Under changed circumstances, Croce was making the same point that he had emphasized many years earlier, in his anti-Fascist manifesto of 1925, calling for a separation of responsibilities that was hard to follow – then or later. "A manifesto of intellectuals, which during February and March 1948 had collected many signatures from different people and had been promoted by the Communist Party under the guise of a text above political considerations, was followed by a bustle of polemics, and then by some comic explanations and recantations of many, who claimed not to have understood the nature of and the reasons for the document which they had signed; all of this compelled me to reassert ... elementary concepts that seemed forgotten and lost."[11] In one of his newspaper articles, Croce told fellow intellectuals that "as philosophers, historians, artists, or writers, they had to strive to serve truth and beauty, according to their disposition, ability, and personal inspiration." In practical matters and political affairs, however, no special privileges can be claimed; "intellectuals are equal to any other citizen, and have to make their choices and assume their positions in the electoral struggle according to the dictates of their conscience."[12] Croce condemned the political support given by intellectuals, as men of culture, to the Popular Front, regarding it as naive at best and abhorrent at worst. "What are then these collective interventions of intellectuals in political and electoral matters? The answer is without doubt: they are either an inconsiderate act or an expression of vanity and a desire for personal attention, or a participation, conscious or unconscious, in the hidden intrigues and subtle deceptions of political parties."[13]

In some instances, even very close friends of Croce who shared his ideals joined the Popular Front as candidates for Parliament. Luigi Russo, a former member of the Party of Action, a well-known literary critic, and a staunch anti-Fascist during Mussolini's dictatorship, was one of them, and probably the most illustrious. His decision was the more surprising since, throughout his career, he had always been unwilling to accept authoritarian discipline, let alone a party line coming from above. Croce judged Russo's choice to run under the banner of the Popular Front as "a deplorable act."[14] Russo rebutted the criticism and defended his action, explaining that in his view the Popular Front was necessary to curtail the influence of the Vatican and to oppose the sectarian abuses of the Christian Democrats; he also maintained that only the Communist Party had the power to bring about the social reforms that were needed in Italy and especially in Southern Italy and Sicily, from whence he came. Croce could not accept such explanations, let alone justify them; for him, the future of freedom was at stake, a matter always paramount among all other issues. "Dear Russo," he wrote in a letter, "I will tell you that I can only deplore your sudden change of electoral allegiance at the last moment (and only for the offer of a Senate seat). I believe that this act of yours cannot be defended by any arguments." Sadly, as a result, their long friendship suffered and ultimately ended, as had happened with Gentile under the Fascist regime, though perhaps with less bitterness.[15]

Beside those intellectuals who took positions for or against the Popular Front, there were also those who preferred to sit on the fence. Croce witnessed personally the pusillanimity of some liberal intellectuals, who feared the consequences for their academic careers of any decision they might make. In a meeting in his house, a well-known writer of fiction, his eyes on the Nobel Prize, refused to sign Croce's and De Sanctis's manifesto "with sophistic arguments"; while a famous literary critic promised to sign the manifesto after 18 April, "that is," Croce observed sardonically, "after the results of the elections have become known."[16]

Croce reserved the strongest criticism for "university teachers who are becoming members of the Communist Party."[17] In particular, he was offended by the justification they gave for their actions. Months before the elections, Croce made acerbic remarks about the political peregrinations of a well-known literary critic whom he knew well. "People accept all sorts of sophistries, and even try to defend them. Tonight, in my house, talking about a certain scholar, who in three years has changed parties four times, a friend of his assured me that he has done so 'for a high moral reason,' because among all the other parties only the Communists are present in all parts of Italian society. Is there any common sense in all of this? Some people believe that there is and praise that kind of behaviour, even when, on their part, they are not supporters of communism. Lack of reason and the march to servitude go together, one reinforcing the other."[18] On other occasions, he spoke with disdain about those Italian scholars who suddenly had embraced Marxism and become admirers of the Soviet Union and supporters of the theories of Lenin and Stalin. In a long essay titled "The Imaginary Passage of Marxist Communism from Utopia to Science," Croce made clear that his polemical stance was not "against Marx, the Socialist movement, the working class, or even Russia." Rather, "my disdain is directed against these ruinous 'intellectuals,' these Italian university teachers … who for many years have remained unaware of Marxism (though it has had a long history), and now rave for it, celebrate it, inculcate it, and apply it in their fallacious writings, after fortune seems to have crowned it in Russia with a glowing mitre." He concluded: "To such an extent can the vanity, the servility, the opportunism … of university teachers reach, particularly those who teach philosophy, whom from long experience I regard as incorrigible."[19]

Croce was not always so harsh. In 1947 Antonio Gramsci's *Letters from Prison* was published to great, and deserved, acclaim. Croce wrote a moving review of the book, full of admiration for Gramsci's character, "for the fortitude, serenity, and simplicity with which he suffered … and accepted dangers, persecution and jail, and death." At the end of his review, he lamented the ruthless polemical criticism, often verging on slander, directed at him both by Communist leaders and by Marxist scholars. "Let me note, without willing to offend anybody, that today's Italian Communist intellectuals are far from following Gramsci's example, his readiness to accept truth from wherever it came, his commitment to accuracy and fair-mindedness, his gentleness and respect for others' feelings, his sincere and dignified style, and in this regard they have much to learn from his pages, while we ourselves, on reading those pages, can feel a sense of human fraternity with him." Croce ended with a piece of advice which he had given once before. "Years ago, I recommended to young Neapolitan Communists, who went around armed with a philosophical catechism written by Stalin, to raise their eyes to the statues, which are in Naples, of Thomas Aquinas, Giordano Bruno, Tommaso Campanella, Giovanbattista Vico, and of all the other great thinkers of ours, and to strive, if they can, to join … Marxism to that tradition. But now I can point not to marmoreal statues but to a man whom many of them have known in person, and whose memory should be kept alive for something better than an empty repetition of his words, or for a tasteless polemics, done in bad faith, abusing his name."[20]

As Gennaro Sasso and other scholars have shown, Croce's advice was ignored. Whereas Gramsci continually engaged Croce's writings and philosophy in a respectful, if critical, manner, other Communist intellectuals and politicians did not. After the war, with few exceptions, they used the name of Gramsci to attack Croce's reputation and to undermine his intellectual standing, showing no respect, let alone admiration, for that "worker of the mind," as the literary critic Gianfranco Contini described the old philosopher.[21]

The elections of 1948 were a resounding defeat for the Liberal Party, and the seeds of that disaster had been sown at a party congress the previous December. At that congress, Croce resigned as president of the party and was elected as honorary president. He was then almost eighty-two years old. He felt tired and was more reluctant to travel than ever before; also, for some time he had wanted a younger man to take his place at the helm of the party. Never enamoured of political work, he wished to devote his last years to cultural activity, particularly to the Italian Institute for Historical Studies, which he had founded in 1946.[22] In his farewell speech to the party, Croce, as on other occasions, was clear on general principles but vague on practical points; he did not offer a well-defined program, nor did he propose concrete policies aimed at upcoming elections. He left those tasks to others. In his speech, Croce recapitulated the Liberal Party's record in the past, both the successes and the failures, before offering advice on the course the party should follow in the future in order to remain true to its traditions and natural vocation. As he had done before, he urged unity in the centre as the ideal position from which to defend freedom and to assure progress. In his view, a division between a right wing and a left wing in the Liberal Party had to be avoided, because each faction would carry its own danger: "a left-wing position could end in 'democraticism,'" while a right-wing position "usually tends to become conservative and more or less reactionary."[23]

But Croce's advice was ignored. One delegate noted with surprise that Croce and Einaudi enjoyed great reputations among the rank and file and their speeches were always greeted with long applause, but then their recommendations were cast aside. Croce did not participate in all the debates during the day's sessions, and he certainly was not present during the nocturnal meetings where electoral strategies were devised. As usual on such occasions, when personal and partisan ambitions clashed, there was a great deal of wheeling and dealing. Promises were made and then broken; alliances were negotiated and then did not materialize; agreements foundered at critical moments because of procrastination. It would seem that Croce's friends, confident of victory, became too complacent and were ultimately outmanoeuvred by their rivals. During the congress the delegates had split into two main factions; one of these proposed conservative policies and an electoral alliance, both of which were contrary to the course that Croce had always favoured. By a small margin, the conservative faction emerged triumphant and chose as leader of the party Roberto Lucifero, a right-wing

Liberal, but otherwise an honourable man with anti-Fascist credentials who had effectively defended liberal principles during the sessions of the Constituent Assembly.[24]

The victory of Lucifero's faction came as a surprise to Croce and left him uneasy. His concern found an outlet in his diary:

> Last night at the congress of the Liberal Party something very serious happened. A right-wing motion has been adopted and Mr Lucifero has been elected secretary-general of the party. The motion passed by a small margin of a few votes, but it passed! I blamed immediately those who have rejected the course that I had proposed for the party and had maintained for the last four years, and with honourable results. This morning I saw my friends Cassandro, Casati, and Morelli, and all of them are sad and worried. I cannot understand why everybody kept urging me to remain in Rome for three days, and then nobody asked my advice and nobody gave me any information. Anyway, for now there is nothing that I can do.[25]

After the congress, Lucifero fashioned an alliance between the Liberal Party and Giannini's right-wing Common Man movement; then the two groups, joined by Nitti's followers, formed a National Bloc to contest the elections. The aim was to create a strong political force on the right of the Christian Democrats to confront the danger of communism and at the same time defend the interests of the middle class. Lucifero ignored Croce's advice "to show an open mind" and "to avoid policies that could compromise the future of the Liberal Party"; instead, he followed his own inclinations and gave the Liberal Party a conservative cast that it did not have before, while also increasing at the same time its anti-Communist polemics.

For some critics, Lucifero "had placed the Liberal Party at the extreme right of Italian politics"; others even accused him of entertaining hopes of a monarchical restoration. Members of the left wing of the party broke away. Some of these were close friends of Croce, but they too acted in defiance of his wishes, and in some cases even ignored his personal entreaties. Croce kept urging his friends "not to abandon the terrain but to offer instead resistance" and "to defend one's position and fight for a new unity." In his correspondence with some of them, he was bitter, even unfair sometimes, accusing them of a "lack of political judgment" and a "lack of discipline" and of having succumbed to "personal vanity," a "spirit of arrogance," and the "sin of pride."[26] Strangely enough, for the unfortunate results of the congress, Croce blamed more his old left-wing friends than Lucifero himself, as we see from letters to Casati written in December 1947. In one, he wrote: "Those who belonged to the left-wing faction are the main culprits of the disturbing outcome." In another letter, he elaborated that "I am in complete agreement with you about what happened, and should not have happened, in Rome. I lay the blame mainly on that group of men who are as arrogant as they are narrow-minded, and who do not possess much political intelligence. I would like very much to discuss and to clarify with you every aspect of that event. I have recommended and still recommend to both factions, which have equal strength, to try reaching an agreement, and also I have shown that elements of an agreement do exist."[27] Croce's criticism rested on a naive assumption: had the left-wing Liberals joined forces with the centrist Liberals, the right-wing Liberals would have lost.

In the following months, the divisions within the Liberal Party placed Croce in a difficult position. He was dismayed by his party's new policies, but he was not in favour of secession, aware of the political damage that it would inflict on the party as whole and even on the very idea of liberalism. In these circumstances, he decided to remain in the party in order to maintain some of its strength for the coming elections. His predicament is evident in another letter to Casati, who shared his view: "I tried to avoid the worst; and with my advice and by threatening my resignation as honorary president, so far I have been successful and avoided another split. After the elections, if Italy does not tumble into complete ruin, we shall try to put the party back on the right track. I have to confess that as official president of the party I endured fewer pains and suffered less anxiety than now, when I am only an honorary president without direct responsibilities!"[28] In the midst of his worries, Croce sought the support of kindred individuals and the counsel of his trusted friend Casati.

> I have a great need to talk and to agree with you about something that torments me greatly: the future of our party, nay, the future of the liberal idea in Italy ... Overcoming my temperament, I sought above all that the Liberal Party would not fall into complete ruin and did not remain absent from the next election. Unfortunately, the participation of the party in the coming election is not as logical and dignified as it was before. But afterwards, we shall restore it to its former dignity and to the right course. This is our duty, and it comes from our tradition, which is sacred to us. Unfortunately, my strength is weakening, more for psychological than for physical reasons, hence the need to talk with you, in order to find the remedies.[29]

Sometime later, in his diary, Croce offered a good description of his quandary as well as a rationale for his decisions. "I saw clearly that if we were going to undertake another split in the party, already unwisely divided, liberalism would come to an end in Italy. So we had to make a virtue out of necessity, and until the elections are over, be quite ready to accept the fact and act accordingly. This solution compelled me to eat many bitter morsels, to the great discomfort of my stomach."[30] Croce's bitterness was on even fuller display in another entry, which read: "The Liberal Party is in such bad shape that, unwilling on my part to contribute to its total demise, I am compelled to swallow bitter pills ... and to accept the new policies and even the newcomers, who are repugnant to me and whom I always kept at bay in their repeated attempts to join our party. Never mind! Let us be patient! After the next elections, we shall see what can be done!"[31]

Before the elections, Croce worked to repair the disarray that the new course was creating among the party's rank and file. "I am very much worried ... because of this new alliance, which never should have been made, with Mr Giannini and with the U.Q., and which now threatens to give the upper hand in our party to peoples without scruples, who even lack elementary forms of good manners." Croce had "meetings and discussions" with trusted friends in Naples "to limit the moral and political damage of this bad alliance." Those friends took the same view as Croce; "they agreed with me that this union with the U.Q. will weaken and not strengthen us."[32] Once, Croce proposed drastic action, the sundering of the alliance with the UQ. "I am irritated by this alliance with Giannini, whose offers and requests of a union with the Liberals I always rejected while I was president of the party. I have proposed now and argued with force the moral necessity and political convenience of breaking up the union with him, negotiated by Lucifero after the small victory at the last congress of the Liberal Party. My Neapolitan friends do agree with me, though they point out the practical difficulties; but these, in my opinion, should be faced at once and surmounted."[33]

Croce's latest suggestion was not accepted; it came too late and was not practical – those running as candidates in the coming elections were unwilling and unprepared to face those very consequences that Croce, not a candidate, wanted to overcome. In fact, the pressure and the timetable of the electoral campaign did not allow for a sudden change in the status of the alliance or for drastic reversal of policy, let alone a new selection of candidates. Despite his frequent complaints, Croce was able to accomplish very little in practical terms, but his efforts were far from useless or irrelevant. Some candidates with unsavoury pasts or questionable reputations were barred from running under the banner of the National Bloc. Even more important, thanks to Croce's and Einaudi's protests, "attempts to extend the alliance to the extreme right were thwarted."[34] In a letter to Casati, Croce wrote, "I tried to avoid the worse, and I have succeeded," adding that "even during the electoral period I stood firm, and opposed the union with right-wing monarchial groups, and also with other groups belonging to the extreme right who openly professed Fascist opinions."[35]

In a diary entry written in March 1948, a mere month before the elections, Croce gave a detailed account of the difficulties he faced in trying to overcome the predicament of the Liberal Party. "In political affairs, it has not been possible to achieve my design of breaking the alliance with Giannini and with the U.Q. It needs to be remembered that I am no longer the president of the party but only an honorary president; so I can only provide advice in a private way. My design was supported by Crispo, Corbino, Cortese, and others, but those friends, who are involved in the electoral campaign, observed that the scandal of a break now would produce dangerous confusion and a lack of public confidence in our party among the electorate. Not being involved in the elections myself, I could not, in conscience, press the point. God help us!"[36]

God was not on the Liberals' side: in the elections, Lucifero's strategy failed miserably. More than 90 per cent of the electorate voted. The National Bloc received fewer votes and won fewer seats in 1948 than the Liberal Party and the Common Man had received separately in 1946. Their combined popular vote went from more than 12 per cent in 1946 to less than 4 per cent in 1948, and their total seats shrank from 71 to a meagre 19. The Liberals could take consolation in the resounding defeat of the Popular Front; it won fewer votes than the total of Socialist and Communist votes in 1946, and its share of the popular vote shrank from 39.6 per cent to 31 per cent. The number of Communist deputies increased from 104 to 131, while that of the Socialists declined from 115 to 52. The Social Democratic Party of Giuseppe Saragat, which had split from the Socialist Party only a few months earlier, did fairly well, adding to the Socialists' pain: it obtained 7 per cent of the vote and elected 33 deputies. The clear winners were the Christian Democrats; they received 12.7 million votes, a large increase from 8.1 million in 1946, their share of the popular vote rose from 35.2 per cent to 48.5 per cent, and they constituted a clear majority in the Chamber of Deputies.[37]

Besides a painful reduction of popular support, the Liberal Party, as Croce recognized, had also suffered moral damage.[38] But the results of the elections proved to be a blessing in disguise for Croce and his friends, providing the excuse needed for removing the old leadership and devising new policies. Soon after the elections, there were meetings among Liberals to achieve that aim, as we learn from Croce's diary. "Long and frequent discussions on the ways and means to get the Liberal Party back to its proper course, which is the one followed in the last four years, when I was president. I and my friends did not abandon the party, because we did not want to damage its chances during the election campaign; we made that sacrifice, overcoming our repugnance for the shameful alliance; but we did not hide our desire of wanting to bring the Liberal Party back to a worthy position in the future."[39] The negotiations were lengthy. Croce had several meetings in Naples with party leaders during the following months and also during his summer holidays in Piedmont. "I have seen again Cassandro and other friends of the Liberal Party, and we discussed the way to bring to a close a bad period, during which people who were not liberals conquered the party and made an alliance which has brought shame and caused damage to our party."[40] Despite the results of the elections, dislodging the old leadership proved difficult. Unwilling to relinquish his position, Lucifero schemed to hold onto power. Promises made in the heat of the moment were later withdrawn when the storm had calmed; opinions often changed when circumstances changed, as Croce observed in a diary entry of May 1948, a month after the elections:

> A Neapolitan friend ... a zealous and intelligent member of the Liberal Party, has informed me of what happened in Rome, where Mr Lucifero with his acolytes is refusing to strike an independent committee in order to organize a free and open congress, not one dominated from the beginning by a single faction. Mr Lucifero, who after the elections promised to me in a most solemn manner his irrevocable resignation from his post of leader, now wants to continue to run the party like a boss: a party that he did not create, that he joined after he was invited in, and of which he became secretary-general by a small majority of seven votes, and only by abusing the good faith of the honest Cassandro, who on his part was deceived by people he trusted.[41]

Undaunted, Croce proceeded with his usual tenacity, using his influence and prestige with old friends and with the membership at large.

He had more meetings with party leaders and with kindred ordinary members, trying to gather around him "the best forces of the party" in the lead-up to the next congress. He made it known that, should his effort fail, he was ready to leave the party and "to found another Liberal Party."[42] At the same time, Croce laid down the principles on which the new course should be based. In his opinion, the new course should avoid "the colour of the right" and "by logical implication should also shun the colour of the left," because, by natural inclination, "the Liberal Party is a party of the centre." For that reason, in its program and political actions, "the Liberal Party, like its founding idea, does not have any preconception, and promotes and accepts in concrete all the reforms and all the progress that the political and historical conditions of the moment allow, and naturally all of them have to be debated, evaluated, and voted in parliamentary assemblies."[43] Croce did not ignore the obstacles that the liberal idea was bound to encounter. "I know that the concept we have of the Liberal Party is very high and rather fine, and for that reason meets incomprehension and is exposed to superficial and silly objections. But I do not believe that we should lower our standards and soil the fine linen in order to please the crowds. We have to sustain our idea with calm and with tenacity, and leave the rest to providence, which for its own reasons likes to torment those who want to do good deeds. Above all, I recommend avoiding any equivocation … and rejecting contradictory formulas bound to generate confusion."[44]

In May 1948 a group of influential Liberals wrote a public letter demanding Lucifero's resignation and a new direction for the party. The next day, Croce joined forces with the group and offered his resignation as the party's honorary president, making clear the reasons for such a gesture: "This new division makes it impossible for me to maintain that position, since I share the feelings and the ideas of the dissident members."[45]

Croce's stand proved decisive. Under pressure from different quarters, Lucifero resigned his leadership position and then left the Liberal Party for good, rejoining more congenial companions on the right, who were promoting the return of the king. Those Liberals who had left the party in opposition to Lucifero returned to the fold. Finally, in 1949, after elaborate negotiations, the bulk of the Liberal Party once again agreed on a common program and a new leadership was put in place. Thanks to Croce's efforts, Italy could count anew on a moderate and responsible Liberal Party. The party remained small and prone to divisions, but at least it was still loyal to the republic and to the democratic order while also remaining faithful to the ideals of the Risorgimento, never entertaining again the notion of an alliance with right-wing movements.[46] In foreign affairs, the Liberals, unlike some Christian Democrats, steered clear of neutralism, instead championing European union and NATO – "an alliance," Croce said in announcing his vote of support in 1949, suggested not by "the will of man" but by "nature and history."[47]

Among the many writings of Croce dealing with the reunification of the party, three small pieces written in 1951 stand out for the light they shed on his political aspirations at the end of his life.[48] In one of these essays, Croce wrote that the Liberal Party had to occupy "the vital centre" of the political system. "Freedom needs both hands, the right and the left, because it holds the whole; it needs to be remembered that conservation and progress are both necessary to life, and both on different occasions serve the ends of freedom."[49] In all their political actions, Liberals had to defend both conservation and progress. The difficult task was to find an appropriate synthesis that did justice to both elements and at the same time promoted freedom, ever increasing its reach and its benefits. "Naturally, the party will discuss and propose policies that have a right or a left connotation, that promote conservation or progress, and each time will have to adopt one or the other ... But Liberals cannot deny this truth, that freedom sometimes is guaranteed and enhanced by conservative policies, and other times by radical and audacious policies of progress."[50] But the guiding star of the Liberal Party, and of every Liberal politician, had to be the defence and promotion of freedom. "In human societies, for liberals, there is one aim more fundamental than conservation or progress, that is, to assure to those two social forms the irreplaceable blessing of freedom ... compared to which those two forms assume, in this respect, a contingent aspect."[51]

In another piece, a message written in September 1951 and sent to the new secretary-general of the Liberal Party, Croce offered a general assessment of the party's contribution to Italian political life during and after the war. "After the fall of fascism," he wrote, "there was a lively return of freedom, as if it had awakened from a short sleep. Yet among such enthusiasm, there did not arise a Liberal Party with a large following; instead, so-called mass parties were formed, based on economic and ideological and sectarian interests, and the duties that belonged more properly to the Liberal Party were entrusted to a group of men highly esteemed for ability and patriotism but rather small in number." Yet, "if the Liberal Party remained small ... it had an importance far superior to its size; this can be seen, [first], in the high positions held by Liberals in public institutions, both in the political and economic fields, [second], in the universally recognized reputation of men who belong to the Liberal Party, [third], in the laws that members of the Liberal Party proposed, and that are regarded as among the best devised, debated and voted in parliamentary assemblies, and, above all, in the [party's] constant care for and the vigilant defence of freedom, which is necessary to the well-being of every civilized country."[52]

In the third piece, his last message to a Liberal Party congress, written in December 1951, one year before his death, Croce was less theoretical. There, he gave concrete advice about the problems of Italy "and proposals to solve them." He stated: "If I had to confess what the observation of the present conditions of Italy and of our times suggest, I would say that the decisions of a left-wing nature, that is, those that favour reforms, are far superior to those that support the necessity of conservation. After two great wars and the profound changes that have occurred in all countries, in the people, and in the classes, this is only natural." To make clear his argument and to indicate with more precision the kind of program he had in mind, Croce mentioned the policies and reforms undertaken in that period in the United Kingdom by the British Labour Party, under Clement Attlee, whose government was much admired in Italy. "England, the mother of the liberal idea, is now giving an example that we in Italy have to learn and to follow, naturally with the necessary adaptations and corrections."[53]

The Liberal Party did not become, then or later, an advocate of nationalization of economic enterprises but remained a staunch defender of private initiative, in a free market, under the rule of law. But, at the very least, those sentences of Croce's message of December 1951 should put to rest the assertion, made by his detractors, that Croce, in philosophy and in politics, was a typical, traditional landlord of Southern Italy. A liberal vision of society and a dialectical conception of life can hardly amount to a rejection of progress or a defence of the status quo. He certainly was a prominent landowner and a member of the upper class. Yet, despite the social status and wealth of his family, he lived simply: work was his life. Not the care or the enjoyment of wealth but work and study gave meaning and coherence to his existence, with reading and writing dictating his daily routine, from early in the morning to late at night. Economic interests of a personal, or class, nature did not influence his political actions, nor did they affect his philosophical thoughts. The promotion and defence of liberty was the inspiration for Croce's participation in intellectual and political activity.[54]

Conclusion

Benedetto Croce died on 20 November 1952. He was eighty-six years of age.

From 1948 to 1952, despite growing frailty, Croce had continued to pursue his cultural and intellectual interests, ranging from literary criticism to philosophical musing During that time he published several more books, including a fifteen-hundred-page anthology of his writings and an imaginary dialogue with Hegel, both works attracting a great deal of attention. Also during this period, he continued to be an adviser for the Laterza publishing house and was actively involved in the affairs of the Italian Institute for Historical Studies, acting for the director in his absence and giving several lectures to students on philosophical and historical topics. Meanwhile, he contributed essays to his new journal, *Quaderni della Critica*, to the monthly periodical *Lo Spettatore Italiano*, published by his daughter, Elena, and to the liberal weekly *Il Mondo*, edited by Mario Pannunzio. He was not a candidate in the elections of 1948, but, by a special constitutional dispensation affecting old parliamentarians of pre-Fascist times, he was made a member of the new Senate. However, he appeared in that body only three times, once in 1948 to support the election of his friend, Luigi Einaudi, to the post of president of the republic, and twice in 1949 to speak in favour of and vote for Italy's membership in NATO.

Over the course of his long life, Croce had been both a witness to European wars and a participant in some of the most momentous events in Italian history. His diaries, both the *Taccuini di Guerra* and the *Taccuini di Lavoro*, provide a wealth of information on politics from 1943 to 1949 and leave no doubt about his remarkable contribution to the rebirth of Italian democracy after the fall of Mussolini. His diaries, published writings, and correspondence shed light on each political crisis and cabinet formation from 1944 to 1947, and are useful to understanding the various parties' politics and changing positions and alliances. His *Taccuini di Guerra*, covering 1943 to 1945, contains insightful observations on the personalities of the time and offers keen judgments on political and social events, large and small. These notebooks also must be regarded as the first historical assessment of those dramatic years, especially valuable coming from a direct participant and a historian of wide interests.

During the chaos and the turmoil that followed the fall of Mussolini, and his replacement with Badoglio, Croce's national and international reputation was one of Italy's few remaining assets. People looked to him for inspiration and advice and expected him to play a prominent role in the new political environment. Every time a position of national importance had to be filled, Croce's name was put forward immediately from different quarters. Had he been a man driven by personal ambition, or more confident in his political abilities, he could have been prime minister in 1944 or even in 1945, and certainly he would have had a good chance of becoming the first president of the republic in 1946.

After the armistice with the Allies in September 1943 and the division of Italy into two warring camps, Croce's villa in Sorrento in Southern Italy became a centre of political activity, and he himself acted as unofficial leader of the opposition to the king and the Badoglio government. As such, Croce used his personal prestige to improve relations with the Allies and collaboration among Italian politicians, showing unsuspected diplomatic abilities. From the fall of 1943 to the spring of 1944, he played a pivotal role in the so-called Kingdom of the South, where the king and Badoglio had sought refuge from the invading German armies. With the help of Enrico De Nicola, he was instrumental in persuading the king to relinquish power and to name his son as lieutenant of the realm. With the support of Togliatti, he was the deus ex machina in the formation of the third Badoglio government, which was supported by all the anti-Fascist parties.

Even after Croce resigned from the government in July 1944, he remained president of the Liberal Party, and in that capacity he continued to have considerable influence on national affairs. From his residence in Naples, letters, notes, and instructions continuously flowed to Rome, entrusted to his friends. When national issues were at stake or important initiatives had to be taken, he took part in meetings of the party's executive in Rome. As a result, no major decisions were taken by the Liberal Party or carried out by the Liberal ministers in the cabinet without previous consultation with him. Under Croce's leadership, aware of their electoral weakness and fearful of the Communists' intentions, the Liberals twice made a strategic decision to join forces with the Christian Democrats and entrust the future of Italy to Alcide De Gasperi, assuring the country's democratic future. In 1945 the alliance between the Liberals and the Christian Democrats made possible the replacement of Ferruccio Parri with De Gasperi as prime minister, putting an end to the Jacobin drift in Italian politics and to the naive, if generous, aspirations of the Party of Action. Two years later, Croce and the Liberals offered De Gasperi essential help in dismissing the Socialists and the Communists from government, and then provided the new cabinet with men who had the authority and competence to implement a coherent economic policy. With the help of Croce and the Liberals, Italy became securely anchored in the economic system and democratic traditions of Western Europe and the Atlantic alliance.

Elected to the Constituent Assembly in 1946, Croce was not among the protagonists who replaced the old Albertine Statute with a new constitution. Yet two of his speeches in the Assembly resonated both in Italy and internationally. In his comments on the first draft of the constitution, he pointed out the document's shortcomings and contradictions, which were to be revealed with more clarity in the future. And his speech against the ratification of the Peace Treaty in 1947, imposed on Italy by the Allied powers, gave expression to feelings that were widely shared inside and outside the Assembly.

Croce, persistent claims to the contrary, was not a champion of conservative interests, let alone a proponent of reactionary policies. He was above all a man of the "radical centre" who valued law and order, respected tradition, and was open to progressive reforms. As president of the Liberal Party, he took his inspiration from the ideals of the Risorgimento and the policies of Cavour and Giolitti, trying to keep both conservative and revolutionary elements at bay while pursuing reforms under the aegis of freedom. In the name of those principles, he opposed political alliances with right-wing movements, even though such alliances might sometimes have been in the electoral interest of his party. When the Liberal Party, under new leadership, entered into that very kind of alliance in 1948, contrary to his wishes, he expended a great deal of effort in ousting the culprits and then used his authority to return the party to its original centrist position.

As Liberal Party president, Croce had shortcomings and suffered disappointments. While he did not have a partisan nature, he did have strong, sometimes inflexible views. He was not a good negotiator, and he was not able to avoid divisions in the Liberal Party or to assure the emergence of a younger and more energetic national leader. He gave undue importance to the surviving politicians of liberal Italy. He provided the party with clear principles and gave good general directions, but he neglected to elaborate a detailed program and an appealing platform, especially important during elections. He was an effective communicator and promoter of his ideas. Yet, by temperament and education, he was not attuned to the requirements of modern politics or to the needs of mass communication and partisan propaganda. Under his leadership, the Liberal Party remained a party of the elite. Still, at the end, he left to the new generation a small but responsible party that was faithful to the new institutions and to the democratic order.

Even more important, Croce left behind the legacy of his publications, spanning the fields of history, literature, politics, and philosophy. In the recent past, these writings inspired those who fought for freedom against tyranny. In our own time, the same writings, and the liberal-democratic ideals and humanistic values underpinning them, can provide a defence against "the return of the ghosts" while also pointing the way to a more equitable society and a more rational polity in the name of a common humanity.

Notes

Introduction

1 Croce, *Contributo alla Critica di me Stesso*, 88.
2 Croce, *Taccuini di Lavoro*, vols. 5 and 6; Croce, *Taccuini di Guerra*; Croce, *Nuove Pagine Sparse*; Croce, *Terze Pagine Sparse*; Croce, *Scritti e Discorsi Politici*; Croce; *Filosofia e Storiografia*; Croce, *Discorsi di Varia Filosofia*; Griffo, ed., *Dall' "Italia Tagliata in Due."*
3 Griffo, ed., *Dall' "Italia Tagliata in Due,"* 288–90.
4 Anonymous, "Relazione sul Congresso dei Comitati di Liberazione"; Fanello Marcucci, ed., *Ivanoe Bonomi dal Fascismo alla Repubblica*; Bonanno and Valentini, eds., *Il Congresso di Bari*; Spagnoletti, ed., *Togliatti e il CLN del Sud.*
5 De Giorgi, ed., *Il Movimento Liberale Italiano*; Riccardi, ed., *Niccolò Carandini*; Einaudi, *La Guerra e L'Unità Europea*; Einaudi, *Riflessioni di un Liberale sulla Democrazia*; Orlando, *Discorsi Parlamentari*; Parente, "Aspettando la Libertà"; Cattani, "Dalla Caduta del Fascismo al Primo Governo De Gasperi."
6 Croce, *Carteggio Croce-Antoni*; Croce, *Carteggio Croce-Arangio Ruiz*; Croce, *Carteggio Croce-Omodeo*; Croce, *Carteggio Croce-Calogero*; Croce, *Carteggio Croce-Pannunzio*; Croce, *Epistolario*, vol. 2, *Lettere a Alessandro Casati*; Croce and Einaudi, *Carteggio*; Cutinelli, ed., *Luigi Russo, Benedetto Croce, Carteggio*; and Setta, "Benedetto Croce e la 'Sinistra' Liberale nel Carteggio con Leone Cattani."
7 Sale, *Dalla Monarchia alla Repubblica*; Sale, *Il Vaticano e la Costituzione*; Sale, *De Gasperi, Gli USA e il Vaticano all'Inizio della Guerra Fredda.*
8 Incisa di Camerana, *L'Italia della Luogotenenza*; Lucifero, *L'Ultimo Re. I Diari del Ministro della Real Casa;* Di Campello, *Un Principe nella Bufera*; Puntoni, *Parla Vittorio Emanuele III.*
9 Lizzadri, *Il Regno di Badoglio*; Carracciolo, *Diario di Napoli.*

10 Bonomi, *Diario di un Anno*; Nenni, *Tempo di Guerra Fredda*; Andreotti, *Concerto a Sei Voci*; Andreotti, *1947*; Zanotti Bianco, *La Mia Roma*.

11 Storoni, *La Congiura del Quirinale*; Piccardi, "I 45 Giorni del Governo Badoglio," in Antonicelli, ed., *Trent'Anni di Storia Italiano*, 322–3; Togliatti, "Il Governo di Salerno," in Antonicelli, ed., *Trent'Anni di Storia Italiano*, 365–77; Salvadori, *The Labour and the Wounds*, 318–23; Valiani, *Tutte le Strade Conducono a Roma*; Craveri, *La Campagna d'Italia*; Barzini, *La Verità sul Referendum*; Monelli, *Il Giorno del Referendum*; Scoppola and Elia, eds., *Colloquio con Dossetti*; Carli, *Cinquant'Anni di Vita Italiana*.

12 Murphy, *Diplomat among Warriors*; Macmillan, *War Diaries*; Loewenheim et al., eds., *Roosevelt and Churchill*.

13 Moorehead, *Eclipse*; Moravia, *La Ciociara*; Mowat, *And No Birds Sang*.

14 Matthews, *The Education of a Correspondent*; Malone, *A Portrait of War, 1939–1943*.

15 *British Documents on Foreign Affairs*, pt. II, series F, vols. 22, 23, 24, 25, 26, January 1942–December 1945; *Foreign Relations of the United States*, 1943, vol. 2, 314–445; 1944, vol. 3, 96–1186; 1945, vol. 1, 681–713, vol. 2, 1079–103; 1945, vol. 4, 955–1331, vol. 5, 85–953; 1947, vol. 3, Italy.

16 Craveri, *De Gasperi*. Craveri is Croce's grandson, son of Elena Croce and Raimondo Craveri.

17 Pombeni, *Giuseppe Dossetti*; Remaggi, *La Nazione Perduta*.

18 Monina, ed., *1945–1946*; Nicolosi, ed., *I Partiti Politici nell'Italia Repubblicana*; Quagliarello and Zaslavsky, eds., "I Liberali e la Repubblica: Una Storia da Scrivere," *Ventunesimo Secolo*, 4, no. 8 (2005): 13–158; Grassi Orsini and Nicolosi, eds., *I Liberali Italiani dall'Antifascismo alla Repubblica*, vol. 1; Berti, Capozzi, and Craveri, eds., *I Liberali Italiani dall'Antifascismo alla Repubblica*, vol. 2; Craveri and Quagliarello, eds., *La Seconda Guerra Mondiale e la Sua Memoria*; Nicolosi, ed., *I Partiti Politici nell'Italia Repubblicana*; Craveri, *De Gasperi*; Pombeni, *Giuseppe Dossetti*; Remaggi, *La Nazione Perduta*; Aga-Rossi and Zaslavsky, *Togliatti e Stalin*; Zaslavsky, *Lo Stalinismo e la Sinistra Italiana*.

19 Chabod, *L'Italia Contemporanea, 1918–1948*; Colarizi, *La Seconda Geurra Mondiale e la Repubblica*; Colarizi, *Storia dei Partiti nell'Italia Repubblicana*; Delzell, *Mussolini's Enemies*; Candeloro, *Storia dell'Italia Moderna*.

20 Sasso, *Benedetto Croce*; Sasso, *Filosofia e Idealismo*; Sasso, *Per Invigilare me Stesso*; Galasso, *Croce e lo Spirito del Suo Tempo*; Sasso, *La Ricerca della Dialettica*; Sasso, *La Fedeltà e l'Esperimento*; Galasso, *La Memoria, La Vita, I Valori, Itinerari Crociani*.

21 Orsina, *Il Partito Liberale nell'Italia Repubblicana*; Orsini, "Riaprire il Cantiere," *Ventunesimo Secolo*, 8 (October 2005): 13–65; Finetti, *La Resistenza Cancellata*.

22 Battaglia, *Storia dell'Resistenza Italiana,* 218–19; Gambino, *Storia del Dopo Guerra,* 8; Lepre, *Storia della Prima Repubblica,* 22; Spriano, *Storia del Partito Comunista Italiano,* vol. 5, 138–77.
23 Ragionieri, *Storia d'Italia dall'Unità a Oggi,* vol. 4, tome 3, 2371.
24 Desiderio, *Vita Affettiva e Sentimentale di Benedetto Croce,* 274–8.
25 Orsini and Nicolosi, eds., *I Liberali Italiani dall'Antifascismo alla Repubblica,* vol. 1; Berti, Capozzi, and Craveri, eds., *I Liberali Italiani dall'Antifascismo alla Repubblica,* vol. 2; Berti et al., eds., *Dizionario del Liberalismo Italiano,* books 1, 2.
26 Orsini, "Croce e il Partito Liberale," in *I Liberali Italiani dall'Antifascismo alla Repubblica,* vol. 2, 579–685.
27 Pera, ed., *Benedetto Croce e la Nascita della Repubblica*; Maggi, *L'Italia Che non Muore*; Craveri, *L'Opera Politica di Croce per l'Italia Che non Muore.*

1 Croce and Italy in 1943

1 De Felice, *Mussolini l'Alleato,* vol. 2; Bianchi, *25 Luglio*; Monelli, *Roma 1943.*
2 By necessity and choice, my attention in this book is concentrated on the most pressing political issues of the period 1943–52; other issues of a different nature, or ones with which Croce had limited involvement, are either not explored or discussed only briefly.

One such issue is Croce's response to the Holocaust. Though some have argued otherwise, the truth is that, unlike the case of Martin Heidegger, there is no sign of anti-Semitism in Croce's diaries or letters, let alone in his books. Quite the opposite: the known and publicly available records offer strong testimony against claims about Croce's attitudes towards Jews and the Holocaust, claims that must be dismissed without hesitation as completely without foundation.

In his long life, Croce was never an anti-Semite, and indeed he always rejected racial theories of any kind and opposed discrimination based on race or ethnic background, not to mention political persuasion. When Mussolini introduced the Racial Laws in 1938 and the persecution of Italian Jews began, Croce condemned, publicly and privately, the legislation and ridiculed the pseudo-scientific theory on which it was based and with which it was defended. He also came to the assistance of numerous Jews who were subjected to discrimination and persecution, earning their gratitude. His diary makes clear that Palazzo Filomarino, his residence in Naples, became almost a place of pilgrimage for many persecuted Jews, usually university teachers, who went there for support, advice, or words of comfort.

In my previous book, *Benedetto Croce and Italian Fascism*, I dealt at length with the persecution of Jews under fascism. There, as was appropriate in a study focused on Croce's position in the Fascist era, I discussed in detail his public opposition to the Racial Laws and his interventions on behalf of persecuted Jews (pp. 221–31). I mentioned Croce's friendship with some leading European and American intellectuals of Jewish descent, including the physicist Albert Einstein, the philosopher Henri Bergson, and the journalist Walter Lippmann. More importantly, I showed the high esteem in which he was held by several leading Jewish anti-Fascists, who, in their opposition to fascism and Mussolini's dictatorship, found inspiration in Croce's writings. Among these individuals were Carlo and Nello Rosselli; Paolo and Pietro Treves, sons of the Socialist leader Claudio Treves; Aldo Garosci; Leo Valiani; and Leone Ginzburg, father of the historian Carlo Ginzburg. Garosci and Valiani were well-known historians. Both wrote extensively on Croce long after the war. In Croce's writings they found much to admire, a few things to criticize, but nothing that was worthy of blame on account of ethnic or racial bias.

In the recently published correspondence between Croce and Giovanni Laterza, there are many revealing letters in which Croce expresses his outrage about the new policy of persecution and discrimination that was creating havoc in the lives of Italian Jews, who were, as he writes, "our friends, our citizens, who love Italy no more and no less than we do." On several occasions, he laments the damage done to Italian culture by banning the circulation of books written by Jewish authors, as well as prohibiting their inclusion in school curricula. He also bemoans the wounds inflicted on the reputation of Italian universities and academies by removing from their ranks scholars with Jewish names, many of whom had international standing. A good example of his feelings on this subject is a letter he wrote to Laterza supporting a business proposal made by two Jewish scholars, Giorgio Tagliacozzo and Rodolfo Mondolfo, for selling Laterza publications in South America: "I believe that their proposal would be advantageous and convenient to you, coming as it does from such intelligent and reputable individuals. I urge you to give it full consideration; should you accept their proposal, it will make me very happy, since you know the interest I take in the misfortunes of these unjustly persecuted people" (Pompilio, ed., *Carteggio Croce-Laterza, 1931–1943*, vol. 4, 897).

It should thus come as no surprise that, after Croce's death, Arnaldo Momigliano, a Jew who had personally experienced his benevolence and solidarity, paid this tribute to him: "Few eminent men were as deeply sympathetic to Jews, Italian and German, the victims of persecution, as

Croce" (Momigliano, *Pagine Ebraiche*, 147). Following the war, Croce offered Momigliano the position of academic director of the Italian Institute for Historical Studies, which he had just founded in Naples and which was housed in a wing of his house.

Charges of anti-Semitism against Croce are probably based on the polemical exchange between Croce and Dante Lattes, cut short by Croce as distasteful but continued by others, including Momigliano. This exchange took place in 1947 after Croce had written a letter to Cesare Merzagora, which the latter then used as an introduction to his book *I Timidi.* There, Croce invited the Jews to choose integration and assimilation into the wider Italian society, abandoning "that distinctiveness and separation in which they have persisted for centuries," in order to avoid any pretext for new persecution, which was always a possibility. The letter may contain unfortunate expressions and questionable advice, which Italian Jews were right to resent and reject, but displays no anti-Semitism. On the contrary, it reaffirms Croce's opposition to anti-Semitism in unequivocal terms (Croce, *Scritti e Discorsi Politici*, vol. 2, 323–6).

Twenty years afterwards, in his *Pagine Ebraiche*, Momigliano described Croce's advice as odd and questionable, while others used stronger language. To my knowledge, Gennaro Sasso has offered the best analysis of this episode, as he has done for other aspects of Croce's life and philosophy. His essay is remarkable for its learning and insight, as well as for its understanding and sensitivity, which the nature of the subject requires and even demands (Sasso, *Per Invigilare Me Stesso*, 179–217). Sasso does justice to Croce's feelings and at the same time explains the reasons for and limitations of his position, which, he argues convincingly, was rooted not in anti-Semitism or racial theories but in his philosophical system and in his personal experience in liberal Italy. What Croce said to the Jews he could have said to any other religious group, and in fact he did exactly that in the case of the Catholics at the time of the modernist movement, which agitated the Catholic Church at the turn of the century, under Pope Pius X. For Croce, Sasso notes, religion was a myth and as such was an inferior form of knowledge that philosophy transcends. True knowledge can be achieved only through philosophy, and only by following the tenets of reason and the requirements of logic.

Sasso also stressed the psychological motivation behind Croce's advice to the Jews. After the war, Croce was harking back to the times and spirit of liberal Italy, when Jews were, more or less, integrated in Italian society, holding prestigious positions in politics, education, the arts, and the professions. In those days, Luigi Luzzati, a respected government minister and parliamentarian, could become prime minister, with no one raising any objection on account of his race or religion.

That said, Sasso points out the weaknesses of Croce's position and recognizes the inadequate and outdated nature of his advice, coming as it did after the persecution inaugurated by the Racial Laws and then the Holocaust, which underlined the precarious conditions in which Jews lived everywhere, whether they were integrated in or separated from the larger society. Integration and assimilation had failed. A peaceful and fruitful cohabitation of different peoples in a liberal society requires a deeper understanding of freedom – something that Croce demonstrated in his discussion of many subjects, but not this one. In any event, in dealing with such a sensitive and highly charged matter, any scholar would be wise to follow Sasso's judicious injunction that one should always recognize the limits and shortcomings of a given position, be open to legitimate criticism, and avoid impugning the personal motives of others and making unfounded accusations against them.

It seems appropriate to conclude this discussion by mentioning an instance of *intreccio storico*, a concept often used by Croce to indicate the unforeseen and unexpected workings of history. During the war Croce befriended in Sorrento a wounded young Polish officer of Jewish descent who had been an enthusiastic student of his philosophy at the University of Warsaw. Gustav Herling-Grudzinski was destined to achieve great renown as the author of *A World Apart* and as editor of the Polish periodical *Kultura*. In 1944 he fought in the battle of Montecassino with the Polish Corps, which he had joined in North Africa after a long journey through Eastern Europe and the Middle East, including a short but harrowing stay in a Soviet concentration camp. In 1954 he married Lidia Croce in London. Today, their daughter, Marta Herling, at Palazzo Filomarino, is the proud custodian of her father's and grandfather's cultural and political legacy.

3 Croce's role in the anti-Fascist resistance is examined in my article "Palazzo Filomarino: Un Centro di Resistenza Antifascista, 1925–1943," *Rivista di Studi Italiani*, 1 (June 2005): 248–62. A revised version of this article, entitled "Benedetto Croce and the Italian Anti-Fascist Resistance," appears in Mosco and Pirani, eds., *The Concept of Resistance in Italy*; another essay can be found, under the title "Antifascismo," in Peluso, ed., *Lessico Crociano*, 58–99. On the same subject, see also Nicolini, *Croce*; Rizi, *Benedetto Croce and Italian Fascism*, 80–245; Sasso, *Per Invigilare Me Stesso*, 77–218; Storoni, *La Congiura del Quirinale*.

4 Croce, *Taccuini di Guerra*.

5 Qt. in Placanica, ed., *1944: Salerno Capitale*, 318–23.

6 Macmillan, *War Diaries,* 459.
7 Salvadori. *The Labours and the Wounds,* 169.
8 Malone, *A Portrait of War,* 194.
9 Sasso, *Prefazione,* 7–33; Griffo, ed., *Dall' "Italia Tagliata.*
10 Caracciolo, *Diario di Napoli,* 79. See also Parente, "Aspettando la Libertà" (unpublished manuscript in Luigi Einaudi Foundation in Rome), 97–108, 119–39, 164–201. Parente explains the reasons that compelled Croce to move to Sorrento. He also gives a good account of political activities undertaken by Croce from his new home. On Alfredo Parente and his diary, see Gerardo Nicolosi, "Un Inedito di Alfredo Parente," in Berti, Capozzi, and Craveri, eds., *I Liberali Italiani dall'Antifascismo alla Repubblica,* vol. 2, 661–74.
11 Croce, *Taccuini di Guerra.*
12 Ibid.; Griffo, ed., *Dall' "Italia Tagliata."*
13 Matthews, *Education of a Correspondent,* 427–8.
14 Pieri and Rochat, *Pietro Badoglio,* 771–824; Bertoldi, *Vittorio Emanuele III*; Delzell, *Mussolini's Enemies,* 223–60; Leopoldo Piccardi, "I 45 Giorni del Governo Badolgio," in Antonicelli, ed., *Trent'Anni di Storia Italiana,* 322–30; Orlando, *I 45 Giorni di Badoglio*; Afeltra, *I 45 Giorni Che Sconvolsero l'Italia*; Kogan, *Italy and the Allies,* 26–41; *Verbali del Consiglio dei Ministri,* vol. I (see especially the introduction by Aldo G. Ricci); Ricci and Bongiorno, *La Rinascita dei Partiti in Italia, 1943–1948*; Mimmo Franzinelli, "Il 25 Luglio," in Isnenghi, ed., *I Luoghi della Memoria,* 219–40.
15 Croce, *Taccuini di Guerra,* 13.
16 Ibid., 14.
17 Ibid.
18 Croce, *Scritti e Discorsi Politici,* vol. 1, 109–13. On Bergamini, see Andrea Ungari, "Alberto Bergamini e i Rapporti Tra Liberali," in Orsini and Nicolosi, eds., *I Liberali Italiani dall'Antifascismo alla Repubblica,* vol. 1, 543–74.
19 Croce, *Scritti e Discorsi Politici,* vol. 2, 108.
20 Ibid., 122–5.
21 Ibid., 125; Simoncelli. *L'Epurazione Antifascista all'Accademia dei Lincei*; Nicolini, *Il Croce Minore,* 98–127.
22 Ciani, *Il Partito Liberale da Croce a Malagodi*; De Giorgi, ed., *Il "Movimento Liberale Italiano"*; Einaudi, *Riflessioni di un Liberale Sulla Democrazia*; Riccardi, ed., *Niccolò Carandini,* 13–52; Antoni, *Tre Saggi Storici*; Gerardo Nicolosi, "Il Nuovo Liberalismo," in Orsini and Nicolosi, eds., *I Liberali Italiani dall'Antifascismo alla Repubblica,* vol. 1, 243–84; Sasso, "Benedetto Croce e il liberalismo," in *Filosofia e Idealismo,* vol. 5, 579–630; Antoni, *La Restauzione del Diritto di Natura.* See also Visentin, *Il Neoparmenidismo Italiano*; Postorino, *Croce e l'Ansia di un'Altra Citta.*

23 Croce, *Scritti e Discorsi Politici*, vol. 1, 103.
24 Ibid., 103–7.
25 Ibid.
26 Ibid., 87; Ragghianti, "Il Partito d'Azione: Il Suo Programma e la Sua Storia," in *Disegno della Liberazione Italiana*, 288–385; De Luna, *Storia del Partito d'Azione*, 17–91.
27 Croce, *Taccuini di Guerra*, 15. See also Calogero, *Difesa del Liberalsocialismo*; Sasso, "Calogero e Croce," in *Filosofia e Idealismo*, vol. 3, 301–414; Delzell, *Mussolini's Enemies*, 131–80.
28 Croce, *Scritti e Discorsi Politici*, vol. 1, 133.
29 Croce, *Discorsi di Varia Filosofia*, vol. 1, 261–76; Croce, *Scritti e Discorsi Politici*, vol. 1, 98–102.
30 Croce, *Taccuini di Guerra*, 64. See also Gigante, ed., *Carteggio Croce-Omodeo*, 205–14.
31 Croce, *Scritti e Discorsi Politici*, vol. 1, 134.
32 Croce, *Taccuini di Guerra*, 16–17; Benzoni, *La Vita Ribelle.*
33 Croce, *Taccuini di Guerra*, 16–18.
34 Ibid., 18. Badoglio officially made his announcement at 7:45 p.m. but Eisenhower made his at 6:30 Italian time from Bizerte. Is Croce making a small mistake or had his wife heard Eisenhower's announcement from a different radio station operated by the Allies? Radio Londra, perhaps? On the armistice and peace negotiations, see also Toscano, *Dal 25 Luglio all'Otto Settembre 1943*; Aga-Rossi, *Una Nazione allo Sbando*, 71–110, 224–60.

2 Waging War

1 Pavone, *Una Guerra Civile*, 8; Rossi, *Una Nazione Allo Sbando*, 111–90; Monelli, *Roma 1943*; Pavone, "1943: 8 Settembre," in *Novecento Italiano*, 89–112; Palermo, *Storia di un Armistizio*; Rossi, *L'Italia nella Sconfitta*, 17–124.
2 Croce, *Taccuini di Guerra*, 55; Della Loggia, *La Morte della Patria*; Isnenghi, *La Tragedia Necessaria*, 61–127; Ciampi, *Da Livorno al Quirinale*, 48–62, 72–4. In his book Ciampi rejects Della Loggia's thesis. For the former president of the republic, Carlo Azeglio Ciampi, in 1943 a young army officer and deeply influenced by Croce's history books and by Guido Calogero's teaching, 8 September marks not the death but the rebirth of the fatherland. See also Galasso, "Ideologia Italiana e Morte dell Patria," in *L'Italia Nuova*, vol. 6, 41–83.
3 Croce, *Scritti e Discorsi Politici*, vol. 1, 97–8; Croce, *Storia d'Italia dal 1871 al 1915*; Croce, *Discorsi di Varia Filoisofia*, vol. 1, 291–300.
4 Bartoli, *8 Settembre*, 55–6; Montanelli and Cervi, *L'Italia della Disfatta*; Bertoldi, *Apocalisse Italia*; Patricelli, *Settembre 1943.*

5 Croce, *Taccuini di Guerra,* 18.
6 Ibid., 19.
7 Ibid.
8 Ibid., 20.
9 Ibid.
10 Ibid., 20–1; De Andreis, *Capri 1943,* 335–44.
11 Gallegos. *And Who Are You?* 61–8; Croce, *Croce, the King and the Allies,* 16.
12 Croce, *Taccuini di Guerra,* 22.
13 Ibid., 20–3.
14 Croce, *Taccuini di Guerra,* 24.
15 Ibid., 389–90. See also Croce, *Croce, the King and the Allies,* 141–9.
16 Croce, *Taccuini di Guerra,* 390–1.
17 Placanica, ed., *Salerno Capitale,* 318–23.
18 Croce, *Taccuini di Guerra,* 391.
19 Ibid., 30. See also Croce, *Croce, the King and the Allies,* 143–9.
20 Croce, *Taccuini di Guerra,* 392–7; Macmillan, *War Diaries,* 459.
21 Croce, *Taccuini di Guerra,* 392–7.
22 Ibid.
23 Ibid.
24 Ibid.
25 Ibid.
26 Griffo, ed., *Dall' "Italia Tagliata,"* 71–2.
27 Ibid., 72–4.
28 Ibid., 74.
29 Ibid., *Dall' "Italia Tagliata,"* 2–69.
30 Croce, *Scritti e Discorsi Politici,* vol. 1, 397–400. See also Croce, *Croce, the King and the Allies,* 149–52.
31 Caracciolo, *Diario di Napoli,* 3–94. See also Valiani, *Tutte le Strade Conducono a Roma,* 60.
32 Croce, *Taccuini di Guerra,* 28.
33 Ibid., 29–30.
34 Pavone, *Una Guerra Civile*; Focardi, *La Guerra della Memoria*; Peli, *La Resistenza in Italia,* 15–54; Finetti, *La Resistenza Cancellata.*
35 Griffo, ed., *Dall' "Italia Tagliata,"* 69–71.
36 Ibid.; Minale, ed., *Carteggio Croce–Arangio Ruiz,* 11–13.
37 Croce, *Taccuini di Guerra,* 36.
38 Battaglia, *Storia della Resistenza Italiana,* 12.
39 Patricelli, *I Banditi della Libertà.*
40 Croce, *Taccuini di Guerra,* 34, 39.
41 Griffo, ed., *Dall' "Italia Tagliata,"* 84.

42 Croce, *Taccuini di Guerra,* 43.
43 Griffo, ed., *Dall'"Italia Tagliata,"* 71, 87.
44 Ibid., 85–8.
45 Craveri, *La Campagna d'Italia e i Servizi Segreti*; Caracciolo, *Diario di Napoli,* 81.
46 Pavone, "I Gruppi Combattenti 'Italia,'" in Amendola et al., eds., *Fascismo e Antifascismo,* 558–65.
47 Croce, *Taccuini di Guerra,* 39.
48 Griffo, ed., *Dall'"Italia Tagliata,"* 84.
49 Craveri, *La Campagna d'Italia,* 125.
50 Smith, *OSS,* 90–9; Craveri, *La Campagna d'Italia.*

3 The Matter of the King

1 See Candeloro, *Storia dell'Italia Moderna,* vol. 10, 234; Delzell, *Mussolini's Enemies,* 315–46; Kogan, *Italy and the Allies,* 50–65; Marcucci, ed., *Ivanoe Bonomi dal Fascismo alla Repubblica*; Ciumi, *L'Italia di Badoglio*; Degli Espinosa, *Il Regno del Sud.*
2 Croce, *Taccuini di Guerra,* 30–1. See also Puntoni, *Parla Vittoria Emanuele III.*
3 Croce, *Taccuini di Guerra,* 51–2, 55–6.
4 Macmillan, *War Diaries,* 282.
5 Croce, *Taccuini di Guerra,* 55–6.
6 Macmillan, *War Diaries,* 256.
7 Croce, *Taccuini di Guerra,* 59–60, 77–8, 167. See also Caracciolo, *Diario di Napoli,* 82–3, 87–8.
8 Bianco, *La Mia Roma,* 241–2. See also Degli Espinosa, *Il Regno del Sud,* 154–92; Zeno, *Il Conte Sforza*; Antonio Varsori, "Carlo Sforza nella Politica Italiana," in Berti, Capozzi, and Craveri, eds., *I Liberali Italiani dall'Antifascismo alla Resistenza,* vol. 1, 145–60.
9 Croce, *Taccuini di Guerra,* 32.
10 Griffo, ed., *Dall'"Italia Tagliata,"* 90–1.
11 Croce, *Taccuini di Guerra,* 36–7.
12 Croce, *Taccuini di Guerra,* 38.
13 Macmillan, *War Diaries,* 270.
14 Croce, *Taccuini di Guerra,* 38–9.
15 Ibid., 46–7, See also Degli Espinosa, *Il Regno del Sud,* 193–228.
16 Baget-Bozzo, *Il Partito Cristiano al Potere,* 45–70; Colarizi, *Storia dei Partiti nell'Italia Repubblicana,* 19–75; Ricci and Bongiorno, *La Rinascita dei Partiti in Italia,* 53–80, 153–70; Guido Formigoni, "La Democrazia Cristiana," in Nicolosi, ed., *I Partiti Politici nell'Italia Repubblicana,* 55–90; Antonio Jannazzo, "Il Partito Liberale Italiano," in ibid., 275–312; Renato Pallini,

"Vita Orgazizzativa e Diffusione Territoriale del PLI (1944–1946)," in Orsini and Nicolosi, eds., *I Liberali Italiani dall'Antifascismo alla Repubblica*, vol. 1, 109–30; Gerardo Nicolosi, "Il Nuovo Liberalismo," in ibid., 243–84.

17 Croce, *Taccuini di Guerra*, 38, 42.

18 Croce, *Scritti e Discorsi Politici*, vol. 1, 24–9.

19 Griffo, ed., *Dall'"Italia Tagliata*," 97. The Aventino was an attempt by the anti-Fascist parties, after the Matteotti murder, to bring down Mussolini by boycotting the sittings of Parliament, a tactic not supported by Giolitti or Croce.

20 Croce, *Scritti e Discorsi Politici*, vol. 1, 30–4.

21 Ibid., 34–6; Craveri, "La Vocazione Arbitrale di Enrico De Nicola," in *La Democrazia Incompiuta*, 85–116.

22 Croce, *Taccuini di Guerra*, 61–3, 71–2.

23 Minale, ed., *Carteggio Croce-Arangio Ruiz*, 14–16.

24 Caracciolo, *Diario di Napoli*, 82–3. See also Andrea Ungari, "I Liberali Visti dai Monarchici," in Orsini and Nicolosi, eds., *I Liberali Italiani dall'Antifascismo alla Repubblica*, vol. 1, 777–816.

25 Croce, *Taccuini di Guerra*, 60.

4 The Congress of Bari

1 Caracciolo, *Diario di Napoli*, 133. See also Ricci, ed., *Verbali del Consiglio dei Ministri*, vol. 1; Degli Espinosa, *Il Regno del Sud*; Ciumi, *L'Italia di Badolgio*; Santarelli, *Mezzogiorno 1943–1944*; Alvaro, *L'Italia Rinuncia 1944*; Puntoni, *Parla Vittorio Emanuele III*; Ricci and Bongiorno, *La Rinascita dei Partiti in Italia*; Mazza, *Il Partito d'Azione nel Mezzogiorno.*

2 Lizzadri, *Il Regno di Badoglio*, 188–9.

3 Malone, *A Portrait of War*, 194.

4 Caracciolo, *Diario di Napoli*, 143.

5 Sasso, "Considerazioni sul Diario di Piero Calamandrei."

6 Macmillan, *War Diaries*, 131; Elwood, *Italy 1943–1945*; Leoni, *Il Paradiso Devastato*; Mercuri, *1943–1945.*

7 Di Nolfo and Serra, *La Gabbia Infranta*, 62–148; Borzoni, *Renato Prunas.* Prunas was secretary general – in practice, minister – of foreign affairs at the time. See also Aga Rossi, "La Politica Estera Americana e l'Italia nella Seconda Guerra Mondiale," in *L'Italia nella Sconfitta*, 17–42; Michael Narinsky, "La Politica Estera Sovietica verso l'Europa Occidentale, 1941–1945," in Aga-Rossi and Quagliarello, eds., *L'Altra Faccia della Luna*, 29–51.

8 Matthews, *The Education of a Correspondent*, 442. See also Harris, *Allied Military Administration in Italy.*

9 Candeloro, *Storia dell' Italia Moderna*, vol. 10, 341. See also Placanica, ed., *1944: Salerno Capitale*; Mazzetti, *Salerno Capitale*.
10 Di Nolfo, *Le Paure e le Speranze degli Italiani*, 79–105; Porzio, *Arrivano gli Alleati*, 26–118; Ponzani, *Guerra alle Donne*, 223–52; Bracalini, *Paisà*; Innocenti, *L'Italia del 1943*. One episode of such violence appeared in Vitttorio De Sica's film *Two Women*, based on Alberto Moravia's book and starring Sophia Loren, for which she won an Oscar.
11 Togliatti, "Il Governo di Salerno," in Antonicelli, ed., *Trent'Anni di Storia Italiana*, 365–77.
12 Nenni, *Tempo di Guerra Fredda*, 89.
13 Mowat, *And No Birds Sang*, 171.
14 Moorehead, *Eclipse*, 60, 76–81.
15 Togliatti, "Il Governo di Salerno," 365–77. See also Macmillan, *War Diaries*, 397. Macmillan also reported an invasion of locusts from North Africa.
16 Croce, *Taccuini di Guerra*, 107–8.
17 Malone, *A Portrait of War*, 231–2.
18 Croce, *Taccuini di Guerra*, 97.
19 Ibid., 91. See also Sasso, "La Riflessione Sulla Civiltà Europea dell'Ultimo Croce"; Pera, ed., *Benedetto Croce e la Nascita della Repubblica*, 36–56; Sasso, *Per Invigilare Me Stesso*, 219–82; Galasso, *Croce e lo Spirito del Suo Tempo*, 418–43.
20 Croce, *Taccuini di Guerra*, 99.
21 Ibid., 281–3.
22 Croce, *Taccuini di Lavoro*, vol. 6, 113.
23 Croce, *Taccuini di Guerra*, 68.
24 Croce, *Taccuini di Lavoro*, vol. 6, 105.
25 Lizzadri, *Il Regno di Badoglio*, 179–81; Buonanno and Valentini, eds., *Il Congresso di Bari*; Degli Espinosa, *Il Regno del Sud*, 240–94; Spagnoletti, ed., *Togliatti e il C.L.N. del Sud*; anonymous, "Relazione sul Congresso dei Comitati di Liberazione."
26 Croce, *Taccuini di Guerra*, 76–9.
27 Griffo, ed., *Dall' "Italia Tagliata,"* 113–14.
28 Caracciolo, *Diario di Napoli*, 115.
29 Macmillan, *The Blast of War*, 479–80.
30 Ellwood, *Italy 1943–1945*, 79.
31 Croce, *Taccuini di Guerra*, 76–81.
32 Ibid., 76.
33 Caracciolo, *Diario di Napoli*, 132.
34 Lizzadri, *Il Regno di Badoglio*, 189.
35 Degli Espinosa, *Il Regno del Sud*, 263.
36 Croce, *Scritti e Discorsi Politici*, vol. 1, 54–62.

37 Ibid., 54–62.
38 Croce, *Taccuini di Guerra,* 76.
39 Degli Espinosa, *Il Regno del Sud,* 262–3.
40 Griffo, ed., *Dall'"Italia Tagliata,"* 211, 303.
41 Ibid. For Croce's views on fascism, see also his *Scritti e Discorsi Politici,* vol. 2, 172–7; and *Storia d'Europa nel Secolo Decimonono.* See also Sasso, *Croce: Storia d'Italia e Storia d'Europa,* 11–59.
42 Croce, *Taccuini di Guerra,* 81.
43 Croce, *Scritti e Discorsi Politici,* vol. 1, 59.
44 Ibid., 54–62; Croce, *Taccuini di Guerra,* 76–84.
45 Buonanno and Valentini, ed., *Il Congresso di Bari,* 79–80.
46 Spagnoletti, ed., *Togliatti e il CLN del Sud,* 122.
47 Buonanno and Valentini, eds., *Il Congresso di Bari,* 79–80.
48 Croce, *Taccuini di Guerra,* 411–12.
49 Caracciolo, *Diario di Napoli,* 132–3; Buonanno and Valentini, eds., *Il Congresso di Bari,* 75–6.
50 Ellwood, *Italy 1943–1945,* 20. See also Buonanno and Valentini, eds., *Il Congresso di Bari,* 117–22.
51 Griffo, ed., *Dall'"Italia Tagliata,"* 157–60.
52 Macmillan, *The Blast of War,* 480.
53 Ibid.
54 For a negative assessment of Croce's position and the Bari congress, see Salvemini, *L'Italia Vista dall'America,* vols. 1 and 2, 531–5, 536–7, 564–70.
55 Macmillan, *The Blast of War,* 482.

5 De Nicola's Negotiations

1 Croce, *Taccuini di Guerra,* 86. See also Artieri, *Umberto II;* Di Campello, *Un Principe Nella Bufera;* "Casa di Savoia," in Croce, *Nuove Pagine Sparse,* vol. 1, 96–106.
2 Croce, *Taccuini di Guerra,* 72–3.
3 Griffo, ed., *Dall'"Italia Tagliata,"* 139–43, 149.
4 Ibid., 139–43.
5 Ibid.
6 Croce, *Taccuini di Guerra,* 91–3.
7 Craveri, *La Democrazia Incompiuta,* 106–7; Ansaldo, *Don Enrico.*
8 Croce, *Taccuini di Guerra,* 92–3.
9 Craveri, *La Democrazia Incompiuta,* 107.
10 Croce, *Taccuini di Guerra,* 92.
11 Ibid., 93.

12 Caracciolo, *Diario di Napoli,* 121–2, 145.

13 Croce, *Taccuini di Guerra,* 93. See also Degli Espinosa, *Il Regno del Sud,* 249–350; Ungari, *In Nome del Re. I Monarchici Italiani,* 1–53.

14 Ellwood, *Italy 1943–1945.*

15 Macmillan, *The Blast of War,* 481.

16 Lizzadri, *Il Regno di Badoglio,* 198; Caracciolo, *Diario di Napoli,* 145.

17 Croce, *Taccuini di Guerra,* 85. See also Croce, *Scritti e Discorsi Politici,* vol. 1, 62–5.

18 Griffo, ed., *Dall' "Italia Tagliaia,"* 145–6.

19 Ibid.

20 Ibid., 150–1. In the State of the Union address delivered on 6 January 1941, President Roosevelt had declared that people everywhere were entitled to four basic freedoms: freedom of speech, freedom of worship, freedom from want, and freedom from fear.

21 Croce, *Scritti e Discorsi Politici,* vol. 1, 62–5.

22 Griffo, ed., *Dall' "Italia Tagliata,"* 148.

23 Croce, ed., *Taccuini di Guerra,* 94.

24 Griffo, ed., *Dall' "Italia Tagliata,"* 149.

25 Croce, *Taccuini di Guerra,* 95.

26 Moorehead, *Eclipse,* 87.

27 Croce, *Taccuini di Guerra,* 95.

28 Ibid., 95–6.

29 Ibid., 77–8.

30 Ibid., 95–6. Croce's friendship with Giovanni Gentile ended because of Gentile's adherence to fascism. See Sasso, *Per Invigilare Me Stesso,* 40–76.

31 Caracciolo, *Diario di Napoli,* 141–3, 145.

32 Loewenheim et al., eds., *Roosevelt and Churchill,* 467–8.

33 Ibid., 619–20.

34 Ibid., 470–1.

35 Croce, *Taccuini di Guerra,* 91; Croce, *Scritti e Discorsi Politici,* vol. 2, 404–11.

6 A Democratic Compromise

1 Macmillan, *War Diaries,* 396. See also Delzell, *Mussolini's Enemies,* 315–46; Candeloro, *Storia dell'Italia Moderna,* vol. 10, 230–40, 273–86; Catalano, *L'Italia dall Dittatura alla Democrazia,* vol. 2, 49–67.

2 Lizzadri, *Il Regno di Badoglio,* 175; Di Nolfo and Serra, *La Gabbia Infranta,* 35–148; Elena Aga-Rossi, "PCI e USSR nel Periodo Staliniano," in Nicolosi, ed., *I Partiti Politici nell'Italia Repubblicana,* 91–116.

3 Macmillan, *War Diaries,* 395. See also Keith, *The Secret History of MI6,* 555–9.

4 Macmillan, *War Diaries*, 395.
5 Ibid., 392–7.
6 Pieri and Rochat, *Badoglio*, 823–60; Ciumi, *L'Italia di Badoglio*, 282–333; Barbagallo, *La Formazione dell'Italia Repubblicana*, vol. 1, 5–130.
7 Croce, *Taccuini di Guerra*, 103. See also Setta, *Croce, il Liberalismo e l'Italia Postfascista*, 41–65.
8 Croce, *Taccuini di Guerra*, 108.
9 Ibid.
10 Aga-Rossi and Zaslavsky, *Togliatti e Stalin*; Aga-Rossi and Quagliarello, eds., *L'Altra Faccia della Luna*; Clementi, *L'Alleato Stalin*, 35–89.
11 Bocca, *Togliatti*, 361–89; Spriano, *Storia del Partito Comunista Italiano*, vol. 5, 282–337; Degli Espinosa, *Il Regno del Sud*, 314–49; Bonomi, *Diario di un Anno, 2 Giugno–10 Giugno 1944*; Santarelli, *Mezzogiorno 1943–1944*, 133–6.
12 Croce, *Taccuini di Guerra*, 109.
13 Ibid.
14 Ibid., 111. On Omodeo, see Mustè, *Adolfo Omodeo*, 379–436; and on Omodeo's relationship with Croce, see Sasso, "Croce e Omodeo 'Quando l'Italia Era Tagliata in Due,'" *La Cultura*, 52, no. 1 (2014).
15 Spagnoletti, *Togliatti e CLN del Sud*, 120–5. See also Mazza, *Il Partito d'Azione nel Mezzogiorno*, 36–76; De Luna, *Storia del Partito d'Azione 1942–1947*, 125–204.
16 Croce, *Taccuini di Guerra*, 111.
17 Ibid., 109–12.
18 Ibid.
19 Croce, *Scritti e Discorsi Politici*, vol. 1, 75–8. See also Griffo, ed., *Dall'"Italia Tagliata,"* 289–90; Zanotti Bianco, *La Mia Roma*, 241–7.
20 Croce, *Taccuini di Guerra*, 111–12.
21 Spagnoletti, *Togliatti e CLN del Sud*, 125–8.
22 Valiani, *Dall'Antifascismo alla Resistenza*, 128. See also Aga-Rossi and Zaslavsky, *Togliatti e Stalin*; Clementi, *L'Alleato Stalin*.
23 Croce, *Taccuini di Guerra*, 112.
24 Ibid., 110.
25 Macmillan, *War Diaries*, 385.
26 Croce, *Taccuini di Guerra*, 113. See also Griffo, ed., *Dall'"Italia Tagliata,"* 165, 289–90; Caracciolo, *Diario di Napoli*, 141; Zanotti Bianco, *La Mia Roma*, 241–7; Jannazzo, *Croce e il Comunismo*; Piero Craveri, "Perchè il PCI non Potè Mai Diventare Forza Egemone nel Sistema Politico Italiano," in Nicolosi, ed., *I Partiti Politici nell'Italia Repubblicana*, 117–34.
27 Ajello, *Intellettuali e PCI*, 3–112; Serri, *I Redenti*, 178–233, 279–322; Mangoni, *La Civiltà della Crisi*, 147–286.

28 Macmillan, *War Diaries*, 395; Ricci, *Aspettando la Repubblica*, 8–37.
29 Griffo, ed., *Dall' "Italia Tagliata,"* 161–2.
30 A short explanation of nomenclature. After September 1943 the Allies established the Allied Control Commission (ACC), with the function of "supervising" the Italian government and provincial authorities, and in September 1944 this body was renamed the Allied Commission (AC). To avoid confusion, the name Allied Control Commission/ACC is used throughout this book. The Allied Advisory Council (AAC) was created in March 1944, mainly to give Russia, France, Greece, and Yugoslavia a voice on Italian affairs. It is mentioned only infrequently here.
31 Macmillan, *War Diaries*, 414.
32 Ibid., 411–12.
33 Croce, *Taccuini di Guerra*, 113–14. See also Griffo, ed., *Dall' "Italia Tagliata,"* 165.
34 Croce, *Taccuini di Guerra*, 124–5. See also Mazza, *Il Partito d'Azione nel Mezzogiorno*, 56–76; Alosco, *Il Partito d'Azione nel Regno del Sud.*
35 Spagnoletti, ed., *Togliatti e CLN del Sud*, 120–3.
36 Croce, *Taccuini di Guerra*, 116–18; Macmillan, *War Diaries*, 417–20.
37 Croce, *Taccuini di Guerra*, 117. See also Croce, *Scritti e Discorsi Politici*, vol. 2, 218; Puntoni, *Parla Vittorio*; Campello, *Un Principe nella Buffera*, 112–15.
38 Antonicelli ed., *Trent'Anni di Storia Italiana*, 365–77. See also Croce, *Scritti e Discorsi Politici*, 218.
39 Croce, *Taccuini di Guerra*, 118–19.
40 Ibid., 126–7.
41 Ibid., 116, 120, 123–4, 152.
42 Ibid., 114; Griffo, ed., *Dall' "Italia Tagliata,"* 137.
43 Croce, *Taccuini di Guerra*, 117. See also Griffo, ed., *Dall' "Italia Tagliata,"* 165–7.
44 Croce, *Taccuini di Guerra*, 121; Maurizio Griffo, "Il Pensiero Politico di Adolfo Omodeo nella Ripresa della Vita Libera 1943–1946," in Berti, Capozzi, and Craveri, eds., *I Liberali Italiani dall'Antifascismo alla Resistenza*, vol. 2, 851–67.
45 Griffo, ed., *Dall' "Italia Tagliata,"* 170–1.
46 Croce, *Taccuini di Guerra*, 122. For a lively account of these negotiations, see Ciumi, *L'Italia di Badoglio*, 312–27.
47 Croce, *Taccuini di Guerra*, 121–52
48 Ibid., 127.
49 Ibid., 129. See also Griffo, ed., *Dall' "Italia Tagliata,"* 163–7.
50 Candeloro, *Storia dell'Italia Moderna*, vol. 10, 273–87; Colarizi, *Storia dei Partiti nell'Italia Repubblicana*, 24–75; De Luna, *Storia del Partito d'Azione*, 125–204;

Ricci and Bongiorno, *La Rinascita dei Partiti in Italia*; Fabio Orsini, "Croce e il Partito Liberale," in Berti, Capozzi, and Craveri, eds., *I Liberali Italiani dall'Antifascismo alla Repubblica*, vol. 2, 579–660.

7 A Government of National Unity

1 Croce, *Taccuini di Guerra*, 130–1; Puntoni, *Parla Vittorio Emanuele III*, 227–9; Di Campiello, *Un Principe nella Bufera*, 116.
2 Croce, *Taccuini di Guerra*, 137.
3 Ibid., 132. For an overview of the government's policy, see Di Nolfo, *Le Paure e le Speranze Degli Italiani*, 79–124. For Croce's views, see Setta, *Croce: Il Liberalismo e l'Italia Postfascista*, 66–87.
4 Croce, *Taccuini di Guerra*, 138; Griffo, ed., *Dall' "Italia Tagliata,"* 173.
5 Croce, *Scritti e Discorsi Politici*, vol. 1, 76–8. See also ibid., vol. 2, 239; Ricci, ed., *Verbali del Consiglio dei Ministri*, vol. 2.
6 Croce, *Taccuini di Guerra*, 135, 138. See also Griffo, ed., *Dall' "Italia Tagliata,"* 173.
7 Griffo ed., *Dall' "Italia Tagliata,"* 178–9.
8 Ibid., 145. Bobbio held the same view. See Bobbio, *Profilo Ideologico del Novecento*, 152–65. A positive re-evaluation of the subject is underway especially with regard to art and architecture.
9 Ricci, *Aspettando la Repubblica*, 24–37. On the purge, see especially Woller, *I Conti con il Fascismo*, 19–186. For a more critical assessment, see Franzinelli, *L'Amnistia Togliatti*. Also valuable is Domenico, *Italian Fascists on Trial*.
10 Croce, *Scritti e Discorsi Politici*, vol. 1, 50–4.
11 Croce, *Taccuini di Guerra*, 134–9; Griffo, ed., *Dall' "Italia Tagliata,"* 154–6; Ricci, ed., *Verbali del Consiglio dei Ministri*, vol. 2, 25–34, 113.
12 Antonicelli ed., *Trent'Anni di Storia Italiana*, 365–77; Ricci, ed., *Verbali del Consiglio dei Ministri*, vol. 2, 172.
13 Croce, *Taccuini di Guerra*, 144–5.
14 Ibid., 145.
15 Ibid., 140. See also Petacco, *A Tragedy Revealed*.
16 Croce, *Scritti e Discorsi Politici*, vol. 1, 80–4.
17 Croce, *Taccuini di Guerra*, 140. See also Borzoni, *Renato Prunas Diplomatico*, 62–146.
18 Croce, *Taccuini di Guerra*, 139.
19 Ibid., 140.
20 Ibid., 143. See also Griffo, ed., *Dall' "Italia Tagliata,"* 174.
21 Macmillan, *War Diaries*, 444. See also Di Nolfo and Serra, *La Gabbia Infranta*, 62–146.

22 Croce, *Taccuini di Guerra,* 130.
23 Ibid., 132.
24 Ibid., 133–4; Griffo, ed., *Dall' "Italia Tagliata,"* 175; Ricci, ed., *Verbali del Consiglio dei Ministri,* vol. 2, 26–7, 35–6, 67–70.
25 Croce, *Scritti e Discorsi Politici,* vol. 1, 78–80.
26 Croce, *Taccuini di Guerra,* 416. See also Artieri, *Umberto II.*
27 Croce, *Taccuini di Guerra,* 147. See also Ricci, ed., *Verbali del Consiglio dei Ministri,* vol. 2, 197–205.
28 Croce, *Taccuini di Guerra,* 137, 178.
29 Antonicelli, ed., *Trent'Anni di Storia Italiana,* 365–77.
30 Moorehead, *Eclipse,* 55. For a different interpretation, see Pavone, *Alle Origini della Repubblica,* 70–184.

8 Rome's Liberation

1 Griffo, ed., *Dall' "Italia Tagliata,"* 181. See also Puntoni, *Parla Vittorio Emanuele III,* 234–9; Di Camerana, *L'Italia della Luogotenenza,* 7–57; Candeloro, *Storia dell'Italia Moderna,* vol. 10, 287–318; Ricci, *Aspettando la Repubblica,* 25–68; Kogan, *Italy and the Allies,* 76–90.
2 Macmillan, *War Diaries,* 450.
3 Nenni, *Tempo di Guerra Fredda,* 84–6; Ricci, ed., *Verbali del Consiglio dei Ministri,* vol. 3; Gambino, *Storia del Dopoguerra,* 3–11.
4 Croce, *Scritti e Discorsi Politici,* vol. 1, 84–6. For a critical, and unfair, view of Croce's position, see Salvemini, *L'Italia Vista dall'America,* vols. 1 and 2, 536–48, 564–74.
5 Nenni, *Tempi di Guerra Fredda,* 84–6; Forcella, *La Resistenza in Convento,* 188–206; Sabbatucci, Introduction to Marcucci Fanello, *Ivanoe Bonomi dal Fascismo alla Repubblica,* 5–12.
6 Croce, *Scritti e Discorsi Politici,* vol. 2, 240.
7 Ibid., 218.
8 Macmillan, *War Diaries,* 463.
9 Ibid.
10 Matthews, *The Education of a Correspondent,* 446. See also Di Nolfo and Serra, *La Gabbia Infranta,* 149–75; Borzoni, *Renato Prunas Diplomatico,* 304–70.
11 Croce, *Taccuini di Guerra,* 157. See also Griffo, ed., *Dall' "Italia Tagliata,"* 184–5.
12 Croce, *Taccuini di Guerra,* 401–2.
13 Macmillan, *War Diaries,* 463.
14 Ibid., 465.
15 Ibid.

16 Ibid., 468.
17 Croce, *Taccuini di Guerra*, 157.
18 Ibid., 168–70.
19 Griffo, ed., *Dall' "Italia Tagliata,"* 198–9.
20 Croce, *Taccuini di Guerra*, 164–5, 175–6; Marcucci Fanello, *Ivanoe Bonomi dal Fascismo alla Repubblica*, 19–54.
21 Di Nolfo and Serra, *La Gabbia Infranta*, 149–75.
22 Croce, *Taccuini di Guerra*, 155. For a more favourable view, see Pera, ed., *Meuccio Ruini*, 3–70.
23 Croce, *Taccuini di Guerra*, 152.
24 Ibid.
25 Ibid., 156. See also Woller, *I Conti con il Fascismo*, 187–302; Domenico, *Italian Fascists on Trial*; Quagliarello and Zaslavsky, eds., "La Pubblica Amministrazione dal Fascismo alla Democrazia," *Ventunesimo Secolo*, 2, no. 4 (2003).
26 Croce, *Taccuini di Guerra*, 163.
27 Ibid., 171; Ricci, ed., *Verbali del Consiglio dei Ministri*, vol. 3, 34–7, 39–42.
28 Croce, *Taccuini di Guerra*, 172.
29 Ibid., 169.
30 Ibid., 170. See also Cardia, *L'Epurazione del Senato del Regno.*
31 Croce, *Taccuini di Guerra*, 172.
32 Ibid., 400.
33 Ibid., 160.
34 Ibid., 177. See also Ricci, ed., *Verbali del Consiglio dei Ministri*, vol. 3, 4, 8–10; Griffo, "Una Polemica fra Croce e Togliatti alla Ripressa della Vita Libera," *L'Acropoli*, 16, no. 2 (2015): 144–51.
35 Croce, *Taccuini di Guerra*, 179.
36 Ibid., 181. See also Pera, ed., *Vittorio Emanuele Orlando.*
37 Zanotti Bianco, *La Mia Roma*, 241–6; Craveri, "L'Eredità dell'Italia Liberale nella Formazione della Repubblica," in Pera, ed., *Benedetto Croce e la Nascita della Repubblica*, 23–36.
38 Croce, *Taccuini di Guerra*, 210.
39 Ibid., 255.
40 Ibid., 193.
41 Ibid., 178. See also "Nuove Coccarde per Missiroli," in Zunino, *La Repubblica e il Suo Passsato*, 538–44; Allotti, *I Giornalisti del Regime*, 169–90.
42 Croce, *Taccuini di Guerra*, 283. See also Woller, *I Conti con il Fascismo*, 187–302.
43 Croce, *Taccuini di Guerra*, 188, 191, 200.
44 Croce, *Scritti e Discorsi Politici*, vol. 2, 80–1. See also Griffo, ed., *Dall' "Italia Tagliata,"* 213.

45 Griffo, ed., *Dall' "Italia Tagliata,"* 214. See also Ortona, *Anni d'America*; Di Nolfo and Serra, *La Gabbia Infranta*, 149–75; Malagodi, *Profilo di Raffaele Mattioli.*

46 Griffo, ed., *Dall' "Italia Tagliata,"* 226.

47 Castronovo, *La Stampa Italiana dalla Resistenza Agli Anni Sesssanta*, 140–4, 182; Nicolosi, *Risorgimento Liberale*, 15–182; Francesco Stagno, "La Stampa Liberale: Dal Crollo del Fascismo al 1948," in Grassi Orsini and Nicolosi, eds., *I Liberali Italiani dall'Antifascismo alla Repubblica*, vol. 1, 131–59.

48 Croce, *Taccuini di Guerra*, 158.

49 Ibid., 200.

50 Ibid., 235.

51 Ibid., 233, 236, 283. See also Piffer, *Gli Alleati e la Resistenza Italiana*, 163–92.

52 Croce, *Scritti e Discorsi Politici*, vol. 2, 79–80.

53 Ibid., 65–7. See also Quaglieni, ed., *Carteggio Croce-Pannunzio*, 34; Pavone, *Una Guerra Civile*; Gerardo Nicolosi, "I Liberali e la Resistenza," in Monina, ed., *1945–1946*, vol. 1, 383–420.

54 Croce's position has given rise to the charge of "appropriation" in some quarters. According to this interpretation, Croce sought to appropriate the "partisan struggle" through his argument that "martyrs" of the Communist Party and others "had died for mankind" and belonged not to a single party but to the nation as a whole. The verb "appropriate" is a loaded and contentious one in modern times, both inside and outside the academic community. There is no need here to enter that minefield, nor to defend the nobility of Croce's patriotic appeal on behalf of a common humanity, which is self-evident to a candid reader. Suffice it to say that the wartime Resistance was led by the Committee of National Liberation, which included representatives of all political parties, and that Communist propaganda urged the Italian people to join forces in a struggle of national liberation against the dictatorship and the German invasion. Accordingly, one can easily argue that Croce's position that the martyrs of that struggle belonged to a national pantheon was more faithful to the Communist position during the war than was Togliatti's partisan stance, and that of his underlings, in the post-war period. Furthermore, on this subject, Togliatti himself, on a different occasion, expressed views that were similar to Croce's. At the National Congress of the Italian Communist Party in late 1945, Togliatti, before thousands of delegates (many of whom had been partisans in Northern Italy), said: "In this struggle we have not been alone, nor do we claim any exclusive merit. Beside us were Socialist workers, as well as workers and intellectuals of the Party of Action, of the Christian Democratic Party, and of the other liberal and democratic movements. To all of these

let us send our warm greetings." He then continued: "In the struggle for the liberation of our country, our party and others have been bound together by a unity of aspirations, which has been one of the reasons for our victory. This unity should not be broken, but rather strengthened; it should endure and become part of the foundation of the new Italy, which all of us want to build" (Focardi, *La Guerra della Memoria,* 125–9). Clearly, during this period of sharp divisions, Croce was not alone in calling for a sense of unity between the dead and the living in order to heal the wounds of the past and to meet the challenges of a difficult present and an uncertain future.

55 Croce, *Taccuini di Guerra,* 159.
56 Ibid., 174.
57 Croce, *Scritti e Discorsi Politici,* vol. 2, 70–1.
58 Croce, *Taccuini di Guerra,* 204.
59 Ibid., 242–3. See also Macmillan, *War Diaries,* 583.
60 Croce, *Scritti e Discorsi Politici,* vol. 2, 87–102; Fabio Grassi Orsini, "I Liberali e la Guerra: Vecchia e Nuove Generazioni a Confronto," in Craveri and Quagliarello, eds., *La Seconda Guerra Mondiale e la Sua Memoria.*
61 Griffo, ed., *Dall' "Italia Tagliata,"* 211–12.
62 Macmillan, *War Diaries,* 550–1, 590–1.

9 From Bonomi to Bonomi

1 See Candeloro, *Storia dell'Italia Moderna,* vol. 10, 287–318; Ricci, ed., *Verbali del Consiglio dei Ministri,* vol. 3; Elena Aga-Rossi, "La Situazione Politica e Economica dell'Italia nel Periodo 1944–1945," in *L'Italia nella Sconfitta,* 125–90, 305–424.
2 Croce, *Scritti e Discorsi Politici,* vol. 2, 72–7.
3 Griffo, ed., *Dall' "Italia Tagliata,"* 200–1. See also Woller, *I Conti con il Fascismo,* 187–302; Di Capua, *Il Bienno Cruciale,* 229–320.
4 Ricci, *Aspettando la Repubblica,* 41–68; Mammarella, *L'Italia dalla Caduta del Fascismo ad Oggi,* 59–100; Gambino, *Storia del Dopoguerra,* 3–68; Craveri, *De Gasperi,* 145–70; Di Nolfo, *Le Paure e le Speranze degli Italiani,* 79–123.
5 Croce, *Scritti e Discorsi Politici,* vol. 2, 72–7.
6 Croce, *Taccuini di Guerra,* 179.
7 Ibid., 214.
8 Ibid.
9 Ibid., 231.
10 Ibid., 305.
11 Ibid., 230–54.
12 Ibid., 250.

13 Macmillan, *War Diaries*, 595.
14 Loewenheim et al., eds., *Roosevelt and Churchill*, 619, 624; See also Di Nolfo and Serra, *La Gabbia Infranta*, 149–75.
15 Croce, *Scritti e Discorsi Politici*, vol. 2, 72–7.
16 Croce, *Taccuini di Guerra*, 247, 301–7. See also Catalano, *L'Italia dalla Dittatura alla Democrazia*, 128–47.
17 Croce, *Taccuini di Guerra*, 243. See also Andreotti, *Concerto a Sei Voci*, 25–43.
18 Croce, *Taccuini di Guerra*, 243.
19 Nenni, *Tempo di Guerra Fredda*, 100–3; Craveri, *De Gasperi*, 152–67; Gambino, *Storia del Dopoguerra*, 11–68.
20 Croce, *Taccuini di Guerra*, 233, 238.
21 Macmillan, *War Diaries*, 585.
22 Croce, *Taccuini di Guerra*, 238.
23 Ibid., 240.
24 Ibid., 231–40.
25 Ibid., 245.
26 Croce, *Scritti e Discorsi Politici*, vol. 2, 72–7.
27 Croce, *Taccuini di Guerra*, 252.
28 Croce, *Scritti e Discorsi Politici*, vol. 2, 79–80.
29 Griffo, ed., *Dall' "Italia Tagliata,"* 200–1.
30 Cattani, "Dalla Caduta del Fascismo al Primo Governo De Gasperi," *Storia Contemporanea*, 5, no. 3 (1974): 737–88.
31 Croce, *Taccuini di Guerra*, 251.
32 Ibid., 251–2.
33 Ciani, *Il Partito Liberale Italiano*; Pallini, "Vita Organizzativa e Diffusione Territoriale del PLI, 1944–1946," in Grassi Orsini and Nicolosi, eds., *I Liberali Italiani dall'Antifascismo alla Repubblica*, vol. 1, 109–30.
34 Croce, *Taccuini di Guerra*, 252–3.
35 Di Nolfo, *Vaticano e Stati Uniti*, 404, 296.
36 Valiani, *L'Avvento di De Gasperi*, 23–4.
37 Craveri, *De Gasperi*; Tupini, *De Gasperi*; and Quagliarello and Zaslavsky, eds., "De Gasperi e la Costruzione della Democrazia," *Ventunesimo Secolo*, 3, no. 5 (2005).

10 The Northern Wind

1 Croce, *Taccuini di Guerra*, 294. See also Candeloro, *Storia dell'Italia Moderna*, vol. 11, 15–53; Catalano, *L'Italia dalla Dittatura alla Democrazia*, vol. 2, 128–221; Delzell, *Mussolini's Enemies*, 493–578; Andreotti, *Concerto a Sei Voci*, 43–90.

2 Croce, *Taccuini di Guerra*, 345. See also Di Nolfo, *Le Paure e le Speranze degli Italiani*, 124–50; Mammarella, *L'Italia dalla Caduta del Fascismo ad Oggi*, 101–24.
3 Cattani, "Dalla Caduta del Fascismo al Primo Governo De Gasperi," *Storia Contemporanea*, 5, no. 4 (1974): 737–88. See also Pansa, *Il Sangue dei Vinti*; Fabio Grassi Orsini, "Questione dell'Ordine Pubblico e Lotta Politica in Italia," in Monina, ed., *1945–1946*, vol. 2, 373–418.
4 Croce, *Scritti e Discorsi Politici*, vol. 2, 216.
5 Ibid., 221.
6 Croce, *Taccuini di Guerra*, 277.
7 Macmillan, *War Diaries*, 711.
8 Croce, *Taccuini di Guerra*, 310. See also Aga-Rossi and Zaslavsky, *Togliatti e Stalin*, 57–134; Aga-Rossi, *L'Italia nella Sconfitta*, 191–260; Elena Aga-Rossi, "PCI e URSS nel Periodo Staliniano: 1944–1953," in Nicolosi, ed., *I Partiti Politici nell'Italia Repubblicana*, 91–116.
9 Ricci, *Aspettando la Repubblica*, 69–150.
10 Croce, *Taccuini di Guerra*, 306.
11 Croce, *Scritti e Discorsi Politici*, vol. 2, 217–20.
12 Ibid., 217–28.
13 Nenni, *Tempo di Guerra Fredda*, 111–26; Tamburrano, *Pietro Nenni*; Piffer, *Gli Alleati e la Resistenza Italiana*, 184–238.
14 Polese Remaggi, *La Nazione Perduta*, 277–318; Boneschi, "Parri: Uomo Solo," *Nuova Antologia*, 563, no. 2173 (1990): 330–4; Aniasi, *Parri*, 166–212.
15 Croce, *Taccuini di Guerra*, 311–12.
16 Ibid., 303. See also Fornaro, *Giuseppe Saragat*, 107–56.
17 Croce, *Taccuini di Guerra*, 297.
18 Ibid., 297. For a different view, see Andreotti, *Concerto a Sei Voci*, 82–9.
19 Croce, *Taccuini di Guerra*, 299. See also ibid., 306–7.
20 Ibid., 299.
21 Cattani, "Dalla Caduta del Fascismo al Primo Governo De Gasperi," 745–6.
22 Nenni, *Tempo di Guerra Fredda*, 111–26; Tamburrano, *Pietro Nenni*, vi, 92.
23 Valiani, *L'Avvento di De Gasperi*, 25–7.
24 Croce, *Taccuini di Guerra*, 308–9.
25 Ibid., 316.
26 Ibid., 310–11.
27 Ibid., 347.
28 Ibid., 316, See also ibid., 309.
29 Matthews, *The Education of a Correspondent*, 485.
30 Croce, *Taccuini di Guerra*, 320. See also Polese Remaggi, *La Nazione Perduta*, 277–318; Gambino, *Storia del Dopoguerra*, 3–111.

31 Croce, *Taccuini di Guerra*, 309.

32 Ibid., 315.

33 Ibid., 318.

34 Croce, *Scritti e Discorsi Politici*, vol. 2, 222–4. See also Gabriella Ciampi, "I Liberali e la Pubblica Istruzione," in Grassi Orsini and Nicolosi, eds., *I Liberali Italiani dall'Antifascismo alla Repubblica*, vol. 1, 405–18.

35 Croce, *Scritti e Discorsi Politici*, vol. 2, 191–4. See also Croce, *Taccuini di Guerra*, 342–3; Croce, *Discorsi di Varia Filosofia*, vol. 2, 291–300; Setta, *Croce: Il Liberalismo e l'Italia Postfascista*, 98–114.

36 Romeo, *Risorgimento e Capitalismo*; Romeo, "Il Risorgimento: Realtà Storica e Tradizione Morale," in *Dal Piemonte Sabaudo all'Italia Liberale*, 249–86; Cafagna, *Dualismo e Sviluppo nella Storia d'Italia*, 135–221; Galasso, *L'Italia s'è Desta.*

11 The Advent of De Gasperi

1 Nenni, *Tempo di Guerra Fredda*, 156–9; Polese Remaggi, *La Nazione Perduta*, 277–318; Gambino, *Storia del Dopoguerra*, 69–126.

2 Cattani, "Dalla Caduta del Fascismo al Primo Governo De Gasperi," *Storia Contemporeanea*, 5, no. 4 (1974): 737–88; Candeloro, *Storia dell'Italia Moderna*, vol. 11, 34–53; Mammarella, *L'Italia dalla Caduta Fascismo ad Oggi*, 101–25; Ricci, *Aspettando le Repubblica*, 99–150.

3 Croce, *Taccuini di Guerra*, 294.

4 Nenni, *Tempo di Guerra Fredda*, 127; Woller, *I Conti con il Fascismo*, 365–437; Franzinelli, *L'Amnista Togliatti.*

5 Ricci, *Aspettando la Repubblica*; Polese Remaggi, *La Nazione Perduta*, 277–318; Nenni, *Tempo di Guerra Fredda*, 111–26; Craveri, *De Gasperi*, 171–234; Di Capua, *Il Biennio Compromissorio*, 193–333.

6 Croce, *Taccuini di Guerra*, 325.

7 Ibid., 364–7.

8 Ibid., 325. On Tarchiani, see Elena Aga-Rossi, "Alberto Tarchiani: Politica, Diplomazia ed Economia di un Liberale Atipico," in Berti, Capozzi, and Craveri, eds., *I Liberali Italiani dall'Antifascismo alla Repubblica*, vol. 2, 209–56.

9 Croce, *Scritti e Discorsi Politici*, vol. 2, 238–42. See also Chabod, *L'Italia Contemporanea*, 186; Setta, *Croce*, 115–21.

10 Cattani, "Dalla Caduta del Fascismo al Primo Governo De Gasperi."

11 Ibid., 759.

12 Valiani, *L'Avvento di De Gasperi*, 23–4.

13 Gambino, *Storia del Dopoguerra*, 69–125; Aniasi, *Parri*, 166–209.

14 Craveri, *De Gasperi*, 193–212. See also Giovanni Orsina, "Translatio Imperii: La Crisi del Governo Parri e I Liberali," in Monina, ed., *1945–1946*, vol. 2, 201–56; Pavone, *Alle Origini della Repubblica*, 70–184.
15 Croce, *Taccuini di Guerra*, 370–1.
16 Ibid., 371.
17 Ibid., 369.
18 Ibid., 378.
19 Cattani, "Dalla Caduta del Fascismo al Primo Governo De Gasperi"; Fanello Marcucci, *Il Primo Governo De Gasperi*, 5–64.
20 Croce, *Taccuini di Guerra*, 378.
21 Ibid., 378–9.
22 Craveri, *De Gasperi*, 206–12; Ciani, *Il Partito Liberale Italiano da Croce a Malagodi*; Fabio Grassi Orsini, "Croce e il Partito Liberale," in Berti, Capozzi, and Craveri, eds., *I Liberali Italiani dall'Antifascismo alla Repubblica*, vol. 2, 579–660.
23 Croce, *Taccuini di Guerra*, 372.
24 Giannnini, *La Folla*; Setta, *L'Uomo Qualunque*; Setta, *La Destra nell'Italia del Dopoguerra*; Dino, "L'Uomo Quallunque: Ragioni e Ritardi di un Movimento Politico sui Generis," *Nuova Storia Contemporanea*, 16, no. 3 (2012): 5–38.
25 Murialdi, *La Stampa Italiana del Dopoguerra*, 43–6.
26 Croce, *Taccuini di Guerra*, 354. See also Imbriani, *Vento del Sud*, 49–84; Tarchi, *Italia Populista*, 171–94; Orsina, "L'Antipolitica dei Moderati."
27 Croce, *Taccuini di Guerra*, 354.
28 Ibid., 368–9.
29 Ibid., 369. See also De Giorgi, *Mons. Montini*, 115–245.
30 Croce, *Taccuini di Guerra*, 350. See also Fornaro, *Giuseppe Saragat*, 107–56; Michele Donno, "I Liberali Italiani e il Socialismo Democratico di Giuseppe Saragat," in Berti, Capozzi, and Craveri, eds., *I Liberali Italiani dall'Antifascismo alla Repubblica*, vol. 2, 749–76.

12 Election and Referendum

1 Croce, *Scritti e Discorsi Politici*, vol. 2, 288–300. See also Amendola, *Intervista sull'Antifascismo.*
2 Croce, *Scritti e Discorsi Politici*, vol. 2, 288–300.
3 Ibid. See also Croce and Einaudi, *Liberismo e Liberalismo*; Quagliarello and Zaslavsky, eds., "I Liberali e la Repubblica"; Setta, *Croce*, 115–56.
4 Croce, *Taccuini di Lavoro*, vol. 6, 30–3; Blasberg, "I Liberali tra CLN e Qualunquismo," in Monina, ed., *1945–1946*, vol. 2, 162–200; Ciani, *Il Partito Liberale Italiano da Croce a Malagodi.*

5 Griffo, ed., *Dall' "Italia Tagliata,"* 256. See also Lucio D'Angelo, "Fra Liberalismo e Socialismo: Il Partito Democratico del Lavoro," in Grassi Orsini and Nicolosi, eds., *I Liberali Italiani dall'Antifascismo alla Repubblica,* vol. 1, 109–58, 159–74, 175–284; and Ghersi, *Benedetto Croce e l'Unione Democratica Nazionale.*
6 Croce, *Taccuini di Lavoro,* vol. 6, 18.
7 Ibid., 19.
8 Ibid., 24, 28, 30.
9 Griffo, ed., *Dall' "Italia Tagliata,"* 256–60; Gaggi, *Vittorio Emanuele Orlando,* 205–26; Paolo Varvaro, "Il Liberalismo come Questione Nazionale: Nitti e il Nittismo nel Secondo Dopoguerra," in Berti, Capozzi, and Craveri, eds., *I Liberali Italiani dall'Antifascismo alla Repubblica,* 687–712.
10 Griffo, ed., *Dall' "Italia Tagliata,"* 256–61.
11 Ibid.
12 Croce, *Taccuini di Lavoro,* vol. 6, 21.
13 Ibid.
14 Croce, *Scritti e Discorsi Politici,* vol. 2, 283–6.
15 Ibid., 300–3. See also Santarelli, *Il Problema della Libertà in Italia.*
16 Griffo, ed., *Dall' "Italia Tagliata,"* 262.
17 Croce, *Taccuini di Lavoro,* vol. 6, 24.
18 Ibid., vol. 6, 36, 38, 39, 40; Candeloro, *Storia dell'Italia Moderna,* vol. 11, 73–82; Mammarella, *L'Italia dalla Caduta del Fascismo ad Oggi,* 125–40; Ballini and Ridolfi, eds., *Storia delle Campagne Elettorali in Italia,* 193–203; Ridolfi et al., eds., *Italia al Voto,* 1–30, 522–3.
19 Croce, *Taccuini di Lavoro,* vol. 6, 30.
20 Fabio Grassi Orsini, "Questione dell'Ordine Pubblico e Lotta Politica in Italia," in Monina, ed., *1945–1956,* vol. 2, 373–418; Zaslavsky, *Lo Stalinismo e la Sinistra Italiana,* 47–82.
21 Di Nolfo, *Le Paure e le Speranze degli Italiani,* 151–268; Di Capua, *Il Biennio Compromissorio,* 333–86; Ricci, *Aspettando la Repubblica,* 151–220; Ciani, *Il Partito Liberale da Croce a Malagodi.*
22 Grassi Orsini, "Riaprire il Cantiere: I Liberali dalla Crisi del Regime alla Ricostruzione del Partito," *Ventunesimo Secolo,* 4 (October 2005): 13–64; Fabio Grassi Orsini, "Croce e il Partito Liberale," in Berti, Capozzi, and Craveri, eds., *I Liberali Italiani dall'Antifascismo alla Repubblica,* vol. 2, 349–504, 579–660, 687–782; Antonio Jannazzo, "Il Partito Liberale Italiano," in Nicolosi, ed., *I Partiti Politici Italiani nell'Italia Repubblicana,* 275–312; Scoppola, *La Repubblica dei Partiti,* 13–132.
23 Croce, *Scritti e Discorsi Politici,* vol. 2, 288–300. See also Mammarella, *L'Italia dalla Caduta del Fascismo ad Oggi,* 125–40; Gambino, *Storia del Dopoguerra,*

127–248; Ricci, *Aspettando la Repubblica 1946*, 151–224; Gabrieli, *Il 1946*, 3–42, 149–204; Sale, *Dalla Monarchia alla Repubblica*.

24 Croce, *Taccuini di Lavoro*, vol. 6, 38.

25 Ibid., 35. See also Setta, *Croce*, 115–40.

26 Croce, *Taccuini di Lavoro*, vol. 6, 27.

27 Ibid., 35. See also F. Tessitore, "Il Percorso Psicologico dalla Monarchia alla Repubblica Attraverso *I Taccuini di Lavoro* di Benedetto Croce," in Pera, ed., *Benedetto Croce e la Nascita della Repubblica*, 57–66.

28 Croce, *Taccuini di Guerra*, 379. See also Artieri, *Umberto II*, 213–68.

29 Croce, *Scritti e Discorsi Politici*, vol. 2, 305–6.

30 Griffo, ed., *Dall' "Italia Tagliata,"* 261.

31 Ricci, *Aspettando la Repubblica*, 194–220; Croce, *Taccuini di Lavoro*, vol. 6, 42; Ungari, *In Nome del Re. I Monarchici Italiani dal 1943 al 1948*, 183–231.

32 Croce, *Taccuini di Lavoro*, vol. 6, 40–2, 44. See also Barzini, *La Verità sul Referendum*; Monelli, *Il Giorno del Referendum*; Sasso, *Per Invigilare Me Stesso*, 266–80.

13 The Constituent Assembly

1 Croce, *Taccuini di Lavoro*, vol. 6, 44.

2 Ibid., 40–1. See also Sasso, *Per Invigliare Me Stesso*, 266–90.

3 Griffo, ed., *Dall' "Italia Tagliata,"* 266.

4 Croce, *Taccuini di Lavoro*, vol. 6, 46–7. See also Nenni, *Tempo di Guerra Fredda*, 233–5; Gambino, *Storia del Dopoguerra*, 256–8.

5 Griffo, ed., *Dall' "Italia Tagliata,"* 265.

6 Croce, *Taccuini di Lavoro*, vol. 6, 46–8. See also Gambino, *Storia del Dopoguerra*, 256–8.

7 Griffo, ed., *Dall' "Italia Tagliata,"* 266.

8 Croce, *Taccuini di Lavoro*, vol. 6, 46. See also Scoppola, *La Repubblica dei Partiti*, 91–9.

9 Croce, *Taccuini di Lavoro*, vol. 6, 48.

10 Ibid.

11 Ibid.

12 Ibid.

13 Ibid., 49. See also Craveri's entry on De Nicola in Nicolosi, ed., *Dizionario del Liberalismo Italiano*, vol. 2.

14 Galante Garrone, *Questa Nostra Repubblica*, 12–28; Falzone, Palermo, and Cosentino, *La Costituzione della Repubblica Italiana*; Paladin, *Per una Storia Costituzionale dell'Italia Repubblicana*, 19–72; Ricci, *Il Compromesso Costituente*, 11–180; Pombeni, *La Questione Costituzionale in Italia*.

15 Scoppola and Elia, *A Colloquio con Dossetti e Lazzati*, 54–63; Scoppola, *La Democrazia dei Cristiani*, 94–146; Craveri, *De Gasperi*, 239–40; Andreotti, *1947*.
16 Sartori, *Corriere della Sera*, 27 February 2009, and Napolitano, *La Repubblica*, 23 April 2009. See also Valerio Onida, *Corriere della Sera*, 9 February 2012; Sabino Cassese, *Corriere della Sera*, 19 September 2011; Scoppola, *La Repubblica dei Partiti*, 179–231; Maranini, *Storia del Potere in Italia*, 315–36, 403–50.
17 Maranini, *Storia del Potere in Italia*, 365–403; Ghisalberti, *Storia Costituzionale d'Italia*, 389–427; Alessandro Vitale, "Luci e Ombre di una Costituzione Nata Vecchia," *Nuova Storia Contemporanea*, 13, no. 2 (2009): 5–28.
18 Croce, *Taccuini di Lavoro*, vol. 6, 176–7. See also Lanaro, *Storia dell'Italia Repubblicana*, 48–56; Baget-Bozzo, *Il Partito Cristiano al Potere*, 105–28, 189–210; Paolo Pombemi, "Il Contribuito dei Cattolici alla Costituente," in Labriola, ed., *Valori e Principi del Regime Repubblicano*, vol. 1, 36–80.
19 Scoppola, *A Colloquio con Dossetti*; Scoppola, *La Repubblica dei Partiti*, 179–231; Sale, *Il Vaticano e la Costituzione*; Candeloro, *Storia dell'Italia Moderna*, vol. 11, 138–56; Guerrieri, "Il PCI e il Processo Costituente," in Monina, ed., *1945–1946*, vol. 2, 51–80; Pombeni, *Giuseppe Dossetti*; Portoghesi Tuzi and Tuzi, *Quando si Fece la Costituzione*, 121–298.
20 Ghisalberti, *Storia Costituzionale*, 389–430; Carlo Ghisalberti, "La Costituzione Repubblicana e la Tradizione Liberale," in Grassi Orsini and Nicolosi, eds., *I Liberali Italiani dall'Antifascismo alla Repubblica*, vol. 1, 343–86; Caperucci, *I Liberali alla Consulta e alla Costituente*; Alberto Giordano, "I Liberali e la Costituzione Italiana," *Materiali per una Storia della Cultura Giuridica*, 41, no. 2 (2011): 361–88; Pera, ed., *Meuccio Ruini*, 43–61, 63–70; Vincenzo Atripaldi, "Luigi Einaudi e la Costituzione Italiana del 1948," in Acocella, ed., *Luigi Einaudi*, 29–36; Lanchester, *Pensare lo Stato*, 141–50.
21 Croce, *Taccuini di Lavoro*, vol. 6, 110. See also Francesco Margiotta Broglio, "I Liberali e la Questione Religiosa alla Costituente," in Berti, Capozzi, and Craveri, eds., *I Liberali Italiani dall'Antifascismo alla Repubblica*, vol. 2, 47–77.
22 Andreotti, *1947*, 50.
23 Croce, *Taccuini di Lavoro*, vol. 6, 110; Andreotti, "Vittorio Emanuele Orlando: Visto da Vicino," in Pera, ed., *Vittorio Emanuele Orlando*, 3–16; Gaetano Quagliarello, "Il Partito e la Forma di Governo nella Riflessione dei Liberali e degli Azionisti nella Stagione Costituente," in Labriola, ed., *Valori e Principi del Regime Repubblicano*, vol. 1, 81–124.
24 Orlando, *Discorsi Parlamentari*, 703–24. See also Gangi, *Vittorio Emanuele Orlando*, 205–25; Alberto Giordano, "I Liberali e la Costituzione Italiana," *Materiali per una Storia della Cultura Giurica*, 41, no. 2 (2011): 361–88; Paolo

Pombeni, "L'Ultimo Orlando: Il Costituente," in Pera, ed., *Vittotio Emanuele Orlando,* 33–58.

25 Croce, *Taccuini di Lavoro,* vol. 6, 123.

26 Ibid., 115, 131.

27 Ibid., 106.

28 Ibid., 131.

29 Ibid., 109.

30 Ibid., 106.

31 Cutinelli-Rendina, ed., *Luigi Russo, Benedetto Croce, Carteggio,* vol. 2, 692. Fifty years later, a Marxist minister of education reinterpreted the meaning of this amended article in a manner favourable to Catholic schools.

32 Croce, *Taccuini di Lavoro,* vol. 6, 110. See also Griffo ed., *Dall' "Italia Tagliata,"* 283–94; Croce, *Scritti e Discorsi Politici,* vol. 2, 357–8.

33 Croce, *Taccuini di Lavoro,* vol. 6, 113. The final wording of this article, achieved after intense negotiations and several drafts, was dictated by Monsignor Montini to Giorgio La Pira, accepted by Dosssetti, and then approved by Togliatti.

34 Griffo, ed., *Dall'"Italia Tagliata,"* 290.

35 Ibid., 291–2; Rodotà, ed., *Alle Orgini della Costituzione,* 43–97.

36 Croce, *Scritti e Discorsi Politici,* vol. 2, 350–8.

37 Ibid.

38 Ibid. See also Calamandrei, *Chiarezza nella Costituzione*; Jemolo, *Chiesa e Stato in Italia negli Ultimi Cento Anni,* 431–548; Pertici, *Chiesa e Stato in Italia,* 333–596.

39 Croce, *Taccuini di Lavoro,* vol. 6, 116. See also Griffo, ed., *Dall' "Italia Tagliata,"* 291–2.

14 The Peace Treaty of 1947

1 See Mammarella, *L'Italia dalla Caduta del Fascismo ad Oggi,* 183–97; Catalano, *L'Italia dalla Dittatura alla Democrazia,* vol. 2, 287–352; Candeloro, *Storia dell'Italia Moderna,* vol. 11, 92–106; Kogan, *Italy and the Allies,* 132–68.

2 See Lorenzini, *L'Italia e il Trattato di Pace*; Ballini, *Il Trattato di Pace all'Assemblea Costituente*; Cattaruzza, *L'Italia e il Confine Orientale,* 283–327; Pastorelli, *La Politica Estera Italiana del Dopoguerra,* 11–122.

3 Croce, *Scritti e Discorsi Politici,* vol. 2, 243–9. See also Romano, *Guida alla Politica Estera Italiana,* 5–54; Mammarella and Cacace, *La Politica Estera dell'Italia dallo Stato Unitario ai Giorni Nostri,* 131–71.

4 Croce, *Scritti e Discorsi Politici,* vol. 2, 244–52.

5 Ibid., 182–7.
6 Ibid., 253–5.
7 Ibid., 404–11. See also Croce, *Taccuini di Lavoro*, vol. 6, 60–1.
8 Croce, *Scritti e Discorsi Politici*, vol. 2, 308–11. See also Gerardo Nicolosi, "1947: Opposizione al Diktat: La Critica Liberale al Trattato di Pace," in Berti, Capozzi, and Craveri, eds., *I Liberali Italiani dall'Antifascismo alla Repubblica*, vol. 2, 161–208.
9 Croce, *Taccuini di Lavoro*, vol. 6, 94–5.
10 Ibid., 101. See also Riccardi, ed., *Niccolò Carandini*, 53–82.
11 Croce, *Taccuni di Lavoro*, vol. 6, 15.
12 Ibid., 136. See also Pastorelli, *La Politica Estera Italiana del Dopoguerra*, 107–209.
13 See Craveri, *De Gasperi*, 235–66; Antonio Varsori, "Carlo Sforza nella Politica Italiana," in Berti, Capozzi, and Craveri, eds., *I Liberali Italiani dall'Antifascismo alla Repubblica*, vol. 2, 149–60; Aga-Rossi and Zaslavsky, *Togliatti e Stalin*, 135–56; Lorenzini, *L'Italia e il Trattato di Pace del 1947*, 107–30; Ballini, *Il Trattato di Pace all'Assemblea Costituente*, 34–40, 63–83.
14 Griffo, ed., *Dall' "Italia Tagliata,"* 300–1.
15 Orlando, *Discorsi Parlamentari*, 685–8. See also Ragionieri, *Storia d'Italia*, vol. 4, tome 3, 244.
16 Griffo ed., *Dall "Italia Tagliata,"* 302–3.
17 Croce, *Taccuini di Lavoro*, vol. 6, 111, 116, 139.
18 Croce, *Scritti e Discorsi Politici*, vol. 2, 384–6.
19 Ibid., 338–9.
20 Ibid., 386–93.
21 Croce, *Taccuini di Lavoro*, vol. 6, 144.
22 Cutinelli-Rendina, ed., *Luigi Russo, Benedetto Croce, Carteggio*, vol. 2, 696–9.
23 Griffo, ed., *Dall "Italia Tagliata,"* 303.
24 Einaudi, *La Guerra e l'Unità Europea*, 153–64.
25 Pastorelli, *La Politica Estera Italiana del Dopoguerra*, 145–259; Varsori, *La Cenerentola d'Europa?* 31–118.
26 Romeo, *Dal Piemonte Sabaudo all'Italia Liberale*, 285. See also Romeo, *Italia Mille Anni*, 187–200; Galli Della Loggia, *La Morte della Patria*, 96–118.

15 A New Course

1 Andreotti, *1947*; Di Capua, *L'Anno delle Grandi Svolte*; Gambino, *Storia del Dopoguerra*, 403–68; Malgeri, *Alcide De Gasperi*, vol. 2, 257–369; Baget-Bozzo, *Il Partito Cristiano al Potere*, 129–88.
2 Croce, *Scritti e Discorsi Politici*, vol. 2, 335–9.

3 Croce, *Taccuini di Lavoro*, vol. 6, 101.
4 See Quagliarello and Zaslavsky, "I Liberali e la Repubblica"; Formigoni, "De Gasperi e la Crisi Politica Italiana del Maggio 1947"; Elena Aga-Rossi, "L'Italia nel Contesto Internazionale, 1945–1948," in Monina, ed., *1945–1946*, vol. 1, 25–60; Degli Innocenti, "I Socialisti," in ibid., vol. 2, 105–41.
5 Acocella, ed., *Luigi Einaudi*, 96. See also Grassi Orsini, "I Liberali, De Gasperi e la Svolta del Maggio 1947." For a contrary view, see Marcello De Cecco, "Economic Policy in the Reconstruction Period, 1945–1951," in Woolf, ed., *The Rebirth of Italy*, 156–80.
6 Croce, *Taccuni di Lavoro*, vol. 6, 129.
7 Ibid., 129. See also Grassi Orsini, "I Liberali, De Gasperi e la Svolta del 1947"; Malagodi, *Profilo di Raffaele Mattioli*, 19–23, 67–80; Gigliobianco, *Via Nazionale*, 217–49; Carli, *Cinquant'Anni di Vita Italiana.*
8 Croce, *Taccuini di Lavoro*, vol. 6, 134–5; Craveri, *La Democrazia Incompiuta*, 85–116.
9 Croce, *Taccuini di Lavoro*, vol. 6, 134–5. See also Croce, *Scritti e Discorsi Politici*, vol. 2, 378–81; Ricci, ed., *Il Compromesso Costituente*, 105–81.
10 Over the years, there were several occasions when Togliatti enthusiastically advanced this fictional narrative in order to achieve his political objectives. In 1944, while both were members of the Bonomi cabinet, Togliatti called into question Croce's anti-Fascist credentials, claiming that his continuous anti-Marxist polemic coupled with timid criticisms of the regime amounted to a hidden connivance with fascism (Rizi, *Benedetto Croce and Italian Fascism*, 208). Challenged by Croce, he offered an apology of sorts, making some excuses for unfortunate language; Croce accepted this apology, though he was not fully convinced of Togliatti's sincerity. In the text (see pp. 127–8) have been noted Togliatti's malicious remarks about Croce's agrarian interests. On another occasion after the end of the war, Togliatti tried to make a mountain out of a molehill when he made disparaging remarks about Croce's expression "Judaic messianism" – an expression that Croce had used to indicate one element of Marx's revolutionary aspirations and ideological outlook. However, Croce never made a direct reference in any of his essays on Marx and Marxism to Marx's Jewish heritage; instead, he always stressed Marx's ties with Hegelian philosophy and the Machiavellian political tradition. Moreover, Togliatti, like his ideological descendants, have ignored another well-known fact, namely that Croce had studied Marx and Marxism in depth, and that this study influenced his future philosophical development. As a result, in his philosophical system, he elevated the useful, under which he subsumed all economic activity, to the dignity of a category, alongside the traditional ones: the beautiful, the good, and the true.

It is also true, of course, that after the war Croce criticized Marx more frequently, especially once Marxism became identified with Leninism, Stalinism, and Soviet ideology. Yet, even so, the old admiration remained more or less intact, as shown in the introductions he wrote to several editions of his book *Materialismo Storico e Economia Marxistica* (the last edition appearing in 1951, a year before his death). For example, in the 1917 edition, he wrote: "Those who study the culture of Italy in the last years of the century have to recognize, in my opinion, the deep and beneficial influence exercised by Marxism on Italian thought between 1890 and 1900." He added: "Now, after more than twenty years, Marx has lost the position of teacher that he then held … But this should not stop us from admiring the old revolutionary thinker (in many respects he was far more modern than Mazzini, with whom in Italy he is often compared and contrasted)" (xii–iv).

It also should be pointed out that there were occasions when Togliatti was more charitably inclined towards Croce, recognizing, in his peculiar way, both his intelligence and his political and cultural contribution to the cause of freedom and Italian liberation. As he said in his speech to the Communist Party's National Congress in 1945, evidently with reference to Croce: "Our contribution to the cause of Italian liberation has been of a particular kind. Yet it is certainly not my intention to deny the importance of the opposition of those who, with their writings during the gloomy years of the tyranny, sustained the struggle for freedom" (Focardi, *La Guerra della Memoria,* 125–9). Later, in the early 1960s, towards the end of his life, Togliatti spoke at a conference in Turin about the "Svolta of Salerno" and the negotiations for the formation of the new Badoglio cabinet. He recounted: "I have to confess that to overcome the obstacles in April 1944 standing in the way of the formation of a new government, Croce collaborated with us and his collaboration was important and effective … He was the most intelligent of our adversaries, and it was perhaps for this reason that working with him was possible" (Antonicelli, ed., *Trent'Anni di Storia Italiana, 1915–1945,* 375). These words of praise are all the more remarkable coming from one who, on both occasions, was extolling the special value – primacy almost – of the Communist contribution to the struggle against fascism and the war of liberation.

11 Cutinelli-Rendina, ed., *Luigi Russo, Benedetto Croce, Carteggio,* vol. 2, 692.

12 Ibid. See also Croce, *Taccuini di Lavoro,* vol. 6, 143–8.

13 Cutinelli-Rendina, *Luigi Russo, Benedetto Croce, Carteggio,* vol. 2, 692. See also Croce, *Scritti e Discorsi Politici,* vol. 2, 382–4; Andreotti, *1947,* 88–9; Craveri, *De Gasperi,* 349–51.

14 Grassi Orsini, "I Liberali, De Gasperi e la Svolta del Maggio 1947," 33–69; Zunino, *La Repubblica e il Suo Passato,* 319–89; Ballini, "1947."
15 Craveri, *De Gasperi,* 268–353; Scoppola, *La Repubblica dei Partiti,* 133–68; Ragionieri, *Storia d'Italia dell'Unità a Oggi,* vol. 4, 2461–72; Galante, *La Fine di un Compromesso Storico*; Amendola, "La Rottura della Coalizione Tripartita."

16 The Elections of 1948

1 Ventresca, *From Fascism to Democracy*; Novelli, *Le Elezioni del Quarantotto*; Mammarella, *L'Italia dalla Caduta del Fascismo ad Oggi,* 203–14; Ricci, *Il Compromesso Costituente,* 220–68; Ricolfi et al., eds., *Italia al Voto,* 1–30, 521–5; Zizola, *Il Microfono di Dio,* 132–52.
2 Croce, *Taccuini di Lavoro,* vol. 6, 186. See also Ventrone, *La Cittadinanza Repubblicana,* 219–92; Giuseppe Galasso, "L'Avvio al Centrismo e Gli Anni di De Gasperi," in ibid., vol. 4, 270–300; Di Capua, *L'Anno delle Grandi Svolte,* 119–94; Gambino, *Storia del Dopoguerra,* 450–522.
3 Croce, *Taccuini di Lavoro,* vol. 6, 185–7. See also Galasso, *Croce e lo Spirito del Suo Tempo,* 410–76.
4 Croce, *Scritti e Discorsi Politici,* vol. 2, 382–4. See also Griffo, ed., *Dall' "Italia Tagliata,"* 284–6; Jemolo, *Chiesa e Stato in Italia Negli Ultimi Cento Anni,* 507–48.
5 Grassi Orsini and Nicolosi, eds., *I Liberali Italiani dall'Antifascismo alla Resistenza,* vol. 1, 132.
6 Croce, *Scritti e Discorsi Politici,* vol. 2, 170–4; Zaslavsky, "Aprile 1948."
7 Croce, *Scritti e Discorsi Politici,* vol. 2, 422–4. See also Lucia, *Intelletuali Italiani del Secondo Dopoguerra,* 15–142; Ajello, *Intellettuali e PCI,* 3–122; Andreucci, *Da Gramsci a Occhetto,* 191–310.
8 Croce, *Scritti e Discorsi Politici,* vol. 2, 424–6. See also Griffo, ed., *Dall' "Italia Tagliata,"* 307, 310, 316–18.
9 Croce, *Taccuini di Lavoro,* vol. 6, 184. See also Serri, *I Redenti*; La Rovere, *L'Eredità del Fascismo,* 258–352.
10 Croce, *Taccuini di Lavoro,* vol. 6, 184–5. See also Antoni, *L'Avanguardia della Libertà*; Capozzi, "Un Modello Politico-Intelletuale Atlantico"; Saunders, *The Cultural Cold War.*
11 Croce, *Nuove Pagine Sparse,* vol. 1, 346–8.
12 Ibid.
13 Ibid.
14 Croce *Taccuini di Lavoro,* vol. 6, 206.
15 Cutinelli-Rendina, ed., *Luigi Russo, Benedetto Croce, Carteggio,* vol. 2, 722.

16 Croce, *Taccuini di Lavoro*, vol. 6, 187.
17 Ibid., 133.
18 Ibid., 11.
19 Croce, *Filosofia e Storiografia*, 279–80. See also ibid., 270–80; Bobbio, *Politica e Cultura*, 160–94.
20 Croce, *Scritti e Discorsi Politici*, vol. 2, 396–9. See also Garin, *Cronache di Filosofia Italiana*, vol. 2, 489–620; Asor Rosa, *Storia d'Italia dall'Unità a Oggi*, vol. 4, 1584–1620; Galasso, *Croce e lo Spirito del Suo Tempo*, 515–60.
21 Sasso, *La Voce dei Ricordi*; Sasso, *La Fedeltà e l'Esperimento*, 215–66; Sasso, "Gramsci e l'Idealismo," in *Filosofia e Idealism*, vol. 5, 513–79; Sasso, "Del Provincialismo negli Studi," *La Cultura*, 53, no. 1 (2015): 5–40; Manzella, ed., *Le Culture della Prima Repubblica*; Galasso, "Togliatti e Croce," in *L'Italia Nuova*, vol. 1, 276–330; Galasso, "Intelletuali e Società di Massa in Italia, 1945–1980," in *L'Italia Nuova*, vol. 3, 195–265; Galasso, *Croce, Gramsci e Altri Storici*.
22 Croce, *Taccuini di Lavoro*, vol. 2, 162–9; Sasso, *Filosofia e Idealismo*, vol. 1, 545–607; Setta, *L'Uomo Qualunque*, 217–88; Setta, *Croce, il Liberalismo e l'Italia Postfascista*, 132–56.
23 Croce, *Scritti e Discorsi Politici*, vol. 2, 431–41. See also Fabio Grassi Orsini, "Croce e il Partito Liberale," in Berti, Capozzi, and Craveri, eds., *I Liberali Italiani dall'Antifascismo alla Repubblica*, vol. 2, 579–660.
24 Griffo, ed., *Dall' "Italia Tagliata,"* 322–3, 332, 334–8; Eugenio Capozzi, "La Destra Liberale e la Segreteria Lucifero (1947–1948)," in Grassi Orsini and Nicolosi, eds., *I Liberali Italiani dall'Antifascismo alla Resistenza*, vol. 1, 309–42; Paolo Bonsi, "Il PLI nelle Pagine del Diario di Anton Dante Coda," in ibid., 575–94.
25 Croce, *Taccuini di Lavoro*, vol. 6, 170.
26 Griffo, ed., *Dall' "Italia Tagliata,"* 322–4, 332, 334–8. See also Teodori, *Pannunzio*, 87–133; Riccardi, ed., *Niccolò Carandini*, 85–143; Antonio Cardini, "Il Liberalismo di Mario Pannunzio," in Grassi Orsini and Nicolosi, eds., *I Liberali Italiani dall'Antifascismo alla Repubblica*, vol. 1, 611–46.
27 Croce, *Epistolario*, vol. 2, 269, 274. See also Setta, "Benedetto Croce e la 'Sinistra' Liberale nel Carteggio con Leone Cattani."
28 Croce, *Epistolario*, vol. 2, 269–70.
29 Ibid., 270–1.
30 Croce, *Terze Pagine Sparse*, vol. 1, 300.
31 Croce, *Taccuini di Lavoro*, vol. 6, 175.
32 Ibid., 181. See also ibid., 171–2.
33 Ibid., 180.
34 Croce, *Nuove Pagine Sparse*, vol. 1, 432–3.

35 Croce, *Epistolario*, vol. 2, 274. See also ibid., 269, 270–1, 273–5.
36 Croce, *Taccuini di Lavoro*, vol. 6, 183.
37 Ricolfi et al, eds., *Italia al Voto*, 522–5.
38 Croce, *Taccuini di Lavoro*, vol. 6, 191; Mammarella, *L'Italia dalla Caduta del Fascismo ad Oggi*, 203–11.
39 Croce, *Taccuni di Lavoro*, vol. 6, 192–3.
40 Ibid., 227.
41 Ibid., 193–4.
42 Croce, *Epistolario*, vol. 2, 272.
43 Ibid., 274.
44 Ibid., 274–5.
45 Croce, *Nuove Pagine Sparse*, vol. 1, 432–3.
46 Croce, *Taccuini di Lavoro*, vol. 6, 190–4, 205, 212, 223, 242, 249, 272; Croce, *Terze Pagine Sparse*, vol. 1, 298–304; Ciani, *Il Partito Liberale Italiano da Croce a Malagodi*; Setta, *Croce, il Liberalismo e l'Italia Postfascista*, 140–228.
47 Croce, *Taccuini di Lavoro*, vol. 6, 274–5. See also Croce, *Epistolario*, vol. 2, 281.
48 Croce, *Terze Pagine Sparse*, vol. 1, 298–310.
49 Ibid., 298–301.
50 Ibid., 307–8.
51 Ibid., 300–1. See also Gennaro Sasso, "Sul liberalismo," in Manzella, ed., *Le Culture della Prima Repubblica*, 53–74; Sasso, "Benedetto Croce e il Liberalismo," in *Filosofia e Idealismo*, vol. 5, 579–630; Bobbio, *Politica e Cultura*, 100–20; 211–68; Salvadori, *Il Liberalismo Italiano*, 43–80; Antoni, *La Restaurazione del Diritto di Natura*.
52 Croce, *Terze Pagine Sparse*, vol. 1, 301–4.
53 Ibid., 308–10. See also Elisa Guidi, "Per l'Unità delle Forze Liberali: Benedetto Croce, il Gruppo de 'Il Mondo' e il PLI (1947–1951)," in Menozzi, Moretti, and Pertici, eds., *Culture e Libertà*, 419–51.
54 Nicolini, *Croce*; Nicolini, *Il Croce Minore*, 39–202; Elena Croce, *Ricordi Familiari*.

Bibliography

Acocella, Nicola, ed. *Luigi Einaudi: Studioso, Statista, Governatore.* Rome: Carocci 2010.

Afeltra, Gaetano. *I 45 Giorni che Sconvolsero l'Italia: 25 Luglio–8 Settembre 1943.* Milan: Rizzoli 1993.

Aga-Rossi, Elena. "Alberto Tarchiani: Politica, Diplomazia ed Economia in un Liberale Atipico." In Giampiero Berti, Eugenio Capozzi, and Piero Craveri, eds., *I Liberali Italiani dall'Antifascismo alla Reppublica.* Vol. 2. Soveria Mannelli: Rubbettino 2010. 209–56.

– "L'Italia nel Contesto Internazionale." In Giancarlo Monina, ed., *1945–1946: Le Origini della Repubblica.* Vol. 2. Soveria Mannelli: Rubbettino 2007. 25–60.

– *L'Italia nella Sconfitta: Politica Interna e Situazione Internazionale durante la Seconda Guerra Mondiale.* Naples: E.S.I. 1985.

– *A Nation Collapses: The Surrender of September 1943.* Cambridge: Cambridge University Press 1993.

– *Una Nazione allo Sbando: 8 Settembre 1943.* Bologna: Il Mulino 2003.

– "PCI e USSR nel Periodo Staliniano, 1944–1953." In Gerardo Nicolosi, ed., *I Partiti Politici nell'Italia Repubblicanna.* Soveria Mannelli: Rubbettino 2006. 91–116.

Aga-Rossi, Elena, and Gaetano Quagliarello, eds. *L'Altra Faccia della Luna: I Rapporti tra PCI, PCF e l'Unione Sovietica.* Bologna: Il Mulino 1997.

Aga-Rossi, Elena, and Victor Zaslavsky. *Togliatti e Stalin: Il PCI e la Politica Estera Staliniana negli Archivi di Mosca.* Bolgona: Il Mulino 1997.

Ajello, Nello. *Intellettuali e PCI, 1944–1956.* Bari: Laterza 1979.

Alosco, Antonio. *Il Partito d'Azione nel Regno del Sud.* Naples: Guida 2002.

Alvaro, Corrado. *L'Italia Rinunzia 1944: Il Meridione e il Paese di Fronte alla Grande Catastrofe.* Rome: Donzelli 2011.

Amendola, Giorgio. *Intervista sull'Antifascismo.* Bari: Laterza 1994.

– "La Rottura della Coalizione Tripartita: Maggio 1947." *Il Mulino,* 22, no. 235 (1974): 780–98.

Amendola, Giorgio, et al., eds. *Fascismo e Antifascismo, 1918–1948.* Milan: Feltrinelli 1961. 2 vols.

Andreotti, Giulio. *1947: L'Anno delle Grandi Svolte nel Diario di un Protagonista.* Milan: Rizzoli 2005.

– *Concerto a Sei Voci: Roma 1944–1945: I Primi Governi dell'Italia Liberata.* Milan: Boroli Editore 2007.

Andreucci, Franco. *Da Gramsci a Occhetto.* Rome: Della Porta Editori 2014.

Aniasi, Aldo. *Parri: L'Avventura Umana, Militare e Politica di Maurizio.* Turin: ERI 1991.

Anonymous. "Relazione sul Congresso dei Comitati di Liberazione (Bari, 28–29 Gennaio 1944)." [Croce papers; marked "Secret."]

Ansaldo, Giovanni. *Don Enrico.* Florence: Le Lettere 2013.

Antoni, Carlo. *L'Avanguardia della Libertà.* Naples: Guida 2012.

– *La Restaurazione del Diritto di Natura.* Venezia: Neri Pozza 1959.

– *Tre Saggi Storici.* Bologna: Il Mulino 1997.

Antonicelli, Franco, ed. *Trent'Anni di Storia Italiana, 1915–1945.* Turin: Einaudi 1961.

Artieri, Giovanni. *Umberto II: Il Re Gentiluomo.* Florence: Le Lettere 2007.

– *Umberto II: Il Re Gentiluomo: Colloqui sulla Fine della Monarchia.* Florence: Le Lettere 2002.

Baget-Bozzo, Gianni. *Il Partito Cristiano al Potere: La DC di De Gasperi e Dossetti. 1945–1954.* Florence: Vallecchi 1978.

Ballini, Pier Luigi. "1947: Il Viaggio di De Gasperi negli Stati Uniti. Gli Studi e gli Appunti Inediti di Alberto Pirelli." *Nuova Antologia,* 140, no. 594 (1990): 333–44.

– *Il Trattato di Pace nell'Assemblea Costituente.* Rome: Camera dei Deputati 2008.

Ballini, Pier Luigi, and Maurizio Ridolfi, eds. *Storia delle Campagne Elettorali in Italia.* Milan: Bruno Mondadori 2002.

Barbagallo, Francesco, ed. *La Formazione dell'Italia Repubblicana.* Vol. 1. Turin: Einaudi 1994.

Bartoli, Domenico. *8 Settembre 1943: L'Italia si Arrende.* Milan: Editoriale Nuova 1984.

Barzini, Luigi. *La Verità sul Referendum.* Florence: Le Lettere 2005.

Battaglia, Roberto. *Storia della Resistenza Italiana.* Turin: Einaudi 1964.

Benzoni, Giuliana. *La Vita Ribelle.* Bologna: Il Mulino 1985.

Berti, Giampiero, Eugenio Capozzi, and Piero Craveri, eds. *I Liberali Italiani dall'Antifascismo alla Reppublica.* Vol. 2. Soveria Mannelli: Rubbettino 2010.

Bertoldi, Silvio. *Apocalissse Italia: Otto Settembre 1943: Fine di una Nazione.* Milan: Rizzoli 1998.

– *Vittorio Emanuele III.* Turin: UTET 1970.

Bianchi, Gianfranco. *25 Luglio: Crollo di un Regime.* Milan: Mursia 1963.

Bobbio, Norberto. *Politica e Cultura.* Turin: Einaudi 1955.

– *Profilo Ideologico del Novecento.* Milan: Garzanti 1990.

Bocca, Giorgio. *Palmiro Togliatti.* Bari: Laterza 1977.

Bonanno, C., and O. Valentini, eds. *Il Congresso di Bari (28–29 Gennaio 1944).* Rome: Sapere 2007.

Boneschi, Mario. "Parri: Un Uomo Solo." *Nuova Antologia,* 125, no. 563 (1990): 330–44.

Bonetti, Paolo. *Il Mondo, 1949–1966: Ragione e Illusione Borghese.* Bari: Laterza 1975.

Bonomi, Ivanoe. *Diario di un Anno: 2 Giugno 1943–10 Giugno 1944.* Milan: Garzanti 1947.

Borzoni, Gianluca. *Renato Prunas Diplomatico, 1892–1951.* Soveria Mannelli: Rubbettino 2004.

Bracalini, Romano. *Paisà: Vita Quotidiana nell'Italia Liberata.* Milan: Mondadori 2008.

British Documents on Foreign Affairs, Pt. 3, Series F, Europe, Italy, and South-Eastern Europe. Vols. 22, 23, 24, 25, 26; January 1942–December 1945.

Cafagna, Luciano. *Dualismo e Sviluppo nella Storia d'Italia.* Venice: Marsilio 1990.

Calamandrei, Piero. *Chiarezza nella Costituzione.* Rome: Edizioni Storia e Letteratura 2012.

Calogero, Guido. *Difesa del Liberalsocialismo.* Milan: Marzorati 1992.

Campanozi, Simona. *Il Pensiero Politico e Giuridico di Meuccio Ruini.* Milan: Giuffrè 2002.

Candeloro, Giorgio. *Storia dell'Italia Moderna.* Vol. 10, *1939–1945: La Seconda Guerra Mondiale, Il Crollo del Fascismo, La Resistenza.* Milan: Feltrinelli 1984.

– *Storia dell'Italia Moderna.* Vol. 11, *1945–1950: La Fondazione della Repubblica e la Ricostruzione: Considerazioni Finali.* Milan: Feltrinelli 1986.

Caperucci, Vera. "I Liberali alla Consulta e alla Costituente." In Fabio Grassi Orsini and Gerardo Nicolosi, eds., *I Liberali Italiani dall'Antifascismo alla Repubblica,* vol. 1, 343–72.

Capozzi, Eugenio. "Un Modello Politico-Intelletuale 'Atlantico': Il Congresso for Cultural Freedom e L'Associazione Italiana per la Libertà della Cultura." *L'Acropoli,* 4, no. 1 (2003): 36–53.

Caracciolo, Filippo. *Diario di Napoli.* Florence: Passigli 1992.

Cardia, Maria Rosa. *L'Epurazione del Senato del Regno, 1943–1945.* Milan: Giuffrè 2005.

Cardini, Antonio. *Tempi di Ferro: "Il Mondo" e l'Italia del Dopoguera.* Bologna: Il Mulino 1992.

Carli, Guido. *Cinquant'Anni di Vita Italiana (Con la Collaborazione di Paolo Peluffo).* Bari: Laterza 1993.

Castronovo, Valerio, and Nicola Tranfaglia, eds. *La Stampa Italiana dalla Resistenza agli Anni Sessanta.* Bari: Laterza 1980.

Catalano, Franco. *L'Italia dalla Dittatura alla Democrazia.* 2 vols. Milan: Feltrinelli 1970.

Cattani, Leone. "Dalla Caduta del Fascismo al Primo Governo De Gasperi." *Storia Contemporanea,* 5, no. 4 (1974): 737–88.

Cattaruzza, Marina. *L'Italia e il Confine Orientale. 1866–2006.* Bologna: Il Mulino, 2007.

Catti-De Gasperi, Maria Romana. *De Gasperi: Uomo Solo.* Milan: Mondadori 1974.

Chabod, Federico. *L'Italia Contemporanea, 1918–1948.* Turin: Einaudi 1961.

Ciampi, Carlo Azeglio. *Da Livorno al Quirinale: Storia di un Italiano.* Bologna: Il Mulino 2010.

Ciani, Arnaldo. *Il Partito Liberale Italiano da Croce a Malagodi.* Naples: E.S.I. 1968.

Ciliberto, Michele, ed. *Croce e Gentile: L'Italia e la Cultura Europea.* Rome: Treccani 2016.

Ciumi, Roberto. *L'Italia di Badoglio, 8 Settembre 1943–5 Giugno 1944: Storia del Regno del Sud.* Milan: Rizzoli 1993.

Clementi, Marco. *L'Alleato Stalin: L'Ombra Sovietica sull'Italia di Togliatti e De Gasperi.* Milan: Rizzoli 2011.

Cofrancesco, Dino. " 'L'uomo Qualunque': Ragioni e Ritardi di un Movimento Politico Sui Generis." *Nuova Storia Contemporanea,* 16, no. 3 (2012): 5–38.

Colapietra, Raffaele. *Benedetto Croce e la Politica Italiana.* 2 vols. Bari: Edizioni del Centro Libraio 1969.

Colarizi, Simona. *La Seconda Guerra Mondiale e la Repubblica.* Turin: UTET 1995.

– *Storia dei Partiti nell'Italia Repubblicana.* Bari: Laterza 1994.

Corbi, Gianni. *L'Avventurosa Nascita della Repubblica: Gli Anni della Costituente: Da Parri al Patto Atlantico.* Milan: Rizzoli 1989.

Craveri, Piero. *De Gasperi.* Bologna: Il Mulino 2006.

– *La Democrazia Incompiuta: Figure del Novecento Italiano.* Venice: Marsilio 2002.

– "L'Eredità dell'Italia Liberale nella Formazione della Repubblica." In Marcello Pera, ed., *Benedetto Croce e la Nascita della Repubblica.* Soveria Mannelli: Rubbettino 2003. 23–36.

– L'Opera Politica di Croce per 'L'Italia Che Non Muore.' " *L'Acropoli,* 4, no. 1 (2003): 98–105.

– "Perchè il PCI Non Potè Diventare Forza Egemone del Sistema Italiano." In Gerardo Nicolosdi, ed., *I Partiti Politici nell'Italia Repubblicana.* Soveria Mannelli: Rubbettino 2006. 117–34.

Craveri, Piero, and Gaetano Quagliarello, eds. *La Seconda Guerra Mondiale e la Sua Memoria.* Soveria Mannelli: Rubbettino 2006.

Craveri, Raimondo. *La Campagna d'Italia: ORI e I Servizi Segreti.* Milan: La Pietra 1980.

Croce, Benedetto. *Carteggio Croce-Antoni.* M. Musté, ed. Bologna: Il Mulino 1996.

– *Carteggio Croce-Arangio Ruiz.* Valerio Massimo Minale and Luigi La Bruna, eds. Bologna: Il Mulino 2012.

– *Carteggio Croce-Calogero.* Cristina Farneti, ed. Bologna: Il Mulino 2004.

– *Carteggio Croce-De Ruggiero.* Angelina Schinaia and Nunzio Ruggiero, eds. Bologna: Il Mulino 2008.

– *Carteggio Croce-Flora.* Enrica Mazzetta, ed. Bologna: Il Mulino 2008.

– *Carteggio Croce-Laterza, 1931–1943,* 2 Vol.. Antonella Pompilio, ed. Bari: Laterza 2009.

– *Carteggio Croce-Omodeo.* Marcello Gigante, ed. Naples: I.I.S.S. 1978.

– *Carteggio Croce-Pannunzio, 1945–1952.* P.G. Quaglieni, ed. Turin: Centro Pannunzio 1998.

– *Contributo alla Critica di Me Stesso.* Milan: Adelphi 1989.

– *Croce, the King and the Allies: Extracts from a Diary, July 1943–June 1944.* London: George Allen 1950.

– *Dieci Conversazioni con gli Alunni dell'Istituto Italiano per gli Studi Storici di Napoli.* Bologna: Il Mulino 1993.

– *Discorsi di Varia Filosofia.* 2 vols. Bari: Laterza 1945.

– *Epistolario,* vol. 2, *Lettere a Alessandro Casati, 1907–1952.* Naples: I.I.S.S. 1979.

– *Filosofia e Storiografia.* Bari: Laterza 1949.

– *History of Europe in the Nineteenth Century.* New York: Harcourt Brace 1933.

– *Lettere a Vittotio Enzo Alfieri.* Milazzo: Edizioni Spes 1956.

– *Nuove Pagine Sparse.* 2 vols. Bari: Laterza 1966.

– *Quando l'Italia Era Tagliatta in Due.* Bari: Laterza 1946.

– *Scritti e Discorsi Politici.* 2 vols., 1943–7. Naples: Bibliopolis 1993.

– *Storia d'Europa nel Secolo Decimonono.* Bari: Laterza 1957.

– *Storia d'Italia dal 1871 al 1915.* Bari: Laterza 1953.

– *Taccuini di Guerra.* 1943–5. Milan: Adelphi 2004.

– *Taccuini di Lavoro.* 6 vols., 1901–49. Naples: Arte Tipografica 1987.

– *Terze Pagine Sparse.* 2 vols. Bari: Laterza 1955.

Croce, Benedetto, and Luigi Einaudi. *Carteggio, 1902–1953.* Turin: Fondazione Luigi Einaudi 1986.

– *Liberismo e Liberalismo.* Milan: Ricciardi 1957.

Croce, Elena. *Ricordi Familiari.* Florence: Vallecchi 1967.

Cutinelli-Rendina, Emanuele, ed. *Luigi Russo, Benedetto Croce, Carteggio, 1912–1948.* 2 vols. Pisa: Edizioni della Normale 1997.

De Andreis, Marcella Leone. *Capri 1943: C'Era una Volta la Guerra.* Capri: La Conchiglia 2007.

De Cecco, Marcello. "Economic Policy in the Reconstruction Period, 1945–1957." In Stuart Woolf, ed., *The Rebirth of Italy, 1943–1948.* London: Longman 1972. 156–80.

De Felice, Renzo. *Mussolini L'Alleato.* 3 vols., 1940–5. Turin: Einaudi 1990–7.

– ed. "I Primi Passi dell'Italia Postfascista." *Storia Contemporanea,* 5, no. 4 (1974): 569–832.

De Giorgi, Fulvio. *Mons. Montini: Chiesa Cattolica e Scontri di Civiltà nella Prima Metà del Novecento.* Bologna: Il Mulino 2012.

De Giorgi, Maria, ed. *Il Movimento Liberale Italiano (Roma 1943).* Lecce: Congedo Editore 2005.

Degli Espinosa, Agostino. *Il Regno del Sud: 8 Settembre–4 Giugno 1944.* Rome: Migliaresi 1946.

Degli Innocenti, Maurizio. "I Socialisti." In Giancarlo Monina, ed., *1945–1946: Le Origini della Repubblica.* Vol. 2. Soveria Mannelli: Rubbettino 2007. 105–41.

De Luna, Giovanni. *Storia del Partito d'Azione: La Rivoluzione Democratica 1942–1947.* Milan: Feltrinelli 1984.

Delzell, Charles F. *Mussolini's Enemies: The Italian Antifascist Resistance.* Princeton, NJ: Princeton University Press 1961.

Desiderio, Giancristiano. *Vita Intellettuale e Affettiva di Benedetto Croce.* Macerata: Liberilibri 2014.

Di Campello, Francesco. *Un Principe nella Bufera: Diario dell'Ufficiale di Ordinanza di Umberto, 1943–1944.* Florence: Le Lettere 2012.

Di Capua, Giovanni. *L'Anno delle Grandi Svolte (Maggio 1947–Aprile 1948): L'Italia di Alcide De Gasperi.* Soveria Mannelli: Rubbettino 2006.

– *Il Biennio Comprommissorio (Maggio 1945–Aprile 1947): L'Italia del "Don Basilio."* Soveria Mannelli: Rubbettino 2006.

– *Il Biennio Cruciale (Luglio 1943–Giugno 1945): L'Italia di Charles Poletti.* Soveria Mannelli: Rubbettino 2005.

Di Nolfo, Ennio. *Le Paure e le Speranze degli Italiani, 1943–1953.* Milan: Mondadori 1986.

– *Vaticano e Stati Uniti, 1939–1952: Dalle Carte di Myron C. Taylor.* Milan: Franco Angeli 1978.

Di Nolfo, Ennio, and Maurizio Serra. *La Gabbia Infranta. Gli Alleati e l'Italia dal 1943 al 1945.* Bari: Laterza 2010.

Domenico, Roy Palmer. *Italian Fascists on Trial.* Chapel Hill: University of North Carolina Press 1991.

Einaudi, Lugi. *La Guerra e l'Unità Europea.* Milan: Comunità 1953.

– *Riflessioni di un Liberale Sulla Democrazia, 1943–1947.* Florence: Olschki Editore 2001.

Ellwood, David. *Italy, 1943–1945.* Leicester, UK: Leicester University Press 1985.

Falzone, V., F. Palermo, and F. Cosentino. *La Costituzione della Repubblica Italiana. Illustrata con i Lavori Preparatori.* Milan: Mondadori 1976.

Finetti, Ugo. *La Resistenza Cancellata.* Milan: Ares 2003.

Focardi, Filippo. *La Guerra della Memoria: La Resistenza nel Dibattito Politico Italiano dal 1945 a Oggi.* Bari: Laterza 2003.

Forcella, Enzo. *La Resistenza in Convento.* Turin: Einaudi 1999.

Foreign Relations of the United States, 1943, vol. 2, 314–445; 1944, vol. 3, 996–1186; 1945, vol. 1, 681–713; 1945, vol. 2, 1079–103; 1945, vol. 4, 955–1331; 1946, vol. 5, 85–953; 1947, vol. 3, Italy.

Formigoni, Guido. "De Gasperi e la Crisi Politica del 1947: Documenti e Interpretazioni." *Ricerche di Storia Politica,* 6, no. 3 (2003): 361–88.

Fornaro, Federico. *Giuseppe Saragat.* Venice: Marsilio 2003.

Franzinelli, Mimmo. "8 Settembre." In Mario Isnenghi, ed., *Luoghi della Memoria Personaggi e Date dell'Italia Unita.* Bari: Laterza 1997. 241–70.

– *L'Amnistia Togliatti, 22 Maggio 1946: Colpo di Spugna sui Crimini Fascisti.* Milan: Mondadori 2006.

Fratta, Arturo. *Così Finì il Regno D'Italia: Dai Taccuini di Croce.* Naples: Di Mauro 1992.

Gabrielli, Patrizia. *Il 1946, le Donne, la Repubblica.* Rome: Donzelli 2009.

Galante, Severino. *Le Fine di un Compromesso Storico: PCI e DC nella Crisi del 1947.* Milan: Franco Angeli 1980.

Galante Garrone, Alessandro. *Questa Nostra Costituzione.* Turin: Loescher 1987.

Galasso, Giuseppe, ed. *Benedetto Croce e il Corriere della Sera.* Milan: Rizzoli 2010.

– *Croce, Gramsci e Altri storici.* Milan: Rizzoli 1969.

– *Croce e lo Spirito del Suo Tempo.* Bari: Laterza 2002.

– "Introduzione e Apparati." In Benedetto Croce, *Filosofia, Poesia, Storia: Pagine Tratte da Tutte le Opere a Cura dell'Autore.* Milan: Adelphi 1996.

– *L'Italia s'è Desta.* Florence: Le Monnier 2002.

– *L'Italia Nuova.* Vol. 1. Rome: Edizioni di Storia e Letteratura 2011.

– *L'Italia Nuova.* Vol. 3. Rome: Edizioni di Storia e Letteratura 2011.

– *L'Italia Nuova.* Vol. 4. Rome: Edizioni di Storia e Letteratura 2011.

– *L'Italia Nuova.* Vol. 6. Rome: Edizioni di Storia e Letteratura 2011.

– *La Memoria, La Vita, I Valori, Itinerari Crociani.* Naples: I.I.S.S. 2015.

Gallegos, Adrian. *And Who Are You?* London: Adelphi Press 1992.

Gallerano, Nicola, ed. *L'Altro Dopoguerra: Roma e il Sud, 1943–1945.* Milan: Franco Angeli 1985.

Galli Della Loggia, Ernesto. *La Morte della Patria.* Bari: Laterza 1996.

Gambino, Antonio. *Storia del Dopoguerra: Dalla Liberazione al Potere DC.* Bari: Laterza 1978.

Gangi, Massimo. *Vittorio Emanuele Orlando.* Rome: La Navicella 1991.

Garin, Eugenio. *Cronache di Filosofia Italiana, 1900–1943: Quindici Anni Dopo.* Vol. 2. Bari: Laterza 1975.

Gavalotti, Enrico. *Il Professorino: Giuseppe Dossetti tra Crisi del Fascismo e Costruzione della Democrazia.* Bologna: Il Mulino 2002.

Gentile, Emilio, et al., eds. *Novecento Italiano.* Bari: Laterza 1996.

Ghersi, Livio. *Benedetto Croce e l'Unione Democratica Nazionale.* Rome: Bibliosofica 2008.

– *Croce e Salvemini: Uno Storico Conflitto Ideale Ripensato nell'Italia Odierna.* Rome: Bibliosofica 2007.

Ghisalberti, Carlo. *Storia Costituzionale d'Italia, 1848–1948.* Bari: Laterza 1974.

Giannini, Guglielmo. *La Folla, Seimila Anni di Lotta Contro la Tirannide.* Soveria Mannelli: Rubbettino 2002.

Gigliobianco, Alfredo. *Via Nazionale: Banca d'Italia e Classe Dirigente: Cento Anni di Storia Italiana.* Rome: Donzelli 2006.

Giordano, Alberto. "I Liberali e la Costituzione Italiana: Storia di un Rapporto Difficile, 1946–1947." *Materiali per una Storia della Cultura Giuridica,* 41, no. 2 (2001): 361–88.

Grassi Orsini, Fabio. "Croce e il Partito Liberale." In Giampiero Berti, Eugenio Capozzi, and Piero Craveri, eds., *I Liberali Italiani dall'Antifascismo alla Repubblica.* Vol. 2. Soveria Mannelli: Rubbettino 2010. 579–660.

– "I Liberali, De Gasperi e 'La Svolta' del Maggio 1947." *Ventunesimo Secolo,* 3, no. 5 (2004): 33–70.

– "Questione dell'Ordine Pubblico e la Lotta Politica in Italia." In Giancarlo Monina, ed., *1945–1946: Le Origini della Repubblica.* Vol. 2. 373–418.

– "Riaprire il Cantiere: I Liberali dalla Crisi di Regime alla Ricostruzione del Partito 1925–1946." *Ventunesimo Secolo,* 4, no. 8 (2005): 13–45.

Grassi Orsini, Fabio, and Gerardo Nicolosi, eds. *I Liberali Italiani dall'Antifascismo alla Repubblica.* Vol. 1. Soveria Mannelli: Rubbettino 2008.

Griffo, Maurizio. "Il Pensiero Politico di Adolfo Omodeo nella Ripresa della Vita Libera, 1943–1946." In Giampiero Berti, Eugenio Capozzi, and Piero Craveri, eds., *I Liberali Italiani dall'Antifascismo alla Repubblica.* Vol. 2. Soveria Mannelli: Rubbettino 2010. 851–67.

– "Una Polemica fra Croce e Togliatti alla Ripresa della Vita Libera." *L'Acropoli,* 16, no. 2 (2015): 144–51.

– ed. *Dall' "Italia Tagliata in Due" all'Assemblea Costituente: Documenti e Testimonianze dai Carteggi di Benedetto Croce.* Bologna: Il Mulino 1998.

Guidi, Elisa. "Per l'Unità delle Forze Liberali: Benedetto Croce e il Gruppo de 'Il Mondo' e il PLI (1947–1951)." In Daniele Menozzi et al., eds., *Culture e Libertà: Studi in Onore di Roberto Vivarelli.* Pisa: Edizioni della Normale 2006. 419–52.

Harris, C.R.S. *Allied Military Administration in Italy, 1943–1945*. London: HMSO 1957.
Imbriani, Angelo Michele. *Vento del Sud: Moderati, Reazionari, Qualunquisti, 1943– 1948*. Bologna: Il Mulino 1996.
Incisa di Camerana, Ludovico. *L'Italia della Luogoteneza: Umberto di Savoia e il Passaggio alla Repubblica*. Milan: Corbaccio 1996.
Innocenti, Marco. *L'Italia del 1943*. Milan: Mursia 1993.
Isnenghi, Mario, ed. *I Luoghi della Memoria: Personaggi e Date dell'Italia Unita*. Bari: Laterza 1997.
– *La Tragedia Necessaria: Da Caporetto all'Otto Settembre*. Bologna: Il Mulino 1999.
Jannazzo, Antonio. *Croce e il Comunismo*. Naples: E.S.I. 1982.
– *Il Liberalismo Italiano del Novecento. Da Giolitti a Malagodi*. Soveria Mannelli: Rubbettino 2003.
Jemolo, Arturo Carlo. *Chiesa e Stato in Italia negli Ultimi Cento Anni*. Turin: Einaudi 1963.
Judt, Tony. *Postwar: A History of Europe since 1945*. New York: Penguin Books 2005.
Keith, Jeffery. *The Secret History of MI6*. New York: Penguin Press 2011.
Kogan, Norman. *Italy and the Allies*. Cambridge, MA: Harvard University Press 1968.
Labriola, Silvano, ed. *Valori e Principi del Regime Repubblicano*. 4 vols. Bari: Laterza 2006.
Lanchester, Fulco. *Pensare lo Stato. I Giuspubblicisti nell'Italia Unitaria*. Bari: Laterza 2004.
Lanaro, Silvio. *Storia dell'Italia Repubblicana*. Venice: Marsilio 1992.
La Rovere, Luca. *L'Eredità del Fascismo: Gli Intellettuali, i Giovani e la Transizione al Postfascismo, 1943–1948*. Turin: Bollati 2008.
Leoni, Alberto. *Il Paradiso Devastato: Storia Militare della Campagna d'Italia, 1943–1945*. Milan: Edizioni Ares 2012.
Lepre, Aurelio. *Storia della Prima Repubblica: L'Italia dal 1945 al 1998*. Bologna: Il Mulino 1998.
Lizzadri, Oreste. *Il Regno di Badoglio*. Rome: Napoleone 1974.
Loewenheim, Francis, Harold Langley, and Manfred Joans, eds. *Roosevelt and Churchill: Their Secret Wartime Correspondence*. New York: F.P. Dutton 1975.
Lorenzini, Sara. *L'Italia e il Trattato di Pace del 1947*. Bologna: Il Mulino 2007.
Lucia, Piero. *Intellettuali Italiani del Secondo Dopoguerra: Impegni, Crisi, Speranze*. Naples: Guida 2003.
Lucifero, Falcone. *L'Ultimo Re: Diari del Ministro della Real Casa, 1944–1946*. Milan: Mondadori 2002.
Macmillan, Harold. *The Blast of War, 1939–1945*. London: Macmillan 1967.

– *War Diaries: Politics and War in the Mediterranean, 1943–1945*. London: Macmillan 1984.
Maggi, Michele. *L'Italia Che Non Muore: La Politica di Croce nella Crisi Nazionale*. Naples: Bibliopolis 2001.
Malagodi, Giovanni. *Profilo di Raffaele Mattioli*. Turin: Aragno 2010.
Malgeri, Francesco. *Alcide De Gasperi*. Vol. 2, *Dal Fascismo alla Democrazia, 1943–1947*. Soveria Mannelli: Rubbettino 2009.
Malone, Richard S. *A Portrait of War, 1939–1943*. Toronto: Totem Press 1983.
Mangoni, Luisa. *La Civiltà della Crisi: Cultura e Politica tra Otto e Novecento*. Rome: Viella 2013.
Mammarella, Giuseppe. *L'Italia dalla Caduta del Fascismo ad Oggi*. Bolgona: Il Mulino 1978.
Mammarella, Giuseppe, and P. Cacace. *La Politica Estera dell'Italia dallo Stato Unitario ai Giorni Nostri*. Bari: Laterza 2006.
Manzella, Andrea, ed. *Le Culture della Prima Repubblica*. Milan: Reset 1998.
Maranini, Giuseppe. *Storia del Potere in Italia, 1848–1967*. Florence: Vallechi 1967.
Marcucci Fanello, Gabriella, ed. *Ivanoe Bonomi dal Fascismo alla Repubblica: Documenti del CLN (Dicembre 1942–Giugno 1944)*. Manduria: Lacaita 2005.
– *Il Primo Governo De Gasperi, Dicembre 1945–Giugno 1946: Sei Mesi Decisivi per la Democrazia in Italia*. Soveria Mannelli: Rubbettino 2004.
Matthews, Herbert L. *The Education of a Correspondent*. New York: Harcourt, Brace 1946.
Mazza, Fulvio. *Il Partito d'Azione nel Mezzogiorno, 1942–1947*. Soveria Mannelli: Rubbettino 1992.
Mazzei, Federico. "De Gasperi e la Santa Sede nella Crisi Italiana, 1942–1943." *Ricerche di Storia Politica*, 14, no. 3 (2011): 303–24.
– "I Partiti e la Consulta: Un'Inchiesta del 1944." *Nuova Antologia*, 146, no. 607 (2011): 12–42.
Mazzetti, Massimo. *Salerno: Capitale d'Italia*. Salerno: Paguro 2000.
Menozzi, D., M. Moretti, and R. Pertici, eds. *Culture e Libertà: Studi in Onore di Roberto Vivarelli*. Pisa: Edizioni della Normale 2006. 419–52.
Mercuri, Lamberto. *1943–1945: Gli Alleati e L'Italia*. Naples: E.S.I. 1976.
Monelli, Paolo. *Il Giorno del Referendum*. Florence: Le Lettere 2007.
– *Roma 1943*. Turin: Einaudi 1993.
Monina, Giancarlo, ed. *1945–1946: Le Origini della Repubblica*. 2 vols. Soveria Mannelli: Rubbettino 2007.
Montanelli, Indro, and Mario Cervi. *L'Italia della Disfatta:10 Giugno 1940–8 Settembre 1943*. Milan: Rizzoli 1982.
Moorehead, Alan. *Eclipse*. New York: Soho Press 1999.

Moravia, Alberto. *La Ciociara.* Milan: Bompiani 2002.

Mosco, Maria Laura, and Piero Pirani, eds. *The Concept of Resistance in Italy.* London: Rowman and Littlefield 2017.

Mowat, Farley. *And No Birds Sang.* Toronto: McClelland and Stewart 1979.

Murialdi, Paolo. *La Stampa Italiana del Dopoguerra, 1943–1972.* Bari: Laterza 1974.

– *La Traversata: Settembre 1943–Dicembre 1945.* Bologna: Il Mulino 2001.

Murphy, Robert D. *Diplomat among Warriors.* New York: Doubleday 1964.

Mustè, Marcello. *Adolfo Omodeo: Storiografia e Pensiero Politico.* Bologna: Il Mulino 1990.

Nassisi, Cosima. "Interpretazioni Storiografiche e Dibattito sull'Azionismo." In Gerardo Nicolosi, ed., *I Partiti Politici nell'Italia Repubblicana.* Soveria Mannelli: Rubbettino 2006. 210–45.

Nenni, Pietro. *Tempo di Guerra Fredda: Diari, 1943–56.* Milan: Sugarco Edizioni 1981.

Nicolini, Fausto. *Croce.* Turin: UTET 1962.

– *Il Croce Minore.* Naples: Ricciardi 1963.

Nicolosi, Gerardo. "Il Nuovo Liberalismo." In Fabio Grassi Orsini and Gerardo Nicolosi, eds., *I Liberali Italiani dall'Antifascismo alla Repubblica.* Vol. 1. Soveria Mannelli: Rubbettino 2008.

– *Risorgimento Liberale: Il Giornale del Nuovo Liberalismo: Dalla Caduta del Fascismo alla Repubblica, 1943–1948.* Soveria Mannelli: Rubbettino 2012.

– ed. *Dizionario del Liberalismo Italiano.* Vols. 1 and 2. Soveria Mannelli: Rubbettino 2011–15.

– ed. *I Partiti Politici nell'Italia Repubblicana.* Soveria Mannelli: Rubbettino 2006.

Novelli, Edoardo. *Le Elezioni del Quarantotto.* Rome: Donzelli 2008.

Oliva, Gianni. *Gli Ultimi Giorni della Monarchia.* Milan: Mondadori 2016.

– *La Resa dei Conti, Aprile-Maggio 1945: Foibe, Piazzale Loreto e Giustizia Partigiana.* Milan: Mondadori 1999.

Operti, Piero. *Lettera Aperta a Benedetto Croce.* Turin: Lattes 1946.

Orlando, Federico. *I 45 Giorni di Badoglio.* Rome: Bonacci 1994.

Orlando, Vittorio Emanuele. *Discorsi Parlamentari.* Bologna: Il Mulino 2002.

Orsina, Giovanni. "L'Antipolitica dei Moderati: Dal Qualunquismo a Berlusconi." *Ventunesimo Secolo,* 12, no. 30 (2013): 91–112.

– *Il Partito Liberale nell'Italia Repubblicana: Guida alle Fonti Archivistiche.* Soveria Mannelli: Rubbettino 2004.

– "Quando Antifascismo Sconfisse l'Antifascismo: Interpretazioni sulla Resistenza nell'Alta Cultura Antifascista, 1955–1965." *Ventunesimo Secolo,* 4, no. 7 (2005): 9–44.

– "Translatio Imperii: La Crisi del Governo Parri e i Liberali." In Giancarlo Monina, ed., *1945–1946: Le Origini della Repubblica.* Vol. 2. Soveria Mannelli: Rubbettino 2007. 201–56.

– ed. *Storia delle Destre nell'Italia Repubblicana.* Soveria Mannelli: Rubbettino 2014.

Ortona, Egidio. *Anni d'America: La Ricostruzione, 1944–1951.* Bologna: Il Mulino 1984.

Paladin, Livio. *Per una Storia Costituzionale Dell'Italia Repubblicana.* Bologna: Il Mulino 2002.

Palermo, Ivan. *Storia di un Armistizio: Gli Avvenimento dell'8 Settembre.* Milan: Mondadori 1967.

Pallini, Renato. "Vita Amministraviva e Diffusione Territoriale del PLI, 1944–1946." In Fabio Grassi Orsini and Gerardo Nicolosi, eds., *I Liberali Italiani dall'Antifascismo alla Repubblica.* Vol. 1. Soveria Mannelli: Rubbettino 2008. 109–30.

Pansa, Gianpaolo. *Il Sangue dei Vinti.* Milan: Sperling and Kuper 2003.

Parente, Alfredo. "Aspettando la Libertà: Pensieri e Ricordi Politici." Naples, 1939–43. [Unpublished mss supplied to author by Fondazione Einaudi of Rome.]

Pastorelli, Pietro. *La Politica Estera Italiana del Dopoguerra.* Bologna: Il Mulino 1987.

Patricelli, Marco. *I Banditi della Libertà: La Straordinaria Storia della Brigata Maiella.* Turin: UTET 2005.

– *Settembre 1943: I Giorni della Vergogna.* Bari: Laterza 2009.

Pavone, Claudio. "1943: L'8 Settembre." In Emilio Gentile et al., eds., *Novecento Italiano.* Bari: Laterza 2011. 89–112.

– *Alle Origini della Repubblica: Scritti su Fascismo, Antifascismo e Continuità dello Stato.* Turin: Bollati 1995.

– "Gruppi Combattenti Italia.'" In Giorgio Amendola et al., eds., *Fascismo e Antifascismo, 1918–1948.* Vol. 2. Milan: Feltrinelli 1961. 558–65.

– *Una Guerra Civile: Saggio Storico sulla Moralità della Resistenza.* Turin: Bollati 1991.

Peli, Santo. *La Resistenza in Italia: Storia e Critica.* Turin: Einaudi 2004.

Pelle, Loredana. "De Gasperi negli Stati Uniti: Nascita di un Leader." *Nuova Storia Contemporanea,* 7, no. 1 (2003): 82–100.

Peluso, Rosalia, ed. *Lessico Crociano: Un Breviaro Filosofico-Politico per il Futuro.* Naples: La Scuola di Pitagora Editrice 2016.

Pera, Marcello, ed. *Benedetto Croce e la Nascita della Repubblica.* Soveria Mannelli Rubbettino 2002.

– *Meuccio Ruini: La Presidenza Breve.* Soveria Mannelli: Rubbettino 2003.

– *Vittorio Emanuele Orlando: Lo Scienziato, il Politico e lo Statista.* Soveria Mannelli: Rubbettino 2002.

Pertici, Roberto. *Chiesa e Stato in Italia: Dalla Grande Guerra al Nuovo Concordato (1914–1984).* Bologna: Il Mulini 2009.

Petacco, Arrigo. *A Tragedy Revealed: The Story of Italians from Istria, Dalmatia, and Venezia Giulia, 1943–1956* (trans. Konrad Eisenbichler). Toronto: University of Toronto Press 2005.

Piccardi, Leopoldo. "I 45 Giorni del Governo Badoglio." In Franco Antonicelli, ed., *Trent'Anni di Storia Italiana, 1915–1945.* Turin: Einaudi 1961. 322–30.

Pieri, Piero, and Giorgio Rochat. *Badoglio.* Turin: UTET 1974.

Piffer, Tommaso. *Gli Alleati e La Resistenza Italiana.* Bologna: Il Mulino 2010.

Placanica, Augusto, ed. *1944: Salerno Capitale: Istituzioni e Società.* Naples: E.S.I. 1986.

Pombeni, Paolo. "Il Contributo Cattolico alla Costituente." In Silvano Labriola, ed., *Valori e Principi del Regime Repubblicano.* Vol. 1. Bari: Laterza 2006. 36–80.

– *Giuseppe Dossetti.* Bologna: Il Mulino 2013.

– *La Questione Costituzionale in Italia.* Bologna: Il Mulino 2016.

Ponzani, Michela. *Guerra alle Donne, 1940–1945.* Turin: Einaudi 2012.

Portoghesi Tuzi, Telemaco, and Grazia Tuzi. *Quando si Faceva la Costituzione: Storia e Personaggi della Comunità del Porcellino.* Milan: Il Saggiatore 2010.

Porzio, Maria. *Arrivano gli Alleati: Amori e Violenze nell'Italia Liberata.* Bari: Laterza 2011.

Postorino, Francesco. *Croce e l'Ansia di un'Altra Città.* Milan: Mimesis 2017.

Puntoni, Paolo. *Parla Vittorio Emanuele III.* Bologna: Il Mulino 1993.

Quagliarello, Gaetano. "Forma di Governo nella Riflessione dei Liberali e degli Azionisti alla Costituente." In Silvano Labriola, ed., *Valori e Principi del Regime Repubblicano.* Vol. 1. Bari: Laterza 2006. 81–124.

Quagliarello, Gaetano, and Victor Zaslavsky, eds. "1947: L'Anno della Svolta." *Ventunesimo Secolo,* 6, no. 12 (2007): 5–81.

– "De Gasperi e la Costruzione della Democrazia." *Ventunesimo Secolo* 3, no. 5 (2005): 5–305.

– "Il Liberali e la Repubblica: Una Storia da Scrivere." *Ventunesimo Secolo* 4, no. 8 (2005): 5–158.

– "La Pubblica Amministrazione dal Fascismo alla Repubblica." *Ventunesimo Secolo,* 2, no. 4 (2003): 9–178.

Ragghianti, Carlo Ludovico. *Disegno della Liberazione Italiana.* Florence: Nistri-Lischi 1962.

Ragionieri, Ernesto. *Storia d'Italia dall'Unità a Oggi.* Vol. 4, Tome 3. Turin: Einaudi 1976.

Remaggi, Luca Polese. *La Nazione Perduta: Ferruccio Parri nel Novecento Italiano.* Bologna: Il Mulino 2004.

Riccardi, Luca, ed. *Niccolò Carandini: Il Liberale e la Nuova Italia, 1943–1953: Con Documenti Inediti.* Florence: La Monnier 1993.

Ricci, Aldo G., ed. *Verbali del Consiglio dei Ministri.* 3 vols., Luglio 1943–Maggio 1948. Rome: Istituto Poligrafico dello Stato 1994.

– *Aspettando la Repubblica: I Governi di Transizione, 1943–1946.* Rome: Donzelli, 1996.

– *Il Compromesso Costituente: 2 Giugno 1946–18 Aprile 1948; Le Radici del Consociativismo.* Foggia: Bastogi Editrice 1999.

Ricci, Aldo G., and Pino Bongiorno. *La Rinascita dei Partiti in Italia, 1943–1948.* Rome: Edizioni Nuova Cultura 2009.

Ricolfi, Luca, et al., eds. *Italia al Voto.* Turin: UTET 2012.

Riva, Valerio. *Oro da Mosca: I Finanziamenti Sovietici al PCI dalla Rivoluzione d'Ottobre al Crollo dell'USSR.* Milan: Mondadori 1990.

Rizi, Fabio Fernando. *Benedetto Croce and Italian Fascism.* Toronto: University of Toronto Press 2003.

Rodotà, Stefano, ed. *Alle Orgini della Costituzione.* Bologna: Il Mulino 1998.

Romano, Sergio. *Guida alla Politica Estera Italiana: Dal Crollo del Fascismo al Crollo del Comunismo.* Milan: Rizzoli 1993.

Romeo, Rosario. *Italia Mille Anni.* Florence: Le Monnier 1981.

– *Dal Piemonte Sabaudo all'Italia Liberale.* Turin: Einaudi 1963.

– *Risorgimento e Capitalismo.* Bari: Laterza 1959.

– *Scritti Storici, 1951–1987.* Milan: Mondadori 1997.

– *Vita di Cavour.* Bari: Laterza 1984.

Rosa, Alberto Asor. *Storia d'Italia: Dall'Unità a Oggi. La Cultura.* Vol. 4, Tome 2. Turin: Einaudi 1975.

Sale, Giovanni. *De Gasperi, gli USA e il Vaticano all'Inizio della Guerra Fredda.* Milan: Yaca Books 2005.

– *Dalla Monarchia alla Repubblica, 1943–1946.* Milan: Jaca Books 2003.

– *Il Vaticano e la Costituzione.* Milan: Jaca Books 2008.

Salvadori, Max. *The Labours and the Wounds.* London: Pall Mall 1958.

Salvadori, Massimo L. *Il Liberalismo Italiano: I Dilemmi della Libertà.* Rome: Donzelli 2011.

Salvemini, Gaetano. *L'Italia Vista dall'America.* Milan: Feltrinelli 1969.

Santarelli, Ezio. *Mezzogiorno, 1943–1944: Uno "Sbandato" nel Regno del Sud.* Milan: Feltrinelli 1999.

– *Il Problema della Libertà in Italia.* Pesaro: Federici 1946.

Sasso, Gennaro. "Benedetto Croce e il Liberalismo." In Gennaro Sasso, *Filosofia e Idealismo.* Vol. 5. Naples: Bibliopolis 2007. 579–630.

– *Benedetto Croce: La Ricerca della Dialettica.* Naples: Guida 1975.

– "Bobbio, Calogero e il Liberalsocialismo." In Gennaro Sasso, *Filosofia e Idealismo.* Vol. 5. Naples: Bibliopolis 2007. 631–62.

– "Calogero e Croce: La Libertà, le Libertà, la Giustizia." In Gennaro Sasso, *Filosofia e Idealismo.* Vol. 3. Naples: Bibliopolis 1997. 301–414.

– "Considerazioni sul Liberalismo." In Andrea Manzella, ed., *Le Culture della Prima Repubblica.* Milan: Reset 1998. 53–74.

– "Croce e Omodeo: 'Quando l'Italia Era Tagliata in Due.'" *La Cultura,* 52, no. 1 (2014): 5–46.

– *Croce: Storia d'Italia e Storia d'Europa.* Naples: Bibliopolis, 2017.

– *La Fedeltà e l'Esperimento.* Bologna: Il Mulino 1993.

– *Filosofia e Idealismo.* Vol. 1. Naples: Bibliopolis 1994.

– *Filosofia e Idealismo.* Vol. 3. Naples: Bibliopolis 1997.

– *Filosofia e Idealismo.* Vol. 4. Naples: Bibliopolis, 2000.

– *Filosofia e Idealismo.* Vol. 5. Naples: Bibliopolis 2007.

– *Filosofia e Idealismo.* Vol. 6. Naples: Bibliopolis 2012.

– "Gramsci e l'Idealismo." In Gennaro Sasso, *Filosofia e Idealismo.* Vol. 5. Naples: Bibliopolis 2007. 513–79.

– *Per Invigilare Me Stesso: I Taccuini di Lavoro di Benedetto Croce.* Bologna: Il Mulino 1989.

– "Del Provincialismo negli Studi." *La Cultura,* 53, no. 1 (2015): 5–40.

– "La Riflessione sulla Civilità dell'Ultimo Croce." In Marcello Pera ed., *Benedetto Croce e la Nascita della Repubblica.* Soveria Mannelli: Rubbettino 2003. 36–56.

– "Sul Diario di Piero Calamandrei." *La Cultura,* 1 (2017): 5–50.

– *La Voce dei Ricordi.* Naples: Bibliopolis 2012.

Saunders, F.S. *The Cultural Cold War: The CIA and the World of Arts and Letters.* New York: New Press 2000.

Scoppola, Pietro. *La Democrazia dei Cristiani.* Bari: Laterza 2006.

– "De Gasperi e la Svolta del Maggio 1947." *Il Mulino,* 22, no. 231 (1974): 25–46.

– *La Repubblica dei Partiti: Evoluzione e Crisi di un Sistema Politico, 1945–1996.* Bologna: Il Mulino 1997.

Scoppola, Pietro, and Leopoldo Elia, eds. *A Colloquio con Dossetti e Lazzati.* Bologna: Il Mulino 2003.

Serri, Mirella. *I Redenti: Gli Intellettuali che Vissero Due Volte, 1938–1948.* Milan: Corbaccio 2005.

Setta, Sandro. "Benedetto Croce e la 'Sinistra' Liberale nel Carteggio con Leone Cattani, 1947–1948." *Storia Contemporanea,* 19, no. 2 (1988): 115–42.

– *Croce, il Liberalismo e l'Italia Postfascita.* Rome: Bonacci Editore 1979.

– *La Destra nell'Italia del Dopoguerra.* Bari: Laterza 2001.

– *L'Uomo Qualunque, 1944–1948.* Bari: Laterza 2005.

Sforza, Carlo. *L'Italia dal 1914 al 1944: Quale Io la Vidi.* Rome: Mondadori 1954.
Simoncelli, Paolo. *L'Epurazione Antifascista all'Accademia dei Lincei.* Florence: Le Lettere 2009.
Smith, Richard Harris. *OSS: The Secret History of America's First Central Intelligence Agency.* New York: Dell Publishing 1973.
Soleri, Marcello. *Memorie.* Turin: Einaudi 1946.
Spagnoletti, Mario, ed. *Togliatti e il C.L.N. del Sud: La Svolta di Salerno nei Verbali della Giunta Esecutiva, Creata dal Congresso di Bari.* Rome: Sapere 1996.
Spriano, Paolo. *Storia del Partito Comunista Italiano.* Vol. 5. Turin: Einaudi 1978.
Storoni, Enzo. *La Congiura del Quirinale.* Florence: Lettere 2013.
Tamburrano, Giuseppe. *Pietro Nenni.* Bari: Laterza 1986.
Tarchi, Marco. *Italia Populista: Dal Qualunquismo a Grillo.* Bologna: Il Mulino 2003.
Teodori, Massimo. *Pannunzio.* Milan: Mondadori 2010.
Tessitore, Fulvio. "Il Percorso Psicologico dalla Monarchia alla Repubblica Attraverso i Taccuini di Lavaro di Benedetto Croce." In Marcello Pera, ed., *Benedetto Croce e la Nascita della Repubblica.* Soveria Mannelli: Rubbettino 2003. 57–66.
Togliatti, Palmiro. "Il Governo di Salerno." In Franco Antonicelli, ed., *Trent'Anni di Storia Italiana, 1915–1945.* Turin: Einaudi 1961.
Toscano, Mario. *Dal 25 Luglio all'Otto Settembre 1943.* Florence: Le Monnier 1966.
Tupini, Giorgio. *De Gasperi: Una Testimonianza.* Bologna: Il Mulino 1992.
Ungari, Andrea. "I Liberali Visti dai Monarchici." In Fabio Grassi Orsini and Gerardo Nicolosi, eds., *I Liberali Italiani dall'Antifascismo alla Repubblica.* Vol. 1. Soveria Mannelli: Rubbettino 2008. 777–816.
– "La Marcia Verso il Centro e la Prospettiva di una Destra Moderata." *Ventunesimo Secolo,* 4, no. 7 (2005): 113–40.
– *In Nome del Re. I Monarchici Italiani dal 1943 al 1948.* Florence: Le Lettere 2004.
Valiani, Leo. *Dall'Antifascismo alla Resistenza.* Milan: Feltrinelli 1960.
– *L'Avvento di De Gasperi: Tre Anni di Politica Italiana.* Turin: De Silva 1949.
– *Testimoni del Novecento.* Florence: Passigli 1999.
– *Tra Croce e Omodeo: Storia e Storiografia nella Lotta per la Libertà.* Florence: La Monnier 1984.
– *Tutte le Strade Conducono a Roma.* Bologna: Il Mulino 1995.
Varsori, Antonio. "Carlo Sforza nella Politica Italiana." In Giampiero Berti, Eugenio Capozzi, and Piero Craveri, eds., *I Liberali Italiani dall'Antifascismo alla Repubblica.* Vol. 2. Soveria Mannelli: Rubbettino 2010. 149–60.
– *La Cenerentola d'Europa? L'Italia e l'Integrazione Europea dal 1947 ad Oggi.* Soveria Mannelli: Rubbettino 2010.

– *L'Italia nelle Relazioni Internazionali dal 1943 al 1992.* Bari: Laterza 1993.

Varvaro, Paolo. "Il Liberalismo come Questione Nazionale: Nitti e il Nittismo nel Secondo Dopoguerra." In Giampiero Berti, Eugenio Capozzi, and Piero Craveri, eds., *I Liberali Italiani dall'Antifascismo alla Repubblica.* Vol. 2. Soveria Mannelli: Rubbettino 2010. 687–712.

Ventresca, Robert A. *From Fascism to Democracy: Culture and Politics in the Italian Election of 1948.* Toronto: University of Toronto Press 2004.

Ventrone, Angelo. *La Cittadinanza Repubblicana, 1943–1948.* Bologna: Il Mulino 1996.

Visentin, Mauro. *Il Neoparmenidismo Italiano.* 2 vols. Naples: Bibliopolis 2005.

Woller, Hans. *I Conti con il Fascismo: L'Epurazione in Italia, 1943–1948.* Bologna: Il Mulino 1998.

Woolf, Stuart J., ed. *The Rebirth of Italy, 1943–1950.* London: Longman 1977.

Zanotti Bianco, Umberto. *La Mia Roma: Diario, 1943–1947.* Manduria: Lacaita 2011.

Zaslavsky, Victor. "L'Apparato Paramilitare Comunista nell'Italia del Dopoguerra (1945–1955)." *Nuova Storia Contemporanea,* 5, no. 1 (2001): 89–124.

– "Aprile 1948, L'Insurrezione Mancata: La Politica Mediterranea di Stalin e i Suoi Riflessi in Italia." *Ventunesimo Secolo,* 1, no. 1 (2002): 9–44.

– *Lo Stalinismo e La Sinistra Italiana: Dal Mito dell'USSR alla Fine del Comunismo, 1945–1991.* Milan: Mondadori 2004.

Zeno, Livio. *Il Conte Sforza.* Florence: Le Monnier 1999.

Zizola, Giancarlo. *Il Microfono di Dio: Pio XII, Padre Lombardi e i Cattolici Italiani.* Milan: Mondadori 1990.

Zunino, Pier Giorgio. *La Repubblica e il Suo Passato.* Bologna: Il Mulino 2003.

Index

www.ingramcontent.com/pod-product-compliance
Lightning Source LLC
LaVergne TN
LVHW090149080826
844660LV00013B/728/J

* 9 7 8 1 4 8 7 5 0 4 4 6 5 *